David Haynes – Judi Vernau (Eds.)

The Human Position in an Artifical World: Creativity, Ethics and AI in Knowledge Organization

ISKO UK Sixth Biennial Conference
London, 15–16th July 2019

T0134349

David Haynes – Judi Vernau (Eds.)

The Human Position in an Artifical World: Creativity, Ethics and AI in Knowledge Organization

ISKO UK Sixth Biennial Conference
London, 15–16th July 2019

ERGON VERLAG

Umschlagabbildung:
© peshkova – stock.adobe.com

Bibliografische Information der Deutschen Nationalbibliothek
Die Deutsche Nationalbibliothek verzeichnet diese Publikation in
der Deutschen Nationalbibliografie; detaillierte bibliografische Daten
sind im Internet über http://dnb.d-nb.de abrufbar.

www.ergon-verlag.de

ISBN 978-3-95650-549-2 (Print)
ISBN 978-3-95650-550-8 (ePDF)

Table of contents

Session 1: OPENING SESSION

Monday 15th July 2019

Knowledge Graphs and Analytics for Data Linking (Keynote paper)

Jem Rayfield, Ontotext, UK

Summary

Combining diverse data from multiple sources is a complex task. Matching concepts and entities across disparate data sources and recognizing their mentions in semi-structured content requires disambiguation of meaning. This is easy for people, but computers often fail to do it correctly.

Ontotext have built Big Knowledge Graphs and apply cognitive analytics to provide entity awareness; a sort of semantic fingerprint derived from interconnected entity descriptions.

Accessing Knowledge Graph data can sometimes feel difficult. SPARQL and RDF are also perceived to be complex, difficult, unstable and a niche technology stack. Appearing by many to be conceived out of a scientific agenda, APIs are settling and moving towards GraphQL and JSON which is simple, declarative and powerful. Developers simply want what we all want: something simple and easy that works most of the time. This talk discusses augmenting KnowledgeGraphs with domain driven GraphQL.

Key Messages:
- Combining prop and non-prop information is important to get business insights
- Linking entities across data and text requires 'awareness'
- Cognitive analytics on big KnowledgeGraphs can provide awareness of importance and similarity
- Demonstration of such analytics with 2B statements with GraphDB
- Knowledge Graph simplification using GraphQL

Fandom, Folksonomies and Creativity: the case of the Archive of Our Own

Ludi Price, City, University of London, UK

Abstract

Over recent years Web 2.0 has brought information into the hands of the public, and we are increasingly seeing non-professionals doing sophisticated information tasks not merely for work, research or personal interest, but also for leisure – and even pleasure. This paper looks at an online fanfiction repository, Archive of Our Own (AO3), and investigates the ways that media fans have co-opted new technologies to build a 'curated folksonomy' (Bullard 2014), in order to organise the fanworks (fan-created creative works) uploaded by fans to the website. Run by volunteers, the site is a fascinating example of how passion, and even obsession, can bring amateur knowledge workers together collaboratively with users to build an intricate 'democratic indexing' system (Hidderley and Rafferty 1997; Rafferty and Hidderley 2007).

Through methods of tag analysis and interviews, the paper explores how *Archive of Our Own's* curated folksonomy allows fans to make full and creative use of their own original, freeform tags, while also building a highly granular and sophisticated taxonomy which, though highly labour-intensive to maintain, serves the community by maintaining a high degree of accuracy while also preserving the folksonomic properties of freeform tagging. As well as building a functioning taxonomy, through standardising its nomenclature, and facilitating the discoverability of AO3's collections to its users, these amateur knowledge workers see their domain expertise and knowledge organisation labour as a type of fanwork that 'gives back to the community', in lieu of other creative works such as fanfiction and fanart.

1. Introduction

Archive of Our Own (AO3) is a fanfiction archive which was developed and is run by fans, for fans – in this case, fans can be defined as followers of media franchises, products or series, such as seen in books, movies, TV, videogames, comics, and so on. AO3 is run by the non-profit Organization for Transformative Works and is maintained wholly by volunteers and donations. The entire archive was recently nominated for a Hugo Award in the Related Works category (Cole 2019). Nomination for such a prestigious award has brought wider recognition for the site, and for its efforts to preserve the many artistic and creative works that fans produce, which are termed 'fanworks'. AO3 mainly hosts the textual format of fanfiction, but it can also host fanart, videos, songs and lyrics, and games, among other creative works.

This paper, based on the doctoral thesis of the author (Price 2017), details the 'curated folksonomy' (Bullard 2014), which is the system used on AO3 for knowledge organisation. This is done using tag analysis, and supplementary interviews with 'tag wranglers' – i.e. volunteer subject experts, who link user-generated tags to synonymous, standardised forms.

The purpose of the paper is to highlight several points: a very successful use of Hidderley and Rafferty's (1997) 'democratic indexing'; the sophisticated practices of the volunteer 'tag wranglers' who perform these indexing and classification tasks; and the ways in which such work can be driven by passion and pleasure. It also presents a fan tag taxonomy, based upon the tag analysis section of the study.

The study detailed in this paper describes a portion of a wider comparative case study of three different online platforms used by fans. AO3 was studied in conjunction with Tumblr and Etsy. To read the entirety of the comparative case study, see Price (2017, chapter 5).

1.1 Tagging on AO3

AO3 allows users to organise and categorise their work using tags. However, in a system dubbed a 'curated folksonomy' by Bullard (2014), volunteers called 'tag wranglers' filter these tags by associating them with established synonyms. This flexible system allows for both individual idiosyncrasies in user tagging behaviour to remain intact, while also enabling efficient search retrieval. It does however require considerable effort on the part of the volunteers to combine user tags with established synonyms.

AO3 implements a combined self-tagging and automanual system. Pre-defined tags are suggested when filling them in, although users are also free to choose whatever terms they wish. Tags do not take a hashtag format, and there are no restrictions on spaces, length or characters. Non-Roman script is also allowed. During this study, an interviewed tag wrangler, Participant D, described their work thus:

When a user creates a new, never-before-used tag, it shows up in what we call the "unwrangled bins" of every wrangler assigned to the fandoms tagged on the work. What wranglers such as myself do is look at those incoming tags, and determine, based on the Wrangling Guidelines, if the tag should be marked as canonical (the form of that concept that will show in the drop down menus and autocompletes), made a synonym of any existing canonical, or left unfilterable as a tag that is too unique to be useful for other users to filter with. As a general rule, any character who exists in canon, and any relationship that involves at least one canonical character, will be canonized on the first usage. More general concepts (such as "Alternate Universe" or "Angst") will generally need to be used by multiple users before being canonized.

Figure 1 shows a random search result of works archived under the 'Remy LeBeau/Rogue' tag. The tags are displayed after the archive warning (in this case, the author chose not to employ any archive warnings, e.g. violence, non-consensual sex, etc.).

Figure 1. Archive entry for an X-Men fanfiction on AO3, "Confessions of a Train Wreck", 8th October 2018. Source: http://archiveofourown.org/ (retrieved 22 April 2019).

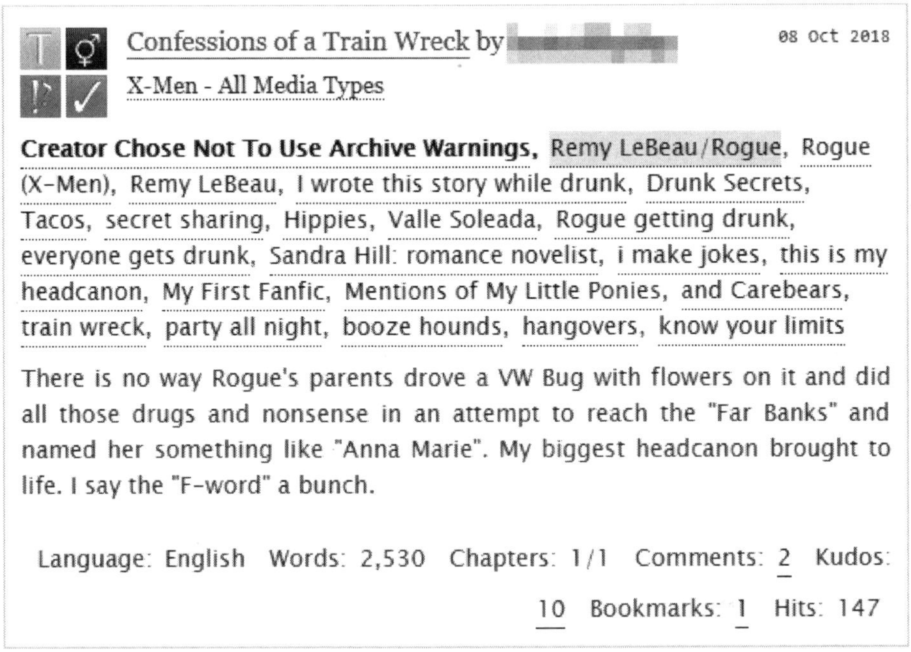

Confessions of a Train Wreck by ▓▓▓▓▓▓▓   08 Oct 2018

X-Men - All Media Types

Creator Chose Not To Use Archive Warnings, Remy LeBeau/Rogue, Rogue (X-Men), Remy LeBeau, I wrote this story while drunk, Drunk Secrets, Tacos, secret sharing, Hippies, Valle Soleada, Rogue getting drunk, everyone gets drunk, Sandra Hill: romance novelist, i make jokes, this is my headcanon, My First Fanfic, Mentions of My Little Ponies, and Carebears, train wreck, party all night, booze hounds, hangovers, know your limits

There is no way Rogue's parents drove a VW Bug with flowers on it and did all those drugs and nonsense in an attempt to reach the "Far Banks" and named her something like "Anna Marie". My biggest headcanon brought to life. I say the "F-word" a bunch.

Language: English   Words: 2,530   Chapters: 1/1   Comments: 2   Kudos: 10   Bookmarks: 1   Hits: 147

In this case greyed out tags denote either a romantic pairing of two characters. Character tags follow, and then descriptive tags. Normally, pre-defined tags start with a capital (e.g. "Hippies", "Drunk Secrets", "Tacos"). There are several tags that the author herself has applied freely to the fanfic. These express themes ("i make jokes", "know your limits") and story elements ("party all night", "hangovers"). These tags are typical examples of how users choose to tag their works on AO3, i.e. using a mixture of pre-defined tags and free ones. If a free tag becomes popular enough, it will be merged by a tag wrangler with a standard, pre-defined one; or a new tag will be entered into the system's taxonomy to accommodate it. For example, in Figure 1, the free tag, "i make jokes" has been made equivalent to the standard tag "Jokes" – if the tag is clicked on, it will lead to all works on the site that have used the tag "Jokes" or their equivalents. Tag equivalencies, once determined by a tag wrangler, are saved automatically in the site's database.

1.2 Fandom, democratic indexing, and curated folksonomies

Since the rise of Web 2.0. during the 2000's, increasingly dynamic information technologies have allowed for a more bottom-up or heterarchical (i.e. unranked) system of online, digital content creation. This more democratic approach is exemplified by cases such as Wikipedia, citizen journalism, open source software programming, amateur videogame development, and basement-made music projects. In terms of fan culture, online communities form around certain franchises or media texts to engage in fantasy and the exchange of common interests, fanworks, and, of course, information (Lee et al 2013). Fans have been prolific users of information technology to create, share and disseminate both information and fanworks (Jenkins 2006). This also extends to knowledge organisation. As Hart et al. (1999) suggest in an early study, fans engage in sophisticated bibliographic control of their creations. Recent work has begun to explore this in more detail. In particular, Julia Bullard (2014, 47), who has been conducting a long-term ethnographical study of an online fanfiction repository, presents the notion of the 'curated folksonomy', which she describes as "a system of tag synonyms and tag relationships that addresses some of the major shortcomings of a pure, unregulated folksonomy". The curated folksonomy involves a degree of structure that mitigates some of the problems associated with pure folksonomies (e.g. the oft-quoted example of tagging photos of oneself with 'me'). This is particularly of note in terms of fandom, because many fanwork repositories, such as Livejournal and Wattpad, use folksonomies as a way of organising documents, and this can be seen most clearly in AO3.

The curated folksonomy is not a new concept and is very similar to the idea of 'democratic indexing' (Rafferty and Hidderley 2007; Hidderley and Rafferty 1997). Here, subject experts evaluate and formalise the indexing choices of a systems' users to create a taxonomy/ontology. Democratic indexing, as Rafferty (2010, 260) explains, "examines the terms or tags attached to each field and creates a collective interpretation for each field based on counting terms". As she also notes, such processes have now been made much more achievable with Web 2.0 technologies, which "could potentially allow for the development of interesting approaches to the retrieval of cultural documentation including fiction" (260). This is, indeed, exactly what takes place on AO3. In their previous study of indexing methods on Flickr, Rafferty and Hidderley (2007, 408) note:

The discourse of user-based indexing is one of democracy, organic growth, and of user emancipation, but there are hints throughout the literature of the need for *post hoc* disciplining of some sort. This suggests that, despite Shirky's claim of philosophical paradigm shifting for social tagging, there is a residing doubt amongst information professionals that self-organising systems can work without there being some element of control and some form of "representative authority". Perhaps all that social tagging heralds is a shift towards user warrant.

I would contend that this is exactly what has happened on Archive of Our Own, where the tag wrangling system enables domain experts to discipline user tags while, as Rafferty (2010, 260) describes it, "still allowing for user interpretation and the recording of historical shifts in our understanding of generic [and, in this case, fan] history". What is perhaps different here, is that the "*post hoc* disciplining" is not performed by traditional domain experts, but by amateur domain experts, i.e. fans who are conversant enough in a certain fandom to be judged competent enough to become that "representative authority". They are not professionals, and hold no qualifications other than being self-taught, and passionate about the domain they are interested in.

To return to the concept of warrant, as mentioned in Rafferty and Hidderley's (2007) quote above, Bullard's research into knowledge organisation in fanfiction repositories has also yielded some fascinating insights into how a curated folksonomy works in practice, and how this collaborative process involves the application of different warrants to create an effective daily classification system that is in constant use. Classification design is always, to some extent, reliant on the concept of warrant. As Bullard (2017, 76) explains, "classification designers express their allegiance with particular theories of classification through their appeals to warrant – the body of evidence and terminology taken as authoritative in the design of a classification system"; or, by Beghtol's (1986, 110) definition, warrant is "the authority a classificationist invokes first to justify and subsequently to verify decisions" in their choice of terms. Different warrants include: 1) literary warrant (classification derived from the field of scholarship that is being classified); 2) scientific or consensus warrant (classification based on current scientific conclusions and consensus between relevant fields); 3) user warrant (classification based on user needs and/or expectations), and; 4) ethical warrant (classification based on ethical considerations regarding users, e.g. minority groups, discriminatory language in current classification systems, potential divergence from consensus terms).

In practice, classification design is more complex, and several types of warrant may be used at any given time. Bullard's (2017) work expands on this by giving examples of how warrant works in an online fanfiction repository where its folksonomy is highly specialised and constantly expanding as users add to it. The volunteers who curate this folksonomy communicate behind the scene to discuss controversial or problematic terms that have been entered by users. The scenarios Bullard describes succinctly indicates the tension classification designers encounter regarding different warrants, and that these tensions are not easily surmountable, especially when a classification system is being collaboratively designed, and even more so when it is being developed on-the-fly. Despite the fluid nature of collaborative and democratic classification design, it can work successfully. Unlike official classification systems, created by professional bodies, the curated folksonomy described in Bullard's work, and seen on sites such as AO3, is not monolithic and does not take years to implement change. Its workers are passionate, expert volunteers. Interviews with AO3's tag wranglers, discussed in section 6.0., show that while the curated folksonomy system is under strain, it is nevertheless a successful one that generally works well, simultaneously both preserving and standardising the terms created by its users (i.e. the fan community). When one considers the vast size and granularity of the folksonomy, AO3 is a stunning achievement, blending all four warrants to build a classification system that both serves its community well and generally describes content accurately.

Here it is also important to note that Bullard's research into her fanfiction repository posits classification work as fun, pleasurable, and recognised by the wider fan community as the efforts of volunteers with a particular expertise. There is still a relative dearth of research acknowledging the important role that fun, passion, obsession and play have in motivating volunteers to take part in collaborative knowledge organisation projects. Activities such as classifying galaxies by shape (GalaxyZoo), editing a wiki article (Wikipedia), or standardising an obscure fandom term (AO3) can be monotonous in the extreme – so why are so many people doing it? Scholarship should perhaps move away from regarding these activities from the sole standpoint of something which constitutes labour, and instead consider creativity, passion and play as a way to understand why people such as amateur experts, enthusiasts and fans engage in this type of activity.

2. Empirical Study

The aim of the empirical section of the study was to understand how the curated folksonomy used on AO3 was being used – how fans chose to tag their work; how tag wranglers controlled the taxonomy, and whether they were effectively preserving the meaning of the original tags when standardising them 'behind the scenes'. This involved: a) ascertaining the meaning of tags, as they had been input by users; b) ascertaining the user's intention in assigning that tag (e.g. was it being used to describe the content of the work, or something else); and c) ascertaining whether the meaning of the original tags was being preserved by tag wranglers. A secondary aim was to engage with the tag wranglers about their work and their opinions on AO3's tagging system. Two methods were used to achieve this: firstly, tag analysis; and secondly, structured interviews.

2.1 Methods

Tag analysis as a research tool has its roots in hyperlink network analysis, or link analysis (Thelwall 2004), which in turn has its roots in social network analysis (Park and Thelwall 2003). Social network analysis (SNA) is a research approach and technique that has been widely used in the social sciences for many decades (Carrington and Scott 2011, 1). It takes as its premise the idea that, as Marin and Wellman (2011, 11) explain, "social life is created primarily and most importantly by relations and the patterns formed by these relations". When people form networks, they bring with them and exchange resources. These resources can be tangible in form: money, goods, and services; or they may be intangible, such as information, expertise, and influence (Haythornthwaite 1996, 323). People become 'nodes' (or vertices) in the network, network members or actors who are linked through relationships, or 'edges' (or links – see Figure 2). Social network analysis studies these relationships within a network for meaningful patterns that can tell us about the nature of the network, such as how connected each node in the network is, which node is the most connected, and through which relationships resource exchange works most efficiently.

Figure 2: The basics of a social network (Source: Hawksey 2017).

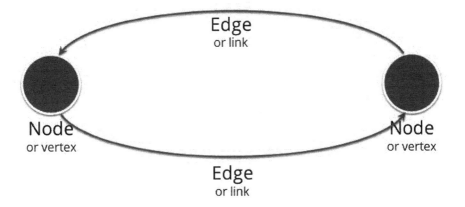

There are several ways in which sense can be made of a network, which are as follows:

- Degree: the number of connections that a node has. The more connections, the higher the degree.
- Betweenness centrality: how often a node appears on the shortest path between two other nodes. The higher the betweenness centrality, the higher the importance of that node in exchanging a resource within the network – thus nodes with a higher betweenness centrality can be considered a more efficient carrier of information between other nodes.

- Clustering: groups of highly interconnected nodes within a network. A cluster denotes nodes that can reach one another in only one step. This is a group of highly influential nodes.
- Density: the degree to which a node is connected to all other nodes in the network.

Social networks are not merely restricted to people. In fact, Marin and Wellman (2011, 11) note that "any units that can be connected to other units can be studies as nodes", and networks can be used to describe the relationships between units of information as well. It is thus not surprising that it has found applications within the field of LIS (Bawden and Robinson 2012, 174; Otte and Rousseau 2002). The potential usefulness of the method in the discipline appears to have first been explicitly suggested by Haythornthwaite (1996). Haythornthwaite (1996, 338-339) noted five aspects of information exchange that SNA is well able to shed light on. These are:

- Information needs: information exchange between certain group members, and the type of information being exchanged, can tell the information provider how best to serve users.
- Information exposure: relationships with highly influential network members can illustrate a person's level of exposure to information.
- Information legitimation: measuring the strength of ties between network individuals can show how information is being passed on to others. The stronger the tie, the more legitimised the information (and therefore its source).
- Information routes: establishing the routes of information exchange within the network is useful not only for describing information flows, but also which routes are most efficient.
- Information opportunities: influential people in the network can control information flows between other individuals within the network, thus becoming information brokers or gatekeepers, regulating both information sources and outlets.

Since then, SNA has been used in a variety of papers within the field of LIS. Johnson (2019) used the method to explore collaborative information seeking between healthcare teams; Jiang, Zhang and Liu (2014) to map the relationships between the editors of LIS journals in China; Jalalimanesh and Yaghoubi (2013) examined an Iranian interlibrary loan service to map the transfer of knowledge between institutions; and Johnson (2004) used SNA to investigate how a group of residents in Ulaanbaatar, Mongolia, searched for information, finding that they often went to people they didn't know very well, but who had higher social capital. This is but a small sample of works in this area – at the time of writing, LISTA lists 65 papers that use or mention social network analysis as a research method.

The growth of social network analysis over the past couple of decades is not surprising, considering the rise of the internet and the fact that it is, in effect, a vast social network in and of itself (Otte and Rousseau 2002, 441). This has led to the method of hyperlink analysis (Park and Thelwall 2003), or simply link analysis (Thelwall 2004), which "casts hyperlinks between Web sites (or Web pages) as social and communicational ties, applying standard techniques from Social Network Analysis to this new data source" (Park and Thelwall 2003, n.p.). Here, the website is the node, and the hyperlink is the edge that connects websites. By analysing a network of hyperlinks, one can discern patterns between individuals, organisations, companies, and even nation states through their website links, much as one would by analysing offline social networks.

Not only can social network analysis methods can be applied to people, organisations and websites, it can also be applied to metadata stored within the Web. One of the ways in which this has taken shape over the past decade or so is in the form of *tag analysis*, where the network properties of tags are analysed. In this case, the nodes in the network are not people or organisations, but tags (or hashtags), for example on Twitter, Flickr, or Delicious. The edges between nodes in a tag network demonstrate when a tag is used in conjunction with another tag in the same post (see Figure 3).

Tag analysis can be used to examine many facets of online phenomena, such as political sentiment on Twitter (Small 2011), usage patterns of bookmarking tags on Del.icio.us (Golder and Huberman 2006), and the semantic information in Flickr tags (Bolognesi 2016). Tag analysis is particularly prevalent in the context of Twitter hashtags, of which there is much literature – recent research includes Malik et al. (2018), Rossi and Giglietto (2016), Wang, Liu and Gao (2016), and Wang and Iwaihara (2015). A growing area of related research involves the merging of tag analysis and social network analysis, where the latter is applied to the analysis of tags in order to visualise and thus better understand the network-type properties of social media folksonomies (Cattuto et al. 2007; Ma and Li 2014). Such analyses are presented in graph form, usually depicting a base tag as a central node in a network, connected to co-occurring tags – these graphs are called *co-occurrence graphs* (see Figure 3). A central node (in this case #glass) represents the base tag; tags that are co-occurring (i.e. that occur in the same post, or tweet) are joined to the central node by an edge.

More complicated relationships between tags, such as group clustering etc., can be visualised by the application of various algorithms, which can depict tag usage amongst different communities, thus elucidating how patterns of tag usage differ between different groups and networks. This gives some insight into information exchange in online and social media settings.

Figure 3: A co-occurence graph of the hashtag #glass. Source: Wang and Iwaihara (2015).

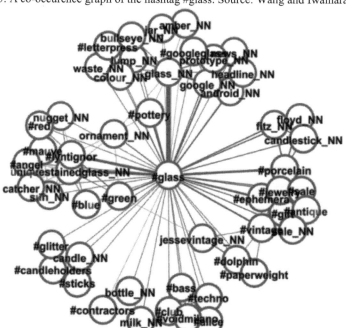

Tag analysis has also been used to describe the tagging behaviours of users within a given information domain. Trant (2009, 23) gave an early overview of LIS and computer science articles on tagging and folksonomy, noting that tools "such as vocabulary analysis and classification, user interaction theory, and social network theory are used to describe and analyse the nature of tagging and folksonomy". Examples of LIS papers which use tag analysis are Ådland and Lykke (2012), Chen and Ke (2013), Vaidya and Harinarayana (2016), and Estrada et al. (2017). Within fan contexts, Johnson (2014), Rose (2013), and Gursoy (2015) have examined tag usage in fanfiction repositories, although these studies did not use social media data/tag analysis specifically.

While tag analysis comprised the bulk of the empirical research presented in this paper, it was felt that a qualitative element would be needed to shed some more light on the tag wranglers' activities. Therefore, some small-scale, structured email interviews were conducted to complement and test the results of the tag analysis.

3. Tag analysis

For this study, one particular tag which is used on AO3 – 'Remy LeBeau/Rogue' – was crawled. This tag describes the romantic pairing between two characters from a multimedia franchise called *X-Men*, which was created by Marvel. The tag was chosen as the author was familiar with these characters, and with the X-Men franchise at large. Since time and resources were scarce for this doctoral project, there was not the luxury of training up a team of assistants in the requisite domain expertise to parse and code the tags. Thus, it was deemed more expedient to perform the analysis on a domain that the author was already familiar with. This subject knowledge allowed the author to more easily navigate the co-occurring tags associated with the 'Remy LeBeau/Rogue' tag. AO3 does not use tags in the same way that they are used on social media platforms such as Twitter or Instagram. Instead, tags are based on their own 'home page', which has its own URL, similar to a traditional authority file (see Figure 4). Tags therefore cannot be harvested in the same way that they might be on Twitter or Instagram. They can only be retrieved via a static URL address.

The crawl was done using SocSciBot 4.1. SocSciBot is a free crawler programme developed by Mike Thelwall specifically for use in the social sciences and humanities. It has seen wide use within information science, especially in webometrics, altmetrics, and link analysis research (recent examples include Thelwall 2017; Hendrikx et al 2016; Saha and Mukhopadhyay 2016). Because the tag is based on a homepage, SocSciBot was easily able to run a crawl, in a way that would have been much more complicated on, for example, Twitter or Instagram, which are hashtag-based.

The crawl of the 'Remy LeBeau/Rogue' tag took place on 29 April, 2016. The maximum number of pages to crawl was 1000, and the max crawl depth was set to 1. This was to limit the crawl only to pages which co-occurred with those using the 'Remy LeBeau/Rogue' tag. To ensure that only web addresses for tags were returned (rather than for the actual works themselves), the crawl was set to collect only pages that began with the URL http://archiveofourown.org/tags/. The difficulty with this crawl is that SocSciBot does not crawl a URL that is composed of special characters. In this case, the URL that needed to be crawled includes asterisks, which SocSciBot does not recognise. Therefore, a workaround was used, wherein the URL for the synonym, 'Romy' (http://archiveofourown.org/tags/Romy) was used to start the crawl, as it automatically loads the 'Remy LeBeau/Rogue' tag homepage in any case.

Figure 4: AO3's 'Remy LeBeau/Rogue' tag homepage. User tags that have been designated synonymous by tag wranglers are shown under 'Tags with the same meaning'. Source: https://archiveofourown.org/tags/Remy%20LeBeau*s*Rogue/ (retrieved 22nd April 2019).

Remy LeBeau/Rogue

Works   Bookmarks

This tag belongs to the Relationship Category. It's a common tag. You can use it to filter works and to filter bookmarks.

Parent tags (more general):

All New X-Factor, Gambit (Comic), Marvel, Marvel (Comics), Marvel 616, Marvel Noir, Marvel Ultimates, Remy LeBeau, Rogue (X-Men), Wolverine (Movies), X-Men (Comicverse), X-Men (Original Timeline Movies), X-Men (Ultimateverse), X-Men - All Media Types, X-Men Evolution, X-Men: The Animated Series

Tags with the same meaning:

Anna Maria LeBeau/RemyLeBeau, Anna Marie/Remy LeBeau, anna-marie/remy lebeau, former Remy LeBeau/Rogue, Gambit / Rogue, Gambit x Rogue, Gambit/Man!Rogue, Gambit/Rogue, Gambito/Rougue, implied Remy Lebeau/Rogue, implied Rogue/Gambit, MAYBE Remy LeBeau/Rogue, mentions of Rogue/Remy LeBeau, mr. and mrs. lebeau, past Rogue/Remy LeBeau, Post Remy LeBeau/Rogue, referenced Remy LeBeau/Rogue, Remy LeBeau | Gambit/Marie D'Ancanto | Rogue, Remy LeBeau/Anna Marie, Remy LeBeau/Anna Marie LeBeau, Remy LeBeau/Anna-Marie, Remy LeBeau/Anna-Marie LeBeau, Remy LeBeau/Rogue (X-Men), Remy/Rogue, Rogue | Marie/Remy LeBeau (Gambit), Rogue/Gambit, Rogue/Gambit (mentioned), Rogue/Gambit (past), rogue/remy, Rogue/Remy LeBeau, Rogue/Remy LeBeau - Pairing, Rogue/Remy LeBeau - Relationship, romy, Rouge/Gambit, slight Gambit/Rogue, slight Remy LeBeau/Rogue

The resulting data was saved as a Pajek file (.net). The Pajek format is a widely used standard within network science, and is interoperable with many programmes, such as SocSciBot, NodeXL, Gephi, and others. The resulting Pajek file was imported into NodeXL. Here the data was cleaned, and the URLs rendered in their plain tag form (e.g. 'archiveofourown.org/tags/kitty*s*kurt' became 'kitty/kurt'). During this process several problems were encountered, as listed below:

- Due to SocSciBot's limitations, some URLs were truncated. For example, all instances of 'in a URL were rendered as &, and the rest of the URL was not rendered. For example, archiveofourown.org/tags/darcy%20likes%20&. In cases such as these, the original tag was often considered irretrievable. Since these examples were now rendered useless, they were removed from the dataset. Some, however, could be reconstructed by searching for the tag via Google (e.g. archiveofourown.org/tags/dracy%20and%20logan%20aren& contained a spelling error ('dracy' instead of 'darcy'), and could easily be found through a Google search (the final tag was 'dracy and logan aren't normal').

- Some tags can be deleted, presumably if the work it was attached to is removed by the author. In such cases, the tag was left in the dataset.
- Due to the dynamic nature of AO3, tags are always being merged with standard synonyms. The dataset therefore does not reflect changes made to tags post-analysis.

The final dataset included a total of 8182 individual tags, with a total of 4368 tag names. The next stage was to create a separate dataset by merging synonyms according to their tag wrangled version (i.e. their standardised form as determined by AO3's tag wranglers). For example, all incidences of 'Romy' were merged with 'Remy LeBeau/Rogue', 'ultimate x-men' was merged with 'x-men (ultimateverse)', 'logan – oc' was merged with 'logan (x-men)/original character', and so on. After merging all synonyms with the standardised form, tags that were not popular enough to have been 'tag wrangled' yet remained. These comprised the 'long tail' of the dataset. The wrangled dataset came to a total of 4946 individual tags, with a total of 2752 tag names. This indicated that 63% of tags that co-occur with 'Romy' had been wrangled.

There were now two datasets – one comprising pre-wrangled tags, and one comprising wrangled tags (if, indeed, a tag was popular enough to have been wrangled), allowing for both sets to be compared. Each tag was then manually coded to a tag type, using an iterative, inductive process. This process was used to develop a fan tag taxonomy (see Table 1), which is described further in the author's doctoral research (Price 2017, chapter 5). This taxonomy was based on a simple, generalised tag taxonomy used by Smith (2008, 67), but has added categories that can be implemented in fan-specific contexts.

Table 1. Fan-tag taxonomy as developed during Price's (2017) doctoral thesis

CODE	TAG TYPE /SUB-TYPE	DEFINITION	EXAMPLES
1	Descriptive	Describes content	vintage; commission; black and white; regram
1.1	Fandom	Describes fandom	X-Men; Marvel; Avengers; Harry Potter
1.2	Ship	Describes characters in a romantic relationship	Romy; Erik Lehnsherr/Charles Xavier; loroki

CODE	TAG TYPE /SUB-TYPE	DEFINITION	EXAMPLES
1.3	Character	Describes characters	Gambit; Rogue; Thor; Wade Wilson
1.4	Genre	Describes genre of resource	drabble; fluff; angst; slash; steampunk
1.5	Event	Describes a 'real world' event	Christmas; Valentines Day; dragoncon
1.6	Person	Describes a 'real world' person	Channing Tatum
1.7	Friendship	Describes characters in a friendship	kitty pryde & kurt wagner; darcy and logan
1.8	Organisation/Team/Group	Describes a group of people	witches; Hydra; X-Men; Illuminati
1.9	Location	Describes a location or setting	Alkali Lake; Xavier Institute; Wakanda
1.10	Plot	Describes a fictional story element	M-Day; Crimson Gem of Cyttorak
1.11	Warning	Describes sensitive content	spoilers; swearing; rape/non-con
2	Resource	Type of resource	comics; drawing; photo; video
2.1	Fanwork	Type of fan resource	fanfic; fanart; cosplay; fanfic rec list
2.2	Title of fanwork	Title of fan resource	In Between; Loki and the Loon
2.3	Citation	Citation of fan resource	Episode: Shadowed Past; X-Men Legacy 272
3	Ownership	Ownership of tagger	mike draws
3.1	Creator/source	Name of fan resource creator	Jim Lee; toyscomics; bbrae; ishandahalf
3.2	Recipient	Name of intended recipient of fan resource	txpeppa
4	Opinion	Opinion on resource	sexy; geeky; quirky; badass; epic
4.1	Communication	Communicates thoughts	I blame Tumblr; I need this shirt; great gift idea
4.2	Explanatory	Explains resource content	this is how I vent; iron fist is shameless
4.3	Affective	Explains emotional reaction	poor Pietro; ineedhelp; theyre so cute omg
4.4	Conversational & enunciative	Instigates or responds to a dialogue	why?; ask me stuff; leah shut up; askbox
4.5	Emoticon	Visual communication	XD; :D; 0:)
5	Self-reference	Reference to tagger/self	personal post; my art; self; my life
6	Task organising	Personal organisation of resource	work in progress; other character tags to be added; queueballs
7	Play & performance	Resource is part of an event, or has some performative aspect	prompt fill; fangirl challenge; frostiron month

4. Supplementary interviews

AO3 interviewees were recruited from tag wranglers. It was decided to interview two tag wranglers who worked specifically on works in the Marvel fandom. This was because: a) they would likely have wrangled the tags in the analysed dataset, and; b) they might shed some light on the tag wrangling process, how it impacts the site, and how they perceived their role in the organisation of fan-related information. Contact with tag wranglers must be made through the Organization for Transformative Works (OTW), who runs AO3. Therefore, a private message was sent to the Communications Team via a contact form on the AO3 site. In order to be approved for scholarly research on the site, information sheets, ethics checklists, consent forms and interview guides were emailed to the Communication Team Co-chair. Once approval was granted, interviews with the tag wranglers (Participants C and D) were mediated electronically by the co-chair. For this reason, interviews were by necessity structured. This was due to the considerable time and negotiation between mediations, and the questions being mediated through a third party. The questions asked were:

1. What do you do as a tag wrangler?
2. What is important about tag-wrangling?
3. Tag-wrangling might be considered a monotonous task – why do you do it?
4. Do you see yourself as a gatekeeper of your fandom, and if so, how?
5. What do you think of AO3's tagging system? Do you think it could be improved?

Interviews were conducted online via email, once consent forms had been returned. When responses highlighted concepts that required further investigation, a follow-up email was sent with further questions.

5. Analysis

There were two different datasets created from the AO3 Romy tag crawl. The first was designated the 'pre-wrangled' dataset – that is, all the tags were the original versions that had been input by the user. The second was designated the 'wrangled' dataset – that is, all tags that had been filtered by a tag-wrangler and merged with a standard, synonymous tag (e.g. all instances of "aggressive flirting" are merged with the standard tag "Flirting"; "team fic" with "Team", etc.). Therefore, the 'wrangled' dataset showed higher levels of homogeneity and much lower tag name counts than the 'pre-wrangled' set. The 'pre-wrangled' dataset comprised a total of 8182 individual tags, and 4638 different tag names. The 'wrangled' dataset comprised a total of 4946 individual tags, and 2752 different tag names. This indicated that well over half of the tags in the data set (63%) had been processed by tag-wranglers.

Figure 5 shows a directed co-occurrence graph for the 'Remy LeBeau/Rogue' tag on AO3, grouped by tag type, laid out using the Fruchterman-Reingold algorithm, as this had the most visual clarity. Edge opacity is denoted by the edge weight; vertex size by betweenness centrality; tag type by colour and vertex shape. Figure 6 depicts all tags with a betweenness centrality of 1 or above (that is, tags that appear to be more efficient carriers of information content within the network). Three hundred and nineteen (11.6%) tags reached this value. Each tag was categorised according to the fan tag taxonomy on Table 1. Most of the tags with a betweenness centrality of 1 or above either described the franchise or property associated with the post (Fandom); relationships between two characters (Ship); the characters themselves (Character); or simply described the content of the story (Descriptive). These figures were similar in both 'pre-wrangled' and 'wrangled' datasets.

This was an important finding. It had been expected that the effect of the tag wrangling process would be evident on the 'wrangled' dataset, thus implying that some form of gatekeeping or inaccurate/biased bibliographical control was being exerted by the tag wranglers. In fact, there was very little difference between pre-wrangled and post-wrangled tag usage. Figures 7 and 8 compare the number of tag names in both pre-wrangled and wrangled datasets – they show very similar patterns, despite the standardisation of the wrangled set.

This would suggest that tag wrangling is not a form of gatekeeping of the vernacular or the taxonomy used in the Romy or wider Marvel fandoms. Nor is it gatekeeping in terms of the bibliographical control of fanworks. Indeed, during the interviews, the tag wranglers did not see themselves as gatekeepers, and confirmed that they tried to follow the original tagger's meaning and intent as closely as possible. Examples from their interviews show considerable expertise in their chosen area (i.e. the Marvel Universe, and therefore it may be concluded that, in order to do their task properly, tag wranglers pride themselves on being able to recognise the obscure references in certain tags, preserve them in the wrangling process, and standardise them if warranted. As Participant D said:

What I do see myself as providing is a chance to make too many years reading a lot of comic books useful. Marvel has a very, shall we say, dense, history. But if you think there aren't users out there who will tag for characters who appeared in one issue of Fantastic Four back in 1973, I want to assure you: you are wrong.

Figure 5. Co-occurrence graph for the 'Rogue/Remy LeBeau' tag on AO3 (from the wrangled dataset).

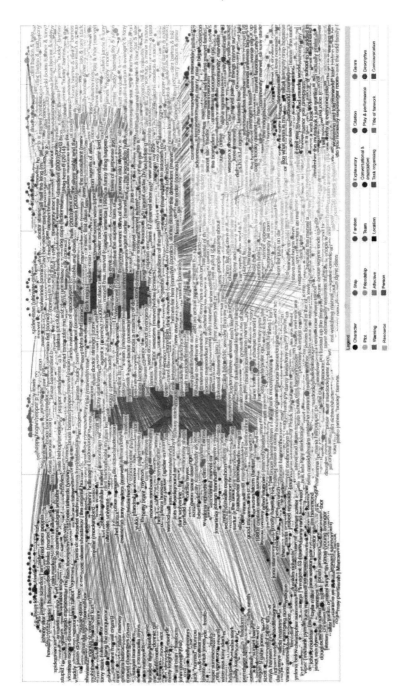

Figure 6: Co-occurrence graph for the 'Rogue/Remy LeBeau' tag on AO3 (from the wrangled dataset). All displayed tags have a betweenness centrality of 1+.

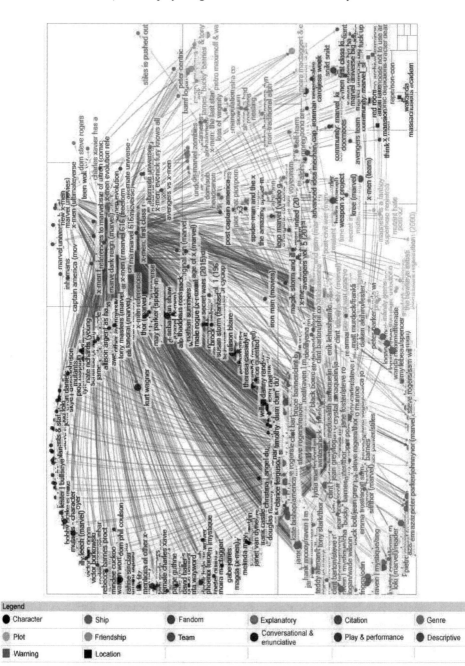

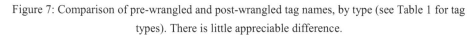

Figure 7: Comparison of pre-wrangled and post-wrangled tag names, by type (see Table 1 for tag types). There is little appreciable difference.

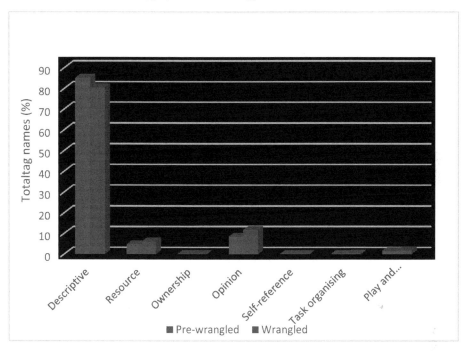

This knowledge capital could equate to some prestige in the fan community, but it is important to note that tag wranglers do not benefit from this, as they are unseen and anonymous.

Ownership type tags (see Table 1) were seldom employed as ownership is inherent in the post itself (i.e. the author of the story is the poster of the content). The Descriptive type was highest, particularly the Character sub-type, which indicated the characters present in the story (arguably characters are the most important aspect of a story, enabling readers to easily find the characters they want to read about). Communication was the second highest tag type employed, and surprisingly this type showed a marked percentage rise post-wrangling. This may be because Communication (sub)-type tags are idiosyncratic, and unlikely to be used more than once. Since their usage is so low, this means that they are rarely tag wrangled and merged with other tags. Therefore, their percentage of the total Communication type tag count tends to remain static, while other tag types, particularly Descriptive and Resource tags, tend to be readily merged with already-existing synonyms, which therefore reduces their percentage of the total tags within the post-wrangled dataset.

Figure 8: Comparison of pre-wrangled and post-wrangled tag names, by sub-type (see Table 1 for tag types).

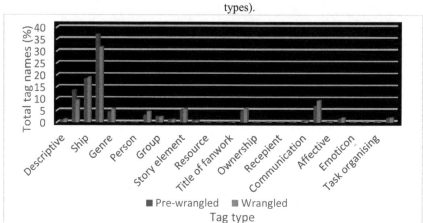

As with Ownership, there was negligible use of Self-reference or Task organising tags (less than 1%) in both datasets. There was some slight use of the Play and Performance tag type, and this was used in very specific contexts (indicating stories written as part of events, competitions, contests, challenges or games, which were mostly hosted on other social media sites). Examples of these were 'i accepted a few prompts', 'community: xmen15', 'secret mutant ficathon 2014' and 'x-men big bang challenge'.

Figures 9 and 10 show a comparison of the total tag count used in the 'pre-wrangled' and 'wrangled' datasets. Figure 9 demonstrates that on the level of tag type, there is an almost negligible difference between the two sets. Figure 10, however, shows some significant disparities at the level of tag sub-type. These are at the following sub-types: Ship, Character, Friendship, Citation and Explanatory Communication.

It seems that this is where the long tail of tags manifests itself most clearly. This long tail is made up of all the tags that are not popular enough to have been wrangled. However, it was noticed during the merging of pre- and post-wrangled tags that several more obscure tags had been 'shoehorned' into a standardised tag that did not encapsulate the specificity of its original meaning. To take the Citation sub-type as an example, the tag 'Star-Lord and Kitty Pryde', which is the title of a comic series, and of low popularity, has been tag-wrangled into a synonym of the much broader Fandom sub-type, 'Marvel'. Likewise, the Ship tag 'loroki' (indicating a romantic pairing between the characters of Loki and Storm) has also been made a synonym of 'Marvel'. In both cases the precise meaning of the original tags have been lost in the process of tag-wrangling, and both have also been classified under an inaccurate sub-type. While examples of this are in the minority, they are still frequent enough that it would suggest that, at the tag sub-type level, tag wrangling is slightly less successful than it is at the tag type level. Such funnelling of less popular tags into inaccurate tag sub-types (even if they are still in the same overall tag type) might account for the unusual spikes in the Friendship, Citation and Explanatory sub-types in the 'wrangled' dataset, and in the Character sub-type in the 'pre-wrangled' dataset.

Figure 9: Comparison of the percentage of the total tag count in the pre- and post-wrangled datasets, arranged by tag type (see Table 1 for tag types). There is little appreciable difference.

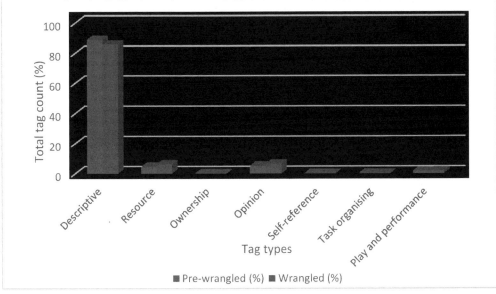

6. Discussion

AO3 tagging practices show high density and granularity, as authors attempt to convey the minute particulars of their fandom, as well as the plots of their stories. Fans are known to be particular about the types of fanworks they will engage with (Driscoll 2006), showing preference according to characters, ships, genres and kinks (i.e. the sexual predilections depicted in fanfic). All these elements and more are of primary importance, both for the reader, who wishes to find a fic that matches her preferences as precisely as possible, and for the creator, who wishes to draw as large an audience as possible to her work. Because of this, tagging – on AO3 in particular – becomes an important finding aid, similar to the subject headings found in library catalogues, except that they are far more granular and far more numerous in scope.

Figure 10: Comparison of the percentage of the total tag count in the pre- and post-wrangled datasets, arranged by tag sub-type (see Table 1 for tag types). Ship, Character, Friendship, Citation and Explanatory sub-types show the most marked difference.

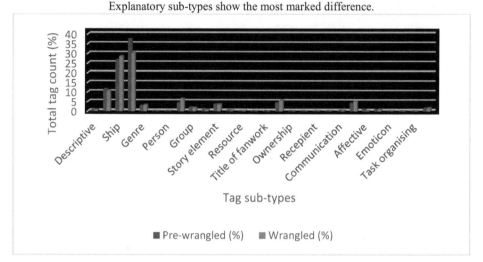

While there is the unique practice of 'tag wrangling' on AO3, this did not generally seem to affect the overall meaning or sense of the original tags used. Tag wranglers in the Marvel fandom appeared to have an in-depth expertise in their area, and, judging by the marked similarity between the pre- and post-wrangled AO3 datasets, they were for the most part correctly able to interpret and maintain the sense of the original tags. Indeed, the tag wranglers appeared to be very dedicated to this mission, and to preserving the authenticity of the original tags, as Participants C and D opined respectively:

The AO3 Terms and Conditions and the Wrangling First Principles both strictly prevent us from being gatekeepery. We can't change tags, we can't tell users how to tag in any official capacity ("describe not proscribe"). Our goal is to organize tags in a way that fans will be able to find what they're looking for. To do that, we have to speak their language and use the words they use.

One of the most important principles of tag wrangling is that we don't alter a user's tags. The beauty of the AO3's system is that everyone can tag for whatever they want, in exactly the format they want. As well, most large fandoms have multiple wranglers assigned to them, and that means that there has to be a general consensus on how to handle any given tag that is for some reason challenging, or requires a judgement call of some kind.

In fact, these tag wranglers strongly felt that their work was a way of giving back to the community, in lieu of more traditional types of fan production, such as writing fanfiction and drawing fanart. Participant C and D respectively offered that:

Tag wrangling is a way I can contribute to a community that I love. I like this kind of work and, with the decline of livejournal, I felt less connected to the community and less like I was pulling my own weight. Wrangling both lets me meet people from across fandom and help out.

I consume a great many fanworks in my day to day life, but I don't really create that many. Tag wrangling is a way that I can feel as though I give something back to the community that has brought me so much joy.

Both interviewees rejected the idea that they were gatekeepers within their fandom. Participant C even went so far as to say "I don't think of myself as a gatekeeper, mostly because I hate that word". Despite this, I would contend that tag wranglers are information gatekeepers in the sense that they are, as Case (2012, 339) says, "shaping, emphasizing, or withholding" information, or the flow of information. This is with the caveat that they do not appear to be actively or intentionally withholding or emphasizing certain aspects of information within their fan community. Rather, they are shaping it in the sense of streamlining its flow and facilitating greater access to it. In fact, Participant C noted that the reason why tag wrangling was important was that it facilitated greater access over a broad community:

Fan writing is increasingly centralized at AO3, while our day-to-day fannish expressions are ever more decentralized. I think fan writing is amazing and important, but there are sometimes some disconnects in how different parts of a fandom talk about a topic or a character. That shouldn't keep them from being able to see each others' work. For example, tagging your fic as "Romy" would keep it from being seen by people who weren't familiar with that smushname [i.e. a portmanteau of two character's names] unless a wrangler hooked them together on the backend.

The idea that tag wrangling assists in the streamlining of information is supported by the fact that far more co-occurring tags in this dataset had a higher betweenness centrality when compared to the other sites studied in the original doctoral study, Tumblr and Etsy (Price 2017, chapter 5). This means that more tags on AO3 acted as points of information exchange than either of the other two. In essence, tags on AO3 were more effective bearers of information. One might deduce, therefore, that both AO3's tag wranglers, and its curated folksonomy, are a very effective method for mitigating the less predictable effects of online tagging.

Further investigation, incorporating the views of more tag wranglers, as well as AO3 users, would be interesting. This would allow a better understanding of the tag wrangler's role as a democratic indexer and would allow us to engage with user perceptions of the system and how it works. While tag wranglers exert a great amount control over AO3's tagging system when compared to platforms such as Twitter and Tumblr, it is an 'invisible control', as on the surface the tags themselves are not changed, but merged with synonym, and categorised under a parent tag. The tag wranglers interviewed had positive views on the tagging system, especially considering the "insane strain it's under" (Participant C). Participant C felt that the filtering system could be better streamlined in order to increase retrieval accuracy. Participant D was largely satisfied with the system, but felt the "most changes that could be proposed would have more to do with changes in policy":

For example, there are an unfortunate number of tags floating about that can't be wrangled because users entered them in the wrong field, [and] if you put "Tony Stark" in the Fandom field, we can't make it a synonym of Tony Stark the character tag. Changing the type of a given tag is changing what a user entered in a way that we don't do as a matter of policy, and it's a policy I have to agree with.

This is very indicative of the trade-off between 'messiness' and control that is so often seen in folksonomic systems (Smith 2008). While AO3 suffers in some ways from maintaining this balancing act, on the whole it seems to be doing it successfully.

7. Conclusions

AO3 shows us that tagging and folksonomies are used by fans in a variety of ways – not merely for reasons of classification and organisation, but also for creative, affective and dialogic purposes. A tagging system should be flexible enough for fans to use it in any of these ways but may be labour-intensive to run. AO3's tag wrangling system seems to be largely effective, having achieved a method for linking synonymous tags, which Lu, Zhang and He (2016, 677), Chen and Ke (2013), and Rafferty (2010) have suggested as a desirable function for improving tag retrieval. This curated folksonomy is an innovative solution to the messiness of folksonomies that on the whole successfully standardises fan taxonomies without losing the original tagger's intended meaning. Such a system may be implemented in wider contexts and should be of great interest to knowledge organisers and information architects. There is much we can learn from AO3's tagging system about the ways in which both platform creators and users can come together to create knowledge organisation systems which are best-geared towards user warrant. This can be a monumental task – but AO3's tagging system shows that with passion and even obsession as a driver, much can be achieved with little. In future studies, it would be useful to interview more tag wranglers about their work, as well as users themselves. It would also be interesting to do more research into the challenges that wranglers face, both in terms of warrant, and the technological 'strain' that Participant C referred to.

References

Ådland, Marit Kristine, and Marianne Lykke. 2012. "Social Tagging in Support of Cancer Patients' Information Interaction". In *Social Information Research*, eds. Gunilla Widen and Kim Holmberg. Bingley: Emerald Group Publishing, 101-128.

Bawden, David, and Lyn Robinson. 2012. *Introduction to Information Science*. London: Facet Publishing.

Beghtol, Clare. 1986. "Semantic Validity: concepts of warrant in bibliographic classification systems". *Library Resources & Technical Services* 30: 109-125.

Bolognesi, Marianna. 2016. "Flickr® Distributional Tagspace: evaluating the semantic spaces emerging from Flickr® tags distributions". In *Big data in cognitive science: from methods to insights*, ed. Michael. N. Jones. Hove: Psychology Press, 144-173.

Bullard, Julia. 2014. "Values and Negotiation in Classification Work". In *CSCW Companion '14: Proceedings of the companion publication of the 17th ACM conference on Computer supported cooperative work & social computing*, 15-19 February 2014, Baltimore, Maryland, USA. New York: ACM, 45-48.

Bullard, Julia. 2017. "Warrant as a Means to Study Classification System Design". *Journal of Documentation* 73: 75-90.

Carrington, Peter J., and John Scott. 2011. "Introduction". In *The SAGE Handbook of Social Network Analysis*, ed. John Scott and Peter J, Carrington. London: SAGE, 1-10.

Cattuto, Ciro, Christoph Schmitz, Andrea Baldassarri et al. 2007. "Network Properties of Folksonomies". *AI Communications* 20: 245-262.

Chen, Ya-Ning, and Hao-Ren Ke. 2013. "An Analysis of Users' Behaviour Patterns in the Organisation of Information: a case study of CiteULike". *Online Information Review*, 37: 638-656.

Cole, Samantha. 2019. "An Internet Fan Fiction Archive Is Nominated for a Hugo". *Motherboard*. April 3 2019. https://motherboard.vice.com/en_us/article/vbw9eb/internet-fan-fiction-archive-ao3-hugo-award

Driscoll, Catherine. 2006. "One True Pairing: the romance of pornography and the pornography of romance". In *Fan fiction and fan communities in the age of the internet*, eds. Karen Hellekson and Kristina Busse. Jefferson: McFarland, 79-96.

Estrada, Liliana Melgar, Michiel Hildebrand, Victor de Boer & Jacco van Ossenbruggen. 2017. "Time-Based Tags for Fiction Movies: comparing experts to novices using a video labeling game". *Journal of the Association for Information Science and Technology*, 68: 348-364.

Golder, Scott A., and Huberman, Bernardo A. 2006. "Usage Patterns of Collaborative Tagging Systems". *Journal of Information Science*, 32: 198-208.

Gursoy, Ayse. 2015. "Evaluating Fan Fiction Metadata for Preservation Use". In *ASIST '15 Proceedings of the 78th ASIS&T Annual Meeting: Information Science with Impact: Research in and for the Community*, St. Louis, MO, USA, 6-10 November 2015, 52: 1-4.

Hart, Chris, Michael Shoolbred, David Butcher, & David Kane. 1999. "The Bibliographical Structure of Fan Information". *Collection Building* 18: 81-89.

Hawksey, Martin. 2017. "Making the Complex Less Complicated: an introduction to social network analysis". *MASHe*, 3 June. https://mashe.hawksey.info/2017/06/making-the-complex-less-complicated-an-introduction-to-social-network-analysis/

Haythornthwaite, Caroline. 1996. "Social Network Analysis: an approach and technique for the study of information exchange". *Library & Information Science Research,* 18: 323-342.

Hendrikx, Bas, Stefan Dormans, Arnoud Lagendijk, & Mike Thelwall. 2016. "Understanding the Geographical Development of Social Movements: a web-link analysis of Slow Food". *Global Networks*, 17: 47-67.

Hidderley, Rob & Pauline Rafferty,. 1997. "Democratic Indexing: an approach to the retrieval of fiction". *Information Services and Use*, 17: 101-109.

Jalalimanesh, Ammar & Seyyed Majid Yaghoubi, 2013. "Application of Social Network Analysis in Interlibrary Loan Services". *Webology,* 10: article 108. http://www.webology.org/2013/v10n1/a108.html

Jenkins, Henry. 2006. *Fans, Bloggers, and Gamers: exploring participatory culture.* New York: New York University Press.

Jiang, Chunlin, Liwei Zhang & Shengbo Liu. 2014. "Social Network Analysis of the Interlocking Editorship among Chinese Library and Information Science Journals". *Journal of the China Society for Scientific & Technical Information,* 33: 481-490.

Johnson, Catherine A. 2004. "Choosing People: the role of social capital in information seeking behaviour". *Information Research,* 10: paper 201. http://www.informationr.net/ir/10-1/paper201.html

Johnson, J. David. 2019. "Network Analysis Approaches to Collaborative Information Seeking in Inter-Professional Health Care Teams". *Information Research* 24: paper 810. http://www.informationr.net/ir/24-1/paper810.html

Johnson, Shannon Fay. 2014. "Fan Fiction Metadata Creation and Utilization within Fan Fiction Archives: three primary methods". *Transformative Works and Cultures,* 17. http://dx.doi.org/10.3983/twc.2014.0578

Lee, So Young, Hyang Mi Kim, Kyounghee Chu & Jungchi Seo. 2013. "Fandom as a Prosumer: study on information behavior of fandom". *The Journal of Digital Policy and Management,* 11: 747-759.

Lu, Chao, Chengzhi Zhang & Daqing He. 2016. "Comparative Analysis of Book Tags: a cross-lingual perspective". *The Electronic Library,* 34: 666-682.

Ma, Feicheng, and Yating Li. 2014. "Utilising Social Network Analysis to Study the Characteristics and Functions of the Co-Occurrence Network of Online Tags". *Online Information Review,* 38: 232-247.

Malik, Aqdas, Aditya Johri, Rajat Handa, Habib Karbasian & Hemant Purohit. 2018. "How Social Media Supports Hashtag Activism Through Multivocality: a case study of #ILookLikeanEngineer". *First Monday* 23. https://doi.org/10.5210/fm.v23i11.9181

Marin, Alexandra & Barry Wellman. 2011. "Social Network Analysis: an introduction". In *The SAGE Handbook of Social Network Analysis*, ed. John Scott and Peter J, Carrington. London: SAGE, 11-25.

Otte, Evelien & Ronald Rousseau. 2002. "Social Network Analysis: a powerful strategy, also for the information sciences". *Journal of Information Science*, 28: 441-453.

Park, Han Woo, and Mike Thelwall. 2003. "Hyperlink Analyses of the World Wide Web". *Journal of Computer Mediated Communication*, 8.

Price, Ludovica Wing Sheun. 2017. *Serious Leisure in the Digital World: exploring the information behaviour of fan communities*. Ph.D. thesis, City, University of London.

Rafferty, Pauline. 2010. "Genre Theory, Knowledge Organisation and Fiction". In *Paradigms and conceptual systems in knowledge organization: Proceedings of the eleventh international ISKO conference*. February 23-26, Rome, Italy, eds. Claudio Gnoli and Fulvio Mazzocchi. Würzburg: Ergon-Verlag, 254-261.

Rafferty, Pauline & Rob Hidderley. 2007. "Flickr and Democratic Indexing: dialogic approaches to indexing". *ASLIB Proceedings* 59: 397-410.

Rose, Sarah Marita. 2013. "There is a Conversation in my Search: differing uses for tags". In *From collections to connections: turning libraries "inside-out". The 21st International BOBCATSSS Conference*, 23-25 January 2013, Ankara, Turkey, eds. Zehra Taskin et al. Ankara: Hacettepe University Department of Information Management, 28-31.

Rossi, Luca & Fabio Giglietto. 2016. "Twitter Use During TV: a full-season analysis of #serviziopubblico hashtag". *Journal of Broadcasting & Electronic Media*, 60: 331-346.

Saha, Arpita & Parthasarathi Mukhopadhyay. 2016. "Ranking OER Providers in India: a webometric analysis". *International Research: Journal of Library & Information Science*, 6: 134-143.

Small, Tamara A. 2011. "WHAT THE HASHTAG? A content analysis of Canadian politics on Twitter". *Information, Communication & Society,* 14: 872-895.

Smith, Gene. 2008. *Tagging: people-powered metadata for the social web*. Berkeley, CA: New Riders.

Thelwall, Mike. 2004. *Link Analysis: an information science approach*. London: Elsevier.

Thelwall, Mike. 2017. "Book Genre and Author Gender: Romance>Paranormal-Romance to Autobiography>Memoir". *Journal of the Association for Information Science and Technology*, 68: 1212-1223.

Trant, J. 2009. "Studying Social Tagging and Folksonomy: a review and framework". *Journal of Digital Information*, 10: 1-44.

Vaidya, Praveenkumar, and N. S. Harinarayana. 2016. "The Comparative and Analytical Study of Librarything Tags with Library of Congress Subject Headings". *Knowledge Organization* 43: 35-43.

Wang, Mengmeng & Mizuho Iwaihara. 2015. "Hashtag Sense Induction Based on Co-Occurrence Graphs". In *APWeb 2015: Web Technologies and Applications*, 18-20 September 2015, Guangzhou, China, eds. Reynold Cheng et al. Lecture Notes in Computer Science, 9313, Cham: Springer, 154-165.

Wang, Rong, Wenlin Liu & Shuyang Gao. 2016. "Hashtags and Information Virality in Networked Social Movement: examining hashtag co-occurrence patterns". *Online Information Review*, 40: 850-866.

Session 2A: AI

Semantic Enrichment of Linked Personal Authority Data: a case study of elites in late Imperial China

Shu-jiun Chen, Institute of History and Philology, Academia Sinica, Taiwan

Abstract

The study uses the Database of Names and Biographies (DNB) as an example to explore how, in the transformation of original data into linked data, semantic enrichment can facilitate research inquiries and enhance engagement in digital humanities. Semantic enrichment is one partial study of LOD (Linked Open Data) in this report, developed by collaborating with historians in converting the DNB from legacy systems to a Linked Data format for the purpose of digital humanities. In the preliminary results of the study, we have defined instance-based and schema-based categories of semantic enrichment. In the instance-based category, in which enrichment occurs by enhancing the content of entities, we further determined three types, including (1) enriching the entities by linking to diverse, cross-domain external resources in order to provide additional data of multiple perspectives, (2) enriching the entities with missing data, which is needed to satisfy the semantic queries, and (3) providing the entities with access to an extended knowledge base. In the schema-based categories, in which enrichment occurs by enhancing the relations between the properties, we have preliminarily identified and implemented two types for the project, including (1) enriching the properties by defining the hierarchical relations between properties and (2) specifying properties' domain and range for data reasoning. In addition, the study implements the LOD dataset in a digital humanities platform to demonstrate how instances and entities can be applied in the full texts where the relationship between entities are highlighted in order to bring scholars more semantic details of the texts.

1. Introduction

Semantic relations between entities are the basic units of knowledge organization (Green 2001; Stock 2010). This paper discusses the issue of semantic enrichment in Linked Open Data (LOD) research. The study will use the Database of Names and Biographies (DNB) as an example to explore how, in the transformation of original data into linked data, semantic enrichment can facilitate research inquiries and enhance engagement in digital humanities. Hosted by the Institute of History and Philology, Academia Sinica (Taiwan), the DNB contains 35,666 records of Chinese historical persons who are cultural and socio-political elites in late imperial China (1368-1911), extracted from various historical archives for the purpose of supporting historians' research. Each metadata record has information including name, alternative name, dates of birth/death, native place, biographical data, work experiences, related persons, specialties, academic background, and job titles. Semantic enrichment is one of the current LOD project's core research streams, developed by collaborating with historians for converting the DNB from legacy databases to Linked Data format for the purpose of digital humanities. The study has deployed the methods of data modeling, data reconciliation, and data enrichment during transforming the legacy metadata records into LOD in order to add value which is structured in machine-processable format and gives more meaning to the dataset (Hyvönen 2016; Van Hooland & Verborgh 2014;

Zeng 2019). The DNB data model is composed of 5 core classes (i.e. agent, event, place, object and time classes), 67 properties from 16 semantic vocabularies (i.e. bio, dbpedia, dcterms, gvp, leo, owl, rdfs, schema.org, skos, etc.), and reuses 3 external resources (i.e. AAT, VIAF, TGAZ). The LOD dataset contains more than 2 million triples and is available to query Linked Data with SPARQL from the LODLab of Academia Sinica (http://data.ascdc.tw/en/sparql.php). The following presents the preliminary results of the study.

2. Instance-based Semantic Enrichment

Instance-based, or entity, enrichment, in the context of LOD is a process to endow the original data with other supplementary or supported knowledge, which is beyond the original data content, from external resources. This is done to extend the perspective of the data itself and also integrate heterogeneous resources into a more complete and sophisticated knowledge. By enriching the entities in the LOD-based dataset, it not only enlarges the knowledge base itself but also inspires new perspectives for further research and interpretation of the study results. There are three approaches identified in the study to achieve entity enrichment as follows.

2.1 Enriching the Entities by Linking to Diverse, Cross-domain External Resources in Order to Provide Additional Data of Multiple Perspectives

In the DNB dataset, which is focused on the information of Chinese historical figures, the Agent Entity is linked to the cross-domain external resources. For instance, in the Agent Entity of Tseng Guo-fan (曾國藩, 1811-1872), a famous literati and high minister of the late Qing period, the AAT (Art & Architecture Thesaurus) concept of "calligraphy" is directly linked with the Agent by the specialty property (dbpedia-owl:specialty). In the original DNB metadata, a specialty of Tseng is presented in literal as "書法" (calligraphy) in Chinese characters. Since the AAT is a multilingual thesaurus including English, Chinese, German, Dutch, and more, the link to the AAT term for "calligraphy" (AAT 300053162) can enrich the Agent Entity in the related property with information on the same concept and its definition in other languages. This could enhance understandability for users who do not know the Chinese language.

2.2 Enriching the Entities with Missing Data Which is Needed to Satisfy the Semantic Queries

As to the information on the native place of a person, since its value shows the historical administrative name of a place and is not entirely equivalent with the current place name, we therefore added a new contextual entity for Place for each agent, when the referred agent has information in the field of "native place." The method of adding a place entity is not only to describe the historical name but also to be enriched by linking to the linked data of the Chinese historical place name in the Temporal Gazetteer (TGAZ) developed by Harvard University, which defines the geographical range and temporal information of the related historical place name with the same-as property (owl:sameAs) under the same entity. Such a place entity is linked to the Agent Entity of this study by the native-place property (ascdc:nativePlace) and also carries the label (rdfs:label) and the link to external resources (owl:sameAs).

Another reason to reuse the terms of Chinese historical place names from TGAZ is that on the SPARQL (SPARQL Protocol and RDF Query Language) interface for DNB dataset the study applied Chinese historical Geographic Information System (GIS) maps for showing an agent's native place in certain examples of SPARQL query. For instance, when one queries "which provenances did the Qing agents ranked as jinshi (進士, "presented scholar", the highest degree of the Chinese Imperial civil service examinations) come from?" Since the current Google Map as open source shows only the global map in modern political and administrative boundaries, it is quite different from the historical map. The location of a city from hundreds of years ago might also be different from its current geographic situation. Since each term in The Temporal Gazetteer contains the longitude and latitude information of a historical place name in different dynasties or periods, the application of TGAZ is reasonable for displaying the related geographic information in the historical GIS-maps.

2.3 Providing the Entities with Extension to a Knowledge Base

The extension of data content in the entities to a knowledge base is regarded in this study as one part of data enrichment. It could not only enable the entities with more detailed information from the external resources but also make linkage of the original entity to an entire knowledge base of a certain subject field, which can inspire new perspectives for further research and interpretation of the study results. For instance, the study makes extension of entities to the time ontology which is one part of the knowledge base. In the current LOD-based dataset of the DNB, the entities relating to the temporal information on the official career of a person is particularly extended to the "term lists of the time and periods", a controlled vocabulary developed by the study for defining the Chinese historical periods and yearly times of all dynasties in China (see Figure 1). The application of such term lists is based on the "Time ontology," which is developed by the study and based on W3C's Time ontology in OWL (Cox & Little 2017).

Figure 1. Extension of DNB entities with the study's time ontology, viewed with classes

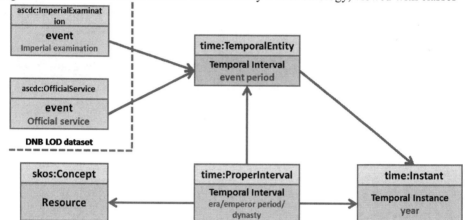

For example, the DNB person agent Ding Bao-zhen (丁寶楨) was appointed as Governor of the Sichuan Province (四川總督) between 1881 and 1886. In the data model design of DNB, a person agent's official career in the government is expressed as entities of Official service (ascdc:OfficialService). To describe the beginning date and end date of Ding's appointment, this entity for official service is linked to an entity of temporal period (time:TemporalEntity) by at-time property (leo:atTime), which further describes the beginning and end date of the related period for official service in the historical Chinese era year, represented by the "time:instant" entity. To extend the knowledge base for that temporal information, the study's time ontology is applied to describe the hierarchical temporal details of the instances as the "7th year of Guangxu" (光緒七年, 1881) and "12th year of Guangxu" (光緒 12 年, 1886) and linked with the entity for era name (光緒), emperor name (光緒皇帝), and dynasty name (清朝) in "time:propertInterval" by the properties "time:intervalDuring" and "time:inside."(see Figure 2)

Figure 2. Extension of the entity with knowledge-based external resource

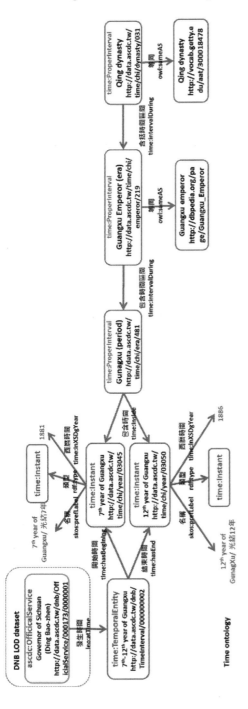

Example: Extension of the entity for official service with hierarchical information on the beginning and end date of Ding Bao-zhen's appointment as Governor in Sichuan between 1881 and 1886

After extending the entity with the temporal terms to describe the beginning and ending year of a certain period of an official position, the information of these mentioned historical years is expressed as entities of thing and can further be linked to the era names, emperor names, and the dynasty names in Chinese history. Therefore, a hierarchically structured knowledge base, which is focused on Chinese historical temporal names, is entirely integrated into the dataset and enriches the data content of each related person agent.

3. Schema-based Semantic Enrichment
Property enrichment in LOD is a process to enable hierarchical or associative meaning within pairs of property, which could create a relationship between related entities and also enable a meaningful and efficient data query in a hierarchical semantic structure.

3.1 Enriching the Properties by Defining the Hierarchical and Associative Relations Between Properties
To a certain extent, the applicability of enriching the properties in the LOD-based datasets depends on whether a hierarchical or associative meaning exists between different data elements of the original metadata. In the data element of the current DNB datasets, such related meaning is especially found in the data element as the "personal relations" (人物關係) of an agent, in which a person's connections to another agent is linked and expressed by reusing suitable properties. As an example, the semantic relationships of an Agent A to his teacher, Agent B, is defined as the 'has-teacher' property (agrelon:hasTeacher), while the relationships of Agent A to his grandparent, Agent C, is expressed as the 'has-grandparent' property (agrelon:hasGrandparent).

In fact, the personal relation between agents is a mutual- or hierarchical-expressible relationship. If A is student of B, then the B should be the teacher of A. In the semantic data model design, such mutual or hierarchical relation can be defined by enriching the definition of the related properties. In the current world of Semantic Web, RDF and Owl are the two types of data vocabularies, which are mostly applied to enrich the relations between properties as the abovementioned cases and also to enhance the efficiency by data reasoning. In particular, the subproperty-of property (rdfs:subpopertyOf) can be used to mark the hierarchical relation between properties, while the 'inverse-of' property (owl:inverseOf) is suitable to describe the mutually affected relations between properties on the same level (see Table 1).

Table 1 Enrich the properties by using rdfs:subpopertyOf and owl:inverseOf

	Properties	Domain	Range	Function of property enriching
1	rdfs:subPropertyOf	Property	Property	Hierarchical relation
2	owl:inverseOf	Property	Property	Mutual relation

Taking the agent Zeng Guo-fan (曾國藩, DNB: NO000000058) in the DNB datasets as an example, the figure is linked to the agent Li Hong-zhang (李鴻章, DNB: NO000002242) by the 'has-student property' ("agrelon:hasStudent). Since the relationship between a teacher and student is mutually referred, if the 'inverse-of' property (owl:inverseOf) is reused and enriches the definition of the 'has-student' property (agrelon:hasStudent), the reverse relation expressed as 'has-teacher' property (agrelon:hasTeacher) would also be findable by data reasoning.

With the same example of Zeng Guo-fan, the figure is further linked to the agent Yuan Bingzhen (袁秉楨, DNB: NO000012514) by "agrelon:hasChildInLaw" and to Zeng Guangquan (曾廣銓, DNB: NO000008193) by "agrelon:hasGrandchild." Since those different types of relations to a person can be clustered in a broader range of properties such as relatives, a hierarchical structure of property can be hence defined by using "rdfs:supropertyOf to structure "agrelon:hasChildInLaw" and "agrelon:hasGrandchild" both under the property as "agrelon:hasRelative.

3.2 Specifying Properties' Domain and Range for Data Reasoning

In the Semantic Web, each item of data can be expressed as a triple, which is composed of subject, property, and object. From them, the major function of a property is to enable the entities of information (subject and object) with a semantic relation, which could enable the data query in a logical, machine-processable and machine-understandable way. In other words, the property plays a role as the bridge to connect the subject with object and thus construct complete, meaningful information in the data. However, the use of a certain property is not arbitrary. Each property has its own definition to which condition or restriction can be applied to link the subject- and object-entities.

In the current data model design for the "Database of Names and Biographies" (DNB), 67 properties from 16 vocabularies are reused to describe the biographic information on Chinese historical figures and relations between figures. The information on the domain and range of all reused properties is described in the specification of DNB ontology, seen in the selected examples in Table 2. Such specification can be used as referential standard by the semantic data model design and also defines which data context that a property could be reused in the data structure.

Table 2 Specifying domain and range of the father property (bio:father) in DNB

bio:father	
URI	http://purl.org/vocab/bio/0.1/father
Label	Father
Type	Property
Comment	To describe information on father of a DNB Agent Entity
Domain	foaf:Agent
Range	foaf:Agent
Quantification	0-1
Data type	Concept/ASCDC
Examples	Liu yun father Liu Ton-hsung

In the semantic data model design, the domain of a property is always the instance of an entity (or a class), which defines the subject of an information. As in the abovementioned example, a property as "bio:father" in the DNB is applied to describe the information on the father of a person. The domain of this property is defined as "foaf:Agent," which means this property is only suitable to be applied by an entity of the agent. In the machine-processable form it could be formulated as "rdfs:domain foaf:Agent." However, the range of a property could be expressed as a different data type, such as the instance of an entity (or a class), literal information, date decimal numbers of measurement, or quantity of item. Again, as in the example (Table 2), the specification also defines the range of "bio:father" as "foaf:Agent", which means that object information should also be an instance of agent entity. In the machine-processable form it could be formulated as "rdfs:range foaf:Agent."

4. Applications of LOD for Digital Humanities

The input of the LOD-based dataset of the Database of the Names and Biographies (DNB) into the system of the Digital Humanities Research Platform (DHRP), developed by the Academia Sinica Center for Digital Cultures (ASCDC), is a Linked Data application to enhance the reusability of the DNB data. Additionally, the study demonstrates the possibility of applying a LOD-based dataset to enlarge the research scope of the scholars in digital humanities and to integrate into digital research tools- using examples in the DHRP.

The DHRP is an open, cloud-based text repository to enhance the research of digital humanities, which is developed as a platform for online services based on the needs of scholars. The platform is equipped with different digital tools for text and visual analytics, such as text annotation, text similarity comparison, N-gram analysis, historical spatiotemporal visualization, or social network analysis. The digital content of the DHRP is currently uploaded with texts from rare Chinese books for a total of more than 220 million words. In the current stage, the DNB dataset is already in the test version of the DHPR-platform. In particular, we use the DNB's data on properties of the person's relations, specialty, and native place as practical cases of studies to map the text passages in the *Qing Shilu* (the Veritable Records of the Qing Dynasty/清實錄) and to demonstrate the semantic relations between different person agents or agent entities with place or concept entities in the historiographical works of the DHPF-platform. In total, more than 20,000 named entities from the 93,431 text passages in the *Qing Shilu* are matched with the instances of entities in the DNB.

In the DHRP-platform, the mapped DNB personal names in the *Qing Shilu* will be marked up in different colors according to their types in the data unit of a triple in the DNB dataset. For instance, the person's name belonging to the subject in a triple will be highlighted in blue, while names of an object in a triple will be shown upon a gray background. The type of semantic relationships (properties) between different agents will be represented in a dotted line, which link the subject entity with its related object entity.

When moving the mouse cursor onto the subject agent in the text, the platform will automatically present the related agents of person names in green with the type of semantic relation. Further, clicking on those names will direct to the website of the LOD-datasets, showing the data content of the related records of the persons.

Figure 3. Revealing the relations between a matched person's name from DNB in *Qing Shilu* on the DHRP platform

(Example: Teacher-student Relationship between Zeng Guo-fan (曾國藩) andd Li Hong-zhang (李鴻章) are shown with a type of sematic relation (hasStudent) in red.)

Figure 4. Linking the matched person's name in Qing Shilu to the external resource in the DNB

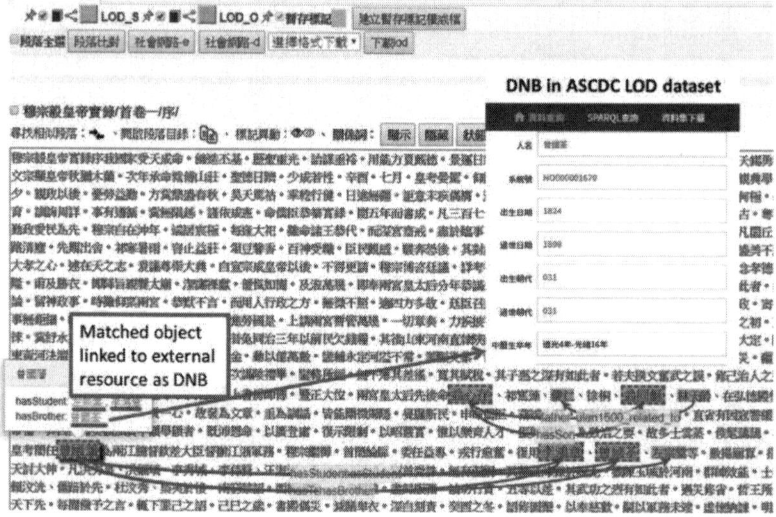

Example: Moving the cursor onto the person name of Zeng Guo-fan (曾國藩) and showing his related persons retrieved in *Qing Shilu*; clicking one of the names as Zeng Guo-chuan (曾國荃) and linking to the equivalent resource in the DNB

For further presentation of the related data in DHRP-platform by using the tools for data visualization, the function of social network analysis (SNA) is integrated into the system to show the matched persons in *Qing Shilu* based on the DNB dataset.

In the original DHRP-platform, the scholars could only execute the text retrieval and comparison based on the literal context uploaded in the system. Users could not find out detailed information or definitions of the retrieved words or text, since the context was not linked to the external resources by a semantic method. After uploading the LOD-based dataset in the originally text-based DHRP-platform, a detailed definition of the matched text (for example, the further biographical information of a person) can be shown in DHRP by reusing the related data in DNB dataset. This is accomplished through the named-entity recognition which is a mapping procedure of the terms in DNB with the text in the platform. The semantic relations of a person to another person, place, or concept will also be notified by endowing the type of relations (properties) in the platform. These could extent not only the knowledge base of a scholar but might also offer other relevant information or inspire research angles, which one might not take notice when retrieving the results merely in a literal context.

Figure 5. SNA-analysis showing the relation types between matched persons in a passage of *Qing Shilu* in different forms of data visualization

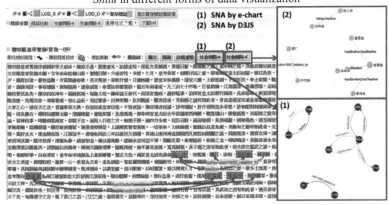

(1) SNA by e-chart; (2) SNA by D3.js data visualization

References

Baca, Murtha and Melissa Gill. 2015. "Encoding Multilingual Knowledge Systems in the Digital Age: the Getty Vocabularies." *Knowledge Organization* 42(4): 232-243.

Bischof, Stefan. 2017. *Complementary Methods for the Enrichment of Linked Data* (Doctoral Dissertation, Technische Universität Wien). https://aic.ai.wu.ac.at/~polleres/supervised_theses/Stefan_Bischof_Dissertation_2017.pdf

Cox, Simon and Chris Little. (2017). *Time Ontology in OWL*. https://www.w3.org/TR/owl-time/

Ding, Li; Joshua Shinavier, Zhenning Shangguan, and Deborah L McGuinness. 2010. "SameAs Networks and Beyond: Analyzing Deployment Status and Implications of OWL:sameAs in Linked Data." In *The Semantic Web: ISWC 2010*, ed. Peter F. Patel-Schneider, et al. Berlin: Springer, 145-60.

Green, Rebecca. 2001. "Relationships in the Organization of Knowledge: An Overview." In *Relationships in the Organization of Knowledge*, ed. Carol A. Bean and Rebecca Green. Dordrecht: Springer, 3-18.

Hyvönen, Eero. 2016. "Cultural Heritage Linked Data on the Semantic Web: three case studies using the sampo model." In *VIII Encounter of Documentation Centres of Contemporary Art: Open Linked Data and Integral Management of Information in Cultural Centres*. Vitoria-Gasteiz, Spain: Artium, 19-20.

Isaac, Antoine, Valentine Charles, Yorgos Mamakis, and Juliane Stiller. 2016. *Europeana Semantic Enrichment Framework*, ed. Hugo Manguinhas

Stock, Wolfgang G. 2010. "Concepts and Semantic Relations in Information Science." *Journal of the American Society for Information Science and Technology*, 61(10): 1951-69.

Subhashree, S., Rajeev Irny, and P Sreenivasa Kumar. 2018. "Review of Approaches for Linked Data Ontology Enrichment." In *International Conference on Distributed Computing and Internet Technology*, 27-49. Cham: Springer.

Van Hooland, Seth and Ruben Verborgh. 2014. *Linked Data for Libraries, Archives and Museums: How to clean, link and publish your metadata*. Chicago: Neal-Shuman.

Zeng, Marcia Lei. 2019. "Semantic Enrichment for Enhancing LAM Data and Supporting Digital Humanities." *El Profesional de la Información*, 28(1).

Towards a Process for Criminal Semantic Information Fusion to Obtain Situational Projections

Valdir Amancio Pereira Junior, São Paulo State University (UNESP), Brazil
Gustavo Marttos Cáceres Pereira, São Paulo State University (UNESP), Brazil
Leonardo Castro Botega, São Paulo State University (UNESP), Brazil

Abstract

Situational Awareness (SAW) refers to the level of consciousness that a human holds about a situation. In risk management domain, SAW failures can induce human to make mistakes in decision making. In addition, criminal domains with dynamic situations are prone to information quality problems, especially when they are provided by humans. Considering the nature of the information and the context, the information may be incomplete, outdated, inconsistent or influenced by cultural and stress factors. Other limiting factors are related to the ability to deal with large scale data, hindering informational processes such as processing, storage and retrieval of information. Information fusion processes present opportunities to improve the quality of information, generating subsidies that can contribute to a more complete SAW. The state-of-the-art presents solutions that involve the representation and processing of high-level information, however applying fusion techniques that are limited to the analysis and integration of information, where the application of semantics, ontological models and the concern with the information quality is limited. The proposal of this work is the development of a semantic information fusion, able to generate better quality information, aiming to make situational projections. Moreover, the new fusion process, as an extension of a previous human-driven fusion model, handles an application ontology, able to represent situations of the risk management domain and enable semantic inferences. Results so far validate the need of semantic-based fusion approaches for the development of useful risk assessment solutions, both to enhance SAW and empower critical decision-making.

1. Introduction

Analyzing human behavior in relation to its forms of interaction with analog and digital environments, information and other humans, there is a perceived dependence between the information that is available in the environment, the mental model of human and the nature of the environment. This can be critical, casual and other variations in the daily situation of individuals. In other words, the context which the human and the information are viewed, will define the degree of relationship between them (Stanton et al. 2001) (Kokar & Endsley 2012).

Bringing this analysis of human behavior with environments and information to the scientific field, searching for sciences and disciplines that sustain this bias, we have reached two main themes: Situational Awareness (SAW) and decision making. According to Endsley (2001), SAW is an important cognitive process for human decision makers in critical situations and environments. It addresses the perception of entities of interest in the environment, the meaning of human and collective actions in Space-time and projection of the current state to the near future.

Considering the criminal domain, SAW becomes a crucial factor in revealing trends, the incidence of threats and the increase or decrease of imminent risks. A limited or flawed SAW can compromise humans understanding of the real state of an environment, leading to poor decision-making, and may result in dire consequences for lives, properties and the environment. While the development of SAW and access to good information about situations cannot guarantee the best human decision making, these factors can collaborate with security analysts and decision makers in order to eliminate uncertainty, maintain a greater knowledge of past criminal events, situations in courses and future activities (Rogova and Bosse 2010).

Acquiring and maintaining a quality SAW is even more challenging when considering the scenario of criminal data in Brazil, due to the large volume and heterogeneity of existing data within the territory. Another critical factor is the source of the data, mostly from human intelligence, as is the case of the main source of data of this work, which are reports of crimes reported to the Centers of Service of security forces. Typically, data provided by humans are incomplete, outdated, inconsistent and sometimes even influenced by cultural factors, affecting the informational and computational processes that capture, organize, categorize, process and represent the data and stimulate the analyst's SAW.

In this context, models and techniques to handle quality limited critical information were developed, aiming to improve subsidies for SAW acquisition and maintenance, and consequently sustained decision-making. These models and techniques are related to various disciplines, such as data quality assessment, information and knowledge representation, data lifecycle and others (Noy and McGuinness 2001) (Batini et al. 2009) (Blasch et al. 2012) (Kokar and Endsley 2012) (Laskey et al. 2012) (Botega et al. 2016).

This paper discusses topics regarding data and information fusion, quality assessment, representation of information and ontologies, towards the proposal of a new approach for crime-related information fusion, deeply influenced by data quality indexes and ontologies to lead the best fit of SAW on a crime situation analysis.

The main contribution of this work is to make feasible the semantic fusion of information, based on the Quantify model (Quality-aware Human-driven Information Fusion Model), working to deal with data from human intelligence, more specifically of situations related to the criminal domain, seeking to improve the quality of these data and positively influence the construction of human SAW, leading them to the state of situational projection. In addition to presenting a means to apply semantic fusion with the Quantify model, this paper also proposes the integration and use of quality indexes and ontologies as parameters of the fusion process.

This paper is organized in the following sections: (2) Situational Awareness, (3) Data and Information Fusion, (4) Data and Information Quality, (5) Semantic Web and Ontologies, (6) The Criminal Domain in Brazil, (7) Related Work, (8) The Process and the Ontology for Criminal Semantic Information and (9) Conclusions.

2. Situational Awareness

Coined by Endsley (1988), the term Situational Awareness (SAW) refers to a fundamental concept that concerns the decision-making process of each individual. This individual in turn may be immersed in an environment that the condition to be under high pressure and exposed to a relevant range of sensitive information, which needs to be analyzed with due attention by the individual so that there is no misinterpretation and consequently can maintain the assertiveness of decision-making. SAW corresponds to a cognitive process of the individual. It does not guarantee that this will produce the best image of the situation and consequently make the most appropriate decision. However, this could improve the quality of decision-making.

The SAW of an individual can be qualified through their experiences, capacities, workload, goals and objectives, among other factors. However, even the most skilled individuals can make mistaken decisions if their SAW is inaccurate. Because of this, Endsley (2016) argues that in order to be more likely to make more definite and more appropriate decision making, it is necessary to continuously improve the SAW, thereby improving the decision-making process.

In the model proposed by Endsley (1988), SAW can be measured by means of three levels, which are directly and indirectly influenced by internal and external factors, as shown in the Figure 1. The levels can be achieved gradually according to the evolution of the situation and better understanding by the individual in relation to it. The SAW levels are:

- Level 1: Perception of the elements in the environment. It is consistent with the perception of existing relevant elements, as well as their characteristics.

54

- Level 2: Understanding the current situation. Based on the composition of the elements found, it is necessary to create a relationship, contextualizing them according to the respective objectives and goals.
- Level 3: Projection of future states. This level refers to being aware of what the elements are and what they mean to the real situation. To achieve this level, it is necessary to have the ability to predict what will be the future states of the elements. Level Three is achieved only successfully when there is a good understanding of the situation, which is incumbent on the previous level. Making projections requires experience in the domain in which the individual is set.

Systems have been developed to promote the continuous development of SAW and provide greater support for decision-making. The systems and mechanisms for collection, storage, representation, processing and visualization of information for the construction of SAW make it possible to deal with information from multiple sources and in different formats delivered transparently and prioritized via a common interface. (Stanton et al. 2001) (Botega et al. 2017).

Figure 1 - Situational Awareness Model from Endsley (1988)

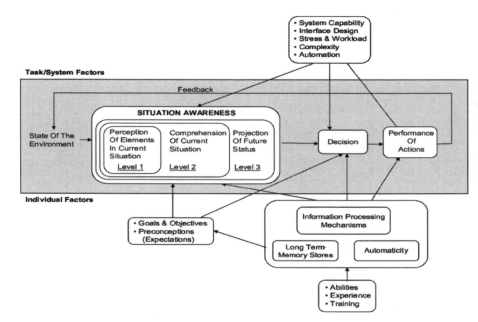

According to Vincen et al. (2009), with technological and scientific advances around this theme, new and increasingly efficient solutions emerge, addressing the entire life cycle of information, from its acquisition and collection from physical and non-physical sensors, persistence, representation, processing, to presentation through an interface. This allows the individual to position him- or her-self itself as an active element and may act during the informational processes. Data Fusion Systems (DFS) and Information Fusion Systems (IFS) are examples of such solutions.

These systems adopt fusion models that resemble some points of the SAW model proposed by Endsley, which in turn can provide synergy between processes, facilitating the development and integration of both models. This approximation of the models favors the informational result that is presented to the individual decision-maker at the end of the SAW process, bringing an image of the real environment much clearer to the digital environment that is monitored (Souza et al. 2015) (Botega et al. 2017).

3. Data and Information Fusion

The data and information fusion can be considered a process of transformation and inference, regardless of the input. The main objective is to maximize the value of information for the individual, whether it is a human or machine. As well as the increase in the value of information, other gains are obtained through the fusion processes, such as reduction in the dimensionality of data, evolution in its representativeness and production of inputs for the analysis of situations. By aggregating advances in the application of data fusion and information processes, it is possible to contribute to the construction of SAW, which offers more informational inputs and stimulating access, use and control of information during the analysis process and favors the analysis of the environment (Steinberg et al. 2008) (Blasch et al. 2012).

For this paper the term Information Fusion Systems (IFS)will be adopted. This due to the content and informational level that the work deals with. Another factor is the literature of the area, which points to data fusion related to physical sensors with lower levels of information. The processes that permeate this work, deal with high-level and even semantic information, mostly from human intelligence (Foo 2013) (Botega et al. 2017).

In the current technological, post-modern scenario there is an increasing number of devices capable of generating, propagating, presenting and interpreting information, together with a growing number of online applications. Together they produce gigantic volumes of information, impacting on daily life, which gives rise to the need for solutions capable of dealing with such abundance and quality of information. IFS, as a multidisciplinary discipline, brings some solutions to remedy the problem of large information volumes (Wurman 1996) (Morville and Rosenfeld 2006) (Blasch et al. 2012).

Where such information is from non-physical sensors, such as human intelligence, diverse databases and information arising from Web, we change the role of the human with the fusion systems. A new term is coined to reflect the role of humans: high-level information fusion (HLIF). This new approach to fusion processes emphasises human action during processes, rules and even in the adequacy of visualization, allowing interfaces to adapt in the best possible way. This supports new forms of inference, classification and data mining of higher-level information, (i.e. arising from non-physical and physical sensors) (Salerno 2002) (Blasch et al. 2012).

Concern about the quality of data and information is also manifested, especially when dealing with data produced by humans. This concern goes beyond the internal processes, which can propagate quality failures, promoting uncertainty and errors in the SAW of users. The need for quality indexes interferes with the user interaction (i.e. in the representation of information, the quality of data and information. (Pereira et al. 2016) (Botega et al. 2019).

Botega et al. (2017) propose a new model of information fusion, which considers the active role of humans within the fusion process, SAW and decision making. The focus of the model is on critical systems for analysis of risk situations, the Quantify model (Quality-aware Human-driven Information Fusion Model), aiming to assist in the construction of SAW during the use of critical systems capable of analyzing complex scenarios. It aims to overcome challenges related to the evaluation and use of quality indexes, such as decision support or risk management systems. This will be the model used as the basis of the discussions and questions of this paper and will be addressed in more detail in Section 7, together with the proposed fusion process.

4. Data and Information Quality in Information Systems

The concept of quality is variable and subjective, aligning the needs, actions and objectives of each domain, characterizing as parameters so that the product or result is in accordance with the needs. Since the analyzed product is free from problems and/or failures, it enables the factors dependent on the analyzed product to run successfully. Since quality is inherent in several domains and can be applied to data, information and other products, the problems and dimensions of quality are also changeable.

Directly addressing the quality of data aims to align it with the needs of the domain that they come from or is applied to. Data that does not faithfully describe the elements of the real environment interferes with the effectiveness of information systems (IS) and can generate failures in the system itself. In real-world activities data quality is an element that enables the SAW and decision-making in a domain.

For Todoran et al. (2015), new questions and problems related to the quantity and quality of data are emerging in a rapidly-changing information and communication technologies (ICT) environment. The authors also make a comparison between the tasks that information system performed and their requirements, highlighting the use for common tasks in the past, such as problems of classification and processing of homogeneous data, and how the requirements and tasks have evolved, if becoming more and more complex, even dealing with SAW.

Considering such changes in information systems, along with changes in the environment, the informational spectrum expands considerably. There are different data sources from different types of sensors, such as physical sensors, robots and mining algorithms, image sensors and human sensors (i.e. from human intelligence). With the increasing amount of heterogeneous data being captured and stored in the most diverse data collections, dealing with all of this data throughout its breadth is no longer the only problem to be solved. Considering, evaluating and improving quality have also become a necessity and concern.

According to English (2009), in recent decades a new concept has been highlighted, the interference of data quality in the execution and capacity of IS. Poor quality negatively impacts several facets of the information environment, from the cost of the IS, through to the representation via graphical interface and affecting more critical levels, such as the of construction of SAW and decision-making.

4.1 Information Quality and SAW in the Fusion Context
Improved data quality can positively influence the process of construction and maintenance of SAW. Allowing humans to use such information can help to achieve the highest level of situational awareness, which in turn can lead to confident decision-making. The greater the SAW of an individual and the better the level of information presented to an individual, the more likely good decisions will be made.

5. Semantic Web and Ontologies
The Semantic Web, Web 3.0, or even Data Web is an evolution of the current web, a document web. The information in the current web does not represent its real value, being

unrelated to context, and therefore irrelevant. This hinders its distribution, access and interoperability. For Berners-Lee (2001), the semantic web is not a separate web, but an extension of the current one. In it the information is given with a well-defined meaning, allowing better interaction between computers and people.

Along with the evolution of the semantic web, another concept arose to fulfill the demands of semantic application to the web: the concept of ontologies. The data web needs richer and more expressive forms and models of dealing with information, and this is where ontologies come in.

There are some accepted definitions for ontologies. For Mizoguchi (2004), an ontology is a set of concepts and their relationships that capture the understanding of humans and their interpretation of a specific domain and makes it formal. The representation of this is understandable by other informational agents, whether they are humans or machines. Another definition is given by Gruber (1993) who brings ontologies as explicit specifications of a conceptualization, we can define an ontology as a formalization of concepts and their relations with the real world, so that it can be represented and understood by computers and without losing essential expressiveness about the domain they represent. That is, it maintains the real meaning of information in any medium that is based on the formal model built and used. (Isotani and Bittencourt 2015).

Together with the representation of the meaning and context, ontologies on the web also act on the reuse and retrieval of information through the formalization, standardization and contextualization information. According to Isotani and Bittencourt (2015), ontologies "[...] provide a common conceptual framework on which we can develop shareable and reusable knowledge bases. And secondly, they facilitate the interoperability and the information fusion, which enables the creation of powerful and smarter computational applications".
Aiming at the construction of an ontology, some essential elements can be noticed and when interconnected represent all the knowledge and power contained in an ontology. For Kiryakov et al. (2005), an ontology can be represented by the notation $O = \{C, R, I, A\}$, where each letter in the set represents an essential element for the formalization of the ontologies. Each letter is defined below:

C - A set of classes that represent the concepts of the domain which ontology represents, bringing the essence of each individual in that context.

R - Represents the set of relationships (or properties) established between the concepts listed, these associations create the essential rules and that structure the base of the represented domain.

I - Set of instances, are the materializations of the classes, bringing a concept or abstraction (class) to one of its forms in the real environment, or concepts and definitions of the ontology itself, for example a factor of quality of the ontology itself.

A - It is the set of domain-related axioms essential to represent the domain in a virtual environment, modeling constraints and rules contained in classes, relationships, and instances.

However, in order to be viable, the semantic web and ontologies must be associated with some technological and computational means, such as programming and mark-up languages. Three of the main technologies are OWL (Web Ontology Language), RDF (Resource Description Framework), RDF-S (Resource Description Framework Schema) and SPARQL. All these languages are for representation and formal description of ontologies (Isotani and Bittencourt 2015).

Of these OWL is the most applied and has the greatest power of representation of the formalities of an ontology, especially when working with semantic web. One of the factors that leads to this is that OWL is based on two other specifications: RDF and RDF-S. It inherits the structure of the RDF, working with triples and Uniform Resource Identifiers (URI), along with the semantic description capacity contained in RDF-S. It has SPARQL as a query and manipulation RDF-S language instantiated in the application and present in other external data sources. It is important to emphasize that OWL is not a programming language, but rather a language aimed at declaring resources, following a certain representation (Hitzler et al. 2009).

When we consider the domain or scenario in which an ontology is inserted, another way of representing the concepts and relationships, as important as the formal representation, is the graphical representation. This representation allows visual interpretation of the classes, relationships (or properties) and instances of the ontology in question. The ontologies represent real and complex environments. Enabling this assessment by individuals is essential, because it brings robustness and greater confidence to the ontology. To demonstrate a graphic representation, Figure 2 shows one example of ontology, with classes of person and object with subclasses, i.e., criminal and weapon.

Figure 2 - Example of ontology with person and object classes.

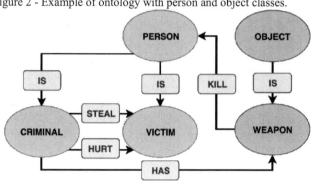

6. Criminal Domain in Brazil

Within the scope of the risk domains, some are present in the Brazilian reality and suffer from problems related to risk situations, such as SAW failures, problem in data quality and information, decision making and data processing from human intelligence. In this work we will deal specifically with the analysis of criminal problems. In Brazil criminal records are based on unstructured data provided by humans. They are unstructured, decentralized and not integrated. They present various problems related to the quality of information (Pereira et al. 2017) (Botega et al. 2019).

One of the biggest problems related to quality in this case is the reliability of the information, because as with any human activity, there is imprecision when the data is recorded. In this scenario it is easy to imagine a situation that causes reliability problem. Take as an example a woman who visits the city of São Paulo and is driving her private car. During her visit her car stolen along with other belongings.

When the victim reports the crime, it will be altered because of anxiety, the large amount of information out of chronological order and possibly some exaggeration. This information is interpreted by a human, a police officer, over the telephone or in person. The report is held within a specific information system, which may be part of a state or city information system. These two steps to report the crime and the human record of what happened opens a margin for error; mainly of the reliability and completeness of the information.

Another problem that can affect the quality of the data during this process is the quality of the electronic system used by the specialist to record the crime. Some of these criminal records systems allow a non-standard field to be filled or even leave some important information out, such as location and time. This information may be relevant to the SAW construction process and decision-making of an expert who goes to consult this data in the future (Pereira et al. 2017).

In critical and risky environments, such as the crime reporting, decision-makers need to perform a concise, clean and accurate assessment of the situation. This is particularly important where there is some risk to the life of a person, property or environment. Focusing primarily on solutions that deal with problems of criminal approach and its various contexts, techniques and processes within IFS is essential, as the filtering, mining, evaluation and data integration helps to produce useful information for the construction and maintenance of SAW (Stanton et al. 2001) (Botega et al. 2019). These techniques are demonstrated in the next section, within a process and its relationship to the domain and problems above, based on the Quantify model (Botega et al. 2017).

7. Related Work

Currently, there is a great interest in the use of non-physical sensors to promote a holistic view of the world. Among these sensors is the use of human intelligence to observe a scenario, which includes knowledge as qualitative sources of data and information, directly or indirectly. Information from human intelligence is subject to trends, inaccuracies and omissions. Interpreting and fusing this information requires the deduction of semantic meaning, which often cannot be inferred by automated functions. It requires human participation in the interpretation and use of information. Examples of these challenges include the interpretation of reports made by witnesses to emergency call systems (Vincen et al. 2009).

Recently, semantic approaches have emerged for data fusion, with the use of ontologies as part of the process of representation and inference. In the work of McGuinness (2001), the first classifications and organizations are presented using ontologies as part of the applications (domain ontology), as well as the use of external ontologies (top ontology), which provide services of vocabularies and controlled glossaries, containing information from different classes, with restrictions on types and values.

Besides the evolution of the human role during the processes of the data fusion model, as reported by Blasch et al. (2013), questions regarding the data and information quality, have also been considered. The aim is to integrate solutions for assessing emergencies in conjunction with data fusion approaches, for better visualizations, user interfaces and data integration (Souza et al. 2015) (Botega et al. 2016).

At the same time, there was an evolution of the models and fusion algorithms, in addition to new areas of application that began to make use of such approaches, especially in the context of critical scenarios. They require extremely reliable information, such as applications related to the domain of emergency management (Vincen et al. 2009) (Blasch et al. 2013). Carvalho et al (2010), makes use of ontologies to represent critical areas characterized by the presence of uncertainty. To this end, a study of techniques capable of representing the complex semantics present in these areas was conducted, along with an analysis of the uncertainty that they contain. The use of a probabilistic ontology (PR-OWL) and a Bayesian network was proposed. The Bayesian network was capable of representing relations between multiple entities present in an ontology and the probability and uncertainty of information.

Costa et al (2012) used data fusion in highly expressive Bayesian models, so that it is possible to process high-level information in a data fusion environment. In addition, the data capture and classification models are compared, relating the positive and negative points between them and as uncertainty factors can arise and affect the data, considering the role of the human and how it will interact and react to the data. Techniques and methods that have the ability to interpret and represent this uncertainty of the data arranged in an ontology, were analyzed regarding the probabilistic relationships existing among the classes. Finally, the work also employs techniques of Bayesian Multi-entity networks, a highly expressive and useful technique for a large quantity and diversity of data to accomplish the fusion process.

Kim et al (2013), conducted an analysis of data capture methods and heterogeneous web information, using the linked data concept, which allowed the connection between data through some common context, ensuring the maximum capture of data extension and retrieval on the web. In this work the RDF technology that allows the classification and structuring of a captured document is also cited. They can be reused by other technologies, such as SPARQL, which allowed the execution of the query in RDF. This allows for greater processing and manipulation of data captured from the web. These techniques allow the human operator to carry out highly complex issues and receive the best possible response in the context of data and information fusion with greater integration of linked data.

8. The Process and the Ontology for Criminal Semantic Information
In order to overcome the challenges of dealing with data and information from heterogeneous and human sources, this work reports on advances in information fusion involving ontologies and data quality assessment.

For such, processes and techniques capable of dealing with SAW, information fusion, semantics, ontologies and quality of information were studied. As a result, some were selected and based on this process capable of dealing with the fusion of semantic information about crimes. Thus, the starting point of this informational process is the Quantify (Quality-aware Human-drive Information Fusion Model) model, aligned to some more processes and informational objects, such as: the methodology of data quality assessment IQESA (Information Quality Assessment Methodology in the Context of Emergency Situational Awareness), the Endsley's SAW model and the Urbanity (Human-Driven Brazilian Crime Ontology) ontology. In addition, this work also shall contribute with the development and evolution of the Urbanity ontology, which already provides for the use and evaluation of information quality. The next subsections will approach in more detail the relationship between the process of semantic assessment and information fusion.

8.1 Quantify Model

According to Botega et al. (2019), the Quantify model is based on two pillars, being the processes for: the continuous data and information quality assessment, which guide the internal processes of the fusion of information; and performing the semantic analysis of the information. The objective is to guide the development of IFS, dedicating itself to support the evaluation of situations that occur in complex scenarios in real time. When there are flaws and low-quality information, it is difficult to collect and use reliable information.

The Quantify model consists on six parts, each playing a well-defined role in relation to the information and role of humans, such as: data acquisition, data and information quality assessment, object evaluation, evaluation of the situation, information representation and SAW-oriented user interface. Below, the Figure 3 demonstrates the Quantify model and the interaction between the stages and also represents the process life cycle.

Figure 3 shows the cycle between each of the steps presented. However, the communication is not sequential and needs to follow in a certain order so that the processing of information, from acquisition, or collection, to the presentation of fused information in the interface to occur. This is because the model predicts independent interaction throughout the process, (i.e. information can repeat the cycle between "quality assessment" and "object assessment" several times), considering some threshold or pattern. Achieving a certain level of quality or presenting some specific attribute are restrictions that are drawn up by a human who is dealing directly within the information fusion cycle.

By guaranteeing this ability of human interaction with the various phases, it is positioned as a key part of the entire process, including directly working in the SAW process, as it can deal with the "information representation" and the "users interface" oriented to SAW.

Figure 3 – Quantify model of information fusion (Adapted from Botega et al. 2019)

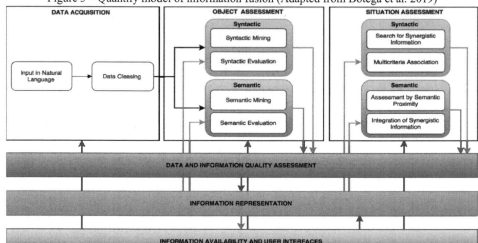

8.2 Quality Assessment by IQESA

The focus of the IQESA methodology is to seek the best way to evaluate and represent the indexes of data and information quality, in order to enable the use of quality in an information evaluation process. This always aims at the construction and maintenance of SAW in situations of the context of risk and emergency, such as the criminal domain, approached in this work. The IQESA process consists of three steps: (1) the survey of the quality requirements of data and information, (2) the definition of the functions and metrics to quantify the quality dimensions and (3) representation of the situational information (Botega et al. 2016).

However, the methodology focuses on increasing the perception and supporting situational comprehension, actions that refer, respectively, to the levels 1 and 2 of SAW, not considering during the process the level 3, the situational projection. With this and considering the model of Endsley (1988), where for the human to reach the projection, it is necessary that he has obtained the Level 2 of SAW. The approach of the present work in relation to the adoption of the IQESA is to integrate the same within the Quantify (Botega et al. 2017), proposing a change and adequacy of the model so that it is possible to perform the semantic fusion with the quality indexes aiming Achieve situational projection (Botega et al. 2016).

According to Botega et al. (2016), IQESA is already prepared to deal with a continuous flow of information to be evaluated and sent to other informational or human processes. When considering the quality assessment as part of the life cycle of a situation assessment process, the information needs to go through other processes, such as the acquisition, or collection of information, before being evaluated. It can then pass through the data and information fusion. After being evaluated the data can be sent on to other processes such as the representation of information, in this case the Urbanity ontology or the user interface.

8.3 Urbanity Ontology

Just as the Quantify model predicts the continuous evaluation of the quality indexes, from its acquisition to the representation via user interface, it also allows the possibility of making the representation of the information, through syntax using relationship structures, such as databases, or through semantic analysis, through ontologies. In this case, by dealing with a semantic process, where the representation of the information must be able to represent the greatest and best possible context, the ontologies will be adopted.

The ontology worked here, takes the name of Urbanity (hUman-dRiven BrAziliaN crIme onTologY), already under development, with the HCIG (Human-Computer Interaction Group), this work aims to evolve this ontology and apply it together with the model Quantify, with the intention To approach more and more of a process of semantic fusion. Another focus of the development of this ontology is the ability to represent and infer quality indexes on the criminal records that will be present, bringing more dynamism and possibility of inferences, together with the methodology of quality assessment IQESA.

Based on the analyses carried out on the criminal data, in this case, official criminal reports (CR) accessed via Law No. 12.527, the Access to Information Act, being regulated by Decree No. 7.724, which are the most complete and with a greater number of relevant information for bringing descriptive and historical data on the events. These bring important details about the real environment, and it is possible to identify and characterize the main elements that compose and are present in the situations of crime, an essential process for the construction of an ontology. It is important to emphasize that only robbery and theft crimes were considered.

The development of this follows the methodology of Noy and McGuinness (2001), the 101 methodology (Ontology Development 101). According to Isotani and Bittencourt (2015), this is the most widely adopted methodology for construction projects of an ontology, due to its simplicity of elaboration, which can be applied to several cases or also accepting changes and adjustments according to the need for each domain. This is composed of seven very clear and straightforward steps that guide the construction process, and this seven-step process is continuous and not accomplished only once, making an iterative and robust process. Figure 4 clearly demonstrates the seven steps, their interaction and the possibility of iteration.

Figure 4 - 101 Methodology Steps (Isotani and Bittencourt 2015)

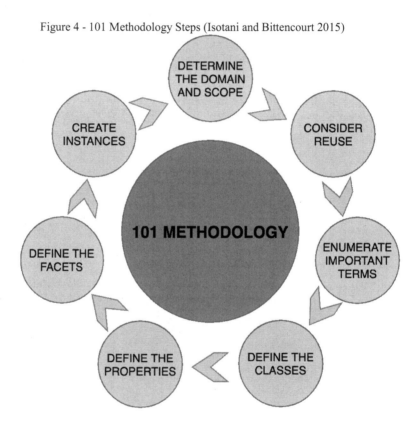

Starting from the very well defined domain, the choice of methodology to be worked in the construction of ontology and the other inputs, dictionary and taxonomy of the domain, the next step was the construction of the ontology through the software Protégé, allowing the development through a computational interface and at the end export the model created, with its, classes, relationship, instances and axioms, in OWL format.

Enabling the deployment and use in other computational systems, with the technologies that support and are compatible with OWL, in this case. Besides this form representation, OWL language, a graphical representation was also generated, aiming to enable easy interpretation by humans, making it more feasible to find flaws, perform corrections and evolve ontology. Figure 5 brings the graphic representation of Urbanity.

Figure 5 - Graphic representation of Urbanity ontology, demonstrating classes and properties

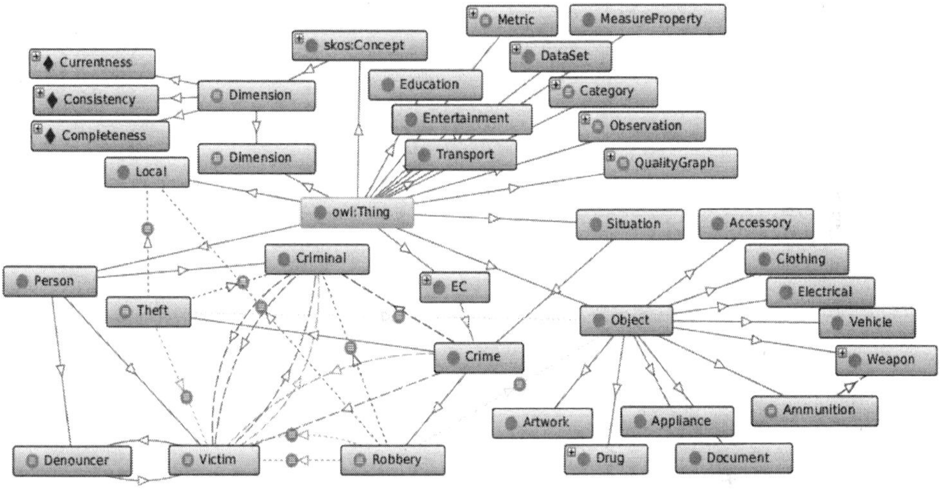

It is classified as an ontology of application, bringing concepts and specific properties of a scenario, being hardly adapted to another, because of its strong rules and axioms that tie all classes and allow inferences more accurate, as well as a better retrieval of the instantiated information, than if it were a top or more abstract ontology (Noy and McGuinness 2001).

8.4 Advances Towards a Process of Semantic Fusion of Information

This section elucidates and consolidate the advances towards a process of semantic fusion of information. Figure 6 represents the advances from the original representation of Quantify from Figure 3 and gives details about the internal process.

The representation of the process is shown as the information lifecycle starting with the acquisition of data, through to the processes of object assessment, situation assessment, quality assessment, representation of information and finally the user interface. Remembering that the user interface is not the focus of this work, it is only present to demarcate the information flow.

The main contribution of this work is the alignment of information retrieval and semantic evaluation of information with the IQESA methodology and the Urbanity ontology, using OWL, RDF, RDF-S and SPARQL. Enabling the algorithm of data and information fusion, already shown by the Quantify model to support semantic processing along with quality indexes. In this fully semantic approach, the internal processes of fusion, "Semantic Object Assessment" and "Semantic Situation Assessment" undergo changes in how they deal with the data. In order to obtain, process, infer and represent semantic information, this becomes even more dependent on an ontology, in this case the Urbanity ontology. Several consultations in ontology via SPARQL were needed to handle the entire exchange of information with the use of RDF and RDF-S.

Figure 6 - Semantic fusion information process based on the Quantify model

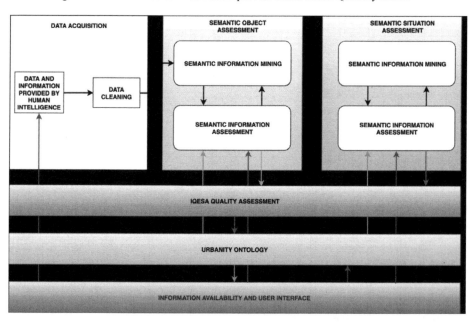

When analyzing the process, it is important to note that the life cycle of the information in this case begins with "Data Acquisition", the leftmost white square. This process collects and preprocesses the data. This represents the input of all necessary data, named "Data and Information Provided by Human Intelligence". At this point the data collected is still heterogeneous, not following any template, pattern, or formatting standard. Even if the data is about an allegation of a crime or a transcribed audio file, it is not possible to analyze them appropriately. After the data acquisition, "Data Cleaning" is performed on the input. This will remove all the accents and unnecessary punctuation so that a semantic analysis of the text can take place. All the text is converted to lowercase.

After the cleaning and standardization, the text undergoes "Semantic Object Assessment", which will identify and classify the objects and the elements found, in the crime reports or statements. The first internal process of this stage, "Semantic Information Mining" segments the texts into chunks, each piece refers to a term, at which point the report is transformed an information object, more specifically an RDF object. The second internal process, "Semantic Information Assessment" analyzes each of the objects created in the previous step and classifies them, giving them a possible class and context. At this point, the process consults the Urbanity ontology, through a SPARQL query. It aligns the information with the ontological model, aggregating classes, properties, instances and axioms of ontology, parameters that will be used for fusion and inference.

The next step is quality assessment, submitting the evaluation result to the "IQESA Quality Assessment", which will evaluate the information according to the dimensions and metrics defined for each object. The representation of the quality indexes should already follow the standards expected by the ontology, enabling quality to be represented, recovered and evaluated appropriately in future processes. With the quality indexes generated, the informational object is sent to the Urbanity ontology, which is responsible for representing and storing the information already analyzed with the quality data.

When the information is properly represented in the ontology, the information process can be followed by three different sub-processes: (1) presenting the information to the user, gray inference frame, (2) returning to the "Semantic Object Assessment" where the input would be reviewed, if, for example, it is not of satisfactory quality, as defined by the user or (3) going to the "Semantic Situation Assessment" process, where the RDF-S object again undergoes the "Semantic Information Assessment" process but now seeking to create a more complete picture taking into account other situations and previously-analyzed information objects. The "Semantic Information Mining" process, which is responsible for semantic searching within the ontology, use as a parameter the RDF-S already created. This makes it possible to do more precise searches, which take into account the context and properties of the current information.

If there are similar situations information, a new situation is created. A new information object is created, containing information referring to both previous situations and aiming to be more complete and of higher quality. This cycle of search and comparison is the fusion of information. New information is associated with objects within the ontology, generating new informational objects with more information, which can improve the quality indexes and feed back into the ontology. The new situation or information object, created, it is submitted again to "IQESA Quality Assessment" and "Urbanity Ontology" completing the information cycle.

When analyzing the information cycle, the quality assessment and ontology were used at various times, characterizing a dynamic evaluation process. This enables the use of both semantic elements and quality indexes, also represented in the ontology, to do search, evaluation, comparison and association of information. Placing the quality and ontology at the core of the process of searching and evaluation of information it is possible to create and use semantic-sized algorithms to deal with information.

9. Final Considerations

This paper presents an approach that moves towards the creation of a process of semantic fusion of information. It aims to help the human who uses the information to reach the level of situational projection, according to the model proposed by Endsley (1988). For this, it requires the support of quality assessment and models of representation of information, in this case an ontology. This represents complex scenarios of the real world in a digital environment.

In order to reach the first steps towards a semantic fusion based on the model Quantify model, the process focused on the continuous evaluation of quality and human interaction dealing with complex data and coming from human intelligence. Having this model as the basis for the fusion process, the IQESA methodology for quality assessment and the Urbanity ontology, an initial process of semantic fusion of information was defined, aiming to validate the proposal.

By consolidating the process, it was found that it is possible to use this model and methodologies to define an information fusion. Further work will be needed to consolidate the process proposed here. This would focus on the definition of the dimensions and metrics for quality assessment with IQESA, as well as the evolution of the Urbanity ontology and the study of effective search techniques and semantic search association.

References

Batini, Carlo, Cinzia Cappiello, Chiara Francalanci, and Andrea Maurino,. 2009. "Methodologies for Data Quality Assessment and Improvement." *ACM Computing Surveys (CSUR)*, 41(3): 16.

Berners-Lee, Tim, James Hendler, and Ora Lassila. 2001. "The Semantic Web." *Scientific American* 284.5: 28-37.

Blasch, Erick P., Dale A Lambert, Pierre Valin, Mieczyslaw M. Kokar, James Llinas, Subrata Das, Chee Chong and Elisa Shahbazian. 2012. "High Level Information Fusion (HLIF): survey of models, issues, and grand challenges." *IEEE Aerospace and Electronic Systems Magazine*, 27(9): 4-20.

Botega, Leonardo. C. and Jéssica. O Souza. and Fábio. R. Jorge, Caio. S. Coneglian, Márcio. R. Campos, Vânia P. A. Neris and Regina. B Araújo. 2016. "Methodology for Data and Information Quality Assessment in the Context of Emergency Situational Awareness." Universal Access in the Information Society, 16(4): 889-902.

Botega, Leonardo. C., Valdir A. P Pereira, Allan. C. Oliveira, Jornda. F Saran, Leandro. A. Villas, and Regina. B. de Araújo, 2017. "Quality-Aware Human-Driven Information Fusion Model." 2017 *20th International Conference on Information Fusion (Fusion)* (pp. 1-10). IEEE.

Botega, Leonardo. C., Allan. C. M. Oliveira, Valdir. A. Pereira Junior, Jordan. F. Saran, Lucas. Z. Ladeira, Gustavo. M. C. Pereira, and Seiji Isotani. 2019. "Quantify: An Information Fusion Model Based on Syntactic and Semantic Analysis and Quality Assessments to Enhance Situation Awareness". *Information Quality in Information Fusion and Decision Making* (pp. 563-586). Springer, Cham.

Carvalho, Rommel N., Shou Matsumoto, Kathryn B Laskey, Paulo C Costa, Marcelo Ladeira, and Laécio L Santos,. 2010. "Probabilistic Ontology and Knowledge Fusion for Procurement Fraud Detection in Brazil". *Uncertainty Reasoning for the Semantic Web* ii (pp. 19-40). Springer, Berlin, Heidelberg.

Costa, Paulo. C., Kathryn B. Laskey, Kuo C Chang, Wei Sun, Cheol Y Park, and Shou Matsumoto. 2012. "High-level Information Fusion with Bayesian Semantics". *Proceedings of the 9th Bayesian Modelling Applications Workshop*.

Endsley, Mica R. 1988. "Design and Evaluation for Situation Awareness Enhancement." *Proceedings of the Human Factors Society Annual Meeting*, 32(2): 97-101.

Endsley, Mica R. 2001. "Designing for Situation Awareness in Complex Systems." *Proceedings of the Second International Workshop on symbiosis of humans, artifacts and environment*.

Endsley, Mica R. 2016. *"Designing for Situation Awareness: an approach to user-centered design"* CRC Press.

English, Larry P. 2009. *"Information Quality Applied: best practices for improving business information, processes and systems"*. Wiley Publishing.

Foo, Pek H. and Gee W Ng. 2013. "High-Level Information Fusion: an overview." *Journal of Advances in Information Fusion*. 8(1): 33-72.

Gruber, Thomas R. 1993. "A Translation Approach to Portable Ontology Specifications." *Knowledge Acquisition*, 5(2): 199-220.

Hitzler, P. M., B. Krötzsch, P.F. Parsia, P. F. Patel-Schneider and S Rudolph. 2009. "OWL 2 Web Ontology Language Primer." *W3C Recommendation*, 27(1): 123.

Isotani, Seiji and Ig I. Bittencourt, 2015. *"Dados Abertos Conectados: em busca da Web do Conhecimento"*. Novatec Editora.

Kim, Haklae, Jungsung Son, and Kisoog Jang. 2013. "Semantic Data Fusion: from open data to linked data." *Proceedings of the European Semantic Web Conference.*

Kiryakov, Atanas, Damyan Ognyanov, and Dimitar Manov. 2005. "OWLIM–a pragmatic semantic repository for OWL". *International Conference on Web Information Systems Engineering.* Springer, Berlin, Heidelberg. p. 182-192.

Kokar, Mieczyslaw M. and Mica R. Endsley, 2012. "Situation Awareness and Cognitive Modeling". *IEEE Intelligent Systems* 27(3): 91-96.

Laskey, Kathryn. B., Gee. W Ng, Rakesh Nagi, Dafni Stampouli, Johan Schubert, and Pierre. Valin, 2012. "Issues of Uncertainty Analysis in High-Level Information Fusion." *Fusion 2012 Panel Discussion.*

Mizoguchi, Riichiro. 2004. "Part 3: Advanced Course of Ontological Engineering." *New Generation Computing*, 22(2): 193-220.

Morville, Peter and Louis Rosenfeld. 2006. "Information Architecture 3.0." *Semantics Studios*, 29.

Noy, Natalya F., and Deborah L. McGuinness, 2001. *"Ontology Development 101: a guide to creating your first ontology".*

Pereira, Valdir A., Jordan F Saran, Lucas Z. Ladeira, João H. Martins, Vagner Pagotti, Allan. M. Souza, Leandro A. Villas, and Leonardo C. Botega. 2017. "Beyond Syntactic Data Fusion in the Context of Criminal Data Analysis." *12th Iberian Conference on Information Systems and Technologies (CISTI)* (pp. 1-6). IEEE.

Pereira, Valdir. A., Matheus. F. Sanches, Jordan. F. Saran, Caio. S. Coneglian, Leonardo. C. Botega, and Regina. B. Araujo. (2016). "Towards Semantic Fusion Using Information Quality and the Assessment of Objects and Situations to Improve Emergency Situation Awareness." *2016 Eleventh International Conference on Digital Information Management (ICDIM)* (pp. 260-265). IEEE.

Rogova, Galina L. and Eloi Bosse. 2010. "Information Quality in Information Fusion." *13th International Conference on Information Fusion.* IEEE.

Salerno, John. 2002. "Information Fusion: a high-level architecture overview." *Proceedings of the Fifth International Conference on Information Fusion*, 1: 680-686.

Souza, Jessica, Leonardo C. Botega, José E Santarém Segundo, Claudia B Berti, Márcio R. Campos, and Regina. B. Araújo, 2015. "Conceptual Framework to Enrich Situation Awareness of Emergency Dispatchers." *International Conference on Human Interface and the Management of Information* (pp. 33-44). Springer, Cham.

Stanton, Neville A., Peter R.G Chambers, and John Piggott. 2001. "Situational Awareness and Safety." *Safety Science* 39(3): 189-204.

Steinberg, Alan N., Christopher L. Bowman, and Franklin E. White, 2008. "Revisions to the JDL Data Fusion Model." *Handbook of Multisensor Data Fusion* (pp. 65-88). CRC Press.

Todoran, Ion-Gorge, Lauren Lecornu, Ali Khenchaf, and Jean-Marc L. Caillec, 2015. "A Methodology to Evaluate Important Dimensions of Information Quality in Systems." *Journal of Data and Information Quality*, 6(2-3): 11.

Vincen, Daniel, Dafni Stampouli, and Gavin Powell, 2009. "Foundations for System Implementation for a Centralised Intelligence Fusion Framework for Emergency Services." *12th International Conference on Information Fusion* (pp. 1401-1408). IEEE.

Wurman, Richard S. 1996. *"Information Architect."* Information Architects.

The Role of Knowledge Organisation Systems in Business Intelligence: a literature review

Tanja Svarre, Aalborg University, Denmark
Marianne Lykke, Aalborg University, Denmark
Ann Bygholm, Aalborg University, Denmark

Abstract

This paper reviews the literature on the cross field between business intelligence (BI), knowledge organisation systems (KOS) and user experience. The purpose is to map where and how KOS have been incorporated into BI systems to support BI users for a better interaction with a BI system. Web of Knowledge, Scopus and Library, Information Science & Technology Abstracts (LISTA) were used to carry out the search for relevant research papers. For the analysis, Zeng's (2008 p. 161) model of the structures and functions of KOS was used to map the distribution of initiatives. The review showed that the focus on the user experience of the implementation of KOS in BI systems is limited. The findings of the review have been used to identify and to discuss where there is still potential for further development and integration in BI.

1. Introduction

Business intelligence (BI) designates the combination of gathering and storing data with knowledge management and analysis to support decision making in organisations (Negash & Gray, 2008). It is a generic term related to designating concepts and methods in the field along with the intrinsic architectures, tools and databases that enable the analyses to be carried out (Lim, Chen, & Chen, 2013). Traditionally, BI has been based on raw data from heterogeneous sources (Vo, Thomas, Cho, De, & Choi, 2018); however, recently, researchers have begun to discuss the next generation of BI systems, also known as BI 2.0 or self-service BI (Varga, Romero, Pedersen, & Thomsen, 2014). A part of this next generation is a change in the data sources used for BI, such as when social media, sensors and devices generate data that are incorporated into a BI system for new and changed analyses (Alpar & Schulz, 2016). One implication of this changed BI landscape is that by 2020, it is expected that artificial intelligence (AI) will be a standard feature in a majority of modern BI platforms (Gartner, 2018).

The use of BI has many benefits for organisations. Perhaps the primary benefit is that when organisational decisions are made on the basis of business analytics, organisations can improve their practices—and more importantly—their performance (Bronzo et al., 2013; Popovic, Turk, & Jaklic, 2010). This also means that data are central to a variety of functions and are used by a diverse span of end users, such as within companies (Wang, 2016) and healthcare (Gaardboe & Svarre, 2018); however, the increased integration with many local systems and the continuously increasing amount of data challenge end users' use of BI (Shiran, 2018). This may explain why many papers present new BI systems or system features with the aim to alleviate the challenge for users and make their use more effective. However, only limited attention has been paid to identify and characterise effective and ineffective use in the literature (Trieu, 2017). Several approaches can be taken to support interactions between users and systems. In this paper, the focus is the use of KOS in BI systems for improved user experience. Therefore, the following research question guides the remainder of this paper:

What characterises the user experience related to the implementation of KOS in BI systems?

The remainder of the paper is organised as follows. In sections 2 and 3, the theoretical foundation of the paper is outlined. In section 4, the methodical approach is described. Section 5 presents the analysis. The paper concludes with a discussion.

2. The notion of user experience and usability

In the user experience (UX) literature, there appears to be a common understanding that task-oriented usability as well hedonic, experience-oriented qualities are essential for the user's perception and evaluation of an interactive system through a user interface (Bargas-Avila & Hornbæk, 2011). The ISO 9241-210 standard defines usability as 'the extent to which a product can be used by specified users to achieve specified goals with effectiveness, efficiency, and satisfaction in a specified context of use' and user experience as 'a person's perceptions and responses that result from the use or anticipated use of a product, system or service…includes all the users' emotions, beliefs, preferences, perceptions, physical and psychological responses, behaviors, and accomplishments that occur before, during, and after use'. Hassenzahl (2010) distinguishes between the system's practical goals, or the do-goals, such as finding a report in an enterprise search system or retrieving data for a specific analysis in BI, and user experience (UX), which refers to the system's hedonic qualities, or the be-goals, such as feeling competent in retrieving a report or feeling engaged when interacting with the BI system. Usability makes a task or system easy and intuitive, whereas user experience makes it meaningful and valuable.

Usability pre-dates user experience, and a well-established framework exists composed of quality criteria, such as learnability, efficiency, memorability, errors and satisfaction (Preece, Rogers, & Sharp, 2015). User experience is a recent concept, and a large and varied set of criteria is used as an indication of the experiential quality of interactive systems, with affect, aesthetics, emotion and enjoyment being the most common (Lykke & Jantzen, 2016).

Many other criteria or variations of already known criteria have been introduced, including relevance and engagement, typically without a clear relation between the criteria, making it difficult to compare studies that investigate similar phenomena within UX.

3. Knowledge Organisation Systems (KOS)

Knowledge Organisation Systems (KOS) are controlled subject languages designed for the specific purpose of indexing and retrieving information (Svenonius, 2000 p. 128-129). Controlled languages are normalised languages. Meanings are restricted, and relationships to other terms are made explicit. The purpose of normalising is to straighten crisscross mappings and to purge natural language of the ambiguities and redundancies that cause precision and recall failures during retrieval. KOS are a means for creating translations to convert the natural language of authors, data producers, indexers and users into a vocabulary that can match the different language usages. KOS bridge meanings, symbols (words used to express meanings) and controlled terms used to express a certain meaning. Used appropriately and correctly, KOS can promote uniformity in terms of formats and in the assignment of descriptive terms (Hlava, 2014). Different contexts and perspectives require different terms, meanings and relationships. Regarding knowledge sharing, KOS are often viewed as 'boundary objects', and the development of boundary objects is an essential part of facilitating knowledge sharing and communities of practice (Lampe, 2007). These KOS can be viewed as knowledge maps or as communication and learning devices that integrate history, expertise and inside information in support of all business activities (International Organization for Standardization, 2013).

Zeng (2008) lists KOS according to their degrees of control and functions. The lowest level, which she refers to as metadata-like models, are alphabetical lists of terms used to express a certain meaning and to eliminate ambiguity. At the same level are synonym rings that are sets of synonymous or almost synonymous variations, any of which can be used to refer to a particular meaning. Synonym lists are used to bridge between or to identify terms used to express the same meaning. Subject headings, classification schemes and taxonomies are categorised as classification systems that are schemes of categories and subcategories that in addition to controlling meanings and synonyms can be used to sort and to hierarchically organise items of information. The final level consists of thesauri and ontologies that are structured vocabularies, with ontologies being the most developed with a detailed, formal specification of properties and relationships, e.g. cause-effect and action properties. In thesauri, meanings are represented by terms and are organised so that relationships between meanings are made explicit, and the relationships are hierarchical, broad and narrow as well as associatively related. Preferred terms are accompanied by lead-in entries for synonyms and quasi-synonyms.

All types of KOS can be useful for BI. User studies show that BI end-users have difficulties in understanding both the BI data and the available analytical tools; what does the data mean and represent, and what do the analytical results show (Venter, 2005; Madsen, 2012; Laursen & Thorlund, 2016)? A system that is easy to learn, easy to use and easy to understand is more important for the user compared to the quality of information. Users are aware of and accept that data may be complex and 'messy', and the users' understanding and the system's usefulness are essential (Gaardboe, Sandalgaard, & Svarre, 2018). A recent study of BI in a municipal context showed that detailed topical knowledge is required to use and to operate BI systems. A lack of this knowledge also affects the end-user's motivation to use BI (Binder, 2018). These findings indicate that the final level of KOS that provide detailed conceptual information in the form of definitions and a diverse set of relationships may be the most suited KOS for BI systems.

4. Methodological approach

Papers were identified that discuss the impact of KOS for user experience in BI systems through a systematic literature review. In this section, the search criteria, the identification of relevant papers and the analytical approach are described.

The collection of papers for the review was based on a structured search of three academic databases: Web of Science (WoS), Scopus and Library, Information Science & Technology Abstracts (LISTA). The databases were selected based on their coverage of academic topics related to the current research problem. A building block search strategy (Markey, 2015) was used to compose the query. Three facets were included: one represented the technology; one represented KOS; and one reflected the user experience dimension of the problem statement. The synonyms representing the three facets are provided inTable 1.

Table 1: Search terms representing the three facets of the building block search strategy

	Facet 1: BI technology	Facet 2: KOS	Facet 3: User experience
Synonyms included in the facet	'business intelligence' OR BI OR 'data analytics' OR 'BI system' OR 'BI systems' OR 'intelligence system' OR 'intelligence systems' OR 'Data warehouse'	Metadata OR 'controlled vocabulary' OR 'controlled vocabularies' OR 'knowledge organization' OR 'knowledge organisation' OR classification OR classify OR ontology OR ontologies OR taxonom*	'user experience' OR UX OR user*

For the technology facet, various synonyms for BI systems were included. The term 'data warehouse' was also included because it is considered to be an element of BI systems (Wixom & Watson, 2010). The KOS facet consisted of terms representing various forms of KOS and related activities (e.g. classify). Lastly, the user experience facet represented terms to reflect a user perspective within the studies. In addition to the search facets, the searches were limited to academic journals and conference papers because the problem statement was studied from an academic perspective. Only papers written in English were considered for inclusion. Finally, the search was limited to the years 2009-2018 to ensure the findings were recent.

Conducting the searches in the selected databases resulted in 450 records from WoS, 710 records from Scopus and 30 records from LISTA, for a total of 1190 results. Some overlap occurred across the databases, and 370 duplicates were removed. Subsequently, first the abstracts and then the full text of the remaining papers were read. Only papers that discuss KOS to support user experience and users in their interactions with BI systems were included. In the selection of papers, empirical studies of users' interactions with the systems under study were emphasised. After reading the abstracts, 762 papers were removed, and after reading the full text of the remaining 58 papers, 51 papers were removed. This left seven papers for review. The process is illustrated in Figure 1.

Figure 1: Flow diagram of the identification of relevant papers

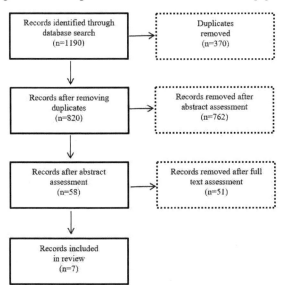

The papers were analysed in two steps. First, a content analysis (Krippendorff, 2004) was conducted to map the occurrence of search terms in the full set of retrieved papers. The purpose of this analysis was to determine the distribution of knowledge organisation elements in the studies along with the representation of users in the studies. Second, an inductive thematic analysis (Jones, Coviello, & Tang, 2011) of the seven papers included for the final review was conducted.

5. Analysis

As shown in Figure 1, 820 unique papers were identified using the building block strategy. Table 2 outlines the representation of the search terms from the KOS facet throughout the 820 papers. As shown, metadata (219 occurrences) along with variations of classifications (391 occurrences) and ontologies (179 occurrences) were the most common knowledge organisation initiatives presented in the papers. The search terms represent knowledge organisation initiatives in the papers. For instance, Al-Aqrabi et al. (2013) applied metadata to enable a facetted search for a BI system, and Demraoui et al. (2015) departed from users' interactions in the development of their metadata model for interoperability in BI. In Zhang et al.'s (2009) study, the classification and the clustering of e-mails were used to identify homogenous groups of users in an organisation.

The search terms also represent language variations irrelevant to the current problem statement. To illustrate, the search term classify* also retrieved papers for which classification was not used in a KOS sense but rather in a rhetorical sense; however, in terms of Zeng's (2008) model of KOS, Table 2 illustrates that KOS on both the low and the high levels are implemented in BI systems to improve functionalities and to support users.

Table 2: Number of papers representing the search terms in the 820 unique results of the KOS facet of the building block search

KOS	Number of occurrences
Metadata	219
Controlled vocabulary	9
Knowledge organization OR knowledge organisation	42
classifi*	391
ontolog*	179
taxonom*	47

In terms of the user perspective, Table 3 illustrates the occurrence of the three search terms of the second facet. Here, it becomes clear that user experience and UX are not common among the 820 papers. On the other hand, users are commonly mentioned in the papers.

After reading first the abstracts and then the full text of the remaining papers, it was evident that most papers have some consideration of the users but not in the way that the users are included in either the development or the evaluation of the solutions proposed in the papers. In the following section, the papers that include the user perspective on the use of KO in BI systems are analysed.

Table 3 Number of papers representing the search terms in the 820 unique results of the user facet of the building block search

User perspective in the 820 papers	Number of occurrences
User experience	38
UX	15
user*	803

5.1 Thematic review of selected papers

Seven papers met the criteria for inclusion in this review. They are listed in Table 4. The papers are evenly distributed across the time period covered by the building block search. They represent the cross field between BI, KOS and user experience in different ways. The papers concerned with metadata correspond well with the general papers covering this type of KOS (cf. Table 2); however, the user focus in studies of classification and ontologies representing the user perspective have a limited focus in BI systems. Thus, only one study from the review investigates users in relation to these two types of KOS, namely Chung, Chen and Reid (2009). The seven papers that are analysed further appears in Table 4.

Table 4: Papers included for the review

Authors	Publication year	KOS	User perspective
Chung, Chen & Reid	2009	Classification	Controlled user test
Even, Kolodner & Varshavsky	2010	Metadata	Controlled user test
Chee, Yeoh & Gao	2011	Metadata	Semi-structured interviews
Blunschi, Jossen, Kossmann, Mori & Stockinger	2012	Metadata	User feedback
Chee, Yeoh, Gao & Richards	2014	Metadata	Semi-structured interviews
Foshay, Taylor & Mukherjee	2014	Metadata	Survey
Dinter, Schieder & Gluchowski	2015	Metadata	Survey

5.1.1 KOS perspective of the reviewed papers

Chung, Chen and Reid (2009) published the only paper using classification. The paper discusses automatic classification used to support managers and business analysts in classifying relevant stakeholders online. The purpose is to facilitate the understanding of the company's competitive environment. The proposed solution extends the already known automated classification of websites to be used to classify business stakeholders online. The process consists of three steps. First, a collection of business webpages is collected. Next, the websites are tagged, and feature extraction is carried out. The purpose is to reduce noisy data and to prepare the websites for automated classification. Last, classification is carried out by means of a classification model.

Metadata are covered to a larger extent in the papers. Thus, six of seven papers concern metadata in various forms. Even, Kolodner and Varshavsky (2010) added value-driven usage metadata to the BI system. Tracking data use, decisions made and their associated value can provide value-driven usage metadata that will improve the users' interactions with BI systems. Upon the assignment of metadata, various approaches can be taken to attribute value to datasets. One approach is to use the BI product and a metadata map (BIP-map) (Chee, Yeoh & Gao, 2011; Chee, Yeoh, Gao & Richards, 2014). Here, metadata supports the production of an extensive framework that enhances the traceability and the accountability of BI for BI users. During the SODA project (Blunschi et al., 2012), the metadata model of a data warehouse was fed into a graph pattern algorithm. The aim was to enable a Google-inspired search experience in data warehouses.

The remaining two papers also investigate metadata in BI systems, though not based on a specific system or technology. Instead, metadata are considered from different perspectives, and the role of metadata in BI systems is investigated. Foshay, Taylor and Mukherjee (2014) investigated four different types of metadata: definitional, data quality, navigational and lineage metadata. They also studied their roles in users' attitudes towards data from the perspective of cognition and affect. Dinter, Schieder and Gluchowski (2015) examined the current situation, benefits, challenges and need for improvement of metadata management (MDM) in BI and big data from various stakeholder viewpoints.

In sum, various views and applications of KOS are represented in the reviewed papers; however, the majority of papers represent the low level of KOS in terms of Zeng's (2008) model. They represent the improvement of existing systems by developing new elements and approaches for various functionalities of BI systems and data warehouses, but there are also examples of general studies that focus on the status of existing BI systems.

5.1.2 The user perspective in the reviewed papers

Various methodical approaches have been used to understand the user perspective and the users' perceptions of the technology in question (cf. Table 4). Two papers present variations of controlled user tests. In Chung, Chen and Reid (2009), the purpose of the evaluation is to verify the accuracy of the classification. Two user groups—university students and business practitioners—are used to classify a number of stakeholders. The classifications are subsequently compared with automated classification and tested for overall accuracy, within-class accuracy and inter-subject agreement. The users' subjective comments regarding the solution are also presented in the paper, providing an understanding of their perceptions of the potential solution proposed by Chung, Chen and Reid (2009). Even, Kolodner and Varshavsky (2010) adopted a similar approach. Here, 200 university students in IS engineering performed controlled tasks using a baseline and an experimental BI system. During the interactions, performance measures, such as decision value, time and clicks, were registered. The analysis was strictly quantitative.

Semi-structured interviews have also been used to obtain insight into users' perspectives. Chee, Yeoh and Gao (2011) and Chee, Yeoh, Gao and Richards (2014) used interviews to evaluate their metadata-based initiatives. The BIP-map was presented to the interviewees, and they subsequently responded to a number of questions in relation to the product. The interviewees included professionals, such as CEOs, CIOs and CTOs. The number of interviewees does not appear in the papers. Similarly, it is unclear whether the two papers refer to the same interviews. Blunschi et al. (2012) combined an experimental setup for the evaluation of their empirical work. They began with a controlled test, where queries from the query log were used to test the SODA system. They evaluated the performance in relation to precision and recall; however, they also reported feedback from various users (computer scientists and business users) in the paper. Apart from having been introduced to the system before providing feedback, the method applied for collecting feedback is not explained further in the paper.

Lastly, for two studies, surveys were used to examine users' perceptions of KOS in BI systems. The purpose of Foshay, Taylor and Mukherjee's (2014) study was to understand the value of metadata in BI systems. Their questionnaire builds upon elements from the IS success model (DeLone & McLean, 2003) and the technology acceptance model (Davis, 1989). The respondents included 455 BI end-users. In their survey, Dinter, Schieder and Gluchowski (2015) included questions about BI and big data in relation to MDM along with background questions. The respondents included 72 BI users, BI developers and BI managers.

In sum, user involvement exists neither in the design nor in the evaluation phase in studies of KOS incorporations into BI systems; however, based on this analysis, it is clear that little is known about user experiences related to the KOS initiatives as defined by Bargas-Avila and Hornbæk (2011). None of the studies specifically investigates the interaction quality of the systems based on actual user experience with BI systems. Elements of usability are included in Even, Kolodner and Varshavsky's (2010) study, but the papers do not provide systematic knowledge regarding the user experience with KOS elements in BI systems. In the following section, the conclusions from the seven studies on the users' perceptions of KOS in BI systems are discussed.

5.1.3 The importance of KOS in users' interactions with BI systems

The general understanding of the users' perceptions of KOS in BI based on the reviewed papers is that they are positive and that users perceive considerable potential. Even, Kolodner and Varshavsky's (2010) study shows that value-driven usage metadata increases decision value and decreases the number of clicks during interactions with the BI system. Users also appear to be positive towards improvements in BI systems that can help them during interactions and that can save time. In Chung, Chen and Reid's (2009) paper, the subjective comments from future users who have not directly interacted with the system are positive towards the potential of automated classification. Apart from the expectation of saving time and being supported during interactions, the users expect more detail and a better understanding from using the functionality. Blunschi et al. (2012) found similar results in their feedback from various audiences but in more detail. Users were positive towards being able to identify data and joins across tables, to document legacy systems and to use the schema to discover relations between entities through the SODA system. This is supported by Dinter, Schieder and Gluchowski (2015), who found that users agree on the need for MDM implementation to improve data quality and to support data interpretation. Foshay, Taylor and Mukherjee (2014) found that in users' assessment of four types of metadata, data quality metadata were the most influential for both cognition and affect.

Implementing KOS into BI systems is also associated with challenges. Thus, Dinter, Schieder and Gluchowski (2015) found that the biggest challenges in implementing MDM are the organisational establishment of metadata curation and integrated metadata modelling. In particular, the BI users also emphasised the importance of providing an intuitive frontend, indicating that the field requires more knowledge regarding what this implies. Understanding data is also a challenge indicated in the papers by Chee, Yeoh and Gao (2011) and Chee, Yeoh, Gao and Richards (2014). Thus, the BIP-map will help users understand how information is collected along with improved data capturing during information generation processes (Chee, Yeoh & Gao, 2011), which could be an indication that these are some of the challenges experienced in the current system. As expressed by the authors, it is risky to make decisions based on data if the decision maker has difficulties in understanding the origin of the data. A lack of an understanding of the data and the systems was also indicated by the users who requested the possibility to identify the personnel responsible for the information products in case of problems (Chee, Yeoh, Gao & Richards, 2014).

6. Discussion and concluding remarks

During this literature review, papers studying users' perceptions of KOS in BI systems were analysed. The analysis has shown that BI systems mainly use KOS from either the lowest level of Zeng's (2008) model in the form of metadata or from the upper level in the form of classifiers or ontologies. Considering the limited number of relevant papers, additional research is needed to understand both how users interact with a large variety of KOS in BI context, but also how different KOS can support the user experience of BI systems, as regard usability and achievement of their specified goals and their experiential perceptions and responses to the system. More knowledge is also needed on how KOS can be integrated in the interface to enable a useful as well as experiential interaction with BI data, functions, and related conceptual information for a better understanding of the data and the analyses carried out.

Based on the review, it is clear that although many of the papers focus on improving BI systems for users, the majority of papers discuss an experimental approach to evaluation. Only a minority of papers actually examines the users in the evaluation of KOS for the systems. System evaluation can be formative or summative (Lewis, 2014). This means that an evaluation that includes users can inform system developers regarding which changes should be made (formative) or whether a system is successful after implementation (summative). Additional studies and user involvement are needed from both perspectives to determine what is needed to support users during interactions with BI systems as well as to determine what actually characterises users' challenges, perceptions, and emotions when using the systems. This knowledge is needed to enable the design and the development of the existing and the next generation of BI systems.

References

Al-Aqrabi, H., L. Liu, R. Hill & L. Cui. 2013. "Faceted Search in Business Intelligence on the Cloud". *Proceedings - 2013 IEEE International Conference on Green Computing and Communications and IEEE Internet of Things and IEEE Cyber, Physical and Social Computing, GreenComiThings-CPSCom 2013*, 842–849.

Alpar, P., & M. Schulz. 2016. "Self-Service Business Intelligence". *Business & Information Systems Engineering*, 58(2): 151–155.

Bargas-Avila, J. A. & K. Hornbæk. 2011. "Old Wine in New Bottles or Novel Challenges: a critical analysis of empirical studies of user experience". *Proceedings of the SIGCHI Conference on Human Factors in Computing Systems*, 2689–2698.

Binder, L. (2018). *Kritiske Succesfaktorer for Business Intelligence i en Kommunal Kontekst*. Aalborg: Aalborg University.

Blunschi, L., C. Jossen, D. Kossmann, M. Mori & K. Stockinger. 2012. SODA: "Generating SQL for business users". *Proceedings of the VLDB Endowment*, 5: 932–943.

Bronzo, M., P. T. V. de Resende, M. P. V. de Oliveira, K. P. McCormack, P. R. de Sousa & R. L. Ferreira. 2013. "Improving Performance Aligning Business Analytics with Process Orientation". *International Journal of Information Management*, 33(2): 300–307.

Chee, C.-H., W. Yeoh, & S. Gao. 2011. "Enhancing Business Intelligence Traceability Through an Integrated Metadata Framework". *ACIS 2011 Proceedings - 22nd Australasian Conference on Information Systems*.

Chee, C.-H., W. Yeoh, S. Gao & G. Richards. 2014. "Improving Business Intelligence Traceability and Accountability: an integrated framework of bi product and metacontent map". *Journal of Database Management*, 25(3): 28–47.

Chung, W., H. Chen & E. Reid. 2009. "Business Stakeholder Analyzer: an experiment of classifying stakeholders on the Web". *Journal of the American Society for Information Science & Technology*, 60(1): 59–74.

Davis, F. D. 1989. "Perceived Usefulness, Perceived Ease of Use, and User Acceptance of Information Technology". *MIS Quarterly*, 13(3): 319–340.

DeLone, W. H., & E. R. McLean. 2003. "The DeLone and McLean Model of Information Systems Success: a ten-year update". *Journal of Management Information Systems*, 19(4): 9–30.

Demraoui, L., H. Behja, E. M. Zemmouri & R. Ben Abbou. 2015. "Towards Integration of the Users' Preferences into the Common Warehouse Metamodel". *Colloquium in Information Science and Technology, CIST, 2015*, 151–154. https://doi.org/10.1109/CIST.2014.7016610

Dinter, B., C. Schieder, & P. Gluchowski. 2015. "A Stakeholder Lens on Metadata Management in Business Intelligence and Big Data - Results of an empirical investigation". *Americas Conference on Information Systems, AMCIS 2015*.

Even, A., Y. Kolodner & R. Varshavsky. 2010. "Designing Business-Intelligence Tools with Value-Driven Recommendations". I Winter, R and Zhao, JL and Aier, S (Eds.), *Global Perspectives on Design Science Research* (p 286-). Univ St Gallen, Inst Informat Management; ACM; ACM SIGCAS; ACM SIGMIS; ACM SIGCHI; ACM SIGDAA.

Foshay, N., A. Taylor & A. Mukherjee. 2014. "Winning the Hearts and Minds of Business Intelligence Users: the role of metadata". *Information Systems Management*, 31(2): 167–180.

Gartner. 2018. *Magic Quadrant for Analytics and Business Intelligence Platforms*. https://www.gartner.com/doc/3861464/magic-quadrant-analytics-business-intelligence

Gaardboe, R., N. Sandalgaard, & T. Svarre. 2018. "Which Factors of Business Intelligence Affect Individual Impact in Public Healthcare?" *Proceedings of the 16th Scandinavian Conference on Health Informatics 2018*, Aalborg, Denmark August 28–29, 2018, 96–100. https://vbn.aau.dk/da/publications/which-factors-of-business-intelligence-affect-individual-impact-i

Gaardboe, R., & T. Svarre. 2018. "BI End-User Segments in the Public Health Sector". I A. Kő & E. Francesconi (Eds.), *Electronic Government and the Information Systems Perspective, 231–242.* Springer International Publishing.

Hassenzahl, M. 2010. "Experience Design: Technology for All the Right Reasons". *Synthesis Lectures on Human-Centered Informatics*, 3(1): 1–95.

Hlava, M. 2014. *The Taxobook: Principles and Practices of Building Taxonomies*. Morgan & Claypool Publishers.

International Organization for Standardization. 2013. ISO 25964-2: *Information and Documentation - - Thesauri and interoperability with other vocabularies -- Part 2: Interoperability with other vocabularies.*

Jones, M. V., N. Coviello & Y. K Tang. 2011. "International Entrepreneurship Research (1989–2009): a domain ontology and thematic analysis". *Journal of Business Venturing*, 26(6): 632–659.

Krippendorff, K. (2004). *Content Analysis: An Introduction to Its Methodology*. SAGE.

Laursen, G. H. N. & J. Thorlund. 2016. *Business Analytics for Managers: taking business intelligence beyond reporting*. John Wiley & Sons.

Lewis, J. R. 2014. "Usability: Lessons Learned … and Yet to Be Learned". *International Journal of Human–Computer Interaction*, 30(9): 663–684. https://doi.org/10.1080/10447318.2014.930311

Lim, E.-P., H. Chen & G. Chen. 2013. "Business Intelligence and Analytics: Research Directions". *ACM Transactions on Management Information Systems*, 3(4): 17:1–17:10.

Lykke, M., & C. Jantzen. 2016. "User Experience Dimensions: A Systematic Approach to Experiential Qualities for Evaluating Information Interaction in Museums". *Proceedings of the 2016 ACM on Conference on Human Information Interaction and Retrieval*, 81–90.

Madsen, L. 2012. *Healthcare Business Intelligence: a guide to empowering successful data reporting and analytics*. John Wiley & Sons.

Markey, K. 2015. *Online Searching: a guide to finding quality information efficiently and effectively*. Lanham: Rowman & Littlefield.

Negash, S., & P. Gray. 2008. "Business Intelligence". In *Business intelligence: Handbook on decision support systems 2*.

Popovic, A., T. Turk & J. Jaklic. 2010. "Conceptual Model of Business Value of Business Intelligence Systems". *Management: Journal of Contemporary Management Issues* 15(1): 5–29.

Preece, J., Y. Rogers & H. Sharp. 2015. *Interaction Design: beyond human-computer interaction*. John Wiley & Sons.

Shiran, T. 2018. "A New Logical Tier for Data Analytics: the data fabric". *Business Intelligence Journal* 23(1): 25–38.

Svenonius, E. 2000. *The Intellectual Foundation of Information Organization*. MIT Press.

Trieu, V. 2017. Getting Value from Business Intelligence Systems: a review and research agenda. *Decision Support Systems*, 93: 111-124.

Varga, J., O. Romero, T. B. Pedersen & C. Thomsen. 2014. "Towards Next Generation BI Systems: the analytical metadata challenge". *Lecture Notes in Computer Science (including subseries Lecture Notes in Artificial Intelligence and Lecture Notes in Bioinformatics)*, 8646 LNCS, 89–101.

Venter, M. I. (2005). "Business Intelligence (BI) Initiatives: failure and success". *Interim: Interdisciplinary Journal*, 4(1): 149–163.

Vo, Q. D., J. Thomas, S. Cho, P. De & B. J. Choi. 2018. "Next Generation Business Intelligence and Analytics". *Proceedings of the 2nd International Conference on Business and Information Management*, 163–168.

Wang, C.-H. 2016. "A Novel Approach to Conduct the Importance-Satisfaction Analysis for Acquiring Typical User Groups in Business-Intelligence Systems". *Computers in Human Behavior*, 54, 673–681.

Wixom, B. & H. Watson. 2010. "The BI-Based Organization". *International Journal of Business Intelligence Research*, 1(1): 13–28.

Zeng, M. 2008. "Knowledge Organization Systems (KOS)". *Knowledge Organization*, 35(2/3): 160–182.

Zhang, C., W. B. Hurst, R. B. Lenin, N. Yuruk & S. Ramaswamy. 2009. "Analyzing Organizational Structures Using Social Network Analysis". *Lecture Notes in Business Information Processing*, 34: 143–156.

Session 2B: ETHICS

Ethical Considerations and Social Responsibility in Library Catalogues

Drahomira Cupar, University of Zadar, Croatia
Ljiljana Poljak, University of Zadar, Croatia

Abstract

Subject cataloguing is the most important part of resource description and knowledge representation in library catalogues. Subject headings provide direct access to subjects within all types of resources (physical or digital) in library collections. Subject headings should be added to a resource without personal views of librarians/subject cataloguers interfering in the process of assigning and choosing "right"/appropriate terms. By using outdated subject headings systems or letting personal feelings and views towards certain topics interfere with the process of assigning terms to a resource, one can be (falsely) accused for hiding or misrepresenting "the truth" written in the described resource.

This research explores how different types of collections/libraries deal with "problematic" topics and whether subject cataloguers can really be seen as biased while applying chosen subject headings to a certain ("problematic") resources or topics. These examples include (but are not limited to): homosexuality, human reproduction / in vitro fertilization (IVF), people with mental illness and drugs (marijuana). The purpose of this paper is to investigate to what extent a subject headings system can limit (or create misconceptions about) the access to potentially controversial and/or taboo topics. This research analyses subject headings created around chosen topics, and the application of those subject headings to a sample of book titles from a library catalogue. This research answers to following research questions:

    1. How are "problematic" / controversial topics represented in the chosen library catalogues?
    2. Which titles have underrepresented or non-represented topics in subject access points?

The method used in this research was content analysis of subject headings from the catalogue records.

1. Introduction

Since the development of online library catalogues, subject access to library resources has become even more important than before for subject cataloguers. Online library catalogues (in Croatia) enable users to access to library materials via searching (and browsing) subject headings, (uncontrolled) keywords-from-the-title and classification numbers (Universal Decimal Classification system). Although none of the catalogues are fully adapted and user friendly, there are possibilities for researching current state of social responsibility and awareness of the importance of creating neutral access points within the system. Controlled subject headings provide direct access to subjects within all types of resources (physical or digital) in library collections.

The professional code of ethics of Croatian Library Association does not address subject cataloguing / indexing specifically. It only states that information professionals should in their work ensure "Accessibility of different types of resources for all groups of users" (HKD, 2013) and that information professionals in their daily jobs should provide "equal access to information for all users, regardless of their personal characteristics, special needs, gender/sex, nationality, religion, political belief and social status", and, "to include their professional judgement, without interference of political, moral or religious views or material interest" (HKD, 2013). The Croatian Library Association accepted and translated IFLA Code of Ethics for Librarians and other Information Workers (2012) and it addresses neutrality in two important issues (under point 5) "Librarians and other information workers are strictly committed to neutrality and an unbiased stance regarding collection, access and service. Neutrality results in the most balanced collection and the most balanced access to information achievable.", and also "Librarians and other information workers distinguish between their personal convictions and professional duties. They do not advance private interests or personal beliefs at the expense of neutrality" (IFLA FAIFE, 2012).

It is a great challenge in achieving 'the most balanced collection and most balanced access to information'. It is embedded in all segments of professionalism that subject access points should be added to a resource without personal views of librarians/subject cataloguers interfering in the process of assigning and choosing the 'right' or most appropriate terms, but there are many possible reasons for assigning 'wrong', biased or misleading subject access points in catalogues/catalogue records and some of them are not even wrong on purpose.

Social responsibility could also be intertwined with censorship in libraries. Bade (2002) researched misinformation in shared library catalogues where he categorized errors as linguistic errors or intellectual errors. Intellectual errors were primarily connected with classification and subject cataloguing. Bade (2002) argues that "linguistic ignorance and errors are a primary source, but not the only source, of intellectual misinformation. Two principal sources of misinformation [are][...] those that result from linguistic disability and those that result from a weak general education or lack of specialist knowledge" Bade (2002, 12).

Both are problematic since the result is "incorrect subjects and classification". Since studies in the area of subject cataloguing/indexing mostly discuss subjectivity or lack of objectivity (Svenonius and McGarry, 1993) in the process of applying subjects to resources, many conclusions stay on the surface of it claiming that there is no right 'solution' for that problem and it is better to stop wasting time on finding suitable heading. Bade (2002) criticizes those types of articles arguing that "Wrong subjects waste a reader's time; lack of the right subject can prevent readers from finding what they want. Subject headings that are too broad leave the record lost in the large number of items retrieved" (Bade 2002, 12). Inconsistency is another issue researched in the area of subject cataloguing. Almost every study of inconsistency in indexing starts with Shera's 'Two Laws of Cataloguing' (Shera 1977):

Law #1 No cataloger will accept the work of any other cataloger.
Law #2 No cataloger will accept his/her own work six months after the cataloging

Although it illustrates power of subjectivity and points at particular circumstances which surround subject cataloguing, there is some interesting research done by Mann (2012) dealing with literature on the topic of (in)consistencies in indexing. Mann analysed in detail reports/research papers which are mostly cited on the topic and concluded that often scholars cite information which is out of context and sometimes not true (Mann 2012).

For example, if using outdated subject headings or unintentionally letting personal feelings and views towards certain topics interfere with 'the process of assigning terms to a resource, one can be (falsely) accused of hiding or misrepresenting "the truth" written in the described resource. Sometimes, achieving neutral stance can be more problematic than ignorance of the controversial or so-called problematic topic(s).

This research explores how different types of collections/libraries deal with problematic topics and whether subject cataloguers can really be seen as biased while applying chosen subject headings to a certain problematic resources or topics. These examples include (but are not limited to): LGBTIQ topics, drugs (e. g. books on marijuana), religious topics, discrimination and violence.

To conclude with Bade's (2002) paper, suggestions regarding evaluation of subject analysis, including classification were accepted and implemented in the methodology. This means that authors of this research followed these instructions "the items must be evaluated with the item in hand, and the evaluator must have an adequate knowledge of: (1) standards (LCSH, Dewey Decimal System, etc.); (2) language(s) of the text; and (3) subject of the text" (Bade 2002, 12).

2. Education and standards for subject cataloguing in Croatia
Croatian subject cataloguers all need to have a university diploma and in addition education in library and information science to be eligible to work in a library, especially on

cataloguing and classification/subject indexing. Many more experienced subject cataloguers are subject specialists. For example, they may have formal education in the Croatian language and literature and librarianship, or history and librarianship or musicology and librarianship. Since the Bologna process in Croatian higher education, the study of librarianship has become a one-subject discipline. Lately it has become obvious that students are missing specific subject knowledge in order to be able to index materials in special collections or on specific subjects. The transition of librarianship programmes into information science programmes has only broadened areas within information sciences field, but narrowed opportunities to specialize in certain areas. After gaining a university diploma, Croatian librarians have the opportunity to continue professional training (CSSU) on different topics. Occasionally there is training in subject cataloguing. Although training in subject access is another important topic, there is not much on that subject in current literature. Intner stated in 1996 that "One of the most important parts of subject analysis is determining the subject content of an item, and this can't be taught" (based on Steinhagen et al. 1996). This might be only partially true, since there are many tools and guidelines which can help overcome knowledge gaps for particular subjects. To conclude Intner she stated that (Steinhagen et. al 1996):

1) subject analysis exhibits some unreasonable dichotomies: some librarians say subject headings are useless, while others clamor for subject headings for fiction, form and genre terms, etc., 2) just because some administrators say we don't need subject headings doesn't mean it's true, and 3) it is unreasonable to insist on using only one kind of subject analysis, considering the variations in materials, users, etc. We should consider using different thesauri for different materials, sometimes more than one at a time. Some people need deep indexing and multi-level classification, while others need only keyword searching

It is known that many of the things stated above were 'corrected' and improved over the period of 20 years because of OCLC and Library of Congress efforts but since it is a constant work, there are lot more to do. Many problems occur when LCSH is used in a different cultural environment, on other continents, for example.

Croatian standards used in subject cataloguing are Universal Decimal Classification (UDC) for classification of library resources and principles and standards for building a subject heading system. The National and University Library Zagreb and libraries in their network started to use and translate LCSH accordingly, but there are four big library systems in Croatia, and each builds and maintains its own subject authority database with subject headings based on standards and principles. In this research, examples from two union catalogues were extracted for analysis: Crolist (http://opak.crolib.hr/) and WorldCat (https://www.worldcat.org/).

3. Warrant(s) in knowledge organization systems

Knowledge organization systems are based on a warrant, which Beghtol (1986, 110) defines as "the authority a classificationist invokes first to justify and subsequently to verify decisions about what classes/concepts to include in the system, in what order classes/concepts should appear in the schedules, what units classes/concepts are divided into [...]." It is important to beware that the fulfilment of the conditions and decisions are conscious or unconscious and depend on a classifier "who must interpret both the document and the classification system in order to classify the document by means of available syntactic devices" (111). Barité (2018), citing Tennis (2005), states that "warrant is based on literature, users, scholarly opinion and is culturally biased".

Knowledge organization systems have to be free from bias, and there are several frameworks and suggestions on decision-making process while classifying (Beghtol 2002, 2005; Hjørland 2008), and are both based on a literary warrant. First introduced by Hulme in 1911, it states that defining and naming classes had to be based on published literature from a certain field, rather than extracted from a preconceived philosophical order of sciences. Over the years, as the theoretical and methodological body, cultural warrant was officially recognized by Library of Congress Classification as a criterion for the revision of its tables. It was also incorporated to Archival Studies and National Information Standards Organization (NISO) standards (Barité 2018).

Although Library of Congress Subject Headings also implement literary warrant, Olsen highlights the inconsistencies in terms of LCSH in several examples, stressing that literary warrant is applied differently in mainstream topics than in others. For example, the term 'woman of color' is not an authority heading, although it has a warrant in literature, and the term used instead is 'minority woman' (Olsen 2002). 'Queer theory' is also disregarded at this point (Martínez-Ávila and Budd 2017).

In context of literary warrant, Hjørland wrote about deliberate bias, suggesting it could be a "naturally occurring phenomenon in the supposedly objective approach to KO in which systems are said to mirror points of view derived by literary warrant" (Smiragila 2015, 3). Respecting the literary warrant, the headings are created on literature that could be biased. Another argument is the slow-adaptation nature of the scheme, noted by Rogers, where headings cover a spectrum of culturally sensitive subjects because it originates in North American 19th century, and reflects prejudices of that time (Dash 2015).

Considering user needs, representation and organization systems, and the process of globalization, Beghtol (2005, 904) notes that "a system that has not been established on an appropriate cultural warrant will not be adopted for information search and retrieval because information seekers will find that it does not match their accepted view of how the world works".

The cultural warrant is determined by the discourse community, knowledge domain or culture. It was first named by Lee in 1976, but based on Hulme, considering that individuals have different needs and ways of interpreting established knowledge regarding their cultural space (Barité, 2018). A cultural warrant could be seen as an extended literary warrant because the existing literature needs to reflect the society in which the literature is published (Beghtol, 1986). In knowledge organization theory, there are numerous kinds of warrants, and Barité (2018) sees cultural warrant as an umbrella term for an indigenous warrant, genre warrant, policy warrant and relation with an ethical warrant.

The process of globalization made knowledge organization systems increasingly used across different cultures. If there is a systemic bias, there is an ethical responsibility to recognize it (Olson 1999 in Bair 2005). The term ethical warrant for global knowledge representation and organization systems was introduced by Beghtol in 2002, and later she has proposed "Ethical decision-making for knowledge representation and organization systems for global use" (Beghtol, 2005). This example uses a warrant as a methodological tool in the decision-making model.

4. Neutrality, bias, considerations of subject cataloguers
Neutrality by definition is "the state of not supporting either side in a disagreement, competition or war" (Oxford Advanced Learner's Dictionary, 2005), is the aim of every knowledge organization and representation system. Neutrality supposes an unbiased and objective approach towards a document and its organization and representation. Objectivity is the first principle of subject cataloging, demanding accuracy and an unbiased approach, but understanding the high probability of subject interpretation (Salvano 2003 in Kinyanjui 2016). Olson (2002, 2) notes that a library catalogue is not a neutral tool and it is constructed so "it does not just passively reflect the dominant values of the society in some neutral or objective manner but selects those values for the expression." Classification systems and controlled vocabularies also "fail to accurately and respectfully organize library materials about social groups and identities that lack social and political power" (Drabinski 2013, 95). Furthermore, it is necessary to think about "how to be ethically and politically engaged on behalf of marginal knowledge formations and identities who quite reasonably expect to be

able to locate themselves in the library." In theory, there are a lot of questions about the same, and neutrality in librarianship could be considered as an outdated approach. Lewis (2008) noted that the meaning of the term 'neutrality' nowadays could be represented with the term 'indifference'.

Hjørland (2008) wrote about deliberate bias, based on pragmatism and critical theory, stating that it is impossible to free knowledge organization systems from bias or to gain complete objectivity, but rather to aim at making it more objective. With people developing systems, and their personal degrees of freedom, and users on the other side with system reflecting their needs – it cannot be developed free from bias or be completely objective.

Among core values and ethical codes of information professionals and librarians, professional neutrality is listed along with equality of access (Koehler et al. 2000). Although it can have several applications, proper subject headings also have to guarantee equality of access. As Olson (2000) points out, the lack of neutral meaning while granting subject access is an obstacle to universal access to information. Moreover, we "seem to realize that these sources have significant biases and exclusions, and that by choosing to follow the convenience of a singular public and the canon of literary warrant we are introducing a bias toward the mainstream status quo that is just as much a bias as any professional judgment we are likely to employ" (Olson 2000, 65). In the same paper Olson speculates that the topics are found to be controversial, rather than the action, and while believing that documents can be described without bias, cataloguers seek some kind of external warrant for establishing subject headings.

The professional codes of ethics provide guidelines merely to develop ethical policies or principles and to guide the one in making the right decision. The Code of Ethics of the American Library Association (2008) has the purpose of guiding ethical decision making, and to provide a framework, not to dictate conduct to cover particular situations. The main problem addressing the existing codes of ethics in information science is that they do not necessarily help while dealing with the specific ethical problem (Shoemaker 2015). The intention is for all information professionals, and cataloguers seek for their own code of ethics. Mai (2014), while discussing ethics in classifications, focuses on the problem of neutrality, which is presumed to be followed by cataloguers, and note that in ALA's Code of Ethics "is constrained to suggest that librarians do-the right-thing when facing an ethical dilemma" (Mai 2014, 246).

The assumption that information can be unbiased has to be re-evaluated in accordance with contemporary theories that have found knowledge organization systems inherently biased. In order to give information professionals ethical framework, Fox and Reece (2012) analysed existing frameworks (utilitarianism, deontology, pragmatism, justice, feminist, and Derridean ethics) and proposed new model, i.e. ethical framework, especially for information organization, which is composed of criteria included in the frameworks they analysed. Fox and Reece's model contains following criteria (applicable to both individual and corporate persons): a duty of care; hospitality, with mitigation; and treatment of people as entities with basic rights and responsibilities. Prescribing no action we are certain is wrong (Fox and Reece 2012, 381-382).

5. Controversial topics in library collection

When a controversial or taboo word is mentioned in the library context, it is often connected to censorship of some kind. If we judge from the users' points of view, every book can be seen as insulting or controversial in some aspect. If the library wants to maintain its collections for all, individual user's attitudes and/or feelings should not be the driving force for building library collections. User studies often refer to user needs and from Cutter to the present highlight the fact that library catalogues and other services should and must be built for users, accommodating all their needs (Spiteri 2012). But cataloguers often don't have contact with library users and can only assume what their needs are or might be, and according to those assumptions can try to assign subject headings to library materials. Spiteri argues "Although cataloguers are given the responsibility to create catalogue records to meet users' needs, their ability to do so is limited by their insufficient understanding of these needs" (Spiteri 2012, 210). Spiteri argues "With an insufficient understanding of user needs, cataloguers must often rely on their own judgment to customize catalogue records for user convenience. The process of customizing records is itself problematic, since in the face of decreasing funding to cataloguing departments, library administrators often discourage cataloguers from this practice, since it is often seen as a time-consuming and inefficient practice; it is cheaper, simpler, and faster to use purchased catalogue records from vendors and cataloguing utilities with minimal modification (Hoffman, 2009; Iliff, 2004)" (Spiteri 2012, 210).

That said, there are legitimate arguments that some books are inappropriate s and there is a public debate about whether such books should be in libraries. Controversial or taboo, or even tricky topics include: (homo)sexuality, or LGBTIQ topics in general, drug use, violence, pornography, discrimination, racism, and so on. Depending on different approaches to the topic (from the author's point of view), books may be acceptable or unacceptable to users (and librarians) and they can be indexed in a way that expresses prejudice or bias in subject headings. On the other hand, if librarians add comment in the record expressing the author's views as presented in the book, the subject headings could be seen as being biased. It could mean that the librarian wants to be 'distanced' from the topics and views expressed in the book. Sometimes, being a subject cataloguer can be a tricky business itself.

When discussing ethical issues in the subject cataloguing, four main approaches or types of analysis can be identified in researches and literature:

1. Analysis of ethics/biases/prejudice embedded in knowledge organization systems itself (subject heading and classification);
2. Usage of knowledge organization systems as tools for analysing and expressing biases/prejudice/controversies contained in library materials;
3. Analysis of attitudes towards (potentially or verified) controversial authors and their published materials; and
4. Analysis of assigned subjects/classification numbers to concrete controversial/harmful titles/books in a certain library.

The literature in this area usually combines two or three approaches because most of the time it cannot be seen separately, or out of context. Ethics in subject cataloguing is often closely connected to censorship and is discussed within that context. Most of the studies concerning removal of books with harmful content were done in public libraries. For instance, Chapman (2013) showed that it is usually to decide upon harmful content when children are in question.

Several research projects were done on treatment of controversial or 'bad' books in libraries. Jatkevicius (2003, 38) supports the theory library records should be enhanced, "with subsequent commentary that enhances understanding of its content and its context", if non-fiction library materials are being criticized by at least two reliable sources. All those commentaries should accompany the book for all activities that involve it. He argues that although librarians think they are not part of the debate and not passing judgement on library materials only because someone 'says it's bad', but he claims that "we [a.k.a. librarians] can make value judgments as library professionals. Actually, we do it all the time – we do it in every reference transaction and every book purchase and every resource allocation. We do it by recommending one particular source of information over another, by gauging how much information a patron wants and its quality" (Jatkevicius 2003, 38). Homan (2012, 348) talks about books compromised due to: age, error, abridgement, expurgation, plagiarism, copyright violation, libel, or fraud.

Homan (2012) takes Jatkevicius's conclusion about 'library catalogue enhancement' and criticizes it by citing the ALA Library Bill of Rights and Labelling and Rating Systems Statement that enhanced content in catalogues "should not be construed to preclude provision of resources and information useful to users ... as long as the criteria for inclusion is viewpoint-neutral" and that librarians "should seek the broadest spectrum of information and evaluative materials as possible" Homan (2012, 352). So called 'bad' books are not always controversial regarding topics and therefore neutral-indexing is not the only place where false treatment can be seen. Questionable situations and actions of people involved in the production of 'bad' book can lead to debate over inclusion of the book in a library collection. On the other hand, there are many topics which are problematic. They can be categorized as controversial, are often challenged, and can be seen on lists of banned books. Some of them may 'only' be age inappropriate, (e.g. children's books with strong language or explicit content), or may be positive towards certain topics such as violence, racism, pornography, drug abuse, etc.

Speaking of controversial topics, Brett and Campbell (2016) wrote a paper on changing of attitudes towards controversial topics in public libraries over few decades in America, using data from General Social Survey (GSS), 1972-2014. Brett and Campbell (2016) investigated attitudes towards controversial topics, i.e. books written by authors who are anti-religion, racist (anti-Black), communist, militarist, gay, anti-American Muslim. They specially investigated connection of answers of people who said they visit the library at least 12 times a year (once a month) and concluded that overall data showed significant positive shift, meaning people who are visiting library are more against removing books from the library. Only topic remained almost unchanged is attitudes towards racism (Brett and Campbell 2016, 28). There were significant differences depending on level of education, geographical data and year of birth. Younger people are more against book removal than older people.

Burke (2008, 2008) has done similar research on GSS data, 1973-2006. Burke (2008) analysed data from GSS, 1973-2006 regarding tolerance for library materials with homosexual content, and written by homosexual authors. GSS data showed increasing tolerance toward books on homosexuality, but Burke (2008) identified that "education level and belief that homosexuality is wrong" are most influential predictors showing people are prone to removing books with topics about homosexuality from the library (Burke 2008, 260). Brett and Campbell (2016) reported that since "support for gay marriage rights increased [...] between 1988-2006, then did support for leaving books by gay authors in the library". So, it seems homosexuality is almost not a controversial issue anymore in American public libraries. However, there is significant amount of literature dealing with subject indexing and access of literature with topic of homosexuality (and LGBTIQ topics in general). Just to name few, Johansson (2008), Johnson (2010), Adler (2009), Bates and Rowley (2011), Pinho, Guimarães (2012), Chapman (2013), Drabinski (2013), Fox (2016), Colbert (2016).

On the other hand, the highly-cited author and passionate critic of Library of Congress Subject Headings, Berman (1971; 1993) and Knowlton (2005) three decades later, analysed prejudice and antipathies incorporated into LCSH. "Berman's intent was to call into question certain subject headings in LCSH– and propose alterations, additions, and deletions of headings and cross-references to more accurately reflect the language used in addressing these topics, to rectify errors of bias, and to better guide librarians and readers to material of interest (Knowlton 2005, 125). Knowledge organization schemes go through constant revisions in order to reflect changes in society more accurately, and Berman's work started a whole movement of professionals who asked for changes in LCSH. Many of them are introduced, but, as Berman himself estimated, "that no more than half of his suggestions have been adopted" (Knowlton 2005, 126). Knowlton states that "Of the 225 headings Berman suggested changes in, 88 (or 39%) have been changed almost exactly as he suggested, while an additional 54 (or 24%) have been changed in the ways to partially reflect Berman's suggestions" Knowlton (2005, 127-128). He also discusses reasons for changes and bias that remained in 80 unchanged items. Knowlton (2005) concluded there are "some patterns of thought that persist in the Library of Congress", for example, for Christian religion remaining unchanged. Other unchanged headings are categorized in several groups that: "simply reflect a difference of opinion on the literary merit of subject headings; a different way of restructuring biased headings (rather than compensate for using Man as an umbrella term for humanity by adding similar subdivisions under Woman, LCSH now uses Human beings)". An alternate view on the link between topics are suggested as cross-references (Knowlton 2005, 128). Lember, Lipkin and Lee (2013) researched radical cataloguing in practice, since the term itself was created (in 2008 by Roberto who also co-edited book of essays with Berman called *Radical cataloging: Essays at the Front.*

6. Research

The purpose of this research is to investigate to what extent a subject headings system can limit (or create misconceptions about) the access to potentially controversial and/or taboo topics in library collections. This research was done in two steps. In the first step, analysis of the: a) subject headings created around chosen topics and b) application of those subject headings on a sample of book titles from a library catalogue in Croatia was done. In the second step, subject headings in Croatian catalogue were compared to LCSH found in WorldCat for the same titles.

6.1 Research questions
This research will answer following research questions:

1. How are "problematic" / controversial topics represented in the chosen library catalogues?
2. Which titles have underrepresented or non-represented topics in subject access points?

6.2 Methodology
For the purpose of this research, following topics were chosen as controversial: homosexuality, human reproduction / in vitro fertilization (IVF), people with mental illness and drugs (marijuana). For each topic, ten books were selected randomly to see how the topics were represented in the catalogue. Chosen titles were searched in the Croatian union catalogue Crolist and compared to results in WorldCat. Subject headings were counted and analysed separately, with explanation of connections within subject pre-coordinated strings. Crolist is an integrated library system used in more than 150 public, university, school and special libraries in Croatia. Subject headings used in Crolist are gathered in subject authority file, which consists of more than a half million subject index terms (personal, corporate body and family names, topics, authors, uniform titles, geographic names and genres). There were some limitations to this research. Crolist has Vero FRBR version of the catalogue (UNIBIS 2015) where it is possible to see hierarchies, connections of each subject heading to different titles, etc. Vero has one 'Google-like box' for searching and enables users to see their results in 'split' facets, and also displays subject headings by listing alphabetically but within the list shows another subject heading assigned to certain title. There is also Classic search where subject headings are displayed strictly alphabetically in the catalogue. Due to this 'feature' of the catalogue display, it is 'easier' to find and count all subjects around one topic – you just need to make 'more clicks'. Since searching is allowed only by the first part/term in the pre-coordinated subject heading (a feature not common in third generation library catalogues) users are advised to use Vero. If users don't pick/write exact string of subject heading assigned to a title, they won't get results.

6.3 Results and discussion
Homosexuality

The first chosen topic 'homosexuality' is (still) a great taboo and controversial in Croatia - in literature and in the real life. When searching Vero version of the catalogue using term 'homosexuality', there are 112 results (titles) and not in all of them have 'homosexuality' as a subject heading. In some results the term itself can be found in any part of the record (i.e. title, author, title, subject, keywords and annotation). Search results show that the term is 'subject' in 100 records, and in 19 titles, but when counting all the subject headings assigned to titles (112 results from the first search) connected with the subject/topic homosexuality, only 93 were listed.

The next most frequently used subject heading is 'homosexuality – history', with 19 results and the third suggested is 'homosexuality – religious point of view' with 13 results.

For the purpose of determining number of subject headings per title, ten first ranked titles connected to chosen subject heading were analysed. It is noted that most titles have a poor number of subject headings assigned. When searching for resources indexed by "homosexuality – history", 5/10 had only one subject heading, and when choosing "homosexuality – religious point of view" as a search term, 8/10 titles had only that one subject heading assigned. Examination of the rest of 91 subject headings showed that ten are assigned to 9, 8, 7, 5 or 4 titles, 7 subject headings were assigned to 3 titles, which leaves 74 subject headings used only once or two times as access points for the topic of homosexuality.

A classic search in Crolist enables users to learn about broader terms (BT), related terms (RT), and related terms (see also), and sometimes there are definitions and scope notes for particular term (see Example 1).

Since there is no exhaustive list of all subject headings (especially not pre-coordinated strings of headings) it is not possible to be sure that all of them are accounted for. There are 79 subject headings altogether dealing with the topic of LGBTIQ people. There are more topics connected with this area but are not presented at all in this list. For example, there are Croatian titles using word 'queer' but there is no subject heading containing it and it is not translated into any of Croatian terms. There is also an umbrella term 'rainbow family' but it is not represented in Croatian subject heading list.

Example 1. Hierarchies and see also for the subject heading *Homosexuals* from Crolist.

See also	Homoseksualci. / Homosexuals.
See also	Homoseksualnost. / Homosexuality.
See also NT:	Lezbijstvo. / Lesbianism.
See also BT:	Seksualna orijentacija. / Sexual orientation.
See also BT:	Seksualno ponašanje. / Sexual behavior.
See also	Istospolna zajednica. / Same sex union. [followed by definition in Croatian law for same sex unions]
See also	Lezbijke. / Lesbians. [Definition in Croatian]

There were ten translated book titles found both in Crolist and WorldCat. From ten titles, three were found without subject headings, and therefore invisible and hard to find for users who don't know the title or author(s). One and two subject headings were assigned to six titles and only one title had more than two, i.e. five subject headings. WorldCat usually had three subject headings per title. Two titles had four, and one had two subject headings. It is significant to see the low number or complete absence of subject headings in the Croatian catalogue. Results are shown in the Table 1.

Table 1. Crolist and WorldCat subject headings for 10 titles with the topic of homosexuality/queer theory

	Book title	Crolist SH	WorldCat LCSH
homosexuality / queer theory			
1.	With Pleasure: Thoughts on the Nature of Human Sexuality (1998)	Sexuality – Psychosocial viewpoint [1 SH]	Sex Sexual excitement Pleasure [3 SH]
2.	Gay life and culture: a world history (2011)	Homosexuality – History Sex identity – History Homophobia – History Lesbianism – History Sexuality – History [5 SH]	Homosexuality – History Gays – Social life and customs Lesbians – Social life and customs [3 SH]
3.	Stonewall: the riots that sparked the gay revolution (2011)	Homosexuality – Activism [1 SH]	Stonewall Riots, New York, N.Y., 1969 Gay liberation movement – United States – History - 20th century Gay men – United States – History - 20th century

	Book title	Crolist SH	WorldCat LCSH
			[3 SH]
4.	The practice of love: lesbian sexuality and perverse desire (2003)	Lesbianism – Feminist viewpoint Lesbianism – Psychoanalytic viewpoint [2 SH]	Feminism Lesbianism Sex [3 SH]
5.	Queer in Europe: contemporary case studies (2013)	Gender equality – Study [1 SH]	Homosexuality – Europe – Case studies Homosexuality Europe [3 SH]
6.	Compulsory heterosexuality and lesbian existence (2002)	Lesbianism – Feminist viewpoint Heterosexuality – Feminist viewpoint [2 SH]	Lesbianism Feminism [2 SH]
7.	The straight mind and other essays (2011)	[0 SH]	Feminist theory Feminism and literature Lesbianism Radicalism [4 SH]
8.	Alles Familie!: vom Kind der neuen Freundin, vom Bruder von Papas freuherer Frau und anderen Verwandten (2013)	[0 SH]	Families – Juvenile literature Intergenerational relations – Juvenile literature Families [3 SH]
9.	The men with the pink triangle: the true, life- and death story of homosexuals in the Nazi death camps (2008)	[0 SH]	Gay men – Germany – Biography Male homosexuality – Germany Concentration camps – Germany [3 SH]
10.	Foucault and queer theory (2001)	Foucault, Michel – Sexual theory Homosexuality – Philosophical viewpoint [2 SH]	Foucault, Michel, – 1926-1984. Homosexuality Postmodernism Queer theory [4 SH]

In vitro fertilization (IVF) / human reproduction

The second topic was 'in vitro fertilization (IVF)', which is an extremely controversial topic among conservative groups and political parties in Croatia. Subject searching for 'in vitro fertilization' (12 results) gave confusing results because the majority of results were related to animal reproduction (for example, in vitro fertilization - bovine (3); embryo (veterinary) – culture in vitro (2); in vitro fertilization – methods (1)). Therefore, the broader term 'human reproduction' was used in second search and there were 34 results. Due to the popularity of the topic and volume of published materials, this is considered a low number for both of subject headings. It was necessary to re-formulate the search by using another popular term – 'artificial fertilization' which gave 8 results. Among these 8 results, there is "in vitro fertilization – moral-theological viewpoint". When selected, it gives 11 results/titles. All of those titles are written from a Catholic point of view, which could lead to the conclusion that in vitro fertilization is term more popular in theological than the medical or psychological literature. To conclude, even the broad term, 'human reproduction' is the most convenient subject heading because it contains word 'human' which excludes animal reproduction from results, and also it (almost completely) deals with the topic from medical point of view. Only one title is connected to the moral-theological perspective, but the subject heading 'human reproduction' is in free form and therefore is not searchable. Example 2 shows hierarchies, broader and narrower terms around the topic of human reproduction

Example 2. See also, broader and narrower terms for subject heading In vitro fertilization in Crolist

See also BT:	Reproduktivne metode (Medicina). / Reproductive methods (Medicine)
See also BT:	Asistirana humana reprodukcija. / Assisted human reproduction
See also BT:	Humana reprodukcija./ Human reproduction
See also BT:	Metode i postupci (Medicina). / Methods and procedures (Medicine)
See also NT:	Embrijski transfer. / Embryo transfer
See also NT:	Indukcija ovulacije. / Ovulation induction
See also NT:	Oplodnja in vitro. / In vitro fertilization

Among ten titles chosen for the subject heading analysis, seven were published in English and three were translated. All of them had subject headings assigned, ranging from one to four per title. Two of the titles had free form headings, and as they are not controlled, they could not be found while searching or browsing the catalogue by subject. Also, there is more similarity among subject headings assigned to original English titles in both catalogues, than to those translated from Croatian. The reason for this lies in the fact that Croatian cataloguers often use WorldCat as a source for cataloguing in general. The number of controlled subject heading assigned to titles is almost the same in both catalogues, variations in numbers are insignificant. The results are shown in Table 2.

Table 2. Crolist and WorldCat subject headings for 10 titles with the topics "human reproduction" and "in vitro fertilization"

	Book title	Crolist SH	WorldCat LCSH
human reproduction / in vitro fertilization			
1.	Enhanced beings: human germline modification and the law (2018)	Genetic engineering – Legal aspect Genetic engineering – Ethical aspect Human reproduction – Legal regulation [3 SH]	Genetic engineering – Law and legislation Genetic engineering – Moral and ethical aspects Human reproductive technology – Law and legislation [3 SH]
2.	Barren in the promised land: childless Americans and the pursuit of happiness (1997)	Childless marriage – United States – – History Human reproduction – Disorders – Sociological viewpoint [3 SH]	Childlessness – Social aspects – United States Childlessness – United States Childlessness – United States – History [3 SH]
3.	Reproductive health and human rights: integrating medicine, ethics, and law (2003)	Sexual Health – Bioethical Viewpoint Genetic engineering – Ethical aspect Genetic engineering – Legal aspect Medical Ethics - Patient Rights [4 SH]	Reproductive health – Moral and ethical aspects Women – Health and hygiene – Moral and ethical aspect. Human rights [3 SH]
4.	The prenatal person: ethics from conception to birth (2002)	Human reproduction – Ethical viewpoint Human reproduction – Theological viewpoint [2 SH]	Bioethical Issues Catholicism Reproductive Medicine [3 SH]
5.	Endowed: regulating the male sexed body (2008)	Human reproduction – Legal regulation Gender equality – Legal regulation [2 SH]	Gender identity Human reproduction – Law and legislation Human reproductive technology – Law and legislation [3 SH]
6.	Birthrights: law and ethics at the beginnings of life (1991)	Right to Life * Human Reproduction [1 SH]	Human reproduction – Law and legislation – Great Britain Fertilization in vitro, Human – Law and legislation – Great Britain Artificial insemination, Human – Law and legislation – Great Britain

	Book title	Crolist SH	WorldCat LCSH
			[3 SH]
7.	Reproductive health: case studies with ethical commentary (2012)	Sexual health – Bioethical viewpoint Human reproduction – Legal regulation Medical Ethics – Patient Rights [3 SH]	Contraception – ethics Sterilization – ethics Maternal-Fetal Relations – psychology [3 SH]
8.	Ethics, reproduction and genetic control (1992)	Ethics * Human reproduction* Genetic control[1 SH]	Humans – Reproduction – Ethics Ethics, Medical Eugenics [3 SH]
9.	Begotten, not made: pastoral care for couples experiencing infertility (2017)	in vitro fertilization – moral-theological viewpoint [1 SH]	Infertility – Pastoral counseling of Infertility – Psychological aspects [2 SH]
10	Les enfants du secret (2000)	Adoption – Psychological point of view Parenting – Medical Assisted Infiltration – Psychological Aspects [2 SH]	Adoption Psychology, Child Reproductive Techniques [3 SH]

People with mental disorders

The third chosen topic was 'people with mental disorders'. The term 'psychiatric patients' is not used as a subject heading itself, but rather as 'people with mental disorders' and as a subject heading it represents only one title in Crolist. Searching in Vero using term 'people with mental disorders' gave 88 results. Frequently used subject headings are 'people with mental disorders – Croatia – legal status' (20) and 'people with mental disorders – quality of life' (10). Term 'psychiatric patients' is used in subject headings with complex string construction, such as 'suicide – psychiatric patients', 'Criminal Procedure – psychiatric patients - legal status' or 'war stress – psychiatric patients'. There are also problems with legal terminology. For the term 'un-accountability' as a legal status in criminal law, in Crolist is used word 'neuračunljivost'. That is not the right term used in Croatian criminal laws, but only in Bosnian laws. Croatian term for it is 'neubrojivost'. Both words are acceptable in Croatian language, but not in legal terminology. This only proves that literary warrant was not respected.

There is no hierarchy between subject terms, just in the case of 'mental disorders' subject heading. The number of subject headings in chosen titles is satisfying, and there is not much difference in comparison with subject headings assigned to the same titles in WorldCat. In one title (no. 10) the subject headings are completely different. The results are shown in the Table 3.

Table 3. Crolist and Worldcat subject headings for 10 titles with the topic people with mental disorders

	Book title	Crolist SH	WorldCat LCSH
people with mental disorders			
1.	Madness in civilization: a cultural history of insanity, from the bible to Freud, from the madhouse to modern medicine (2018)	Psychiatric disorders – History Psychiatric disorders – Therapy People with mental disorders – History Psychiatrics – History [4 SH]	Mental illness – History Mental illness – Treatment – History Mental illness [3 SH]
2.	Mental health today and tomorrow: exploring current and future trends in mental health care (2015)	Mental health People with mental disorders – Social status Health psychology – Psychosocial viewpoint Psychiatric disorders – Manual [4 SH]	Mental health services Mental illness – Treatment Political science – Public Policy – Social Security [4 SH]
3.	The man who closed the asylums: Franco Basaglia and the revolution in mental health care (2016)	Basaglia, Franco – Integrative psychiatry Psychiatry – Italy – 20. ct. People with mental disorders – Quality of life – Improvement [3 SH]	Basaglia, Franco Mental health services – Italy – History – 20th century Psychiatric hospitals – Italy – History – 20th century [3 SH]
4.	Mental health: a person-centred approach (2014)	Mental health – Manual People with mental disorders – Social status Health Psychology – Psychosocial Viewpoint Psychiatric disorders – Manual [4 SH]	Mental health [1 SH]

	Book title	Crolist SH	WorldCat LCSH
5.	Key concepts in mental health (2014)	Mental health People with mental disorders – Social status Health Psychology – Psychosocial Viewpoint Psychiatric disorders – Manual [4 SH]	Mental health Mental health services Health and Fitness [3 SH]
6.	Straight talk about your mental health (2002)	Psychiatric disorders – Advice book Mental health – Advice book [2 SH]	Psychiatry – Popular works Mental health services – Popular works Mental health services [3 SH]
7.	Teaching ethics in psychiatry: case vignettes (2012)	Psychiatrist ethics – Patient's rights People with mental disorders – Legal protection [2 SH]	Psychiatric ethics Psychiatry – Law and legislation Involuntary treatment – Moral and ethical aspects [3 SH]
8.	Asylums: essays on the social situation of mental patients and other inmates (2011)	People with mental disorders – Social status [2 SH]	Psychiatric hospitals – Sociological aspects Mentally ill [2 SH]
9.	Crazy: a father's search through America's mental health madness (2006)	Psychiatric disorders People with mental disorders – Family relations Psychiatrics – USA [3 SH]	Psychology Psychology – Psychopathology – General [2 SH]
10.	Breaking points (1985)	People with mental disorders – Criminality [1 SH]	Hinckley, John W Reagan, Ronald – Assassination attempt, 1981. Hinckley, Jack [3 SH]

Marijuana

The fourth topic chosen for this research is 'marijuana'. It is mostly used in the context of medical/therapeutic use or abuse (as a recreational drug). In Croatia, it is an attractive topic at the moment, with many people advocating legalization of growing and using it for medical purposes. Searching in the Vero catalogue using the term 'marijuana' resulted in 18 hits.

Frequently-used subject headings are 'marijuana – medical use' (4) and 'marijuana – abuse' (3). Also, the term 'cannabis' (14) is sometimes used as a broader term, and often as synonym for 'marijuana – medical use'. It can be concluded that subject headings regarding marijuana legalization in general or medical use of marijuana has not yet introduced to the Crolist union catalogue. In the comparison on the sample of ten titles between subject headings in Crolist and WorldCat some inconsistencies can be noted. Of the ten titles, two were found without subject headings in Crolist, and therefore are not visible to the user while searching or browsing the catalogue by subject. In one example (no. 6 in Table 4), subject headings assigned are completely different between compared catalogues. Also, the number of subject headings assigned in Crolist is lower than in WorldCat. The results are shown in Table 4.

Example 3. Hierarchies, broader and narrower terms around the topic "marijuana"

See also BT:	Psihoaktivne droge. / Psychoactive drugs. [Definition in Croatian.]
See also BT:	Kanabis. /Cannabis. [Definition in Croatian, with variation of slang.]
See also NT:	Marihuana. / Marijuana.

Table 4. Crolist and Worldcat subject headings for 10 titles with the topic "marijuana"

	Book title	Crolist SH	WorldCat LCSH
Marijuana			
1.	Marihuana, the forbidden medicine (1997)	Marijuana – Medical use [1 SH]	Marijuana – Therapeutic use Marijuana – Therapeutic use – Social aspects Marijuana – Therapeutic use – Law and legislation – United States [3 SH]
2.	Marihuana (2004)	Marijuana – Study [1 SH]	Marihuana – zlouporaba [marijuana – abuse] [1 SH]
3.	Cannabis pharmacy: the practical guide to medical marijuana (2016)	Cancer – Alternative Medicine Marijuana – Medical use [2 SH]	Marijuana – United States Marijuana – Law and legislation – United States Marijuana – Psychological aspects [4 SH]
4.	Understanding marijuana: a new look at the scientific evidence (2005)	Marijuana – Study Marijuana – Abuse Cannabis – Abuse [3 SH]	Marijuana Cannabis Marijuana abuse [3 SH]

	Book title	Crolist SH	WorldCat LCSH
5.	The Benefits of Marijuana: Physical, Psychological and Spiritual (2014)	Cancer – Alternative Medicine Marijuana – Medical use [2 SH]	Marijuana – United States Marijuana – Law and legislation – United States Marijuana – Psychological aspects [3 SH]
6.	On hashish (2006)	Cannabis- Usage – Psychological effects Psychoactive drugs – Philosophers – Experimenting [3 SH]	Benjamin, Walter, – 1892-1940 – Drug use Benjamin, Walter, – 1892-1940 Benjamin, Walter [3 SH]
7.	Doktore, je li istina da trava čisti pluća?: odgovori na vaša pitanja [Doctor, is it true that weed cleanses the lungs? : Answers to your questions] (1995)	[0 SH]	Substance abuse Substance abuse – Treatment [2 SH]
8.	Strong without substance: everything you want to know about drugs (2004)	Narcotic Drugs – Classification Addictions – Adolescents – Prevention and Control [2 SH]	Book Kinder/Jugendliche ab 10 Jahre bis 50 Jahre [Book Children / adolescents from 10 years to 50 years] [1 SH]
9.	Fire from within (2004)	Psychedelic Drugs – Religious Experience Indians – Religion – Mexico [2 SH]	Mind and body therapies Body, mind and spirit – General [2 SH]
10.	Healing with medical marijuana: getting beyond the smoke and mirrors (2015)	[0 SH]	Marijuana – Health aspects Marijuana – Therapeutic use [2 SH]

7. Conclusions

Croatian subject cataloguing practice has many problems since there is no official subject heading system or authorized list of headings that can be used in all Croatian libraries. Subject authority files are built within integrated library systems, based on common standards (IFLA and ISO standards, and national guidelines) for creating and assigning subject headings, but between different systems there is no 'communication'. Librarians participate in cooperative cataloguing within each system, but there is no rigorous control of created subject headings, not to mention the different practices in assigning subject headings adjusted to individual libraries. Although Crolist has almost half a million subject headings in the subject heading 'list' within the subject authority file, it is not possible to know if the search managed to 'hit' all of the relevant headings during the searches. Results from this research showed that each chosen title usually has up to 3 subject headings, and that they appear to be more general than the topics presented in chosen titles. There is a lack of terminological consistency and there are many examples of outdated headings and misrepresented topics. Croatian subject indexing is not developing fast enough to reflect contemporary society but reveal conservative attitudes to certain topics.

This research has several limitations. Only catalogue records (and sources) and subject headings were analysed. In order to gain more insight into specifics of ethical consideration around creation and assigning of subject headings to sources, it is necessary to research subject cataloguers' views and practices and to find out what specific terms users adopt to perform a search on a controversial or 'problematic' topic. Crolist went through turbulent times while National library changed IT systems, resulting in broken links for some records. Sometimes users can be confused by the inconsistencies and 'empty' subject headings which are not connected to any records. There are also many records without subject headings for no obvious reason. There are also many examples of duplicated records, because some libraries joined the Crolist system later. These issues are affecting the ethical foundations of the catalogues because of misrepresentation of library materials. This can also be considered at the technical level of the ethical decision-making model (Beghtol 2005). Croatian information professionals are in very challenging times: due to a new law on library activities and libraries. There are new standards, procedures and regulations being written, there are many systems used in libraries, there are new cataloguing rules waiting to be introduced, and new rules for subject indexing system, yet to be written. Librarians are following old rules and in parallel trying to learn new ones. Ethical standards were always high in librarians' profession and omissions found in this research could be corrected once collaborative cataloguing becomes a reality.

References

Adler, Melissa. 2009. "Transcending Library Catalogs: a comparative study of controlled terms in Library of Congress Subject Headings and user-generated tags in LibraryThing for transgender books." *Journal of Web Librarianship* 3/4: 309-31.

Code of Ethics of the American Library Association. 2008. http://www.ala.org/united/sites/ala.org.united/files/content/trustees/orgtools/policies/ALA-code-of-ethics.pdf

Bair, Sheila. 2005. "Toward a Code of Ethics for Cataloging." *Technical Services Quarterly* 23 (1): 13-26.

Barité, Mario. 2018. "Literary Warrant". *Knowledge Organization* 45: 517-36. Also available in ISKO Encyclopedia of Knowledge Organization, ed. Birger Hjørland, coed. Claudio Gnoli.http://www.isko.org/cyclo/literary_warrant

Bates, Jo and Jennifer, Rowley. 2011. "Social Reproduction and Exclusion in Subject Indexing: a comparison of public library OPACs and LibraryThing folksonomy." *Journal of Documentation* 67: 3431-448.

Beghtol, Clare. 1986. "Semantic Validity: concepts of warrant in bibliographic classification systems." *Library Resources & Technical Services* 30: 109-25.

Beghtol, Clare. 2002. "A Proposed Ethical Warrant for Global Knowledge Representation and Organization Systems." *Journal of Documentation* 58 (5): 507-32. DOI:

Beghtol, Clare. 2005. "Ethical Decision-Making for Knowledge Representation and Organization Systems for Global Use." *Journal of the American Society for Information Science and Technology* 56 (9): 903–12.

Berman, Sanford. 1993. *Prejudices and Antipathies: a tract on the LC subject heads concerning people.* McFarland; Reprint Edition. http://www.sanfordberman.org/prejant.htm

Brett, Jeremy & Campbell, Mary E. 2016. "Prejudices Unshelved: variation in attitudes toward controversial public library materials in the General Social Survey, 1972–2014." *Public Library Quarterly* 35 (1): 23-36.

Burke, Susan K. 2008. "Removal of Gay-Themed Materials from Public Libraries: public opinion trends, 1973–2006." *Public Library Quarterly* 27 (3): 247-264.

Burke, Susan K. 2010. "Social Tolerance and Racist Materials in Public Libraries." *Reference and User Services Quarterly* 49 (4): 369–79.

CannCasciato, D. 2010. "An Essay on Cataloging." *Library Philosophy and Practice* 1. http://digitalcommons.unl.edu/cgi/viewcontent.cgi?article=1486&context=libphilprac

Colbert, Jessica. 2016. "The Search That Dare not Speak its Name: LGBT information and catalog records." Poster presented at *BOBCATSSS 2016*, Lyon, France. https://www.ideals.illinois.edu/handle/2142/95667

Dash, Chloe Gisela Jane. 2015. *A Matter of Context: an investigation into the representation of bias in social tags and Library of Congress Subject Headings.* PhD diss., Aberystwyth University.

Drabinski, Emily. 2013. "Queering the Catalog: queer theory and the politics of correction." *The Library Quarterly: Information, Community, Policy* 83 (2): 94-111.

HKD. 2013. *Etički Kodeks Hrvatskog Knjižničarskog Društva.* https://www.hkdrustvo.hr/hr/eticki_kodeks/

Fox, Melodie J. 2016. "Legal Discourse's Epistemic Interplay with Sex and Gender Classification in the Dewey Decimal Classification System." *Library Trends* 64 (4): 687-713. DOI:

Fox, Melodie J. and Reece, Austin. 2012. "Which Ethics? Whose Morality?: an analysis of ethical standards for information organization." *Knowledge Organization* 39: 377-83.

Homan, Philip A. 2012." Library Catalog Notes for "Bad Books": ethics vs. responsibilities." *Knowledge Organization* 39: 347-55.

Hjørland, Birger. 2008. "Deliberate Bias in Knowledge Organization." *Advances in Knowledge Organization* 11: 256-61.

IFLA *Code of Ethics for Librarians and other Information Workers* (full version), 2012. https://www.ifla.org/publications/node/11092

Kinyanjui, Daniel. 2016. *Subject Cataloguing and the Principles on which the Choice of Subject Headings Should be Based.* Munich: GRIN Verlag.

Jatkevicius, James. 2003. "When 'Good' Books Go 'Bad': opportunities for progressive collection management in public libraries." *Public Library Quarterly* 22 (4): 31-40.

Johansson, Anna. 2008. "The Consequences of the Heterosexual Norm — How we organize and retrieve gay literature." *LIBREAS. Library Ideas* 12.https://libreas.eu/ausgabe12/003joh.htm

Johnson, Matt. 2010. "Transgender Subject Access: history and current practice." *Cataloging & Classification Quarterly* 48 (8): 661-683.

Knowlton, Steven A. 2005. "Three Decades Since Prejudices and Antipathies: a study of changes in the Library of Congress Subject Headings." *Cataloging & Classification Quarterly* 40 (2): 123-145.

Koehler, Wallace C., Jitka M. Hurych, Wanda V. Dole and Joanna Wall. 2000. "Ethical Values of Information and Library Professionals—an expanded analysis." *The International Information & Library Review* 32 (3/4): 485-507.

Lember, Heather; Suzanne Lipkin & Richard Jung Lee. 2013. "Radical Cataloging: from words to action." *Urban Library Journal*, 19 (1).

Lewis, Alison M. 2008. Introduction. In A.M. Lewis (Ed.). *Questioning Library Neutrality: essays from progressive librarian*, 1-4. Duluth, MI: Library Juice Press.

Mai, Jens-Erik. 2014. "Ethics, Values and Morality in Contemporary Library Classifications". *Knowledge Organization* 40: 242-253.

Mann, Thomas. 1997. "Cataloging Must Change! and Indexer Consistency Studies: misreading the evidence at our peril." *Cataloging & Classification Quarterly* 23 (3/ 4): 3-45.

Martínez-Ávila, Daniel, and John M. Budd. 2017. "Epistemic Warrant for Categorizational Activities and the Development of Controlled Vocabularies." *Journal of Documentation* 73: 700-715.

Olson, Hope A. 2002. *The Power to Name: locating the limits of subject representation in libraries.* Dordrecht: Springer Science & Business Media.

Oxford Advanced Learner's Dictionary of Current English. 2005. 7th ed. Oxford, U.K: Oxford University Press.

Pinho, Fabio Assis & José Augusto Chaves Guimarães. 2012. "Male Homosexuality in Brazilian Indexing Languages: some ethical questions." *Knowledge Organization* 39: 363–69.

Svenonius, Elaine, & Dorothy McGarry. 1993. "Objectivity in Evaluating Subject Heading Assignment". *Cataloging & Classification Quarterly* 16 (2): 5-40.

Schultz-Jones, B., K Snow, S. Miksa & R.L. Hasenyager Jr. 2012. "Historical and Current Implications of Cataloguing Quality for Next-Generation Catalogues." *Library Trends* 61 (1):49-82.

Shoemaker, Elizabeth. 2015. "No One can Whistle a Symphony: seeking a catalogers' code of ethics." *Knowledge Organization* 42: 353-64.

Smiraglia, Richard P. 2015. "Ethics in Knowledge Organization: two conferences point to a new core in the domain." *Encontros Bibli: revista eletrônica de biblioteconomia e ciência da informação* 20: 1-18.

Steinhagen, Elizabeth N., Linda C. Ewbank, Carolynne Myall & Valerie Bross. 1996. "Cataloging News." *Cataloging & Classification Quarterly* 22 (2): 89-100.

UNIBIS. 2015. FRBR – Knjižnični katalozi nove generacije. URL: http://www.unibis.hr/FRBROPAC.html

Ethical Challenges in Archival Knowledge Organization: the description of personal data for long-term preservation

José Augusto Chaves Guimarães, São Paulo State University (UNESP), Brazil
Natalia Tognoli, Fluminense Federal University (UFF), Brazil
José Augusto Bagatini, São Paulo State University (UNESP), Brazil
Daniel Martínez-Ávila, São Paulo State University (UNESP), Brazil

Abstract

Today, archives face an ethical dilemma: they must facilitate access to information but they also must protect the privacy of those who create and access information. Archival records often include personal data that can be sensitive when revealing religious or political convictions, sexual life, biometrics, genetic data, health, and racial origin. These have ethical implications for archival knowledge organization and more specifically to archival description.

In order to verify whether the archival description standards address the ethical challenges that archivists are facing in relation to the protection of privacy, we conducted a comparative diplomatic analysis between the Regulation 679/2016 - European Parliament, and a group of two international archival KOS (Knowledge Organizing Systems): ISAD(G) and ISAAR(CPF).

The results revealed conflicts between the areas Context and Contents of ISAD(G), and the articles 5, 6, 9, 12, 13, 16, 17, and 32 of the European Regulation, in aspects related to adequacy, relevance, accuracy, compliance, consent, categories of personal data, transparency, access, erasure, and security of processing. Regarding ISAAR(CPF) the most vulnerable fields are related to the description of the context, history, and activities of the corporate body or person. None of the two archival standards present any explicit mention of privacy or data protection issues.

Considering that contextual information is a vital component of archival description, the protection of personal data, as a way to avoid harm should also be the object of careful attention within archival KOS in order to guarantee an ethical stance regarding the archival knowledge organization.

1. Introduction

Today, archives are facing an ethical dilemma. On the one hand, they must facilitate the access to information. On the other, they must protect the privacy of those who create and access the information. This question is evident both in government archives, in which a huge volume of data is stored and processed, and in special collections of other kinds of institutions, where professionals face the dilemma of preserving and providing access to the documents and information while at the same time protecting the privacy of the people whose lives are reflected in the records. Those documents often include personal data produced by and about a singular, natural, and identifiable person that can be sensitive when reflecting aspects such as religious or political convictions, sexual life, biometry, genetics, health, racial origin, ethnicity, among others (Canada 2000, World Economic Forum 2011).

These aspects have ethical implications for knowledge organization and more specifically archival description, which can be considered one of the two core activities of archival knowledge organization (Tognoli et al. 2013) together with archival classification and arrangement. This activity permeates aspects that are addressed by the Regulation 679/2016 from the European Parliament on the protection of natural persons regarding to the processing of personal data. The declassification of documents in archives and other information units can be seen as an ethical responsibility and commitment to pluralism in society (García Gutiérrez 2007, 2011, 2014). However recent cases such as Wikileaks or the recent announcement about the UK police secretly harvesting all data from the phones and cloud accounts of suspects, victims, and witnesses and insecurely storing them forever (Privacy international 2018), also raise concerns related to the security and privacy of people. In this sense, the research question of this paper involves the guidelines that archivists receive from professional organizations and the standards to deal with these privacy issues. Do these guidelines and standards reflect and address the new challenges that archivists are facing in the new digital contexts ruled by artificial intelligence? What are the conflicts that are found in these standards that affect the archival knowledge organization activities?

Our hypothesis is that these standards do not completely address the ethical challenges that archivists are facing in relation to the access to information and the protection of privacy. In order to test our hypothesis, we conducted a comparative diplomatic analysis (Duranti 1998, MacNeil 2000) of two instances: a group of two international archival Knowledge Organization Systems, the General International Standard Archival Description – ISAD(G) and the International Standard Archival Authority Records for Corporate Bodies, Persons and Families – ISAAR(CPF), and the aforementioned Regulation 679/2016 from the European Parliament, as well as other documents and statements from the literature.

2. Personal data and artificial intelligence

Several authors have studied the relationship between artificial intelligence and information science (e.g., Mendes 1997, Martins 2010, Silva and Nathansohn 2018), and more specifically between artificial intelligence and knowledge organization (Martínez-Ávila et al. 2014, Martínez-Ávila 2015). As Martínez-Ávila (2015) recounts, the term "artificial intelligence" (AI) was first coined in 1955 by McCarthy and others in "A Proposal for the Dartmouth Summer Research Project on Artificial Intelligence" (1955). However, the birth of the artificial intelligence field is generally established in the summer of 1956 (Crevier 1993; Russell and Norvig 2003; McCorduck 2004), when the Dartmouth conference was actually held. A definition of artificial intelligence given by McCarthy (2007) was "the science and engineering of making intelligent machines, especially intelligent computer programs. It is related to the similar task of using computers to understand human intelligence, but AI does not have to confine itself."

Although the AI field had some years of growth, optimism and plenty of funding during the following decades (with success in some applications such as computer chess and more recently gaming and self-driven cars), it has also had some setbacks due to the impossibility of achieving some of its ambitious goals. This may be due to the complexity of replicating the human brain (and perhaps the inability to resemble the social conditions that affect this intelligence). In addition to several small episodes that gradually undermined the trust of the field in the past, research on artificial intelligence had two major crises: one in 1973-1980 due to cutbacks to academic AI research in the UK and in the US, and another one in 1987-1993 with the collapse of the Lisp machine market and the cancellation of new spending on AI by the Strategic Computing Initiative. These major setbacks in the history of AI received the name of "AI winters." Within the field, the threat of a new AI winter, together with the classical problems to be described below, put almost any new major AI project for decades under suspicion. This is believed to be one of the reasons why some AI researchers have historically chosen to call their work by different names even when the same technologies are being used.

According to Russell and Norvig (2003), some of the main problems that led the AI field to these AI winters in the past are common-sense knowledge and reasoning. Many of these problems related to disambiguation and machine translation are still open today. Another major problem in artificial intelligence is knowledge representation, concerned with representing knowledge in symbols to facilitate the inference (reasoning) from those knowledge elements and the creation of new elements of knowledge. From the AI point of view, the concept of knowledge representation is the same as in knowledge organization and the semantic web. However, Berners-Lee (1998) urged the community to clarify from the beginning that a semantic web is not artificial intelligence, as well as to clarify the differences between his web and past AI technologies such as The CYC Representation Language (CycL) and the Knowledge Interchange Format (KIF): "A Semantic Web is not Artificial Intelligence. The concept of machine-understandable documents does not imply some magical artificial intelligence which allows machines to comprehend human mumblings. It only indicates a machine's ability to solve a well-defined problem by performing well-defined operations on existing well-defined data. Instead of asking machines to understand people's language, it involves asking people to make the extra effort."

As argued in Martínez-Ávila (2015), many of the problems that affected knowledge representation in the AI past (such as centralization, scalability, merging separate knowledgebases, the need to use the same terms for common English words, etc.) could be worked out with ethics. This includes the ethical participation of people, something that has characterized the discourse of some knowledge organization practices and authors (Guimarães 2008; Martínez-Ávila et al. 2015), together with the global use and decentralized description of resources using supported technologies and standards that enable interoperability. In the context of the semantic web, many of these standards would be developed in a social way under the coordination of the W3C. Indeed, this social participation for knowledge representation in the connected world seems to be just an extension of Berners-Lee's original view of the World Wide Web as a social tool (1999, 123): "The Web is more a social creation than a technical one. I designed it for a social effect to help people work together—and not as a technical toy. The ultimate goal of the Web is to support and improve our web-like existence in the world." In the context of archives, many of these standards that could facilitate the automatic processing of information and machines and agents are developed by organization bodies such as the International Organization for Standardization and professional organizations such as the International Council on Archives. In practice, some of these technologies and standards of the semantic web can be applied to archives (Matienzo 2009).

On the other hand, the importance of the social and cultural aspects in the creation and representation of knowledge is something that is also starting to be recognized in the AI field. For instance, Clocksin (2003) outlined some elements of a new conceptual framework for AI that were shaped by Weizenbaum's observation (1976) that intelligence manifests itself only relative to a matrix of social and cultural contexts. It is indeed in this social and cultural context that the ethical aspects that affect privacy in archives collide with the artificial intelligence applications that underlie some knowledge organization practices and technologies.

During the last decade, artificial intelligence has established a strong link with Information Science, especially in relation to aspects such as the organization, management, and retrieval of information. In this context, due to the cultural impact of the wide use of computers and the world wide web among the population, there has been and exponential growth of information that also brought an equally exponential growth of problems related to its organization and retrieval (Martins 2010, Silva & Nathansohn 2018).

Using "expert systems," the artificial intelligence is built upon a set of rules that reproduce the knowledge of an expert on a given domain that is used to solve problems. These systems are especially useful for answering questions, requesting and providing information, making recommendations and assisting in the decision-making processes; using heuristics that correspond to the knowledge of a particular domain, ideally gathered automatically by the machine, and analysing and generating new rules and thus expanding their ability to solve problems.

In the specific context of the organization and representation of knowledge, artificial intelligence provides technical support for the analysis of information, mainly for classification, description, and indexing of documents in a digital environment. This is growing exponentially. As a consequence, its instrumentality in information retrieval can result in a greater exhaustivity and specificity, providing greater quantities of more relevant contents for the user.

Today we are living in an effective "culture of personalization" (Pariser, 2012) in which the expert systems collect personal information to offer relevant contents according to their inferences and knowledge, a process that is not free from the most diverse interests and manipulations. In this sense, it is essential for archivists and information professionals to adopt critical and ethical attitudes regarding artificial intelligence, especially in the context of personal data, in a way that the potential harms related to privacy violations are minimized.

In this sense, it is important for archives to adopt a culture of protection of the privacy of the producer, although without disregarding the rights of the user, in relation to personal data, that are understood as "information that permits identification of a person directly or indirectly, in particular by reference to an identification number or two or more factors specific to his physical, physiological, mental, economic, cultural or social identity (European Parliament. Council of the European Union, 2016).

In this context, we highlight the six questions proposed by the General Data Protection (GDPR) Coalition:

a) What type of personal data do you gather? (Are you gathering sufficient data for the purpose; are you gathering too much or irrelevant data for the purpose? Can you identify ways to minimize the data you gather?); b) Why do you gather it? (What is the purpose? Have you specified the purpose to be individuals? Do they have full knowledge and understanding of what happens to their data once it is passed to your organisation?); c) Do you regularly review the data for accuracy? (Do you have a procedure in place for auditing the data you hold and updating it where necessary?); d) How do you store it? (Do you have appropriate physical and technical security measures in place to keep the data safe and secure? Is access to the data in you organisation restricted to only those who process it? Do you have an off-site back-up for your server? Where is it located? Do you hold data in the Cloud, and if so where is the cloud server located?); e) How long do you keep it? (Do you have measures in place to ensure you do not hold data for longer than is necessary for the specified purpose? Do you have a Data Retention Policy?); f) Can you readily comply with individuals' rights to access, erasure and portability? (Is your system of storing and filling suitable for easily identifying all data you hold so you can respond fully to individuals' requests, and within statutory deadlines where applicable?)

Romansky (2015) proposes a Life Cycle of Personal Data (Figure 1) which, by its configuration, is an important tool for information professionals to protect the privacy of the user and meet the questions of the GDPR Coalition.

Figure 1: Life Cycle of Personal Data (Romansky 2015)

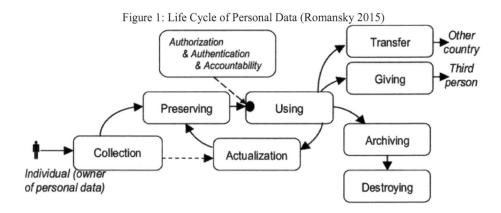

In relation to this, Romansky also highlights some requirements that are essential in this process: a) collection of personal data: based on a legitimate reason and with the consent of the individual; b) preserving of collected data: realized in registers based on preliminary defined purposes and criteria; c) using: only by legitimate persons and based on principles of information security (authentication, authorization, and accountability); d) actualization: integrity and content management of the personal data in terms of correctness, comprehensiveness and actuality; e) transfer: strictly based strong rules; f) archiving: in accordance to the law and for a limited period of time only; and g) destroying: after realization of the goal.

3. Personal data protection: ethical challenges for the archival description e long-term preservation

The protection of the integrity of the archival material and the guarantee to access the archive have been the two main imperatives in archival ethics. Today, the main ethical challenge for archivists seems to oscillate between the openness of information, which is the mission of archives, and the protection of personal data, as it is mandated by new regulations.

Although the discussions on personal data protection are on the rise, especially after the Regulation 679/2016 of the European Parliament and notably due to the increasing of technological innovations, the concerns about privacy and how it is related to accessibility in archives have been addressed as an essential element of the archival access practice since the first code of ethics for archivists.

In this sense, the first Code of Ethics was approved by The Society of American Archivist (SAA) in 1980 (revised in 1992, 2005, and 2012), and with regards to privacy, it states that the "archivist must establish procedures and policies to protect the interests of the donors, individuals, groups, and institutions whose public and private lives and activities are recorded in their holdings" (Society of American Archivists 2012). The professional archivist must also enforce access restrictions on collections to ensure that privacy and confidentiality are maintained.

The International Council of Archives (ICA) code of ethics for archivists also proposes the respect to access and privacy as one of its ten principles. According to this code of ethics (1996) "archivists should take care that corporate and personal privacy as well as national security are protected without destroying information […] They must respect the privacy of individuals who created or are the subjects of records" (International Council on Archives 1996).

The two aforementioned codes highlight the importance of privacy regarding access as a principle and value in archival ethics. The code of ethics recently approved by the UK and Ireland Archives and Records Association (ARA) emphasizes the importance of open and equitable access to records and archives so long as archivists respect the privacy of information subjects and their institutional context (Archives and Records Association 2018).

Based on these three examples, we agree with Tessler (2004) when she says that privacy is the crux of any archive's collection policy, as it is connected directly to personal data protection. If we are dealing with personal data protection, the concept of privacy must be addressed.

The concept of privacy is fluid, varying from country to country, within cultural groups or information spaces. In libraries, for instance, privacy policies are determined having the privacy of the user in mind, and do not consider the author's or creator's privacy when determining collection practices (Tessler 2004). In archives, the responsibility goes beyond the users of archival materials reaching the protection of the privacy of the creators' collection as well.

Regarding the creator's privacy, special attention must be paid by the archivist when describing archival holdings or collections. In this phase, the archivist must balance the access to the holdings under his/her custody – allowing their availability to the largest number of users – while not forgetting his/her commitment with the protection of the privacy of people related to the documents.

Since very few authors in the literature on Archival Science address ethical concerns that are directly related to the archival knowledge organization, and especially arrangement and description systems, a discussion on the protection of the personal data as an ethical imperative in archival description systems has not been addressed in the archival research agenda yet. Actually, according to Zhang (2012 333) "the structure of archival description has not been seriously challenged ethically in its development over the century".

The process of archival description privileged the representation of context over content, which means that contextual information, which includes information about the creator, its nature, and relationships with records is more desirable than the content of the record per se.

The contextual information is based on the application of the principle of Provenance, which according to Gilliland (2012, 341) is "the primary mechanism though which the identity of the creator is established and also the main intellectual access point to a collection of archival materials". Furthermore, Gilliland adds that "the act of designating provenance is an acknowledgment of the authority and responsibility of the official creating entity over any other party involved in the creation of the materials" (Gilliland 2012, p. 342).

Understanding the importance of the creator of the archival material for the representation of contextual information, the ICA Ad Hoc Commission on Descriptive Standards (ICA/DDS) developed the International Standard Archival Authority Record for Corporate

Bodies, Persons and Families – ISAAR (CPF) "as a guidance for preparing archival authority records which provide descriptions of entities associated with the creation and maintenance of archives" (International Council on Archives 2004). This standard must be considered and used together with another document, the ISAD(G): General International Standard Archival Description (International Council on Archives 1999, 2000), which provides guidance for the inclusion of contextual information within the description of archives at any level.

Michael Cook (2006) sees a parallel between the interest of the ICA in codes of ethics and their interest in technical standards during the 1990s: "the ICA developed its widely accepted standards for archival description over much the same period as its code of ethics. The two developments are certainly linked".

The ISAD (G) proposes rules for a multilevel description based on a hierarchy from the fonds to item. The rules are organized as follows:

3.1. Identity Statement Area (3.1.1 reference code; 3.1.2 Title; 3.1.3 Date(s); 3.1.4 Level of description; 3.1.5 Extent and medium of the unit of description),

3.2. Context Area (3.2.1 Name of creator(s), 3.2.2 Administrative / Biographical history; 3.2.3 Archival history; 3.2.4 Immediate source of acquisition or transfer);

3.3. Content and Structure Area (3.3.1 Scope and content; 3.3.2 Appraisal, destruction and scheduling information; 3.3.3 Accruals; 3.3.4 System of arrangement);

3.4. Condition of Access and Use Area (3.4.1 Conditions governing access; 3.4.2 Conditions governing reproduction; 3.4.3 Language/scripts of material; 3.4.4 Physical characteristics and technical requirements; 3.4.5 Finding aids);

3.5. Allied Materials Area (3.5.1 Existence and location of originals; 3.5.2 Existence and location of copies; 3.5.3 Related units of description; 3.5.4 Publication note)

3.6. Note Area (3.6.1 Notes);

3.7. Description Control Area (3.7.1 Archivist's Note; 3.7.2 Rules or Conventions; 3.7.3 Date(s) of descriptions).

These 7 areas are covered by 26 elements of which only 6 are essential for international exchange of descriptive information: a. reference code; b. title; c. creator; d. date(s); e. extent of the unit of description; and f. level of description.

Regarding the protection of personal data, the context and content areas have presented some critical points especially related to the Name of creator(s) and Administrative/Biographical history; and the Scope and content that can present some sensitive information in aspects related to adequacy, relevance, accuracy, compliance, consent, categories of personal data, transparency, access, erasure, and security of processing.

According to the ISAAR (CPF) (International Council on Archives 2004), the elements of description for an archival authority record are organized into four information areas:

5.1 Identity Area - which defines standardized access points for the record (5.1.1 Type of entity; 5.1.2 Authorized form(s) of name; 5.1.3 Parallel forms of name; 5.1.4 Standardized forms of name according to other rules; 5.1.5 Other forms of name; 5.1.6 Identifiers for corporate bodies)

5.2. Description Area - where relevant information is conveyed about the nature, context and activities of the entity being described (5.2.1 Dates of existence; 5.2.2 History; 5.2.3 Places; 5.2.4 Legal status; 5.2.5 Functions, occupations and activities; 5.2.6 Mandates/Sources of authority; 5.2.7 Internal structures/Genealogy; 5.2.8 General context),

5.3. Relationships Area - where relationships with other corporate bodies, persons and/or families are recorded and described (5.3.1 Names/Identifiers of related corporate bodies, persons or families; 5.3.2 Category of relationship; 5.3.3 Description of relationship; 5.3.4 Dates of the relationship)

5.4. Control Area - where the authority record is uniquely identified and information is recorded on how, when, and by which agency the authority record was created and maintained (5.4.1 Authority record identifier; 5.4.2 Institution identifiers; 5.4.3 Rules and/or conventions; 5.4.4 Status; 5.4.5 Level of detail; 5.4.6 Dates of creation, revision or deletion; 5.4.7 Language(s) and script(s); 5.4.8 Sources; 5.4.9 Maintenance notes).

Similar to the case of the ISAD (G), the ISAAR also has some critical points regarding the description of personal data, such as the areas 5.1, 5.2, and 5.3 of the standard. In this sense, area 5.3 must be especially considered for those cases of information exchange between institutions.

In order to avoid sensitive issues related to the description of archival materials, the description should be at the level of series, avoiding describing items that would require more detailed description. However, this higher level of contextual information may sometimes infringe the rights of the individual's data protection as well.

Assuming the impact of the aforementioned regulations for Archives, especially in the case of public archives, the UK National Archives have prepared a guide to archiving national data, "concerning records that contain or consist of personal data that has been acquired by an archive service for preservation as part of its collections or is being assessed for this purpose" (The National Archives 2018, 8). This guide is an important initiative within the archival area, which needs to call the responsibility for itself. According to the guide, "online catalogues and finding aids made available to the public are covered by the Data Protection Act 2018 if they include entries containing personal information," and "if the information is sensitive it may not be suitable to provide public access to all metadata and finding aid content if individuals are identifiable" (The National Archives 2018, 29). As Tessler (2014) pointed out, the scenario is even more complicated when it involves materials gathered by government agencies about a third party as the third party may not be willing to share with the general public.

As previously stated, the access to archival materials as an ethical imperative in archival practices suggests vigilance is required when it comes to privacy and protection of personal data. Privacy relates to the creator of the archival material and also to what Gilliland called 'co-creator'. According to Gilliland (2012, 341), "the archival concept of co-creatorship has been proposed as a way to acknowledge, give voice to, and describe the roles of those who were involved with the creation of the record and its metadata as contributors, subjects, victims, or legatees rather than as the official authors".

The description of the co-creator is also another ethical challenge that archivists face when representing archival knowledge representation, as they must consider all the people involved in the creation of fonds, series or items – the third party – in order to also guarantee the protection of their personal data.

4. Conclusion

The results of the evaluation of the regulations and the two KOSs revealed conflicts between the areas 3.2 and 3.3, Context and Contents of ISAD(G), and the articles 5, 6, 9, 12, 13, 16, 17, and 32 of the European Regulation, in aspects related to adequacy, relevance, accuracy, compliance, consent, categories of personal data, transparency, access, erasure, and security of processing. Regarding ISAAR(CPF) the most vulnerable fields are also related to the description of the context, history, and activities of the corporate body, person and family, identified as Description area (field 5.2) with information such as legal status, functions, occupations and activities, mandates/sources of authority, internal structure/genealogy and general context. The Relationship area (5.3) is also problematic since it exposes the relationship with other corporate bodies, persons and families, encompassing other entities. None of the two standards presents any mention of privacy or data protection issues. This suggests the need for continuous review of archival knowledge organization systems, especially for digital environments.

Considering that contextual information is a vital component of archival description, as shown in the ISAD(G) and the ISAAR(CPF), the protection of personal data, as a way to avoid harm (Adler and Tennis 2013, Fox and Reece, 2012) should also be the object of careful attention within archival knowledge organization systems. This would help to establish an ethical stance regarding archival knowledge organization.

The new technological contexts and artificial intelligence applications have made it necessary caused the necessity to reflect carefully about the protection of personal data, and especially regarding its use. In this new scenario, archival science, in spite of the prominent role that archives play in the society promoting accountability, memory, and social justice, seems to have shown a timid performance in the discussions on the protection of personal data, which has led the area to a lack of concerns and specific actions on archival ethics regarding archival knowledge organization systems. Consequently, the archival knowledge organization systems present themselves as outdated and unprepared to deal with new regulations and laws on personal data protection.

Acknowledgements
This research was supported by São Paulo Research Foundation - FAPESP (Proc. 2017/00584-3 2017/12561-8 and by the National Council for Scientific and Technological Development – CNPq (Proc. 302605/2015-0)

References
Adler, Melissa and Joseph T Tennis. 2013. "Towards a Taxonomy of Harm in KOS". *Knowledge Organization* 40(2): 266-272.

Archives & Records Association (ARA). 2018. *Code of Ethics.* https://www.archives.org.uk/images/ARA_Documents/ARA_Code_Of_Ethics.pdf

Berners-Lee, Tim. 1998. *What the Semantic Web can Represent.* http://www.w3.org/DesignIssues/RDFnot.html.

Berners-Lee, Tim. 1999. *Weaving the Web: the original design and ultimate destiny of the world wide web by its inventor.* New York: Harper-Collins.

Canada. 2000. *The Personal Information Protection and Electronic Documents Act.* https://www.parl.ca/DocumentViewer/en/36-2/bill/C-6/royal-assent

Clocksin, William. 2003. "Artificial Intelligence and the Future." *Philosophical Transactions: Mathematical, Physical and Engineering Sciences* 361(1809): 1721-48,

Cook, Michael. 2006. "Professional ethics and practice in archives and records management in a human rights context". *Journal of the Society of Archivists* 27(1): 1-15,

Crevier, Daniel. 1993. *AI: the tumultuous search for artificial intelligence.* New York: BasicBooks.

Duranti, Luciana. 1998. *Diplomatics: new uses for an old science.* Lanham: Scarecrow.

European Parliament. Council of the European Union. 2016. *General Data ProtectionRegulation* (EU) 2016-679. Brussels.

Fox, Melodie J. and Austin Reece. 2012. "Which Ethics? Whose Morality?: an analysis of ethical standards for information organization". *Knowledge Organization* 39(5): 377-383.

García Gutiérrez, Antonio. 2007. *Desclasificados: pluralismo lógico y violencia de la clasificación*. Barcelona: Anthropos.

García Gutiérrez, Antonio. 2011. "Desclassification in Knowledge Organization: a post-epistemological essay". *TransInformação* 23(1): 5-14.

García Gutiérrez, Antonio. 2014. "Declassifying Knowledge Organization". *Knowledge Organization* 41(5): 393-409.

Gilliland, Anne J. 2006. "Contemplating Co-Creator Rights in Archival Description". *Knowledge Organization* 33(5): 340-6.

Guimarães, José Augusto Chaves, Juan Carlos Fernández-Molina, Fabio Assis Pinho and Suellen Oliveira Milani. 2008. "Ethics in the Knowledge Organization Environment: an overview of values and problems in the LIS literature". In *Cultural and Identity in Knowledge Organization*, ed., Clement Arsenault and Joseph T. Tennis. Advances in Knowledge Organization 11. Würzburg: Ergon Verlag, 340-346

International Council on Archives. 1996. *Code of Ethics*. https://www.ica.org/sites/default/files/ICA_1996-09-06_code%20of%20ethics_EN.pdf

International Council on Archives. 1999. *ISAD(G): General International Standard Archival Description*.

International Council on Archives. 2000. *ISAD (G): General International Standard Archival Description*, 2nd ed. http://www.icacds.org. uk/eng/ISAD(G).pdf

International Council on Archives. 2004. *ISAAR (CPF): International Standard Archival Authority Record for Corporate Bodies, Persons and Families*. 2nd ed. https://www.ica.org/sites/default/files/CBPS_Guidelines_ISAAR_Second-edition_EN.pdf

MacNeil, Heather. 2000. *Trusting Records: legal, historical and diplomatic perspective*. London: Kluwer.

Martínez-Ávila, Daniel. 2015. "Knowledge Organization in the Intersection with Information Technologies". *Knowledge Organization* 42(7): 486-498.

Martínez-Ávila, Daniel; José Augusto Chaves Guimarães, Fabio Assis Pinho, and Melodie J. Fox, 2015. "The Representation of Ethics and Knowledge Organization in the WoS and LISTA Databases". *Knowledge Organization* 42(5): 269-275.

Martínez-Ávila, Daniel, Rosa San Segundo, and Francisco A. Zurian, 2014. "Retos y Oportunidades en Organización del Conocimiento en la Intersección con las Tecnologías de la Información." *Revista Española de Documentación Científica* 37(3): e053.

Martins, Agnaldo Lopes. 2010. "Potenciais aplicações da Intèligência Artificial na Ciência da Informação". *Informação & Informação* 15(1): 1-16.

Matienzo, Mark. 2009. "Archives and the Semantic Web". Presented at the *Annual Meeting of the Archivists' Round Table of Metropolitan New York*, June 23, 2009. https://www.slideshare.net/anarchivist/archives-the-semantic-web/41-Using_HTTP_WebURIs_tells_us

McCarthy, John. 2007. *What is Artificial Intelligence?* http://www-formal.stanford.edu/jmc/whatisai/whatisai.html

McCarthy, John, Marvin L. Minsky, Nathaniel Rochester, and Claude E. Shannon, 1955. *A Proposal for the Dartmouth Summer Research Project on Artificial Intelligence.* http://www-formal.stanford.edu/jmc/history/dartmouth/dartmouth.html.

McCorduck, Pamela. 2004. *Machines Who Think.* 2nd edition. Natick, MA: A. K. Peters.

Mendes, Raquel Dias. 1997. "Inteligência Artificial: sistemas especialistas no gerenciamento da informação". *Ciência da Informação* 26(1).

National Archives. 2018. *Guide to Archiving Personal Data.* http://www.nationalarchives.gov.uk/documents/information-management/guide-to-archiving-personal-data.pdf

Pariser, Eli. 2011. *The Filter Bubble: what the internet is hiding from you.* New York: Penguin Press

Privacy International. 2018. *Digital Stop and Search: how the UK police can secretly download everything from your mobile phone.* https://privacyinternational.org/sites/default/files/2018-03/Digital%20Stop%20and%20Search%20Report.pdf

Romansky, Radi. 2015. "Social Computing and Digital Privacy". *Communication & Cognition* 48(34): 65-82.

Russell, Stuart J. and Peter Norvig. 2003. *Artificial Intelligence: A Modern Approach.* 2nd edition. Upper Saddle River, New Jersey: Prentice Hall.

Silva, Narjara, Bárbara Xavier & Bruno Macedo Nathansohn. 2018. Análise da Produção Científica em Inteligência Artificial na Área da Ciência da Informação no Brasil. In *XIX Encontro Nacional de Pesquisa em Ciência da Informação – ENANCIB 2018.* http://www.brapci.inf.br/index.php/res/v/103730.

Society of American Archivists (SAA). 2012. *Core Values Statement and Code of Ethics.* http://www2.archivists.org/statements/saa-core-values-statement-and-code-of-ethics#core_values.

Tessler, Camila Z. 2014. "Privacy, Restriction, and Access: legal and ethical dilemmas". *SLIS Student Research Journal*, 4(1).

Tognoli, Natália, José Augusto Chaves Guimarães, and Joseph T. Tennis, 2013. "Diplomatics as a Methodological Perspective for Archival Knowledge Organization". *NASKO* 4(1): 204-212.

World Economic Forum. 2011. *Personal Data: the emergence of a new asset class.* http://www3.weforum.org/docs/WEF_ITTC_PersonalDataNewAsset_Report_2011.pdf

Weizenbaum, Joseph. 1976. *Computer Power and Human Reason.* London: Penguin.

Zhang, Jane. 2012. "Archival Context, Digital Content, and the Ethics of Digital Archival Representation." *Knowledge Organization* 33(5): 332-9.

Developments in Ethics of Knowledge Organization: from critical approaches to classifications to controlled digital communication practices

Joana Casenave, Université de Lille, France

Widad Mustafa El Hadi, Université de Lille, France

Abstract

We propose in our paper to examine the evolution of Knowledge organization domain and show how it is currently involved in the ongoing advances in automatic classification techniques. The aim of our work is to see how the ethical issues resulting from the introduction of Artificial Intelligence in the digital communication are rooted in the practices of universal classifications, their cultural, linguistic and racial biases. What practical implications do these ethical issues have in the automation of classifications?

We first provide a critical review of the use of the term ethics, its coverage and its scope, as well as the main focus under which we examine it, that is in KOSs and AI automated classifications. The two dimensions covered by the term Ethics do not constitute a continuity or a continuum but they rather function in a parallel mode. In our paper we suggest establishing a parallel between the control conducted by the mainstream universal classifications the naming power and the power of the algorithms used by today artificial intelligence.

Then, we will focus on the question of ethics in the universal classifications, as an early critique of these models and how they evolved through time. Finally, we examine the current trends on ethical issues related to the ICT and namely artificial intelligence and their impact in delineating ethical issues in KO. We conclude by suggesting some directions of work and plead for an ethical AI based on a combination of legal, technical and social strategies. Initiatives are growing in the academic and professional worlds to set up a responsible AI: the creation of research institutes focusing on AI ethics, algorithm auditing and all sorts of actions to curb biases.

1. Introduction

Knowledge organization is currently involved in the ongoing advances in automatic classification techniques. The aim of our work is to see how the ethical issues resulting from the introduction of Artificial Intelligence in the digital communication are rooted in the practices of universal classifications, their cultural, linguistic and racial biases. What practical implications do these ethical issues have in the automation of classification?

It is crucial to clarify the two dimensions which the term *ethics* covers in our field Information Science. Experience showed that authors who write on Information ethics deal mainly with the impact of Information & Communication Technology ICT and the Internet on information flows even if a few studies have been devoted to the cultural, social and linguistic dimensions of ethics in Information and Knowledge Organization (KO).

We shall first give a critical review of the use of the term ethics, its coverage and its scope, as well as the main focus under which we shall examine it. Then, we will focus on the question of ethics in the universal classifications, as an early critique of these models and how they evolved through time. Afterwards, we will examine the current trends on ethical issues related to the ICT and namely artificial intelligence and their impact in delineating ethical issues in KO.

2. Ethics in traditional classifications and knowledge organization

The concept of Ethics covers two essential dimensions in Information Science: the first is related to the move to a largely digital information environment. It is considered to be more related to the explosion of ICT and the internet access. For example, the use of computerized issuing systems, the availability of many resources in digital form, and the use of RFID identifiers in printed materials falls under that heading. In this respect, the main areas of concern within information ethics as Bawden and Robinson (2012) pointed out include: the contradiction between censorship and intellectual freedom; privacy, confidentiality and data protection; ownership of information, and the possible commercial use of public information; universal access, information poverty and the digital divide; respect for intellectual property combined with fair use; and issues of balance and bias in information provision, collection development and metadata creation. Concerning information science, these ethical issues have been identified and were typically grouped under the term of "information ethics" (Floridi 2013). This concept has grown from an initial focus on the activities of librarians and information specialists to cover a wide concern for information in society as a whole; about which, information specialists feel obviously a particular responsibility *(ibid)*. Some of these aspects are looked at by laws such as copyright and censorship rules and regulations, while others are covered by professional codes of conduct. The second dimension, concerns ethics of knowledge organization as an intimate process linked to language and cultures. This dimension considers ethics under their cultural linguistic and social frames. Most of the literature on-KO focuses on the functionality of Knowledge Organization Systems (KOSs). This functionality is related to the structure of the KOSs and its semantics. Our interest in ethics in KO is rooted in the early criticisms addressed to classification systems. Most of them are based on the fact that these systems do not offer a particular representation of language and that their structure alters our interpretation of language in a way that is unnecessary or false. For this reason, we must take into account the weight of cultures and languages in the design of KOSs as suggested by Tennis (2003, 2013, 2015).

2.1 Historical note

In Information Science, ethics is framed by the philosophy of information, a domain which investigates the conceptual nature and basic principles of information, including its ethical consequences (Floridi, 2011). It is based on two simple ideas: Information is something as fundamental and significant as knowledge, being, validity, truth, meaning, mind, or good and evil, and so equally worthy of autonomous, philosophical investigation. Floridi considers it as the branch of the philosophy of information that investigates, in a broad sense, the ethical impact of Information and Communication Technologies (ICTs) on human life and society. ICTs whose impact is common-place such privacy and freedom of expression, digital divide to surveillance society.

It is crucial to give some elements regarding the appearance and the evolution of the term *Information Ethics* (IE) in the literature of our domain and to show how it is gaining momentum and importance as ITC technologies develop and grow.

Ethics as reflection on morality is widely accepted among philosophers beginning with Aristotle, the founder of ethics as an academic discipline. As Rafael Capurro (2008), who heads the International Center for Information Ethics (ICIE), defines it: "As a self-referential process ethics is an unending quest on explicit and implicit use of the moral code, that is to say of respect or disrespect, with regard to individual and social communication. In other words, ethics observes the ways we communicate with each other as moral persons and the ways this moral identity is understood. There is, indeed, no unbiased ethical observer" (Capurro 2008, 21).

Since the late 1980s, it was often referred to as the *ethics of information in society*. Since the first appearance of the term in 1988, this topic more commonly has been referred to as *Information Ethics* (IE). The history and the professional and scholarly literature of IE ethics in its first 20 years were increasingly intertwined with library ethics; information systems ethics; computer ethics; cyberethics; journalism, communication, and media ethics; image ethics; Internet ethics; and Web ethics. Each of these areas of applied ethics shares roots and relationships with the others and with a wide variety of fields, including engineering ethics and business ethics (Carbo 2008, 1112).

2.2 Critical approach to classifications: ethical biases in traditional classifications

Considering the broad and diverse uses of terms relating to information as a phenomenon, the term *Information Ethics* covers as well as dimensions related to knowledge organizing. We shall go back to ISKO's founder Dr. Ingetraut Dahlberg's position (1992) when she expressed her concern about ethics in KO, she said, "What, generally, is meant by "ethics"? According to my encyclopedia it is a discipline of philosophy which searches for the principles by which it becomes possible to determine reasonably whether something or some subject is valuable or worthless (value theory) or whether a human action is good or evil (Der Neue Herder, Vol.2, Freiburg, Germany, 1970, p.397). [...] What would an ethics of knowledge organization consist of? This question I would very much like to see treated in this journal in several articles" (Dahlberg 1992). We can say that his wish has been fulfilled given the broad contribution from KO community and mainly its journal *KO*.

Later, Hope Olson gave a historical talk at the 3rd International ISKO Conference in Washington DC at the Library of Congress (Olson 1996): *"Dewey Thinks Therefore He Is"*. She continued in the same vein and published later many seminal articles in which she discussed the main reasons for biases in Classification, in terms of race, gender, sexuality nationality and other facets (Olson et al., 1999, 2001, 2002). In her work Olson showed how classification systems can privilege the mainstream, majority view. In another publication, (Olson, 2001, 2002) she based her critical approach to classifications on a critical feminist perspective to key issues in knowledge organization. The title of her book, *The Power to Name* shows that: "the assignment of a subject to a document is not a neutral act but is a policy act contributing to facilitate certain uses of that document at the expense of other uses", as Hjørland highlighted (2016, 313). Hope Olson's work on marginalization and exclusion of specific topics and groups of people in large library classification has inspired many authors such as King (1997) who argued that "Intersectionality is transformative, not additive, in that it does not merely pile up oppressions but creates a new manifestation. [...] each discrimination has a single, direct, and independent effect" on women's status, "racism, sexism, and classism constitute three, interdependent control systems" (King 1997). She also inspired Jens-Erik Mai (2013, 2016), but mainly her PhD student Melodie Fox (2015, 2016), Smiragilia (2012, 2013), Tennis (2016), the Brazilian Team at the State University of St Paulo at Marilia led by Guimaraes, Avila (2010, 2014, 2015, 2016), Tennis (2013), Adler & Tennis (2013) among many others. Our own research at Geriico at the university of Lille is inspired by the "capitalization" on all this international research on Ethics: seminars, Master 2 and PhD research (an ongoing PhD on "Marginality and Non-Uniformity in Subject Representation: An Analysis of Human Rights Concepts").

Instead of the traditional library values of neutrality and universality, Hope Olson suggested a foundation that is based on plurality and diversity (Olson 2001; Clare Beghtol 2000, 2002, 2005) called for the same ethical values. Current approaches are expressed at many conferences (see Smiragilia 2013). Hope Olson and her followers also inspired the "Taxonomy of Harm", built by Adler and Tennis (2013). Harms identified by the authors relates to the many types of biases outlined in different publications. All these publications and stances are in line with Dahlberg's when she earlier introduced the concept and its understanding in Knowledge Organization. Considering her definition and the current state of the art, we can say that the concept of Ethics covers two essential dimensions.

2.3 The link between the two dimensions covered by the term *Ethics*
The two dimensions covered by the term Ethics do not constitute a continuity or a continuum but they rather function in a parallel mode. In our paper we suggest establishing a parallel between the *control* conducted by the mainstream universal classifications systems *the naming power* and the power of the algorithms used by today artificial intelligence.

Wilson (1968, 21) quoted by Mai (2016) suggested that "knowledge organization is driven by the practicality of providing users with "the *best textual means* to his end." In Wilson's vocabulary, this ability requires that librarians and knowledge organization systems have a special power, namely the "power to produce the best textual means to one's ends." But this *power to name* inspired by Wilkins' project to develop a universal language of all human thought: "Librarians call such a constructed universal language a *controlled vocabulary*" and that knowledge organization systems ought to become "neutral' intermediaries" (Olson 2001, 640). This stance has been questioned by Olson. "The main challenge, according to Hope Olson, is that this commitment to neutrality cloak the biases of classifications and hinder conversations about the cultural effects of classifications that marginalize and exclude views outside of the political, social, and ethical mainstream. This core belief among information scientists and librarians that they should remain neutral and the belief that knowledge organization systems ought to be neutral and universal has brought about the understanding that knowledge organization systems appear unbiased and universally applicable but they actually hide their exclusions under the guise of neutrality… [which] disproportionally affects access to information outside of the cultural mainstream and about groups marginalized in our society", (Olson 2001, 640 quoted by Mai 2016, 327).

Here we would like to establish the parallel between the two dimensions and show the comparison between the two types of controls, through algorithms (see below section 4.0 of our paper), causing *unintentional biases*. It more concerns the supremacy of a language and its culture. Bowker and Star (1999) consider that all classifications and, library schemes are "powerful technologies" which, once they are embedded in working infrastructures can "become relatively invisible without losing any of that power". Our position regarding the control by the *power of naming* i.e. classification and categorization and IA algorithms control resonates with Bowker's stance. The power to name given to mainstream classifiers is comparable to the algorithms control over functions such as filtering, machine translation using English as the pivot language (Kaplan 2015), text and image automatic classification, etc. We here translated in English some element from the original text in French: "In December 2014, when one asked Google Translation the equivalent of "*this is a pretty girl*" in Italian the program gave "*Questa ragazza e abbastanza*" which literally meant "*This girl is enough*". What was the cause of this error? The two meanings of the word "pretty" in English, a word which can mean "*beautiful*" or "*rather, to a large extent*". The correct choice should have been the first meaning but the context-blind program chose the second. But there was worse: *the query had not been made in English but in French*. And it meant that the translation algorithms, instead of being closely linked to both initial and final languages were mediated by an English intermediary. Other queries gave similar results. So an attempt at translating into French from English "It is raining dogs and cats" English "*It is raining very heavily*" gave "*il pleut des chiens et des chats*", literally meaning that live cats and dogs were falling screaming from the heavens onto the heads of terrified Frenchmen…" (Kaplan 2015).

3. Ethical issues in automatic classifications and the use of algorithms

While the organization of knowledge is based on classification systems that are well known in traditional documentary circles, it is taking new paths on the Internet. Transposed to the world of the web, what happens to the organization of knowledge? How the documentation is classified and prioritized? It seems that knowledge organization is exploring two areas in particular: the automated process and the participatory one. Far from being separated from each other, they in fact sustain each other.

3.1 Knowledge organization on the web

As early as the 1950s, cultural institutions used automated mechanisms to process their documentation, such as the Library of Congress, which launched The Presidential Papers Program in 1957. Led by the librarian Fred Shelley at the Manuscript Division, this project aimed to automatically index the archives of 23 presidents of the United States, from George Washington to Calvin Coolidge (Shelley 1962). Research in terms of automation applied to documentation has also focused on automatic cataloguing. In 1977, Maurice Freedman already proposed a review of current advances in the field of "automated bibliographic control" in his article "The automation of Cataloging – 1976". His article had highlighted the "data base management system" developed at the University of Chicago and implemented by the Washington Library Network. In 1988, Eric de Grolier reported, in his article "Taxilogy and Classification", on research work in artificial intelligence that it has the potential to redefine traditional knowledge classification systems. Today, research in the field of automated documentation processing regularly sustain new techniques to improve existing systems, for automatic indexing, document categorization and automatic image recognition.

As for the evolution of the organization of knowledge towards the participatory model, it has been achieved through collaborative indexing, since the advent of the first sites associated with the concept of Web 2.0, in the early 2000s (Crepel 2008). Internet users commonly use these techniques for indexing digital content using free keywords, which are part of natural language techniques commonly known as "folksonomies". Since Internet users do not use controlled languages, we are here in a completely different perspective from the traditional documentary classifications used in libraries. However, this social tagging technique targets two quite classic objectives for knowledge organization: defining and categorizing content on the one hand and prioritizing it on the other hand. The first step is to describe the document content, so that it can be classified and processed in relation to the documentary set to which it is associated. The categorized and classified documents are then proposed to users according to classification hierarchies in accordance with their interests. This is the concept of hierarchization, which constitutes "the natural foundation of the organization of knowledge" (Maniez 2002, 278).

These participatory indexing practices can occur in two different contexts: 1) digital content indexing available online, which is undertaken upon the request of a third party - usually cultural and heritage institutions, or academic institutions; and 2) content indexing simultaneous to its publication carried out by its own author.

3.2 Collaborative indexing and heritage enhancement
Cultural and heritage institutions have long called on the Internet community to process their digitized mass of documents and assist in their indexing (Broudoux, 2012). We can evoke the well-known example of the Flickr Common project, in which, in 2008, the American Library of Congress shared its photographs collections so that they could be more easily accessible and indexed by the web community. The project was an immediate success, and 5 years later, 250,000 images uploaded by the library were enriched with more than 2 million tags (Paraschakis, 2013; Earle, 2014). The motivations of indexers are diverse: "three broader motivational categories in comparison with the existing tagging schemes motivations: (a) personal, (b) affective, and (c) social" (Kipp 2017), linked both to the interest of the subjects handled by the photographs and to the interest of participating into a cultural heritage endeavor.

Archival preservation institutions have also followed this trend of participatory data enrichment. Recently, a major collaborative indexing project for archival documents was completed in France. This is the *Memory of People* platform, launched on the occasion of the centenary of the First World War by the Department of Heritage, Memory and Archives (DPMA) of the Ministry of the Armed Forces. The objective was to index the death records of soldiers who died for France during the First World War (Aufray 2014). Started in 2013, the project was accomplished in April 2018. All of the 1.4 million records were indexed thanks to the collaboration of 2506 volunteer indexers.

When collaborative indexing is used in these cultural and heritage contexts, it primarily meets the objectives of categorizing and defining content. Properly indexed, the documents are then described by enriched metadata which will contribute to improve information retrieval systems in the institution databases.

3.3 Collaborative indexing and social media

Apart from these culturally oriented uses, free indexing mainly occurs on the web, within the framework of social networks. They have based their internal content organization modes on their direct categorization by the publications of authors. The use of indexing techniques and hashtags represent a form of classification of published documents. This is the case for photographs and images on Instagram, as well as for publications on Twitter. Once categorized, the labelled data are prioritized, based on the hashtag combinations used and the interactions they give rise to. They are thus directly linked to related publications and they take part of broader user discussions and information-sharing networks.

These collaborative indexing models can be directly linked to the automated part of knowledge organization, when classification and automatic document recognition systems are data-driven from collaborative tagging resources.

This is the case for Facebook, which uses data published on Instagram to train its own image recognition algorithms. This way, Facebook benefits from a particularly large image database, already indexed thanks to the hashtags provided by Instagram users. The social tagging carried out on a social network forms the basis for the development of the automatic image recognition system or the classification system of another social network. This example can be easily transposed outside social networks: a library that uses free indexing can use the collected data to develop automatic indexing algorithms based on it and run them on a larger document set.

3.4 Knowledge organization and societal impacts of the use of artificial intelligence

In the field of knowledge organization, there are three types of interests in the use of artificial intelligence techniques: (1) interests in terms of information management and organization, (2) economic interests, (3) security interests. As the data to be processed is growing and taking on significant quantitative proportions, the use of automation techniques is above all a necessity in terms of information mass management. For nearly ten years now, we have been witnessing the "zettabyte era" (Gantz and Reinsel 2011, Floridi, 2013) and without technical support, it is impossible to process the documentation as it is being produced. In addition to these information management interests, the economic impacts of automation can also be highlighted: the faster the data processed, the more accessible the information is, and the greater will be the economic benefits realized by the institutions or companies responsible for data processing. Finally, security interests are often invoked, especially when it comes to automatic image recognition. This is particularly the case in China, where the government justifies the use of facial recognition techniques in order to control citizens and identify the perpetrators of incivilities or even offences.

But when we examine the field of automatic classification through the lenses of ethics, other questions arise: what are the ethical issues raised by automatic classification systems? Do the benefits of using algorithms sufficiently pay off for the observed biases? Is the use of these techniques justified, from a moral and ethical point of view?

4. Biases in controlled communication algorithms and practices

Academic research has focused for several years now on the ethical issues related to AI and their philosophical and moral foundations (Bostrom and Yudkowsky 2014). There are many problematic issues, including privacy protection, algorithm interpretation, equity of service and system robustness (Kizza 2010).

In the context of our study, what is crucial for us are the ethical biases supported by algorithms. In fact, just as there are cultural, linguistic and racial biases in documentary classification methods (marginalization, stigmatization, exclusion, segregation, ghettoization), there are also biases conducted by artificial intelligence. Researchers have recently been multiplying studies on classification systems to identify their biases. Since algorithms are used in many fields and intrude into our daily lives, it becomes a key societal issue to ensure neutrality, equity and efficiency of algorithms (Bertail et al. 2019).

4.1 Bias and discrimination

In their article "AI can be sexist and racist - it's time to make it fair" (Zou and Schiebienger 2018), the authors begin by giving a series of examples of algorithmic biases, including

Google Translate's sexist bias, which, when converting articles written in Spanish to an English translation, "sentences referring to women often become "he said' or "he wrote"".

Also, in the field of classification, algorithms can be prejudicial. Buolamwini and Gebru have recently examined the biases in facial recognition algorithms that are supposed to determine a person's gender from their photograph. They showed that, depending on the complexion of the people, the algorithms are more or less efficient. To conduct their study, they used three commercial gender classification systems that they mapped to a dataset they built. These set are equally composed of black and white people, women and men. It's the Pilot Parliaments Benchmark (PPB), that "consists of 1270 individuals from three African countries (Rwanda, Senegal, South Africa) and three European countries (Iceland, Finland, Sweden) selected for gender parity in the national parliaments" (Buolamwini and Gebru 2018, 5). As a result, the darker the skin tone of people is, the higher the error rate of algorithms is. While the algorithms achieve an extremely low identification error rate for white males (0.8% error), their identification error rate for black females (34.7% error) is more than 43 times higher (Bulamwini and Gebru 2018).

4.2 Bias vectors
There are many examples of algorithmic errors leading to discrimination and, according to the literature in the field, there are three main vectors of algorithm biases (INRIA 2017, CERNA 2018, Bertail et al., 2019):

- data training;
- the algorithms;
- the use of data and algorithms, subject to manipulation or misuse.

Since artificial intelligence is partly based on deep learning techniques, algorithms learn to process information depending on the data they collect as input. If these data are culturally and racially biased, the automatic classification system will reproduce them (Villani et al., 2018). For example, the dataset may over-represent one type of person / document and under-represent another type of person / document. In many cases, social categories already suffering from marginalization or discrimination in civil society are under-represented. Concerning the algorithms used for facial recognition of gender, Buolamwini and Gebru observed that the datasets available on the web (IJB-A and Adience datatsets) have a major bias, that of being made up of a very large majority of white male persons. If algorithms are trained on this type of datasets, how can they take into account the diversity of the human race?

Likewise, input data may not be properly defined or labelled. This is particularly true in social networks where users themselves produce the published content. When Facebook uses Instagram data to train its own image recognition algorithms, the quality of the automatic classification system depends directly on the image categorization done by Instagram users. The approximations or errors present in the input data partly condition the defects of the algorithm.

The algorithms themselves are very difficult to evaluate. According to Pégny and Ibnouhsein (2018), algorithmic transparency is based on "four fundamental meanings (loyalty, equity, explicability, intelligibility), grouped into two families (prescriptive and epistemic)". These algorithms themselves carry cognitive biases, resulting from the modeling decisions made by their designers: "The results of the algorithms depend on how the programmers wrote them. However, they remain human beings, and many studies in psychology and cognitive sciences show the existence of cognitive biases in decision-making (Khaneman and Tversky, 1974). These cognitive biases can lead to biases in algorithms" (Bertail et al., 2019): bias of anticipation, confirmation, illusory correlation or stereotype.

Finally, some algorithms raise questions about their usefulness and about the use made of it. This is the case of sexual orientation recognition algorithm developed by researchers at Stanford University, applied to a dataset of photographs and data from an American dating site (Wang and Kosinski 2017). The algorithms are based on the "facial feature"" observed in the photographs to categorize people according to their sexual orientation. Beyond the results displayed by their classification system, the use of such an algorithm raises questions: in what way is it useful, and above all, to what extent can it lead to drifts?

The use of algorithms can serve unethical purposes or lead to voluntary manipulation of information and users (e.g. voluntary application of algorithms on irrelevant datasets). It is up to the users to take the commitment of ensuring the fair use of these technologies and putting in place procedures for improving algorithms and ethical control of their use.

4.3 Controlled communication practices.
In parallel with the reproduction of ethical biases, the use of artificial intelligence techniques in the field of knowledge organization leads to increased control of communication modes, particularly on social networks and sites using collaborative indexing.

At first glance, when users practice collaborative indexing, they are completely free to choose the keywords or tags they use. This is the very principle of folksonomy: indexers are solely responsible for the keywords they use. They do not use controlled languages, thus departing from any standard practice (Le Deuff 2006). But unlike traditional documentary classifications, which remain the task of information professionals, all users have the power to name on the web through collaborative and social indexing.

4.4 Crowdsourcing and scientific guarantee

Of course, depending on websites that use collaborative indexing, this guiding principle varies. We have seen that cultural institutions - libraries, archives, museums - use crowdsourcing to index their digitized documents and thus benefit from tenfold forces to process a large amount of data. In this case, collaborative indexing aims to produce a common knowledge and share it. These indexing practices are clearly supervised and controlled to ensure the scientific accuracy of the data collected (Fitzpatrick 2016). Indexing control can be carried out by librarians and staff involved in these projects, but it can also come from the users themselves. Thus, in the *Mémoire des Hommes* project, by signing the participation charter, each indexer agrees to report any indexing errors he/she may come through, so that they can be corrected by the team of archivists involved in the project.

4.5 Social networks, community rules and tag trends

If we examine now social networks, largely based on open indexing practices, the control mechanisms are multifaceted. Of course, the hashtags that accompany tweets publications or photographs are chosen by the Internet users themselves and their number is not limited, as long as they do not exceed the number of characters allowed, if any. But the seeming full freedom of these indexing techniques conceals plural and discrete forms of control: 1) internal control within the network, 2) social control, 3) self-control.

All social networks have an internal legal framework that must be approved by each user upon registration. But what ethical principles govern the establishment of rules for the use of social media, and therefore the publication of content? These may include questions of morality - pornographic, sexual, violent or racist content is prohibited -, privacy or the protection of individuals against intrusive commercial techniques and spam. This internal control takes the form of the establishment of lists of prohibited topics, censoring the communication of Internet users. AI techniques are used by social networks to check each new publication. They assess the adequacy of the hashtags chosen to the rules of the social network and remove, if necessary, publications that contravene them.

Another form of control over content publishing on social networks is social control, especially effective in the choice of hashtags: users choose keywords according to existing trends within their community (Yang 2012). If they use a hashtag that is already widely used, it guarantees a better visibility of their publication, but at the same time it slows down the development and semantic richness of folksonomy.

In addition, self-censorship is a common practice on social networks. Several studies have explained the mechanisms of self-censorship, which generally occur immediately after the publication of content: users then edit this content to modify or delete it, seeking to provide a relevant and appropriate publication (Madsen 2016). According to the 2013 study of 3.9 million Facebook users, 71% of the sample used self-censorship practices (Das and Kramer, 2013).

4.6 Censorship and filtering of conversations

Finally, in some cases, social networks are subject to official censorship, organized at the state level. Authoritarian political regimes can use artificial intelligence techniques to filter Internet users' conversations and block the publication of messages comprising certain keywords incriminated by the regime. This is the case, for example, of the WeChat instant messaging application in China. The Wechatscope research project, developed at the University of Hong Kong, aims precisely at "making censored articles of WeChat's public accounts in China open access" (https://wechatscope.jmsc.hku.hk/). Of course, these practices are part of the implementation of a more global censorship, which leads these political regimes to totally prohibit access to certain websites and applications, particularly Western social networks.

5. Conclusion

Faced with the constraints represented by the use of automation techniques, it is necessary to adopt a responsible stance towards artificial intelligence. The pledge of all the actors is essential for the effective implementation of responsible artificial intelligence, whether it is the authors of algorithms and designers of computer applications or users, insofar as they are the ones who produce the data.

An ethical AI is based on a combination of legal, technical and social strategies. Initiatives are growing in the academic and professional worlds to set up a responsible AI: the creation of study institutes focusing on AI ethics, algorithm auditing and all sorts of actions to curb biases (such as the AI Now Institute at the New York University, or the Alan Turing Institute that is the National institute of Great Britain for data science and artificial intelligence).

Likewise, there has been a explosion of reports and ethical codes of conduct (*Montreal Declaration for the Responsible Development of Artificial Intelligence, AAAI Code of Professional Ethics and Conduct, Livre blanc de l'INRIA sur l'intelligence artificielle*, and so on).

Users of applications also have an important role to play and there are many possibilities for action: avoidance strategies set up by Internet users to by-pass censorship practices (spelling changes to keywords incriminated by authoritarian political regimes, use of remote connection systems), awareness of quality issues and data openness, citizen initiatives that can influence the foundation of an ethical AI. Even within large companies that use AI, there are employee-specific initiatives that can change the situation. This is the case for Google employees who, in recent years, have put pressure on the company's managers to refrain from conducting projects considered unethical (for example, in 2018, a petition issued by Google employees on the *New York Times* that led to putting an end to Maven Military AI Program, which was to make it possible to analyze military drone images).

Finally, the support of the political class is essential for the establishment of a legal framework regulating data ethics. Examples include governments appeals to render algorithm codes public and open. Moreover, a very recent initiative of New York City whose city council adopted a bill in May 2018 launched a working group on algorithmic biases.
Research in AI ethics is growing dynamically and the field of knowledge organization is fully involved in automatic classification practices and ethical issues. We hope that Knowledge organization will make a scientific breakthrough in supporting these initiatives.

References

Adler Melissa and Joseph T. Tennis. 2013. "Toward a Taxonomy of Harm in Knowledge Organization Systems". *Knowledge Organization*. 40, 4.

Arboit, Aline E., José Augusto C. Guimarães. 2015. "The ethics of knowledge organization and representation from a Bakhtinian perspective". *Knowledge Organization*, 42, 324-331.

Aufray, Sandrine. 2014. "Le site Mémoire des hommes et ses évolutions: entre mémoire et histoire". *Gazette des archives* 236 (4): 71-83.

Bawden, David and Lynn Robinson. 2012. *Introduction to Information Science*, Facet, London, Chicago, IL: Neal-Schuman, 351p.

Beghtol, Clare. 2005. "Ethical Decision-Making for Knowledge Representation and Organization Systems for Global Use". *Journal of the American Society for Information Science and Technology*, 56(9): 903–12.

Beghtol, Clare. 2008. "Professional values and ethics in knowledge organization and cataloging". *Journal of Information Ethics* 17(1): 12–19.

Bertail, Patrice, David Bounie, Stephan Clémençon, and Patrick Waelbroeck. 2019. *Algorithmes: biais, discrimination et équité.* Télécom ParisTech.

Bostrom, Nick and Eliezer Yudkowsky. 2014. "The Ethics of Artificial Intelligence". *The Cambridge handbook of artificial intelligence* 1: 316–334.

Bowker, Geoffrey C. and Susan Leigh Star. 1999. *Sorting Things Out: classification and Its consequences.* Cambridge, MA: The MIT Press.

Broudoux, Evelyne. 2012. "Indexation Collaborative: traces de lecture et constitution de communautés". *Bibliothèques 2.0 à l'heure des médias sociaux,* 125-34. Paris: Editions du Cercle de la librairie. https://archivesic.ccsd.cnrs.fr/sic_00715878.

Buolamwini, Joy and Timnit Gebru. 2018. "Gender Shades: Intersectional Accuracy Disparities in Commercial Gender Classification". *Proceedings of Machine Learning Research* 81: 1-15.

Carbo, Toni and Martha M. Smith. 2008. "Global Information Ethics: Intercultural Perspectives on Past and Future Research", *Journal of the American Society for Information Science and Technology* 59(7): 1111–1123.

Capurro, Rafael. 2008. "Information Ethics for and from Africa". *Journal of the American Society for Information Science and Technology* 59 (7): 1162-70.

Chen, Irene, Fredrik D. Johansson and David Sontag. 2018. "Why Is My Classifier Discriminatory?" in *32nd Conference on Neural Information Processing Systems proceedings*, 3543-54.

Crépel, Maxime. 2008. "Les Folksonomies Comme Support Émergent de Navigation Sociale et de Structuration de l'Information sur le Web". *Reseaux* n° 152 (6): 169-204.

Das, Sauvik and Adam Kramer. 2013. "Self-Censorship on Facebook". In *Seventh International AAAI Conference on Weblogs and Social Media,* 120-27. https://www.aaai.org/ocs/index.php/ICWSM/ICWSM13/paper/view/6093.

Earle, Evan Fay. 2014. *Crowdsourcing Metadata for Library and Museum Collections.* Cornell University.

Fitzpatrick, Kathleen. 2016. "Peer Review". *A New Companion to Digital Humanities*, 439-48. John Wiley & Sons, Ltd.

Floridi, Luciano. 2013. *The Ethics of Information.* Oxford Scholarship Online. Oxford: Oxford University Press.

Frankish, Keith and William M. Ramsey. 2014. *The Cambridge Handbook of Artificial Intelligence.* Cambridge University Press.

Freedman, Maurice J. 1977. "The Automation of Cataloging-1976". *Library Trends* 25 (3): 703-21.

Gantz, John and David Reinsel. 2011. "Extracting Value from Chaos". *IDC's Digital Universe Study.*

Grolier, Éric de. 1988. "Taxilogie et classification". *Bulletin des Bibliothèques de France.* http://bbf.enssib.fr/consulter/bbf-1988-06-0468-005.

Guimarães, José Augusto C., Natalia B. Tognoli. 2015. "Provenance as a Domain Analysis Approach in Archival Knowledge Organization". *Knowledge Organization*, 42, 562-569.

Hjørland, Birger. 2008. "Deliberate bias in knowledge organization?". *Culture and identity in knowledge organization: Proceedings of the Tenth International ISKO Conference*, 5-8 August 2008, Montréal, Canada. Advances in Knowledge Organization, v. 11. Würzburg: Ergon, p. 256-61, 2008.

INRIA. 2017. *Intelligence Artificielle, les défis actuels et l'action d'Inria*. Inria. https://www.inria.fr/actualite/actualites-inria/intelligence-artificielle-les-defis-actuels-et-l-action-d-inria.

Kipp, Margaret E. I., Jihee Beak and Inkyung Choi. 2017. "Motivations and Intentions of Flickr Users in Enriching Flick Records for Library of Congress Photos". *Journal of the Association for Information Science and Technology* 68 (10): 2364-79.

Kizza, Joseph Migga. 2010. *Ethical and Social Issues in the Information Age*. 6 ed. Texts in Computer Science. Springer International Publishing.

Le Deuff, Olivier. 2006. "Folksonomies". *Bulletin des Bibliothèques de France*, n° 4: 66-70.

Lee, Hur-Li. 2009. *The Ethics of Information Organization*. Taylor and Francis. (Also published as *Cataloging & Classification Quarterly* 47(7))

Lee, Wan-Chen. 2015. "Culture and Classification". *Knowledge Organization* 42(5).

Madsen, Vibeke Thøis and Joost W. M. Verhoeven. 2016. "Self-censorship on Internal Social Media: A Case Study of Coworker Communication Behavior in a Danish Bank". *International Journal of Strategic Communication* 10 (5): 387-409.

Mai, Jens-Erik. 2013. "Ethics, Values and Morality in Contemporary Library Classifications". *Knowledge Organization* 40(4): 242-53.

Mai, Jens-Erik. 2016. "Marginalization and Exclusion: Unraveling Systemic Bias in Classification". *Knowledge Organization* 43(5).

Maniez, Jacques. 2002. *Actualité des langages documentaires: les fondements théoriques de la recherche d'information*. Paris: ADBS.

Martínez-Ávila, Daniel, José Augusto Guimarães C., Pinho F. A. and Melodie J. Fox. 2015. "The representation of ethics and knowledge organization in the WOS and LISTA databases: A bibliometric and Bardinian content analysis". *Knowledge Organization*, 42: 269-275.

Martínez-Ávila, Daniel, José Augusto C. Guimarães. 2013. "Library Classifications Criticism: Universality, Poststructuralism and Ethics". *Scire* 19: 21-26.

Milani, S. de Oliveira, José Augusto. C. Guimarães, and Hope A. Olson. 2014. "Bias in Subject Representation: convergences and divergences in the international literature". *Knowledge organization in the 21st century: between historical patterns and future perspectives*, W. Babik (ed). Wurzburg: Ergon Verlag, p. 335-344.

Milani, S. de Oliveira, José Augusto C. Guimarães. 2010. "Bias in indexing languages: theoretical approaches about feminine issues". *Paradigms and conceptual systems in knowledge organization*, C. Gnoli, F. Mazzocchi eds., pp. 424-429. Wurzburg: Ergon Verlag.

Olson, Hope A. 1999. "Exclusivity, teleology and hierarchy: our Aristotelean legacy". *Knowledge Organization* 26(2): 65-73.

Olson, Hope A. 2001. "Sameness and Difference: A Cultural Foundation of Classification". *Library Resources & Technical Services* 45:115-22.

Olson, Hope A. 2002. *The Power to Name: Locating the Limits of Subject Representation in Libraries*. Dordrecht, The Netherlands: Kluwer Academic Publishers.

Olson, Hope A. and Melodie J. Fox. 2010. "Gayatri Chakravorty Spivak: Deconstructionist, Marxist, feminist, postcolonialist". *Critical Theory for Library and Information Science: Exploring the Social from across the disciplines*. Santa Barbara, CA: Libraries Unlimited, 295-310.

Paraschakis, Dimitris. 2013. *Crowdsourcing Cultural Heritage Metadata through Social Media Gaming*. http://muep.mau.se/handle/2043/16114.

Silva, Andrieli. P., José Augusto C. Guimarães, Natalia B. Tognolli. 2015. "Ethical values in archival arrangement and description: an analysis of professional codes of ethics". *Knowledge Organization* 42: 346-352.

Shelley, Fred. 1962. "The Presidential Papers Program of the Library of Congress". *The American Archivist* 25 (4): 429-33.

Smiraglia, Richard P. 2012. "Epistemology of Domain analysis". *Cultural frames of knowledge* Smiraglia, Richard P. and Lee, Hur-Li eds. Würzburg: Ergon, p. 111-24.

Smiragilia, Richard. 2015. Encontros Bibli: *Revista eletrônica de biblioteconomia e ciência da informação* 20(1 special): 1- 18.

Tennis, Joseph. T. 2012. "Le poids du langage et de l'action dans l'organisation des connaissances: Position épistémologique, action méthodologique et perspective théorique". *Organisation des connaissances: épistémologie, approches théoriques et méthodologiques*, Michèle Hudon et Widad Mustafa El Hadi eds. p. 15-40.

Tversky, Amos and Daniel Kahneman. 1974. "Judgment under Uncertainty: Heuristics and Biases". *Science* 185 (4157): 1124-31.

Villani, Cédric. 2018. "Donner un sens à l'intelligence artificielle: pour une stratégie nationale et européenne". *Rapport public*. http://www.ladocumentationfrancaise.fr/rapports-publics/184000159/index.shtml.

Wang, Yilun and Michal Kosinski. 2017. "Deep neural networks are more accurate than humans at detecting sexual orientation from facial images". *Journal of Personality and Social Psychology* 114 (2): 246-57.

Zou, James and Londa Schiebinger. 2018. "AI Can Be Sexist and Racist — It's Time to Make It Fair". *Nature* 559 (7714): 324.

Cochrane: Using Linked Data Micrographs to Power Clinical Evidence Discovery, Meta-analysis and Interoperability
Julian Everett, Data Language, UK

Danish National Police: Improving Search and Findability Through Information Architecture, Governance and Taxonomy
Cecilie Rask, Danish National Police, Denmark

Using Knowledge Graphs to Model Standards and Business Processes in the Test and Inspection Industry
Ian Davis, SGS, UK

Using Distributed Ledgers (AKA Blockchain) for Trusted Exchange of Commercially Valuable Information Across a Defence Consortium
Marcus Ralphs, Byzgen Limited, UK

How Not to Implement Taxonomy and Search in O365 - A Disaster Story
Agnes Molnar, Search Explained, UK

John Wiley: Developing a Specialist Taxonomy as a non-SME
Niké Brown, John Wiley, UK

Session 5: CREATIVITY

Tuesday 16th July 2019

Digital Creativity Support: designing AI to augment human creativity

Neil Maiden, Cass Business School, London, UK

Summary

This keynote will report research being undertaken to design and evaluate AI mechanisms to augment human creativity in different realms of professional work. Contrary to most press coverage, new AI mechanisms in the workplace are more likely to augment rather than replace human professionals. One challenge is to determine what aspects of creative work are more amenable to automation, what aspects should continue to be undertaken by people, and how digital creativity support should be designed to augment this human creativity. To explore this challenge, the keynote will summarise how a set of AI mechanisms have been embedded in digital tools to augment human creativity in different professional work - from manufacturing health-and-safety and caring for people with dementia to training elite athletes and journalism. These AI mechanisms combine natural language parsing, sense-making, translation, creative search and recommendation algorithms in simple-to-use tools that have been evaluated in professional settings. The keynote will also report on key findings from these evaluations.

The Respective Roles of Intellectual Creativity and Automation in Representing Diversity: human and machine generated bias

Vanda Broughton, University College London, UK

Abstract

The paper traces the development of the discussion around ethical issues in artificial intelligence, and considers the way in which humans have affected the knowledge bases used in machine learning. The phenomenon of bias or discrimination in machine ethics is seen as inherited from humans, either through the use of biased data or through the semantics inherent in intellectually-built tools sourced by intelligent agents. The kind of biases observed in AI are compared with those identified in the field of knowledge organization, using religious adherents as an example of a community potentially marginalized by bias. A practical demonstration is given of apparent religious prejudice inherited from source material in a large database deployed widely in computational linguistics and automatic indexing. Methods to address the problem of bias are discussed, including the modelling of the moral process on neuroscientific understanding of brain function. The question is posed whether it is possible to model religious belief in a similar way, so that robots of the future may have both an ethical and a religious sense and themselves address the problem of prejudice.

1. What is artificial intelligence?

There are many and varied definitions of artificial intelligence, and various synonyms for it. Poole et al. (1998, p.1) note that 'the term "artificial intelligence" is a source of much confusion', preferring to call it 'computational intelligence', although it is likely that artificial intelligence is today the more widely recognised term. Other names include 'machine intelligence', 'synthetic intelligence' (Brachmann 2005; Gorg et al. 2014), 'augmented intelligence' (Ojala 2018; Albrecht et al. 2015; Hannay 2014)

The *Encyclopedia Britannica* (Copeland, 2019) defines artificial intelligence in the following manner:

Artificial intelligence (AI) [is] the ability of a digital computer or computer-controlled robot to perform tasks commonly associated with intelligent beings. The term is frequently applied to the project of developing systems endowed with the intellectual processes characteristic of humans, such as the ability to reason, discover meaning, generalize, or learn from past experience.

The same article identifies five key aspects of intelligence, whether human or machine: learning, reasoning, problem solving, perception and language. At the operational level, machine intelligence can take a number of forms: pattern recognition, voice recognition, image (including facial image) recognition, and machine translation. Copeland's definition (above) tends towards the narrower field of machine learning: 'a form of AI that enables a system to learn from data rather than through explicit programming' .... 'After a model has been trained, it can be used in real time to learn from data' (Hurwitz & Kirsch 2018 p.4, 5).

For the purposes of this paper, artificial intelligence is considered mainly within the context of information retrieval, specifically document retrieval, and the ways in which document content can be automatically identified using intelligent agents. This may involve the construction of automatic classifiers through machine learning and the way in which document content is processed.

2. Artificial intelligence as a complement to human activity

Artificial intelligence has impacted on many areas of human activity, in part because of the speed with which it can process information in an overloaded world, saving human effort and apparently offering a more objective way to assess and respond to a variety of situations.

Information management is only one of such uses of AI, where it may promise to solve the perennial problem of organization and retrieval in a situation where there is 'too much to know'. This situation has been acknowledged since the early modern period (Blair, 2010), began to be addressed by mechanization in the mid-twentieth century, and in the twenty-first century prompted numerous studies of the way in which machines might automatically analyse, categorize, index and classify documents and other information objects, through a process generally referred to as automatic metadata generation or AMG (Broughton, Palfreyman & Wilson 2008; Greenberg et al. 2005).

During that period there had also been a good deal of research into the relative roles of controlled vocabularies and automatic indexing, generally leading to the conclusion that a hybrid model offered the best balance between efficiency and effectiveness; a number of studies demonstrated that the use of a controlled vocabulary improves the performance of the tool or system (Liang et al. 2006; Cheung et al. 2005; Aula & Kaki 2005; Ko et al. 2004). Another major theme was the automatic building of classificatory structures such as ontologies, independently of humans, from text corpora or other sources. The extraction of data from text continues to be a common means of constructing semantic tools, but, as we may see below, the assumption that terms in text are value free, and mean exactly what they say, presents a danger to the usefulness and efficiency of such exercises.

As AI gains ground as an established tool for processing and decision making, particularly with respect to personal data, some questions have been raised as to the acceptability of AI in this role, the ethics of AI, and the extent to which machines can function as intelligent, and as ethical agents. Associated ideas, such as the personhood of robots, and whether they can be said to assume responsibility for their actions, have also been considered.

3. Ethical considerations in knowledge organization

It is now well established that the business of knowledge organization, whether that is classification, indexing, subject representation through headings, or visualization tools, brings with it some ethical concerns. Recently attention has focussed on fake news, or controversial thinking, such as holocaust denial, and how such material show be represented, but more generally concerns are with the misrepresentation or under representation of minority groups, leading to disadvantage and disempowerment. There is now a growing body of literature on the ethical theory and philosophy of KO (Olson 1998; Szostak 2014; Mai 2010, 2013a, 2013b, 2016), and a substantial number of studies of the way in which it can discriminate on the basis of gender (Foskett 1971; Marshall 1977; Olson & Ward 1997; Olson 2007), sexual orientation (Drabinsky, 2013; Fox, 2016; Howard & Knowlton 2018), race and ethnicity (Duarte & Belarde-Lewis 2015; Adler & Harper 2018), political status (Lacey 2018) and religion (Broughton 2000; Broughton & Lomas 2019).

All of such bias is problematic in a world of increasing diversity, and the major players in conventional KO are seen to address some of the worst excesses. Factors which exacerbate the bias include: unequal provision either of terminology or (in a coded system such as a classification) unequal distribution of notation; failure to name at all certain groups or perspectives; and language which has a strong flavour of one particular favoured perspective or culture. Where culture is a powerful element, as in religions, language is a specific problem.

4. Ethical considerations in artificial intelligence

There has been substantial research into the phenomenon of machine ethics, that is the potential ethical or moral behaviour of intelligent agents. It should be carefully differentiated from computer ethics which is concerned with the behaviour of humans in the context of computing and information technology, and with roboethics which refers to ethical behaviour of humans in the design and construction of intelligent machines, and in human-machine interaction. Although there are some twentieth-century discussions of the possibility of moral - or immoral - actions of machines, the field really begins with the 2005 *AAAI Symposium on Machine Ethics*, where the problem is clearly stated, and named by Anderson et al. (2005):

Past research concerning the relationship between technology and ethics has largely focused on responsible and irresponsible use of technology by human beings, with a few people being interested in how human beings ought to treat machines. In all cases, only human beings have engaged in ethical reasoning. We believe that the time has come for adding an ethical dimension to at least some machines. Recognition of the ethical ramifications of behavior involving machines as well as recent and potential developments in machine autonomy necessitate this. We explore this dimension through investigation of what has been called machine ethics.

In Anderson et al.'s paper they consider the implementation of two systems of machine ethics, based on philosophical principles as displayed in the work of W. D. Ross (theory of prima facie duties), and Jeremy Bentham (Utilitarianism), both of which can be expressed as a series of rules. Utilitarian ethics and the basis of its decision-making is of particular interest, since in the form of Bentham's *Felicific calculus,* or *Calculus of pleasures* (1789), it was designed to be computable, and indeed, one of the themes of the Symposium was the computability of ethics. At the time of Anderson et al.'s research, the likely guarantee of 'good' machine ethics was the imposition of better and more considered rules for the machine's operation, derived from traditional systems of ethics and the practice of professional ethicists. As they say in a subsequent paper (2007, p.25):

Ensuring that a machine with an ethical component can function autonomously in the world remains a challenge to researchers in artificial intelligence who must further investigate the representation and determination of ethical principles, the incorporation of these ethical principles into a system's decision procedure, ethical decision making with incomplete and uncertain knowledge, the explanation for decisions made using ethical principles, and the evaluation of systems that act based upon ethical principles.

5. Where machine ethics falls short: bias in intelligent agents

The general assessment of machine information processing and machine decision-making has been that it may avoid the subjectivity associated with humans. In practice this has turned out not to be the case, since, despite the emphasis on machine independence in artificial intelligence, intelligent agents are not created spontaneously, but require some degree of human participation, and no system of machine learning can avoid the use of information which has been at some stage processed by humans. The problem affects equally machine learning where the agent has learned from data or a prepared model or training set, or in the case of knowledge organization systems, where human-constructed vocabularies or ontologies have been sourced by the agent. Additionally, human intervention often supports the machine-learning process through iteration with the 'teacher', usually through a technique of query-by-example accompanied by feedback to the machine.

Too often the result of this human input is that the machine inherits the prejudices of the human, so that the bias is hard-wired to the machine (Crawford 2016; Kirchner et al. 2016; Sears 2018; Kochi 2018).

Designed and used well, machine learning systems can help to eliminate the kind of human bias in decision-making that society has been working hard to stamp out. However, it is also possible for machine learning systems to reinforce systemic bias and discrimination and prevent dignity assurance. (World Economic Forum 2018, p.3)

The likelihood of such bias has considerable implications for human rights, for the proper management of social diversity, and for the fair treatment of diverse groups in society. Such inequity is a long-standing problem in conventional information management, and has been addressed at length in the research literature of knowledge organization in particular. It seems, however, especially insidious in the machine intelligence context, perhaps because of the expectation that higher levels of neutrality and objectivity apply.

6. Bias and discrimination derived from data

Much of the literature in this area is centred on machine decision-making based on demographic data, and the concern arises from a human rights perspective where some groups are disadvantaged or marginalized by the way in which the data is set up (Obama White House 2016a, 2016b; World Economic Forum 2018). Generally in these cases, the data is factual and the decision-making is based on a combination of values in different categories, and the identification and recognition of patterns embedded in data, especially latent associations between one group of attributes and another.

Particularly prominent in the discussion of bias in AI is gender discrimination, also a feature of early research into bias in KO. A recent major study by Criado-Perez (2019) reveals that data itself is often biased, because the sample is in some way flawed. Criado-Perez's principal concern is with gender imbalance, and it is clear that a female perspective is often omitted because the data is derived from studies that dealt only with males. Criado-Perez provides examples of where, for example, diagnostic thresholds based on biomarkers are inaccurate for women because average figures are based on predominantly male data (as in Khamis et al., 2016), since the inclusion of female data may be as low as 14% of studies in some fields (Pinnow et al. 2014).

This may explain many examples of bias detected in machine intelligence where the agents have been trained on datasets that lack comprehensiveness in one or more respects.

7. Bias and discrimination derived from semantics

A much-cited paper by Caliskan et al. (2017) establishes that not only is any incompleteness or skew in the data sample passed on to intelligent systems, but that semantics is also an inheritable factor. Using measurable associations between pairs of words, Caliskan builds on the work of some prior studies investigating human-like biases in textual corpora, particularly that of Greenwald (1998), who studied 'biases that they consider nearly universal in humans and about which there is no social concern' (Caliskan p.183). Clear associations between 'flowers' and 'pleasant', and 'insects' and 'unpleasant', were replicated by Caliskan's team, as were similar links between 'weapon' (unpleasant) and 'musical instrument' (pleasant), proving the soundness of the methodology. Caliskan et al. were also able to replicate more socially significant connections between European American names and African American names with pleasantness and unpleasantness respectively, a phenomenon confirmed in practice by Bertrand and Mullainathan (2004) who tested employers' response to job applications varying only in the attached European or African sounding names.

Comparable work was also replicated in the area of gender, associating female names with 'family' as opposed to 'career', when compared with male names (Nosek et al. 2002a), and the correlation of women with the arts, rather than mathematics (Nosek et al. 2002a), or with the sciences (Nosek et al. 2002b).

Studies of inherent discrimination based on religion are much less frequent, perhaps because religious affiliation is much less immediately obvious than gender or ethnicity. However, Binns (2018, p.1) places it on a level with gender and race as a potential factor for discrimination, using the example of disparate treatment of nationals from Muslim-majority countries because of a perceived association of Islam with terrorism (p.4). Since such examples of religious prejudice are not uncommon and the problem is one with high public awareness, it is surprising that, to date, there is little or no research into bias associated with religious affiliation.

The existence of such semantic bias has considerable implications for information retrieval because so many automatic classifiers build structures on the back of text corpora on the assumption that these present a neutral and objective picture of the world. The existence of these biases seem to be clearly acknowledged in the world of corpus linguistics, but did not seem to be taken into account at all in the field of automatic classification or term extraction tools, perhaps because work on these originated in the sciences rather than the social sciences and humanities. Automated lexicography is now a very well-established methodology for building such semantic tools, whether the lexical data is sourced from other lexical tools such as dictionaries or extracted from text corpora, and the problem of inherited bias could consequently be a serious impediment to both effective retrieval and ethical practice.

8. Inherited semantic bias in religious terminology: the example of WordNet

WordNet is a vocabulary database, maintained at Princeton University, and used extensively as semantic content for all kinds of automatic indexing and classification tools. It defines itself in the following way (Princeton University, 2010):

WordNet® is a large lexical database of English. Nouns, verbs, adjectives and adverbs are grouped into sets of cognitive synonyms (synsets), each expressing a distinct concept. Synsets are interlinked by means of conceptual-semantic and lexical relations. The resulting network of meaningfully related words and concepts can be navigated with the browser. ... WordNet's structure makes it a useful tool for computational linguistics and natural language processing.

WordNet is displayed in a thesaurus-like format, although the tags it uses are not the conventional ones of information science, but rather offer a more analytical and nuanced range of inter-term relations. Nevertheless, it approximates to the standard tags through its use of the categories hypernym (= broader term, superordinate class), hyponym (= narrower term, subordinate class), and synsets (equivalence relationships). Other relationships include Types (= narrower term generic), Instances (= narrower term instantive) and Meronymy (= narrower term partitive). Opening up a 'Sister term' reveals terms in the same array, comparable with some kinds of related, or associative terms. This suite of relationships provides the vocabulary with a robust logical structure, and verbs as well as nouns are thus organized into hierarchies. Unlike most controlled vocabularies, WordNet also includes adjectives and adverbs in its database. However, there is quite limited use of associative term type links, so the navigation tends to be, on the whole, hierarchical.

WordNet is a good example of a resource that has inherited content. Although initially it was intellectually constructed, it draws on older sources such as thesauri (Barocas et al, 2018) that themselves may contain bias, and because of its widespread use in computational linguistics it passes on that bias.

In some applications, researchers repurpose an existing scheme of classification to define the target variable rather than creating one from scratch. For example, an object recognition system can be created by training a classifier on ImageNet, a database of images organized in a hierarchy of concepts. ImageNet's hierarchy comes from Wordnet, a database of words, categories, and the relationships among them. Wordnet's authors in turn imported the word lists from a number of older sources, such as thesauri. As a result, WordNet (and ImageNet) categories contain numerous outmoded words and associations, such as occupations that no longer exist and stereotyped gender associations.

Even a cursory examination of WordNet's religious categories reveals some very evident examples of bias. As with many humanities and social science disciplines, particularly those where there is a strong cultural dimension, language is a source of some problematic classes and linguistic expressions. Similarly, the precise analytical structure of WordNet, based on linguistics principles, while it is highly suitable for the sciences, does not always serve the rather messier humanistic domains nearly as well. Accurate and comprehensive category structure is not necessarily to be found, and in many cases the arrays are incomplete.

If we consider the standard criticisms of biased Religion classes in standard bibliographic classifications, many of the same shortcomings are evident in WordNet. For example, if we look at the hierarchical display of hyponyms (subordinate classes) under Religion (disregarding the annotations, and further levels of hierarchy) we find:

Noun

- S: (n) **religion**, faith, religious belief (a strong belief in a supernatural power or powers that control human destiny) *"he lost his faith but not his morality"*
- S: (n) **religion**, faith, organized religion (an institution to express belief in a divine power) *"he was raised in the Baptist religion"; "a member of his own faith contradicted him"*
    - *direct hyponym / full hyponym*
        - S: (n) church, Christian church (one of the groups of Christians who have their own beliefs and forms of worship)
        - S: (n) Judaism, Hebraism, Jewish religion (Jews collectively who practice a religion based on the Torah and the Talmud)
        - S: (n) Hinduism, Hindooism (the religion of most people in India, Bangladesh, Sri Lanka, and Nepal)
        - S: (n) Taoism (religion adhering to the teaching of Lao-tzu)
        - S: (n) Buddhism (a religion represented by the many groups (especially in Asia) that profess various forms of the Buddhist doctrine and that venerate Buddha)
        - S: (n) Khalsa (the group of initiated Sikhs to which devout orthodox Sikhs are ritually admitted at puberty; founded by the tenth and last Guru in 1699)
        - S: (n) Scientology, Church of Scientology (a new religion founded by L. Ron Hubbard in 1955 and characterized by a belief in the power of a person's spirit to clear itself of past painful experiences through self-knowledge and spiritual fulfillment)
        - S: (n) Shinto (the native religion and former ethnic cult of Japan)
        - S: (n) established church (the church that is recognized as the official church of a nation)
        - S: (n) sect, religious sect, religious order (a subdivision of a larger religious group)
        - S: (n) cult (followers of an unorthodox, extremist, or false religion or sect who often live outside of conventional society under the direction of a charismatic leader)
        - S: (n) cult (followers of an exclusive system of beliefs and practices)
    - *domain term category*
    - *direct hypernym / inherited hypernym / sister term*
    - *derivationally related form*

When compared with the standard 'big twelve' religions acknowledged by most sources (for example, Hinnell 2017; Boyett 2016), WordNet fails to mention Baha'i, Confucianism, Jainism, Sikhism (other than through its subset Khalsa), Zoroastrianism, and, amazingly, Islam. Expanding the list to include 'full hyponyms' expands the hierarchy and brings in various Christian denominations, movements within Judaism and Buddhism, and under sects, Anglican High Church, Sunni and Shi'a Islam, the Society of Friends or Quakers, Jainism and Hare Krishna. Perhaps surprisingly, Scientology appears, but not the Mormon Church.

Needless to say, the omissions, odd associations and peculiar language (Hindooism looks very antiquated and mildly offensive) would be unacceptable in a modern thesaurus or bibliographic classification.

Many of the definitions and verbal qualifications of entries exhibit some odd if not doubtful attitudes, as in the definition: 'Hindooism (a body of religious and philosophical beliefs and cultural practices native to India and based on a caste system'. There are differing schools of thought about the caste system, and whether it arises from socioeconomic rather than religious forces, and this is a very contentious statement. Similarly, Paganism (synonyms: pagan religion, heathenism) is defined as 'any of various religions other than Christianity or Judaism or Islamism' which is certainly inaccurate in respect of modern pagans, and potentially offensive to followers of the non-monotheistic faiths. Perhaps the worse sufferer is Islam, which is provided with the synonyms Muslimism, Mohammedanism, Muhammadanism, and Islamism. The Oxford English Dictionary says of Mohammedanism that 'its use is now widely seen as depreciatory or offensive', and none of these terms feel very appropriate or polite. It seems likely that this rather uncomfortable content has been imported from much older dictionaries without review or amendment.

Along with such archaic uses of language, there is also a leaning towards a strongly Christian-flavoured understanding of religious terminology, as opposed to a more multi-faith approach; examples of this can be seen in the table below. The terms have been chosen as relatively neutral ones which occur in a variety of religions, but in defining the terms or providing synonyms WordNet imposes a broadly Christian interpretation.

In fairness to WordNet, it does contain many religion specific terms (bhakti, Gemara, hajj, lama, menorah, nirvana, shaman, Sufi, synagogue, etc.) but because of the mainly hierarchical structure these are not easily accessed through the parent religion. This positive feature needs also to be set against the general Christian tenor of the vocabulary, and the evident tendency to view religion through a Christian lens.

There are also some straightforward factual inaccuracies in WordNet, for instance the qualifier of Hinduism '(the religion of most people in India, Bangladesh, Sri Lanka, and Nepal)', whereas the dominant religion in Bangladesh is Sunni Islam, followed by 83.4% of the population (WorldAtlas 2019).

Source term	Synonyms
altar	Communion table, Lord's table
baptism	a Christian sacrament signifying spiritual cleansing
bless	make the sign of the Cross over someone
festival	religious festival, church festival
monk	Brother, Carthusian, Trappist, Cistercian
preaching	an address of a religious nature usually delivered during a church service
scripture	Bible, Christian Bible, Holy Writ, Word (the sacred writings of the Christian religions)
service	church service, prayer meeting, chapel service, vesper
sin	mark of Cain

These significant shortcomings demonstrate a very considerable bias, and a disregard for fairness and sensitivity towards minority groups. The gravity of bias in WordNet is considerably magnified by its widespread use as a lexical source for automatic classifiers, which implies that the prejudices will indeed have been inherited and reinforced by a great number of other intelligent agents.

9. What solutions exist to the problem of bias?

As is the case in library and information science, where the interests and priorities of the user community demand a privileging of those interests, bias is not always regarded as a bad thing. It is generally agreed that the very fact of a specific perspective unwittingly and unavoidably generates bias towards the favoured group (such as classification schemes for libraries with specific religious affiliations). Given the importance of meeting user expectations and the needs of the user community, bias can be seen as an ethically-neutral phenomenon.

In other cases the investigation of bias is simply a part of the scholarly study of society and the legitimate search for patterns and trends in human cultures. For example, a paper by Kozlowski et al. (2018) shows how the machine analytical technique of word embedding can help to reveal changes in social attitudes over time and historic changes in word meanings (p.38). In different situations, the identification of bias may be the preliminary to addressing it in a social and political context and is a useful tool in highlighting social inequalities.

In a wider context however, bias should be energetically tackled if the system is not to appear as the tool of a particular cultural, political or disciplinary community. Bias inherent in data is generally regarded as undesirable and has generated an area of research activity under the general heading of machine-learning fairness. Barocas, Hardt & Narayanan (2018) provide a broadly-based survey of a number of problems and potential solutions, based on statistical adjustment. The book 'offers a critical take on current practice of machine learning as well as proposed technical fixes for achieving fairness'.

Mancuhan & Clifton (2014) also propose a statistical solution to bias in data used for automatic financial decision-making, employing Bayesian techniques to identify and automatically correct bias. This is incidentally one of the few papers to reference religion as an attribute subject to bias, although the authors do not go on to include it in their study.

10. A moral and religious solution

As with every other area of human life, machine intelligence has impacted religious communities, apart from the general philosophical questions of whether robots can act as moral agents. A number of applications exist which aim to support religious practice, such as the Roman Catholic Confession app (Rau 2011) and Muslim Pro which can tell you prayer times and the direction of Mecca in your own town or village (Muslim Pro 2019), and attempts have already been made to use robots in ritual. Most of the literature here is in popular journals and the press, so it may be difficult to assess how serious these efforts are. We learn of a Christian robot priest in Wittenberg which radiates light from its hands and pronounces blessings in five languages as part of an exhibition to celebrate 500 years since the invention of printing technology, instrumental in the Reformation and the rise of Protestantism (Sherwood 2017). Other cases include a robot Buddhist monk in China (Tatlow 2016) which reads scripture and can answer questions, and another in Japan (Field, 2017) which can 'chant prayers and tap drums as part of a funeral ceremony'.

There is also a literature in the overlap between religious philosophy and AI which considers the nature of the relationships between intelligent agents, humans and the person of God, typically whether the creation of intelligent agents in some sense mirrors the creation of humans (Herzfeld 2003), and if the possibilities of transhumanism through the technological alteration of species are realizable (Dumsday 2017). Vidal (2007, p.930) makes a comparison between man's interaction with artificial beings and his interactions with the gods, asking whether the similarities are not caused by uncertainty:

But it is also true that where interaction is supposed to exist between the gods and their worshippers, there always remains a strong element of uncertainty which cannot easily be dismissed concerning the exact ontological nature of the hybrid arrangement by which the divinity's presence is made manifest. It is precisely the same sort of ontological uncertainty that one finds expressed in the field of robotics. And this is also why robots both fascinate and worry the general public.

11. The moral and religious life of machines

A pressing question is whether a real sense of moral responsibility can be developed in intelligent agents, or, more fancifully perhaps, a proper religious sense. In human beings it may seem obvious that ethical decisions differ in some significant respect from other kinds of decisions, and that intellectual reasoning is subordinate to, or at least strongly influenced by, emotional intelligence. As Liao (2016) says:

.... a central area of intellectual inquiry across different disciplines involves understanding the nature, practice, and reliability of moral judgments. For instance, an issue of perennial interest concerns what moral judgments are and how moral judgments differ from nonmoral judgments. Moral judgments such as "Torture is wrong" seem different from nonmoral judgments such as "Water is wet." But how do moral judgments differ from nonmoral, but normative judgments such as "The time on the clock is wrong" or "Talking with one's mouth full is wrong"?

However, work in neuroscience has questioned whether this distinction between cognitive and emotional aspects of moral judgements is valid, suggesting instead that all such decisions depend on reasoning through complex calculation rather than a response to stimulus (Woodward 2016).

Perhaps the most surprising finding to date is that core emotional structures, including the midbrain dopamine system and insula, decompose uncertain choice contexts along the statistical dimensions that are the cornerstone of FDT [Financial decision theory] .... recent findings suggest that the encoding of value in midbrain dopamine areas might underlie an early implicit encoding that is signaled to orbitofrontal cortex, where it guides choice. (Quartz 2009, p.214)

Recent studies have shown that it is possible to identify precisely areas of the human brain responsible for social and moral behaviour, and to link deficits in brain function to immoral, or amoral, behaviour (Damasio 1994; Shoemaker 2012):

The basic limbic emotions are those present in all mammals emanating from phylogenetically analogous brain structures collectively called the limbic system. ... These are fear, anger, disgust, sadness, and happiness; they function chiefly to promote the survival of the individual. The moral emotions, the product of the social brain network, arise later in development and evolution (Adolphs 2003). They are guilt, shame, embarrassment, jealousy, pride, and altruism; they function to regulate social behaviors, often in the long-term interest of a social group rather than the short-term interest of the individual person (Adolphs 2003). (Shoemaker 2012, p.807)

Such work has considerable implications for the development of ethically responsible machines, since if the nature of decision-making can be made explicit and the process modelled, then it is, at least theoretically, possible to replicate this process in machine decision-making.

A further and more difficult question is whether it is possible to inculcate religious sensibility in machines by a similar methodology. In the speculative *Age of spiritual machines* (1999 p.6) Kurzweil, technologist and futurist, suggests that in the distant future this will happen spontaneously as the result of technological evolution:

Even if we limit our discussion to computers that are not directly derived from a particular human brain, they will increasingly appear to have their own personalities, evidencing reactions that we can only label as emotions and articulating their own goals andpurposes. They will appear to have their own free will. They will claim to have spiritual experiences. And people—those still using carbon-based neurons or otherwise—will believe them.'

Some specific studies of the relationship between AI and religion include William Sims Bainbridge's *God from the machine* (2006), which investigates the question of whether religious activity might occur spontaneously in machine learning. Bainbridge and Stark (1987) proposed a general theoretical framework for the scientific study of religion, which included, among many other propositions, reasons for the emergence of cults and for cult affiliation; individuals characterized by high levels of education and social isolation, it is suggested, are more likely to participate in cults, a theory supported in part by practical testing (Bader & Damaris 1996). In 1995 Bainbridge employed the technique of neural network modelling to test his theory, and to identify the reasons for human religious behaviour. The idea of religion, however, is not part of the data supplied:

While not denying the possibility of God's existence, our theory attempts to explain human religious behavior without assuming the truth of religion. Therefore, there is no axiom asserting the existence of the supernatural (p.484).

The program attempts to formalise communication and models a community who seek exchanges with each other in search of the basics of existence, and of beneficial exchanges leading to personal rewards.

In the scenario accompanying the program, they are called *energy, water, food, oxygen,* and *life*. Some people are producers of one or another of the first four rewards, and the simulation models the development of a little economy based on exchange of these consumable rewards. But none of the 24 people can provide each other with eternal life (p. 486).

Bainbridge describes how, in the attempt to find suitable exchange partners for these more intangible rewards, the concept of the supernatural, within the context of a folk religion, may emerge spontaneously.

In the subculture-evolution model, an intensely interacting group of individuals commits itself to the attainment of rewards, some of which are very difficult or even impossible to obtain. As they exchange rewards among themselves, they also exchange explanations about how to get other rewards, and in the attempt to satisfy each other, they magnify slightly their positive evaluation of explanations. Those explanations that can be evaluated empirically will be rejected, leaving the nonempirical (supernatural) explanations that cannot readily be evaluated. Faith will spiral upward, and the group will create a folk religion through a series of thousands of tiny communication steps. (p. 492)

In a more developed version of the methodology Bainbridge (2006) concludes that this is a natural, and to some extent inevitable, process which he is able to model in various ways. He posits that it is quite feasible that, primed with appropriate theological information, machines might also 'communicate ideas as if they were exchange partners engaged in theological discussion with each other' (p. 137), and that 'once separated to some degree from external control, the evolving cult develops ... the end point of successful cult evolution is a novel religious culture' (p.139).

12. Conclusion

The phenomenon of bias is found to be widespread in machine intelligence, both in data per se and in semantic content derived from text corpora. Most of the studies of machine bias have focussed on demographics such as gender, race, and occasionally, social class. Although it is mentioned in a few papers as another potential focus for bias, religious affiliation has not been investigated in the same way, despite the obvious existence of religious prejudice in society. However, examination of the well-established and influential resource WordNet shows high levels of bias in its structural associations and use of language, almost certainly as a result of inheritance from vocabularies used in its original construction. Because of its widespread use in the creation of search and discovery tools, particularly automatic classifiers, WordNet is likely to have passed on these prejudices.

Addressing the problems of bias has mainly concentrated on technical solutions, but recent research in modelling the ethical behaviour of humans suggests that intelligent agents may be able to develop a sense of fairness and moral responsibility independently of humans, and one not assuming pre-programming with specific rules. Several writers speculate that, in time, a sense of the religious could also emerge, and can provide a detailed demonstration of how this might happen using similar neural network methodologies. In time robots themselves might be equipped to deal with the phenomenon of religious prejudice.

References

Adler, M. & L. M. Harper, 2018. "Race and Ethnicity in Classification Systems: Teaching Knowledge Organization from a Social Justice Perspective." *Library Trends* 67: 52-73.

Adolphs, Ralph. 2003. "Cognitive Neuroscience of Human Social Behavior." *Nature Neuroscience Reviews* 4: 165–78.

Albrecht, S. V., A. M. S Barreto, D Braziunas, D. L. Buckeridge M.D., H. Cuayáhuitl, N Dethlefs & J. Zhang. 2015. "Reports of the AAAI 2014 Conference Workshops." *AI Magazine* 36: 87-98.

Anderson, M., & S. L. Anderson. 2007. "Machine Ethics: Creating an Ethical Intelligent Agent." *AI Magazine* 28(4): 15-26.

Anderson, Michael, Susan Leigh Anderson & Chris Armen. 2005. "Towards Machine Ethics: Implementing Two Action-Based Ethical Theories" In *Papers from the 2005 AAAI Fall Symposium on Machine Ethics.*

Aula, A. & M. Kaki, 2005. "Findex: Improving Search Result Use Through Automatic Filtering Categories", *Interacting with Computers* 17: 187-206.

Bader, Chris & Alfred Demaris. 1996. "A Test of the Stark-Bainbridge Theory of Affiliation with Cults and Sects" *Journal for the Scientific Study of Religion* 35: 285.

Bainbridge, W. 1995. "Neural Network Models of Religious Belief." *Sociological Perspectives,* 38: 483-495.

Bainbridge, William Sims. 2006. *God from the Machine: Artificial Intelligence Models of Religious Cognition.* Lanham, MD: Altmira.

Barocas, S., Moritz Hardt & Arvind Narayanan. 2018. *Fairness and Machine Learning* Available at: http://www.fairmlbook.org.

Bentham, Jeremy. 1789. *An Introduction to the Principles of Morals and Legislation.* Oxford: Clarendon.

Bertrand, Marianne & Sendhil Mullainathan. 2004. "Are Emily and Greg More Employable Than Lakisha and Jamal?" *American Economic Review* 94: 991-1013.

Binns, R. 2018. "Fairness in Machine Learning: Lessons from Political Philosophy" *Journal of Machine Learning Research* 81: 1-11.

Blair, Ann. 2010. *Too Much to Know.* New Haven, Conn. ; London : Yale University Press.

Boyett, Jason. 2016. *12 Major World Religions: The Beliefs, Rituals, and Traditions of Humanity's Most Influential Faiths.* Berkeley, Calif: Zephyros.

Brachman, R. 2005. Getting Back to "the Very Idea". *AI Magazine* 26(4), 48-50.

Broughton, V. 2000. "A New Classification for the Literature of Religion." *International Cataloguing and Bibliographic Control* 4 (Paper read at the 66th IFLA Council and General Conference Jerusalem Israel 13-18 August).

Broughton, V., M. Palfreyman & A. Wilson. 2008. Automatic Metadata Generation for Resource Discovery. JISC. http://www.jisc.ac.uk/media/documents/programmes/resourcediscovery/metgenreport_final_v5.doc

Caliskan, A., J. Bryson & A. Narayanan. 2017. "Semantics Derived Automatically from Language Corpora Contain Human-Like Biases." Science 356, 183-186 14 April 2017.

Cheung, C. F., W. B. Lee & Y. Wang. 2005. "A Multi-Facet Taxonomy System with Applications in Unstructured Knowledge Management." *Journal of Knowledge Management* 9(6): 76-91.

Copeland, B. J. 2019. "Artificial Intelligence." *Encyclopaedia Britannica.* (accessed 14.04.2019)

Crawford, Kate. 2016. "Artificial Intelligence's White Guy Problem." New York Times. 25 June.

Criado-Perez, Caroline. 2019. *Invisible Women: Exposing Data Bias in a World Designed for Men.* London: Vintage Digital.

Damasio, Antonio. 1994. *Descartes' Error: Emotion, Reason and the Human Brain.* New York: Grosset/Putnam.

Drabinski, E. 2013. "Queering the Catalog: Queer Theory and the Politics of Correction." *Library Quarterly* 83: 94.

Duarte, Marisa Elena and Miranda Belarde-Lewis. 2015. "Imagining: Creating Spaces for Indigenous Ontologies." *Cataloging & Classification Quarterly Special Issue on Indigenous Knowledge Organization* 53: 677–702.Dumsday, T. 2017. "Transhumanism, Theological Anthropology, and Modern Biological Taxonomy" *Zygon: Journal of Religion and Science.* 52: 601-622.

Field, Matthew. 2017. "This Japanese Robot Can Host Low-Cost Buddhist Funerals." *Daily Telegraph* 24 August 2017.

Foskett, A. C. 1971. "Misogynists All: a study in critical classification." *Library Resources and Technical Services* 15: 117-121.

Fox, M. J. 2016. "Legal Discourse's Epistemic Interplay with Sex and Gender Classification in the Dewey Decimal Classification System." *Library Trends* 64: 687-713.

Görg, C., Z. Liu & J. Stasko. 2014. Reflections on the Evolution of the Jigsaw Visual Analytics System. *Information Visualization* 13(4): 336-345.

Greenberg, J., K. Spurgin & A. Crystal, 2005. *Final Report for the AMeGA (Automatic Metadata Generation Applications Project.* University of North Carolina & Library of Congress. http://www.loc.gov/catdir/bibcontrol/lc_amega_final_report.pdf

Greenwald, A. G., D. E. McGhee & J. L. K. Schwartz. 1998. "Measuring Individual Differences in Implicit Cognition: the Implicit Association Test." *Journal of Personality and Social Psychology* 74(6): 1646-1480.

Hannay, T. 2014. "The Digital Academy and Augmented Intelligence." *Information Today* 31: 25.

Herzfeld, Noreen. 2003. "Creating in Our Own Image: Artificial Intelligence and the Image of God." *Zygon: Journal of Religion and Science* 37: 303-316.

Hinnells, John. 2017. *A New Handbook of Living Religions.* Wiley Online.

Howard, S. A. & S. A. Knowlton. 2018. "Browsing Through Bias: The Library of Congress Classification and Subject Headings for African American studies and LGBTQIA Studies." *Library Trends* 67: 74-88.

Hurwitz, Judith & Daniel Kirsch. 2018. *Machine Learning for Dummies.* Hoboken, NJ: Wiley.

IBM. 2019. *Data Science and Machine Learning.* https://www.ibm.com/analytics/machine-learning

Khamis R.Y., T. Ammari & G.W. Mikhail. 2016. "Gender Differences in Coronary Heart Disease." *Heart* 102: 1142-1149.

Kirchner, Julia, Surya Angwin, Jeff Mattu & Lauren Larson. 2016. "Machine Bias: There's Software Used Across the Country to Predict Future Criminals. And it's Biased Against Blacks." ProPublica 23 May.

Ko, Y., J. Park, & J. Seo. 2004. "Improving Text Categorization Using the Importance of Sentences." *Information Processing and Management* 40 (1): 65-79.

Kochi, Erica. 2018. "AI is Already Learning How to Discriminate". Quartz at Work. https://qz.com/author/erica-kochi/

Kozlowski, Austin C., Matt Taddy, & James A. Evans. 2018. "The Geometry of Culture: Analyzing Meaning through Word Embeddings." Available online at https://arxiv.org/abs/1803.09288

Kurzweil, Ray. 1999. *The Age of Spiritual Machines: When Computers Exceed Human Intelligence.* New York, NY: Penguin.

Lacey, E. 2018. "Aliens in the Library: The Classification of Migration." *Knowledge Organization* 45: 358-379.

Liang, Chun-Yan et al. 2006. "Dictionary-Based Text Categorization of Chemical Web Pages", *Information Processing and Management* 42: 1017–1029.

Liao, S. Matthew. 2016. *Moral Brains: the Neuroscience of Morality.* Oxford: OUP.

Mai, J-E. 2010 "Classification in a Social World: Bias and Trust." *Journal of Documentation* 66: 627-642.

Mai, J-E. 2013a. "Ethics, Values, and Morality in Contemporary Library Classifications." *Knowledge Organization* 40: 242-253.

Mai, J-E. 2013b. *Ethics and Epistemology of Classification.* http://jenserikmai.info/Papers/2013_EEofClass.pdf

Mai, J-E. 2016. "Marginalization and Exclusion: Unraveling Systemic Bias in Classification." *Knowledge Organization* 43: 324-330.

Mancuhan, K. & Chris Clifton. 2014. "Combating Discrimination Using Bayesian Networks." *Artificial Intelligence Law* 22:211–238.

Marshall, J. 1977. *On Equal Terms: A Thesaurus for Non-Sexist Indexing and Cataloging.* New York: Neal Schuman.

Muslim Pro. 2019. www.muslimpro.com

Nosek, B. A., M. R. Banaji & A. G. Greenwald. 2002a. "Harvesting Implicit Group Attitudes and Beliefs from a Demonstration Website." *Group Dynamics* 6: 101 –115.

Nosek, B. A., M. R. Banaji & A. G. Greenwald. 2002b. "Math = Male, Me = Female, therefore Math ^= Me." *Journal of Personality & Social Psychology* 83: 44 –59.

Obama White House. 2016a. *Big Risks, Big Opportunities: the Intersection of Big Data and Civil Rights.* 4 May 2016. https://obamawhitehouse.archives.gov/blog/2016/05/04/big-risks-big-opportunities-intersection-big-data-and-civil-rights

Obama White House. Executive Office of the President. 2016b. Big Data: *A Report on Algorithmic Systems, Opportunity, and Civil Rights.* May 2016. https://obamawhitehouse.archives.gov/sites/default/files/microsites/ostp/2016_0504_data_discrimination.pdf

Ojala, M. 2018. "Digital Ethics in the STM Publishing World." *Information Today* 35: 10-11.

Olson, H. A. 1998. "Mapping Beyond Dewey's Boundaries: Constructing Classificatory Space for Marginalized Knowledge Domains." *Library Trends* 47: 233-254.

Olson, H. A. 2002. *The Power to Name: Locating the Limits of Subject Representation in Libraries.* Dordrecht, The Netherlands: Kluwer.

Olson, H. A. 2007. "How We Construct Subjects: A Feminist Analysis." *Library Trends* 56: 509-541.

Olson, H. A. and D. B. Ward. 1997. "Feminist Locales in Dewey's Landscape: Mapping a Marginalized Knowledge Domain." In *Knowledge Organization for Information Retrieval: Proceedings of the Sixth International Study Conference on Information Research.* The Hague: International Federation for Information and Documentation, 129-133.

Pinnow, E., N Herz, N. Loyo-Berrios & M. Tarver. 2014 "Enrollment and Monitoring of Women in Post-Approval Studies for Medical Devices Mandated by the Food and Drug Administration." *Journal of Women's Health* 23(3). Published Online: 10 Mar 2014 https://doi.org/10.1089/jwh.2013.4343

Poole, David, Alan Mackworth & Randy Goebel. 1998. *Computational Intelligence: A Logical Approach.* New York: Oxford University Press.

Princeton University. 2010. "About WordNet." WordNet. Princeton University. https://wordnet.princeton.edu/

Quartz, Steven R. 2009. "Reason, Emotion and Decision-Making: Risk and Reward Computation with Feeling." *Trends in Cognitive Sciences* 13(5): 209-215

Rau, Andy. 2011. "Should we use a Confession App?" *Think Christian Website* 24 February 2011. https://thinkchristian.reframemedia.com/should-we-use-a-confession-app

Sears, Mark. 2018. "AI Bias and the 'People Factor' in AI Development". *Forbes* November 13. https://www.forbes.com/sites/marksears1/2018/11/13/ai-bias-and-the-people-factor-in-ai-development/#555088e59134

Sherwood, Harriet. 2017. "Robot Priest Unveiled in Germany to Mark 500 Years Since Reformation." *Guardian* 20 May. https://www.theguardian.com/technology/2017/may/30/robot-priest-blessu-2-germany-reformation-exhibition

Shoemaker, William J. 2012. "The Social Brain Network and Human Moral Behaviour." *Zygon: Journal of Religion and Science* 47: 806-820

Stark, R. & W. S. Bainbridge, 1987. *A theory of religion.* New York: David Lang.

Szostak, R. 2014. "Classifying for Social Diversity." *Knowledge Organization* 41: 160-170.

Tatlow, D. K. 2016. "A Robot Monk Captivates China, Mixing Spirituality with Artificial Intelligence" *New York Times* 27 April. https://www.nytimes.com/2016/04/28/world/asia/china-robot-monk-temple.html

Vidal, D. 2007. Anthropomorphism or Sub-Anthropomorphism? An Anthropological Approach to Gods and Robots. *The Journal of the Royal Anthropological Institute* 13: 917-933.

World Economic Forum. Global Future Council on Human Rights 2016-2018. 2018. *How to Prevent Discriminatory Outcomes in Machine Learning.* http://www3.weforum.org/docs/WEF_40065_White_Paper_How_to_Prevent_Discriminatory_Outcomes_in_Machine_Learning.pdf

Woodward, James. 2016. "Emotion Versus Cognition in Moral Decision-Making: A Dubious Dichotomy" In S. Matthew Liao *Moral Brains: the Neuroscience of Morality.* Oxford: OUP.

WorldAtlas. 2019. *Religious Beliefs in Bangladesh.* www.worldatlas.com.

Session 6A: CREATIVITY

Creating an Ontology of Risk: a human-mediated process

David Haynes, City, University of London, UK

Abstract

It can be argued that creation of any kind of knowledge organization system requires human judgement and creativity. An ontology is a representation of reality and is one form of knowledge organization that allows for many different types of relationship between concepts. This paper examines the process of ontology creation as exemplified by the development of an ontology of online risk. This is part of a wider project on the nature of risk and the privacy calculus. The paper explores the degree to which human intervention is required at each stage in the development process. AI is useful for discovering patterns and clustering of concepts. AI is also used for merging different ontologies, because of their ability to process large masses of data. Humans are necessary for defining explicit relationships that might be inferred from the data. Ontologies are widely used to prime AI systems so that they can 'make sense' of big data.

1. Introduction and background

One of the challenges of dealing with risk is trying to pin down definitions and relationships between concepts. Work of this kind must start with some key assumptions from which a model of risk can be constructed. Previous work to develop typologies of risk have become difficult to track because of the complex interactions between vulnerabilities, threats, risk incidents and their impact. Ontologies allow the modelling of the very complicated interactions between entities and can be used to develop rules on the behaviour of predictive systems. They can also be used for navigating linked data sets.

Haynes and Robinson (2015) developed a model of personal risk associated with online social networks which attempts to map the relationships between different types of risk. It was clear from that work that a simple hierarchical structure was insufficient to represent the complex web of cause and effect that a risk analysis requires. Arp, Smith and Spear (2015, 27) describe the extended role of ontologies in the following terms:

"An ontology, as we conceive it, is a representational artifact aimed at representing universals, defined classes, and relations among them."

In this case the risk model was developed from the perspective of the individual as opposed to corporate, governmental or societal interests. This means that where there is a conflict between risk to an individual and risk to society, the risk to the individual is considered. For example, risks associated with a breach of personal privacy may be bad for an individual but could be desirable from the point of view of the security services. In this case the risk to the individual might be loss of liberty, for instance.

2. Purpose

The purpose of this research is to test a manually-based method for ontology development, and to explore the opportunities for AI or machine learning to contribute to the development of the ontology.

In any discussion about AI in the context of ontologies, there are two important considerations: What role does AI play in the development of an ontology? and What role do ontologies play in the establishment of AI systems? There is a wider ethical debate about accountability. The inputs to an AI system may be known, for instance a large data set, and the outputs may be known, for instance in a diagnostic system. However, the processes that take place to arrive at that output may not be clear, the so-called "black box problem". This is a particular concern for instance in profiling criminal suspects, where the prejudices of the programmers may be reflected in the way in which individual suspects are identified. It also has serious implications in medical diagnostics where the reason for a diagnosis may not be clear to a medical practitioner. In this case the use of AI as a decision-support system may be more appropriate. This is one reason why the EU General Data Protection Regulation (GDPR) protects the right of individuals to have decisions that affect them made by humans, bypassing automated decision-making systems (European Parliament and European Council 2016).

3. Literature
3.1 Models of risk

Zhou et al (2008) established key risk categories from a critical review of the literature, using published case studies to develop the risk factors model in project management. Aven and Renn (2009) examine different definitions of risk and come to the conclusion that risk can be defined as "uncertainties about events and consequences and severity of these events and consequences (outcome stakes)" without specifying whether those outcomes are good or bad. Hubbard (2009) takes issue with a neutral rendering of risk definitions, suggesting that it is contrary to a general understanding of risk and probably meaningless.

Risk models can be developed in a variety of ways. For instance, Draghici and Draghici (2013) adopt a mind-mapping approach to develop a model of risk in the industrial safety sector. On the other hand, Mazri (2017) discusses emergent risks and concludes that they are a part of the lifecycle of all risks and this needs to be acknowledged in any risk management framework. An analytical approach is adopted by Freund and Jones (2015) who started with a Bayesian inference, which was later informed by Monte Carlo modelling of probabilities. This is shown in Figure 1, which describes the FAIR risk taxonomy.

Figure 1 - FAIR secondary risk taxonomy (Freund and Jones, 2015)

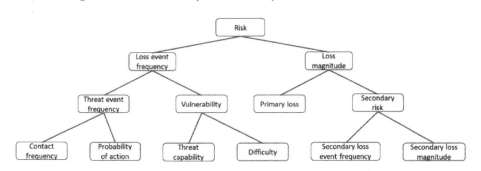

3.2 The nature of an ontology

The term 'ontology' can cover a variety of purposes. An ontology is a representation or model of reality. This can be at the very simple level of a classification system which groups together like entities with a simple hierarchical structure. This type of taxonomy might be a starting point for a more detailed model. The next level is a model of relationships that extends beyond a simple hierarchy. This could be cause and effect relationships and other kinds of association between terms. The third type of ontology is a representation of reality that can be used to detect patterns in new sets of data and to make predictions or suggest courses of action that are appropriate to those sets of data. This third type includes axioms or rules about the behaviour of systems and the relationships between entities.

Ontology evokes the idea of semiotics such as the Pierce ternary or the meaning triangle where there is a concept (in someone's mind), a reference (the actual object or entity that corresponds to the concept) and a symbol (its representation), for instance as a term in a controlled vocabulary.

Studer, Benjamins and Fensel (1998, p.184) talk about ontologies as "a formal, explicit specification of a shared conceptualization". By formal they mean machine-readable, by explicit they mean clearly defined, and by shared they mean consensual. Ontologies consist of classes and concepts describing objects or instances of a class. They have properties or attributes with specific values. Relationships between objects or classes provide the structure. At the simplest level they might be subsumption 'is-a' or meronymy 'is-part-of' as seen in hierarchical taxonomies. At a more complex level they may include domain-specific relationships and cause-and-effect relationships such as 'leads-to' and 'is-caused-by' reciprocal relationships that connect a risk event with the consequence of that event.

Ontologies are widely used in medical and genetic research. They have been used for modelling complex relationships and predicting behaviour of novel compounds. With the recent advances in AI, ontologies are being developed in new areas such as finance and pharmaceutical research. In the 1980s with the research into 'expert systems', there was a great deal of interest in capturing human expertise in a digital system. One strand of the Alvey programme was Intelligent Knowledge Based Systems (Rutherford Appleton Laboratory 2015). The feeling then was that by formalising the knowledge held by humans and concentrating on verifiable facts, it would be possible to improve decision-making by removing the subjective and emotive aspects of human-mediated activity. This depends on axioms or assertions of knowledge that are considered true. Theorems can be deducted from axioms and the rules used for combining them. Multiple axioms and deducted theorems make up a theory. In other words, ontologies deal with entities that have relationships with other.

4. Methodology

A human-mediated approach to ontology development was used in this project. At each stage there was a reflection on the methods adopted and ways in which AI or machine learning techniques could have been applied to facilitate the development of an ontology. The proposed ontology has a defined subject scope which makes it a domain ontology rather than an upper ontology. However, foundational ontologies such as SUMO and DBpedia will be consulted in order to map out the domain of personal online risk.

Yang and Farag (2014) reviewed different approaches to ontology development, which they call ontology engineering. This research follows the iterative approach described by Noy and McGuiness (2001), which has been widely adopted. This is based on seven steps and has been tested in different environments. It has a level of granularity that will ensure that all the necessary processes are likely to be identified:

1. Determine scope
2. Reuse existing ontologies
3. Enumerate important terms
4. Define classes and class hierarchy
5. Define class properties
6. Define facets of the slots
7. Create instances

Two ontology development systems were considered: Protégé, an open source ontology editor from Stanford University, and Synaptica's Graphite system, a commercial system for ontology creation and maintenance. The objective was to find a system capable of supporting the construction of a typology in a formal, structured way. A platform that would facilitate the development of the typology into an ontology that could be applied to wider data sets was also sought. Although both systems were considered suitable for this, the high level of support offered by Synaptica was the deciding factor.

5. Results
5.1 Domain and scope of the ontology of personal online risk

The main purpose of the ontology is to map different types of hazards that individuals face and the possible mitigating actions that they could take. Another purpose is to detect similarities between different hazards and to identify ways in which they might be addressed. A longer-term aim is to populate the ontology with instances based on actual online transactions. It may eventually be possible to estimate the probabilities of a particular outcome.

The ontology covers hazards faced by online users and the resulting consequences. It will model the relationships between different types of hazard and will help users to navigate through the cascade of cause and effect that often occurs as a result of an online incident. It will also provide some insight into similarities between hazards and shared characteristics that might lead to common solutions. For example, a risk ontology could be used to address the following types of question:

- What other risks might be associated with a particular event (such as downloading malware)?
- What kind of mitigating actions are associated with a particular risk?
- Are there recognizable characteristics in online transactions that signal a risk?
- What risk rating would you give for a particular activity?

The ontology is designed to help those responsible for improving the online safety of the public to make evidence-based decisions and judgements. It could eventually be used as a tool for use by safety planners or the cyber insurance industry. An example would be profiling online behaviour of individuals or identifying the risks associated with different demographic characteristics such as age, gender or location. This could be used to generate a risk score for each individual. Certain types of behaviour for instance might increase the risk score (for example social media activity) in a similar way that credit scores are based on demographics, financial resources and behaviour.

5.2 Re-use of existing ontologies

Noy and McGuiness (2001) and Pease (Pease 2011) advocate the re-use of existing ontologies as the starting point for populating a domain specific ontology.. Upper level ontologies were identified from the BARTOC database (Basel University Library 2017) and other sources. They can be used to provide the framework for the development of domain-specific ontologies such as the online risk ontology being developed here.

The upper level ontologies aim to encode common knowledge about the world as observed by humans. Some have been adopted by specific domains, such as the Basic Formal Ontology which has been widely used for the development of medical ontologies (Arp, Smith, and Spear 2015). The Suggested Upper Merged Ontology (SUMO) sponsored by IEEE is also known as 'Standard Upper Merged Ontology'. It has about 25,000 terms and 80,000 axioms (Niles and Pease 2001). This is a candidate source of terms and relationships that could be incorporated into the specialist ontology. The US government funded the development of Cyc which was intended to be an ontology of common-sense facts. It is a proprietary system from Cycorp, but it is not clear whether its core vocabulary is available for public use. ResearchCyc incorporates the ability to test new axioms harvested automatically from Wikipedia and to determine whether they are compatible with existing axioms (Sarjant et al. 2009). This is an example of where a machine-learning approach could work very effectively. Research Cyc is available to the research community. DBpedia is another ontology based on an estimated 270 million triples derived from Wikipedia.

Some of the generic ontologies are more like metadata standards or resemble authority lists rather than providing a set of axioms or rules that can be used to organise concepts. For instance, schema.org provides a core vocabulary of 862 properties. FOAF (friend of a friend) deals with different types of network: social, information and representational. DCAT facilitates interoperation between vocabularies, and VIAF (Virtual International Authority File) is widely used for bibliographic information.

Sources of vocabulary for online risk tended to focus on cybersecurity, simply because most effort has been expended in this area. There are few ontologies on risk, but many typologies and taxonomies about risk of different types. People like Solove (2006) have categorized different types of privacy, including privacy risk, and previous work on privacy and social media identified risks and consequences (Haynes and Robinson 2015). Less-structured lists appear in other sources such as the UK Government's Online Harms White Paper (DCMS 2019). National agencies (sometimes supported by security companies) have developed lists such as the Sophos Threatsaurus (Sophos Ltd 2014) and the National Vulnerabilities Database (NIST 2019).

The opportunities for automation of this step might focus on search and retrieval. Because there are very few upper level ontologies, the opportunities for scaling effects of automation or deployment of AI techniques are limited.

5.3. Enumerate important terms

Terms derived from existing vocabularies were imported into a spreadsheet, along with definitions where available. A total of 342 terms were assessed and grouped together in categories and this helped in the development of a generic model of risk (abstract model) that can be applied to a variety of scenarios. One of the challenges is to eliminate the overlap between terms and to deal with variances in definitions. Eventually it is hoped that the abstract model of risk will be illustrated by multiple scenarios illustrating the relationships between specific threats, vulnerabilities, risks, harms and mitigating actions. Many of the highly technical terms from the National Vulnerabilities database reflected a system perspective rather than the vulnerability of individuals, and it is likely that many of these very specific terms will be weeded out of the ontology of personal online risk. The abstract model could be applied to any new concepts that the researcher becomes aware of during this project. There was some overlap between terms and some terms were very specific and not particularly helpful for providing a high-level view of the domain.

Existing ontologies represent a variety of perspectives. Even if the domains overlap, the intended audience and use of the ontology will affect definitions of concepts, their relationships to one another and their properties. Euzenat and Shvaiko (2013) surveyed 100 ontology-matching systems that were designed to get over the problem of the heterogeneity of overlapping ontologies. Most of the systems surveyed attempted to merge the terms in two input ontologies, although some dealt with multiple ontologies. The majority of systems reviewed were schema-based. This means that the schemas were compared. About a quarter were instance-based systems, more typical of an AI approach, and the remainder used mixed methods.

This step of the process was based on individual judgement on the adoption of specific terms, and was conducted as a manual exercise. Because the domain is very specific, the relevant vocabulary is likely to be small and the opportunities and benefits of a machine-learning approach may be limited. For larger vocabulary sets, it might be possible to explore the links between terms in different taxonomies and vocabularies and attempt to assess the best fit in terms of compatibility with an existing ontology or model of risk. The instance-based approach for merging ontologies needs further exploration in this project.

5.4. Define classes and class hierarchy

An initial attempt at setting up an ontology on Synaptica's Graphite system was based on a core vocabulary from the Sophos Threatsaurus. The next iteration of the design is based on a layered approach: eventually the Ontology will have three layers:

- Abstract layer – describing the nature of relationships between entities, and inferences that can be made as a result of the abstract model
- Scenario layer – specific risks are described in terms of the abstract model
- Instance layer – based on a mass of data (e.g. online reports of incidents or transaction logs) – initial set used to test the model and modify it (iterate) and then used against a larger data set to make sense of actual occurrences.

Figure 1- Layer model

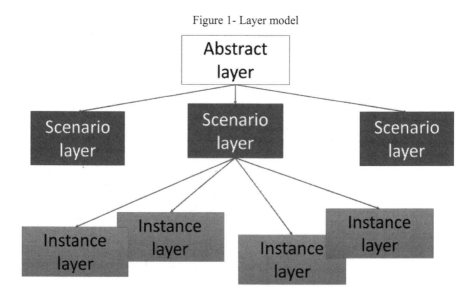

Figure 2 shows the hierarchical nature of the layer model. The scenarios are based on the concepts in the abstract model and the instance layer links specific examples of risk events to a particular scenario. The figure does not show the relationships between concepts within each scenario. So, for example, a harm such as financial loss could appear in several different scenarios. Each risk scenario could have several possible threats that could lead to the event. This project concentrated on the development of these first two layers. The instance layer will be developed in the next phase of this project.

Figure 3 shows the abstract layer in detail. This is a model of risk that will be applied to different scenarios that illustrate generic risk types. This is constructed manually and is based on human judgement.

Figure 3 - Abstract layer

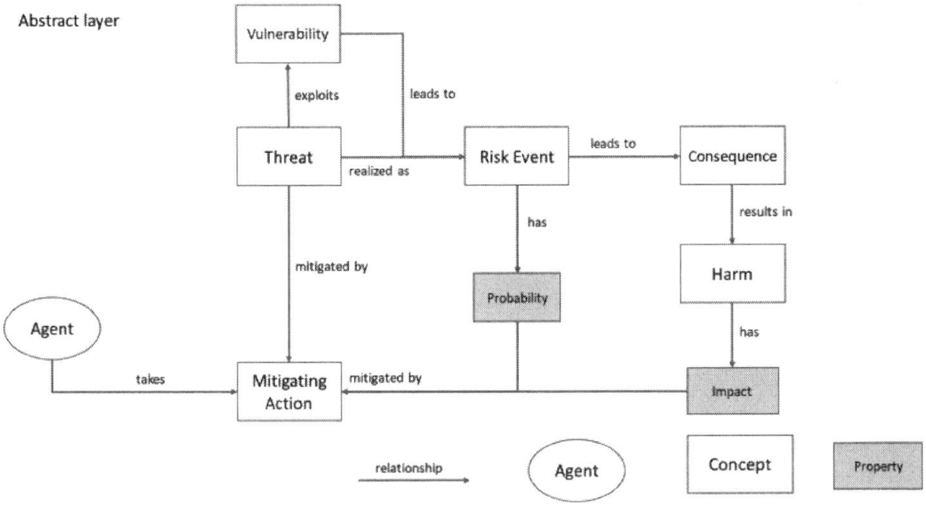

Categorization and creation of hierarchies is a human-centred activity. Neural networks and other machine-learning techniques depend on statistical approaches to cluster or link items together. The relationship between entities is not explicit and in effect by-passes this step in the process of ontology development. An alternative approach would be to use AI to interrogate a large data set to discover patterns of association between entities. To some extent the relationships, say between Threats and Harms would be opaque to a human observer, but the system might learn that a harm could be associated with several different threats and that a threat could be associated with several different harms. For instance, a phishing attempt (a threat) could lead to harms such as loss of privacy, loss of money, and time spent dealing with the consequences of stolen bank details (harms). A harm such as psychological damage might result from threats such as 'doxing', cyberbullying or a data breach.

The use of a machine-learning system which does not explicitly reveal the reasons for its decisions may be disconcerting. However, it might provide to be an effective way of identifying online risks and by association the different mitigating actions that would be appropriate. There are two challenges to be addressed in order to achieve this. Firstly, it would be necessary to find a suitable data set, such as online transactional data or network traffic data. Secondly, a machine-learning system would need to be designed in order to investigate the data set and deduce the relationships that exist between reported activities. It might eventually be possible to predict the conditions that lead to online harm.

The scenario layer is illustrated by a scenario where someone responds to a phishing email and lands on a malicious site that elicits login details for an online bank account (Figure 2). The multiple boxes represent one to many relationships. So, for instance a breach of a personal bank account could lead to several harms – only one of which is explicitly shown here. An ontology would be able to capture this network of connections and help to identify other types of association between concepts that had not been explicitly encoded by the ontology manager.

Figure 2 - Example of a risk scenario

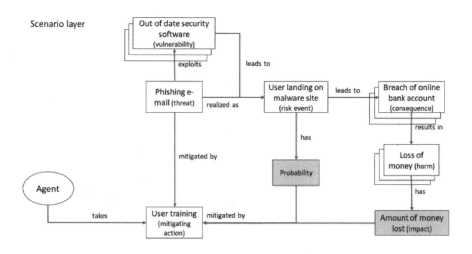

6. Discussion and conclusion
6.1 Use of AI in Ontology Creation

There was a lot of work in the early 2000s to look at ways of automating the creation of ontologies. Gómez-Pérez and Manzano-Macho (2004) identified three types of semi-automated method for ontology building: methods based on linguistics, on statistics, and on machine learning. However, they concluded that "A detailed methodology that guides the ontology learning process regardless of the source used for learning or the approach considered does not exist yet." (p207). They also concluded that human intervention is needed to evaluate ontologies developed with machine-learning techniques. In a more restricted sense Sanchez and Moreno (2004) devised a system for generating taxonomies from content on the World Wide Web. As taxonomies are important components of ontologies, this is a type of automation that could have a significant impact on ontology development. Latterly the focus has shifted towards the use of ontologies to train AI systems.

6.2 Further work

The methodology adopted for this project envisages the following additional steps to the creation of an ontology:

- Define class properties – although some initial work has been completed here e.g. risk events have a probability and harms have an impact, the properties of other concept groups has to be determined. Agents might for instance have a 'name' property that allows for agents to be organizations or people. There may be additional identifiers to uniquely identify individual people or organizations. Existing metadata standards such as schema.org and FOAF are possible sources of appropriate properties.
- Define facets of the slots
- Create instances – a specific incident identified from a transaction log for instance, or from an online resource such as reports in the press or Twitter activity around a specific incident. Further work is needed to develop a schema for linked data sets that could be interrogated using the ontology defined above. It would be interesting if there were a way of associating different types of incident via ontology rules or axioms. There may be a relationship between different scenarios that could affect which mitigating actions are taken, for instance.

6.3 Validating the ontology

Fault tree analysis and event tree analysis of different scenarios would be a start for validating the ontology. This will be conducted during the next phase of the project. This type of analysis can help to highlight inconsistencies in the scenario models and refine the models accordingly.

The ontology will be tested by applying it to online transaction logs. If it is possible to identify events such as downloading software, searching on a topic, or banking transactions, it might be possible to highlight the risks associated with each type of event. In other words, what sort of activities have risks associated with them and what is the nature of those risks?

The models will also be tested at a research seminar to be held in September 2019. Researchers active in the privacy and ontology domains will be invited to attend along with cybersecurity researchers. A series of exercises will be designed to elicit the views of participants, both individually and as a group.

6.4 The relationship between ontologies and AI

This project has identified some of the opportunities for use of AI in ontology creation, by following an established methodology for manual ontology development. At each stage of development, the potential use of AI was considered.

It has become clear that the methodology chosen for manual ontology development cannot be simply translated into an AI environment. Their ways of working are entirely different and the explicit steps to define relationships that a manual approach would require can be bypassed in a machine-learning environment. A manual approach requires explicit relationships or links between entities. These can form axioms or rules for associating specific types of entity with other types. For instance, a risk event leads to a consequence which results in a harm. A harm has the property 'impact'. In an AI system a statistical approach is used to cluster entities together without explicitly stating the relationship between them. It may have as good or better predictive power than a manual system, but it does not explain cause and effect in the way a manually-constructed ontology might. The statistical approach could be used to identify potential relationships by highlighting co-occurrence of concepts. This would allow a human ontology manager to investigate further, and if appropriate assign a relationship type to associate them with one another.

Based on the experience of building an ontology, it could be argued that humans are an essential element in the process, because they are able to define explicit relationships between entities in a way that AI does not. However, AI has a role to play in uncovering inconsistencies in the network of connections between entities and in reviewing large data sets to identify co-occurrence of entities where there may be a potential causal relationship. A variety of ontology matching techniques is reviewed by Euzenat and Shvaiko (2013), and represents one area where AI can contribute to ontology building. There remains a question of whether AI can be integrated into ontology building by identifying associations between terms through clustering and other techniques based on knowledge graphs, linked data and the semantic web.

One of the reasons for the recent resurgence of interest in ontologies is the current high profile of AI. Ontologies provide one means of priming machine-learning systems so that they can start to 'make sense' of the data that they process. It also provides a framework for the development of new rules or axioms that predict future behaviour or inform automated decision-making. Whether it will contribute to autonomous intelligence in the future or even machine consciousness remains to be seen.

Acknowledgement
This research was supported by the Royal Academy of Engineering and the Office of the Chief Science Adviser for National Security under the UK Intelligence Community Postdoctoral Fellowship Programme (Grant No. ICRF1718\1\54). The Graphite system used to develop the ontology was provided by Synaptica Ltd.

References
Arp, Robert, Barry Smith, and Andrew D. Spear. 2015. *Building Ontologies with Basic Formal Ontology*. Cambridge, MA: MIT Press.

Aven, Terje, and Ortwin Renn. 2009. "On Risk Defined as an Event Where the Outcome Is Uncertain." *Journal of Risk Research* 12 (1): 1–11.

Basel University Library. 2017. *Basel Register of Thesauri, Ontologies and Classifications*. 2017. https://bartoc.org/.

DCMS. 2019. *Online Harms White Paper. London*. https://doi.org/978-1-5286-1080-3.

Draghici, Anca, and George Draghici. 2013. "Cross-Disciplinary Approach for the Risk Assessment Ontology Design." *Information Resources Management Journal* 26 (1): 37–53.

European Parliament, and European Council. 2016. *General Data Protection Regulation - EU 2016/679*. EU: OJ L 119 04.05.2016 pp1-88.

Freund, Jack, and Jack Jones. 2015. *Measuring and Managing Information Risk: A FAIR Approach*. Oxford, UK: Butterworth-Heinemann.

Gómez-Pérez, David, and Asuncion Manzano-Macho. 2004. "An Overview of Methods and Tools for Ontology Learning from Texts." *The Knowledge Engineering Review* 19 (3): 187–212.

Haynes, David, and Lyn Robinson. 2015. "Defining User Risk in Social Networking Services." *Aslib Journal of Information Management* 67 (1): 94–115.

Hubbard, Douglas W. 2009. *The Failure of Risk Management: Why It's Broken and How to Fix It.* Hoboken, NJ: John Wiley & Sons, Inc.

Mazri, Chabane. 2017. "(Re) Defining Emerging Risks." *Risk Analysis* 37(11): 2053–65.

Niles, Ian, and Adam Pease. 2001. "Towards a Standard Upper Ontology." In *Proceedings of the International Conference on Formal Ontology in Information Systems - Volume 2001*, 2–9. FOIS '01. New York, NY, USA: ACM.

NIST. 2019. *National Vulnerability Database.* 2019. https://nvd.nist.gov/.

Noy, N. F., and D. L. McGuinness. 2001. *Ontology Development 101: A Guide to Creating Your First Ontology.* Stanford CA. https://protege.stanford.edu/publications/ontology_development/ontology101.pdf.

Pease, Adam. 2011. *Ontology: A Practical Guide.* Angwin, CA: Articulate Software Press.

Rutherford Appleton Laboratory. 2015. *The Alvey Programme.* 2015. http://www.chilton-computing.org.uk/inf/alvey/overview.htm.

Sánchez, D, and A Moreno. 2004. "Automatic Generation of Taxonomies from the WWW." In *Practical Aspects of Knowledge Management. Lecture Notes in Computer Science*, Vol 3336, edited by D Karagiannis and U Reimer, 208–19.

Sarjant, S, C Legg, M Robinson, and O Medelyan. 2009. "'All You Can Eat' Ontology-Building: Feeding Wikipedia to Cyc." In *Proceedings of the 2009 IEEE/WIC/ACM International Joint Conference on Web Intelligence and Intelligent Agent Technology*, edited by Paolo Boldi, Giuseppe Vizzari, Gabriella Pasi, and Ricardo Baeza-Yates, 341–48. Milan: IEEE Computer Society.

Solove, Daniel J. 2006. "A Taxonomy of Privacy." *University of Pennsylvania Law Review* 154 (3): 477–564. https://doi.org/10.2307/40041279.

Sophos Ltd. 2014. *Threatsaurus: The A-Z of Computer and Data Security Threat.* Oxford.

Yang, Seungwon, and Mohamed Magdy Gharib Farag. 2014. "Ontologies." In *Digital Library Technologies*, edited by Edward A Fox and Ricardo da Silva Torres, 63–88. Morgan & Claypool Publishers.

Zhou, Lihong, Ana Vasconcelos, and Miguel Nunes. 2008. "Supporting Decision Making in Risk Management through an Evidence-Based Information Systems Project Risk Checklist." *Information Management & Computer Security* 16 (2): 166–86.

Human-In-The-Loop Topic Modelling: Assessing topic labelling and genre-topic relations with a movie plot summary corpus

Paul Matthews, UWE Bristol, UK

Abstract

A much-used but not yet mainstream text analysis approach, topic modelling supports the identification of lexical themes for a document collection. Against principles for interpretable AI and sociotechnical design, there are definite strengths from its speed and ability to discover structure, but there remain challenges in how results can be interpreted, whether this be by analysts, domain experts, or potential end users. Automated coherence and labelling measures go some of the way toward bridging the understanding and trust gap, and user empowerment through visualisation and design intervention is starting to show how the remaining ground might be made up. This study uses topic modelling on a corpus of Wikipedia movie summaries to illustrate challenges and potential. Topic labelling for naive users was found to be easy in only a quarter of cases, and difficulty increased markedly with 100 topics compared to 50. While automated measures suggested 88 topics, the number manageable by users was closer to 50. The unsupervised topic model was compared to the movie genre labels and indicated that the two might work together well to complement genres, match content across genre and highlight within-genre variability. It is suggested that unsupervised models might work better for creativity and discovery than semi-supervised versions.

1. Introduction

Topic modelling is a machine learning technique for inferring structure across a corpus of documents by detecting a number of characteristic topics each containing clusters of typical words. While a range of approaches and accompanying algorithms now exist, many of those used are based upon the modelling part being "unsupervised", that is the lexical patterns across documents are detected without reference to any prior human- or content-determined constraints. This has both pitfalls and advantages. A naive clustering fails to take account of prior knowledge about the material and about other metadata that can have a clear bearing on its topical variability. Also, being purely statistically-driven, the method can lead to results that are hard for humans to interpret as resulting topics do not necessarily correspond to coherent concepts or add value to an analysis (Bakharia et al. 2016). That said, the approach can be seen in some ways to be objective and to have the potential to uncover useful hidden patterns which might be exploited to improve classification, discovery or theory-building.

The utility of topic models stems from the property that the inferred hidden structure resembles the thematic structure of the collection. This interpretable hidden structure annotates each document in the collection—a task that is painstaking to perform by hand—and these annotations can be used to aid tasks like information retrieval, classification, and corpus exploration. In this way, topic modeling provides an algorithmic solution to managing, organizing, and annotating large archives of texts. (Blei 2012)

As a "bag of words" approach that focuses on word occurrence and usually ignores word order (Blei 2012), topic modelling has been seen as too scattergun by linguists:

The value of the technique for genuine discourse analysis is thus very limited because the 'topics' are either too general or too incoherent to be useful (Brezina 2018)

This paper will elaborate on some of the tensions described above and the ways in which they are being explored by bringing humans and prior knowledge together with the algorithmic results. Decisions such as the number of topics to detect, the labelling of topics and correspondence to human categorisation will be illustrated with reference to a labelled corpus of film plot summaries from Wikipedia.

1.1 Topic model algorithms and typology

Topic models assume that the documents in a corpus contain a number of discoverable topics, and that those topics are distributed across the corpus in certain proportions (Figure 1). The topics themselves are a probability distribution of words, where a high probability of appearing in the topic make it a characteristic or "key" word for that topic. One of the classic processes in the field, Latent Dirichlet Allocation (LDA) (Blei, Ng, and Jordan 2003), starts by assuming the above and that the words and topics have an estimable distribution. A number of algorithms can then be used to build the posterior likelihoods of words being associated with topics and topics with documents. As an unsupervised model, usually the only inputs to LDA are the number of topics one wants to identify (the K value), and some "hyperparameters" that encapsulate some a priori assumptions or goals for the resulting topic and document assignments. The result of a model run is a list of documents with their topic distributions, and a list of topics with their word distributions.

While already having a good deal of power in surfacing lexical themes from text, the LDA algorithm has been developed in a number of ways for specific applications and to address certain limitations. The problem of not knowing the optimal topic number, for example, was addressed through the development of the Hierarchical Dirichlet Process (HDP) model, which adds a slot for the topic number and outputs this together with word-topic and topic-document distributions. Notably, the process for optimising the topic number is based on lexical features rather than any particular user goals. A different hierarchical approach (hLDA) is used to progressively output increasing number of topics with each run.

Figure 1: Topics built up from word distributions in a document set (Blei 2012)

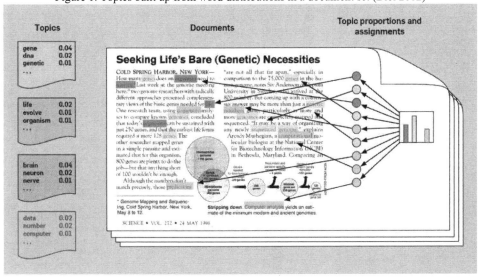

A further family of models make use of metadata and prior knowledge to guide the process. The labelled LDA, the author-topic model and an increasing number of domain-specific models do this by having the LDA as just one subsystem within the model. These are therefore semi-supervised models as they provide as guidance some labelled training examples of different document types. The Stuctural Topic Model (STM) (M. E. Roberts, Stewart, and Tingley 2018; Roberts et al. 2013) is used in the analysis for this study and enables both pure unsupervised modelling and also the analysis and visualisation of interactions between metadata and topic distributions.

So, while more "supervised" versions of topic modelling exist, this paper will focus largely on the unsupervised versions, in order to better draw out the pitfalls and potential advantages for human users and to compare the results with categories applied by people to document collections.

1.2 Interpretable AI and human factors computing

Artificial intelligence and specific machine-learning approaches are often criticised for their opacity of operation and the lack of human agency involved. Doshi-Velez and Kim (2017) argue that machine- learning explanation is needed when algorithmic and application-oriented objectives are not aligned, or there is a need for decisions to be made over the trade-offs between such objectives. They provide a continuum of evaluation approaches toward interpretability that range from formal proxy tasks not involving users, through the use of simplified tasks for real users to test, to the most desirable approach of real humans using the technology for real tasks (figure 2), though cost and time increase along this continuum.

Figure 2: Taxonomy of evaluation approaches for interpretable AI (Doshi-Velez and Kim 2017)

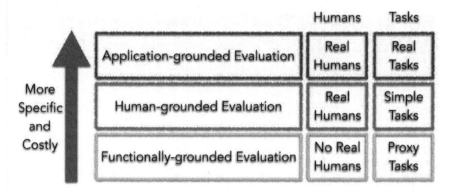

For humans to work effectively with AI-based tools, it is important to develop design guidelines aimed at optimising the mutual relationship. Read et al (2015) sought to develop design principles for systems based on a unification of sociotechnical systems theory and cognitive work analysis. Their derived methodological attributes were ranked by subject matter experts and the top seven resulting attributes were: creative, holistic, structured, efficient, iterative, integrated and valid. Systems need to provide scope for opportunistic and exploratory analysis. The outputs need to justify the expenditure of time and energy. System design should be coherent, with structures enabling communication and means-end accountability. At the same time systems should accommodate changes over time as understanding grows.

1.3 Functional evaluation: Automated measures
At the automated end of topic model evaluation, approaches started at the model-centric level but have moved more recently toward measures which better approximate human judgement. For some time the standard evaluation methods for topic modelling was "held out likelihood" (or log-likelihood), wherein a subset of documents which were not used to train the model were used to predict topical composition. A "perplexity" metric can then be used to score how well the existing model fits these new texts. This tends to give a lower score for higher numbers of topics which provide a closer fit to the training set. However, it does not correspond well to interpretability and may in fact be antagonistic to human understanding (Jacobi, Van Atteveldt, and Welbers 2016).

Coherence is a more recent and important interpretability metric for topics (Röder, Both and Hinneburg 2015). A popular method of evaluating coherence is pointwise mutual information (PMI), which scores words within a resulting topic according to their likelihood of co-occurrence in a reference corpus such as Wikipedia (or within the corpus text itself). The overall coherence of a topic is then a sum of these scores. The score may be further improved by normalisation to a score in the range from -1 to 1, where -1 means the words are never found together and 1 means they always are.

While coherence may tend toward more homogeneous topics, other metrics such as FREX can be used to rate the exclusivity of topics based on the mean of composite word exclusivity and frequency (M. E. Roberts, Stewart, and Tingley 2018). This is quite an important balancing metric as the topic modeller usually wants the topics to be in some way distinctive.

1.4 Human evaluation: which humans and where in the loop?
People may be involved in the topic modelling process at generation, evaluation and end use stages. At the generation stage, the typical actor is the data scientist / information specialist who has access to, and an understanding of the data, tools and methods needed to run the model. Modelling consists of importing text into the corpus, some processing and preparation of the text and then fitting the model (Figure 3). There are then some further steps to evaluate, understand and visualise the model output.

Further evaluation may take place with people, where evaluators might be subject matter experts or more general users. The same groups may then form the intended target audience for the product or service that the model is applied to, although often modelling is done only during a research project and not implemented in consumer products or services.

In practice, generation and evaluation usually proceed iteratively, with repeated runs of the modelling process based on an evaluation of the results. The data scientist and domain expert may be part a research team working together on this. With large data sets, the model runs may take some time (as the algorithms are themselves iterating over the documents repeatedly to derive topics) and this stage forms something of a black box, as most algorithms do not have the ability to absorb parameter changes during a run, though with some flavours of algorithm the analyst can provide a priori constraints as to how words and topics are treated (Bakharia et al. 2016).

Figure 3: Steps in a topic modelling workflow (M Roberts, Stewart, and Tingley 2018)

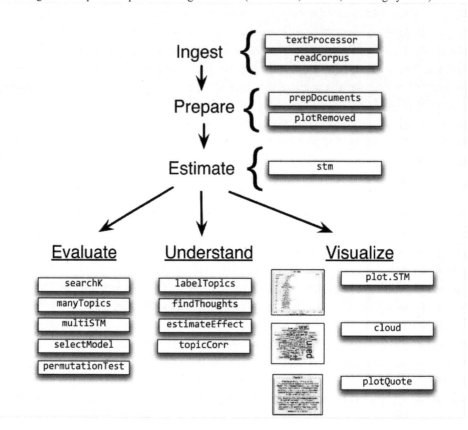

A further, though more indirect, way of combining prior domain knowledge comes though combining modelling outputs with human-generated metadata or document labels. This provides some triangulation between the human and machine classifications and is where interesting insights can be obtained. Such labels may be incorporated into the model a priori as a semi-supervised aspect or compared a posteriori after modelling. In some ways, as the work reported below suggests, the post-hoc analysis might be more interesting, as incorporating prior knowledge into the model at the start may bias it toward expected outcomes.

The majority of topic model-based studies in the literature, such as those in Table 1, use automated evaluation measures such as those described in the previous section. Lee et al (2017) however provide a rare attempt to bridge the gap between machine-based topic building and human interpretability and usefulness. They provided a custom interface to non-specialist users to evaluate 20 and 30 topics and document allocations on a corpus of newspaper articles, with the option to select refinement operations on the results. They found that the most common desirable operations were to remove words from topics, to remove documents from topics, and to change the order of words appearing in topics. Notably, with the first two operations evaluators tended to pick lower probability words and documents, indicating some implicit agreement with the machine-based ranking. In another study of more interactive modelling algorithms, Bakharia et al (2016) noted that the "Topic Creation Rule" was most widely applied by users, allowing them to supply seed words for new topics of interest to their analysis.

1.5 Visualisation for understanding and interaction

While the immediate output of a topic model process are matrices of probability assignments for words and topics, these are not useful or easily interpretable by humans. Work has therefore been required to provide visual summaries of the model outputs to enable evaluation and action by users. Many visualisation interfaces are part of relatively ephemeral research projects, but some are available within open source ecosystems.

The "Termite" tool (Chuang et al 2012) enabled visualisation of term salience (filtering out less informative terms within a topic) and seriation (better highlighting of clustered key terms in a topic). An example is shown in Figure 4. LDAExplore, presented by Ganesan et al (2015) enabled the visualisation of word and topic distributions via interactive graphs and treemaps. Users could filter on and examine topics alongside their representative documents and keywords. A small-scale evaluation indicated that the visualisations improved understanding of the keyword composition of topics. Another tool, LDAvis (Sievert and Shirley 2015), works with the R statistical programming environment and, like the other tools above, works with the output of an LDA modelling run. It provides ways to view the relative size of topics and inter-topic distance, measured as Jensen-Shannon divergence. It also provides a view of representative terms for a topic, and these are ranked both by probability and the use of the "lift" weighting that promotes less common terms characteristic of the topic (Figure 5). LDAvis also allows topics to be clustered to help make sense of a model using larger numbers of topics. A further R tool, stmInsights (Schwemmer 2018), used in the analysis below, takes the output of Structural Topic Modelling (STM) and provides several sense-making and visualisation functions. These include topic labelling, topic distributions and visualisation of model diagnostics and effects.

Figure 4: Termite term comparison (Chuang, Manning, and Heer 2012)

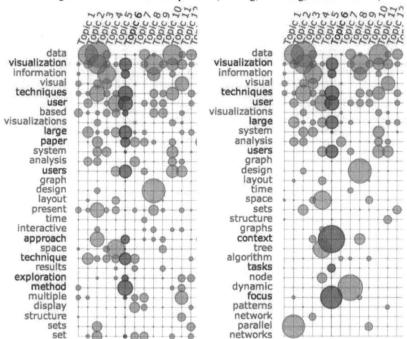

All of the above techniques are post hoc and do not allow the user to affect the actual topic modelling process, only to better understand the results. It is much harder for human interactions to feed back into the algorithm as it is running. That said, recent work by El-assady and colleagues (2019) provides some interesting approaches into how this might be achieved. They use "speculative execution" and model quality feedback from the user to influence and predict the affects of alterations to the topic clusters produced with a hierarchical topic model (Figure 6). Their analytics dashboard allows the user to step through the model run and make alterations or view the affect of alterations on the model quality.

Figure 5: LDAvis topic relationships (left) and term distributions (right) (Sievert and Shirley 2015)

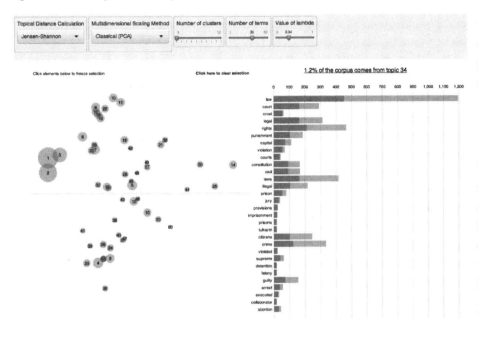

Figure 6: Visual analytics workspace for user-led hierarchical modelling (El-assady et al. 2019)

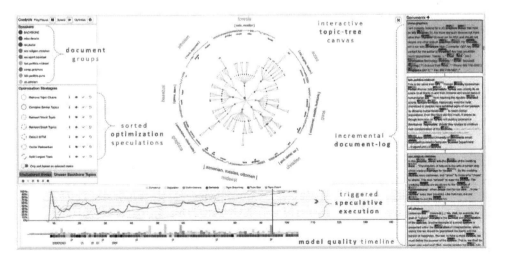

1.6 Human-grounded decisions and evaluation
1.6.1 Topic numbers

As mentioned above, the choice of topic numbers (commonly denoted as the K value) is often a tradeoff between model accuracy and human interpretability. As with other unsupervised methods, the received wisdom is that there is no "correct number" as this is an application and context-dependent issue (M. E. Roberts, Stewart, and Tingley 2018). In a sample of recent studies, researchers have tended to select a relatively small K of 10-50, independent of corpus size (Table 1).

Table 1: Comparison of recent studies showing topic numbers, model types and validation approaches

Reference	Application	No. of Documents	No. of Topics	Method	Evaluation
Park et al (2017)	Medical prescriptions	180,000 and 2,000,000	15	Extended LDA (with diagnosis and medication)	Perplexity (5-fold Cross validation)
Wang et al (2017)	Herbal Medicine Cases	3800	Not selected (though ~60 optimal from evaluation)	LDA v Extended LDA (with symptoms and herbs)	Perplexity
Giaquinto2018 & Banerjee (2018)	Personal medical journals	9,010,623 journals written by 200,388 authors	50 (15 author personas)	Rapid Dynamic Author-Persona (DAP), compared to other methods	Per-word log likelihood
Ren et al (2016)	Suicide blogs	907	Unclear: top 20 reported (5 emotion intensities)	CET – Topics + emotion and emotion intensities	Perplexity
Lee & Kang (2018)	Journal articles	12000	50	LDA	Subjective
Grajzl & Murrwll (2018)	Bacon's works	282	16	STM	Held-out likelihood, coherence, exclusivity
Faisal & Petoniemi (2018)	Video games wikis	15000	31	Multitask, Non parametric LDA	
Pomeda et al (2018)	Interviews	25	10	LDA	

Arnold et al (2016) found 100 topics to work best on a word intrusion-based evaluation for specialists and non-specialists on their corpus of medical reports. While claiming that a greater number of topics allows more interesting topics to emerge, Lee and Kang settled on a relatively conservative 50 (Lee and Kang 2018)

1.6.2 Topic interpretability, coherence and labelling

The word intrusion method has been used to good effect to evaluate topic interpretability (Lau, Newman, and Baldwin 2014). Here, an intruder term is added to the top words for a topic and a human evaluator is asked to identify words that appear out of place. The successful identification of intruders is an (indirect) indication of the coherence of the remaining topic terms.

Topic coherence evaluation on topic models of medical reports by Arnold et al (2016) showed that clinical experts (primary care physicians) performed better than students at identifying mismatched words and topics, indicating for the authors that the models were successfully capturing specialised concepts that the subject experts were better at identifying. The authors note that the system was still far from complete in being able to flexibly absorb new documents with new potential topics, where relearning would be needed.

Whilst topic intrusion was designed as a human-oriented evaluation measure, Lau et al (2014) show that this approach can be successfully used as a machine-learning task to predict which words are likely to be detected as intruders, given a labelled training set and the ability to automate coherence measures using pointwise mutual information (PMI) and conditional probability (CP). For the PMI measure, the topic terms are compared to a reference corpus, but for CP the coherence can be calculated from the documents being used to generate the model. Lau et al also noted that the correlations between human judgements of overall topic coherence and word intrusion are only mild, revealing subtle differences in how the tasks are approached.

Selection of labels is another task that can be fully human-controlled, machine-assisted or machine-determined. "Eyeballing" is perhaps most commonly used (Morstatter, Rey, and Ave 2018), whereby labels are selected by the user / analyst based on a visual inspection of the most common words for a topic. This is nevertheless considered a non-trivial task (Lee and Kang 2018) and in their work these authors used expert consensus to derive agreed labels, where 39 of 50 proved easy but the remaining 11 required "in-depth discussion". In tools such as STM, the most common words can be accompanied by the most exclusive words to give an idea of the distinctiveness of the topic. Machine-oriented approaches include choosing hypernyms and representative words from the topic terms or comparing the terms using reference knowledgebases or ontologies (Boyd-graber, Mimno, and Hu 2017)

2. Analysis using the movie summaries corpus

What do topics mean to a naive audience and how (easily) do they label them? What size of K provides the most useful output for a given corpus? How does unsupervised topic output relate to received and widely-used and shared human-generated categories? In order to investigate these questions, the following section outlines the application of topic modelling to a corpus of movie plot summaries.

2.1 Dataset

In order to combine unsupervised modelling with a posteriori analysis, a labelled dataset was used. This was the CMU Movie Summaries corpus from Carnegie Mellon University (Bamman, O'Connor, and Smith 2013, 2014). This consists of movie plot summaries (1900-2014) from Wikipedia together with matched movie and character metadata from Freebase (now part of Wikidata). Once imported and cleaned, there were 42,206 records in the dataset, though for some of the analysis this was further subsetted or sampled as mentioned below.

2.2 Methods

The dataset was imported into R and topic models were developed using the STM (M Roberts, Stewart, and Tingley 2018) package. The standard workflow recommended by the STM documentation (M Roberts, Stewart, and Tingley 2018) was followed, with text processing followed by document preparation before modelling commenced. At the processing step, a custom name filter was applied to remove as many first names as possible, as these were found to lead to a number of "junk" topics based around names. The first names were retrieved from the dataset of US baby names 1880-2008 (Wickham 2009) and the top 0.05% and above used as the filter list. At the document preparation step, a lower threshold of ten-word occurrences across the corpus was used in order to make the processing more efficient.

To investigate automated topic interpretability measures, two modelling runs were used, firstly with K = 20, 30, 50, 100 and 200 with a random subsample of 1000 movie plots (for K diagnostics, below), then topic models with K = 0, 20, 30, 50 and 100 were generated for the entire corpus for the user testing and genre analysis (200 proved too computationally expensive). The STM default (spectral initialisation) was used, with a maximum iteration of 75 per model. Hyperparameters were set as default. The zero K option is particular to the STM package and enables an estimate of optimal topic numbers using dimensionality reduction on the word co-occurrence matrix followed by an algorithm to find the minimum number of points to encompass this reduction (M Roberts, Stewart, and Tingley 2018).

For user evaluation, generated topics at each level of K from 20-100 were presented to users on the Amazon Mechanical Turk platform, with the top 12 most probable words from each topic being presented to 3 distinct evaluators. People were asked to provide a label that best represented the group of words in the topic and then to rate how easy they found the topic to label (from 1-very easy to 6-impossible). They were advised that the label could be one of the topic words if that represented the group well, otherwise it could be their own word or short phrase. They were allowed to use the label "impossible" if they could not see any link between the terms. Evaluators were not made aware that the words came from movie summaries in order not to bias the results toward established movie genre terminology.

For investigation of genres and their relation to output topic distributions, modelling output (the theta distribution corresponding to the proportion of each topic predicted for the document or movie) was joined back to the movie metadata. In most cases the K=50 model run was used for this analysis.

3. Results
3.1 Automated interpretability and number of topics
The STM diagnostics allow the comparison of models for topic semantic coherence and exclusivity (Figure 6). Semantic coherence is related to how often words appear together in the same source document and tends to increase when there are fewer topics with more common words. Exclusivity is calculated from a weighted mean of the constituent words' frequency and exclusivity (ie. tending to appear in only one topic). Figure 7 clearly illustrates the nature of the tradeoff in terms of topic numbers, with a reasonable optimal estimate being between 50 and 100 topics, where there is still good coherence but topics are also sufficiently different to be useful.

Figure 7: Topic coherence and exclusivity for different K

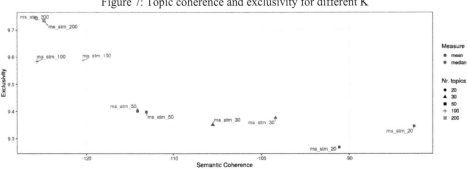

This was supported by the K=0 modelling run mentioned above, where K is estimated based on the dimensionality of the document-term matrix. This indicated a K of 88, within this range.

3.2 Topic labelling

Evaluators found most of the topics of average difficulty to label. Of those judged very difficult or impossible, more came from the K=100 set, with K=20 containing the fewest (Table 2)

Table 2: Topic labelling - percentage of topics judged to be hard or impossible to label

Topics	Labelling - % hard or impossible
20	12.963
30	18.391
50	14.074
100	23.273

At the other end of the difficulty spectrum, there was less differentiation in the ease of labelling across K (Table 3), though K=30 was marginally reported as the easiest.

Table 3: Topic labelling - percentage of topics judged to be easy or very easy to label

Topics	Labelling - % easy or very easy
20	25.926
30	24.138
50	28.889
100	27.636

Table 4 shows some examples of topics that were classed as relatively easy to label, together with the labels applied by different evaluators. While we see quite good agreement in labels, there is clearly variability in the emphasis given to the topic terms by evaluators (particularly in the second topic, labeled as "hobbies", "writing" and "work" respectively).

Table 4: Examples of topics judged to be easy to label, with labels suggested

Topics	No.	Keywords	Difficulty (1=very easy, 6=impossible)	Label
20	1	war, soldier, armi, american, german, men, kill, forc, unit, general, order, british	2	world war II
20	1	war, soldier, armi, american, german, men, kill, forc, unit, general, order, british	2	war
20	1	war, soldier, armi, american, german, men, kill, forc, unit, general, order, british	3	World war

Topics	No.	Keywords	Difficulty (1=very easy, 6=impossible)	Label
20	2	book, max, letter, write, read, paint, jenni, find, publish, tell, art, work	3	hobbies
20	2	book, max, letter, write, read, paint, jenni, find, publish, tell, art, work	2	writing
20	2	book, max, letter, write, read, paint, jenni, find, publish, tell, art, work	3	work
20	3	school, student, high, teacher, colleg, class, friend, girl, univers, parti, becom, professor	3	college
20	3	school, student, high, teacher, colleg, class, friend, girl, univers, parti, becom, professor	3	school
20	3	school, student, high, teacher, colleg, class, friend, girl, univers, parti, becom, professor	3	teachers and education
20	4	ship, island, captain, boat, crew, sea, water, find, gold, rescu, take, fish	3	maritime
20	4	ship, island, captain, boat, crew, sea, water, find, gold, rescu, take, fish	3	being on sea
20	4	ship, island, captain, boat, crew, sea, water, find, gold, rescu, take, fish	3	Ships

In Table 5 are some examples of topics that evaluators found very difficult or impossible to label. Here, topics seemed to be more likely to contain noise from character names used disproportionally highly in the dataset. Interestingly, even topics containing some linked terms e.g. topic 13, containing "magic", "witch" and "spell" was judged by one evaluator as impossible, perhaps due to the distraction of the names and verbs also in the topic keywords.

Table 5: Examples of topics judged to be difficult or impossible to label, with labels suggested (or 'impossible' if no suggestion feasible)

Topics	No.	Keywords	Difficulty (1=very easy, 6=impossible)	Label
20	6	love, get, marri, come, father, take, son, fall, friend, kill, meet, villag	6	Dramatic relationships
20	10	dave, camp, lake, ted, buddi, find, phil, get, josh, willi, ned, elli	6	Camping
20	12	tell, get, leav, see, back, say, car, ask, find, hous, goe, call	5	commands and places
20	13	magic, castl, simon, stone, find, witch, sir, back, franki, return, spell, take	7	impossible
20	14	dog, get, back, bug, cat, run, tri, see, fall, head, come, tree	6	Pets and outdoors

Topics	No.	Keywords	Difficulty (1=very easy, 6=impossible)	Label
20	16	king, babi, queen, princ, princess, tell, take, find, love, palac, lord, duke	7	impossible
20	17	alien, earth, plane, fli, use, crash, destroy, space, pilot, one, control, bomb	5	strome
30	1	van, miller, mile, junior, nina, willi, pink, davi, anderson, ransom, panther, bishop	5	Character names
30	1	van, miller, mile, junior, nina, willi, pink, davi, anderson, ransom, panther, bishop	7	impossible
30	1	van, miller, mile, junior, nina, willi, pink, davi, anderson, ransom, panther, bishop	6	people
30	2	max, freddi, abbi, puppet, neil, tell, mauric, valentin, lenni, philipp, hugo, alli	7	impossible
30	2	max, freddi, abbi, puppet, neil, tell, mauric, valentin, lenni, philipp, hugo, alli	7	impossible

3.3 Correspondence to received genres

As documents are considered to be composed of a combination of topics derived from the unsupervised process, we can see how the results compare to general category groupings, notably the genre to which the film has been assigned in Wikipedia. Most of the films in the dataset were associated with at least one genre, many with several, with overall 363 genres used in the dataset. That said, many were quite niche with only a few films assigned to them.

Taking the learned document-topic distribution matrix (theta) for the K=50 model, we clustered the matrix into 20 centres using K-means. This results in 20 distinct topic combinations for the full movie corpus. These were then compared to the top (32) movie genres and visualised as a heat map (Figure 8). Here, a high value or deep colour indicates that a large number of films in that cluster were associated with a particular genre.

Taken together, the results show that the topic signatures of the clusters correspond quite well to the genres. For many genres there is a distinct cluster associated. This is especially the case were the topic is likely to have quite distinctive associated vocabulary (e.g. science fiction). The heatmap also identifies genres where there are no particular distinct topic signatures (e.g. world cinema, film adaptation) and that intuitively tallies with the knowledge that these are somewhat "catch-all" genres.

Figure 8: Heat map of topic clusters by genre (topic model K=50, k-means=20)

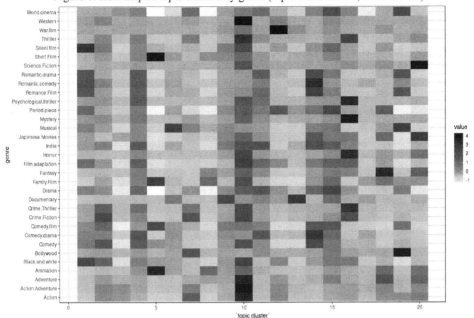

By visualising the distribution of films over topics for a particular genre, we are able to see "typical" or "prototypical" examples of a genre, together with outliers which might be either misclassified or to some extent "genre busters". Figure 9, for instance, visualised the topic distributions for westerns, with two examples highlighted: *A Fistful of Dollars*, perhaps a classic example of a western, and *Brokeback Mountain*, a potential genre buster which was criticised following its release for being stereotypically characterised as a "gay cowboy movie", this characterisation detracting from its importance as a standalone work (Spohrer 2009). We see from Figure 9 that *A Fistful of Dollars* is itself an outlier, on topic 46 (perhaps due to its Mexican focus) and topic 9 (it does contain an excessive amount of shooting). *Brokeback Mountain* is also an outlier on a number of topics, notably topics 19, 30 and 45 (relationship and romance-related). It is in the bottom quartile for the leading topic of westerns overall (topic 42). It is fairly median for violence on topic 9, though notably the violence in the film is directed toward the main characters as homosexuals rather than being instigated by them (Wikipedia 2019).

Figure 9: Topic distribution for the 'Western' Genre with two instances compared

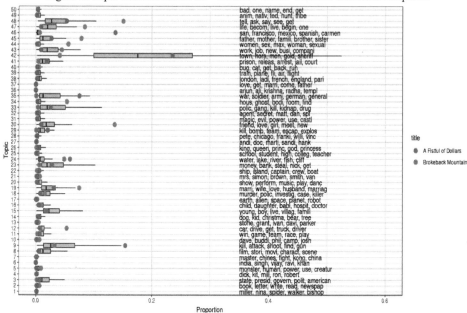

Another interesting aspect is that new genres emerge over time despite earlier works being very much in the mold. Thereafter, movies are made with the specific genre in mind. Road movies are one example of such a genre (Hurault-Paupe 2015). Figure 10 shows the topic distributions for road movies in the corpus. We see a characteristic emphasis on roads and transport (topic 12) but also on relationships (30) and aspects of self-actualisation (topic 47).

Figure 10: Topic distribution for the 'Road movie' Genre

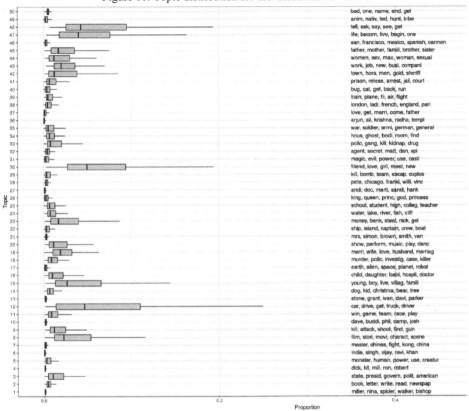

The time-bound and perhaps quite flexible assignation of movies to the "Road movie" genre provides potential to identify works that contain these elements, but which have not been explicitly labelled as such. We might define a prototypical movie as the median topic distribution for the genre, with distance from the median calculated as a squared difference weighted by the topic proportion. To remove the effect of short summaries, we only include summaries of 4000 characters or more. Table 6 shows the most prototypical examples of the genre in the left column with other films from the corpus in the right column that have not been explicitly labelled with the genre. Many of these are closer to the median distribution than the road movies themselves. While some time would be needed to ascertain whether these truly qualify as road movies, some have clear elements of travel and transport as well as self-actualisation, though others have been identified by virtue of multiple mentions of motorcycles, cars and diners.

Table 6: Road movies - labelled and unlabelled candidates

In road movie genre	Distance from median	Not in genre	Distance
My Name is Khan	0.000	Gadar: Ek Prem Katha	0.000
O Brother, Where Art Thou?	0.000	Alien from L.A.	0.000
A Canterbury Tale	0.000	The Stepford Children	0.000
Little Miss Sunshine	0.000	Arthur and the Vengeance of Maltazard	0.000
Blues Brothers 2000	0.000	Wake in Fright	0.000
Singh Is Kinng	0.000	Hum Ek Hain	0.000
The Last Detail	0.000	Kim Possible: A Sitch in Time	0.000
Space Truckers	0.000	Cat's Eye	0.000
Sullivan's Travels	0.000	Just Imagine	0.000
Five Dollars a Day	0.001	The Petrified Forest	0.000
The Darjeeling Limited	0.001	Stand by Me	0.000
Cannonball Run II	0.001	The Business	0.000
To Wong Foo, Thanks for Everything! Julie Newmar	0.001	Role Models	0.000
The Brave Little Toaster	0.001	My Beautiful Laundrette	0.000
Adventures of Power	0.001	Passion Play	0.000
The Motorcycle Diaries	0.001	Handle With Care	0.000
Tashan	0.001	Highlander	0.000
Kabul Express	0.001	Epic Movie	0.000
Until the End of the World	0.001	The Happening	0.000
Serving Sara	0.001	Garfield: The Movie	0.000

3.4 Further analysis using covariates and visualisation

As was indicated by the human evaluation task, topic labelling is not straightforward or necessarily intuitive. For movie plot summaries it nonetheless tended to group themes relating to activities and settings. This has the interesting side effect of identifying significant action sequences that may be outside the genre classification. Figure 10, below, shows the topic distribution for *Bridget Jones's Diary* (labels by author, K=20, random sample of 1000 movies). The topics were labelled using the STMInsights package (Schwemmer 2018), which shows examples of document instances with high proportions of that topic. As the "Rocky" topic was mostly inspired by the Rocky series it was so named. Nevertheless, there is a pivotal fight scene in Bridget Jones between the two male protagonists, played by Colin Firth and Hugh Grant. This example indicates the potential of this approach to provide content-based visualisation and also perhaps could be used for recommendation (e.g. "show me romantic comedies with a bit of fighting!").

Figure 11: Topic proportions for Bridget Jones' Diary

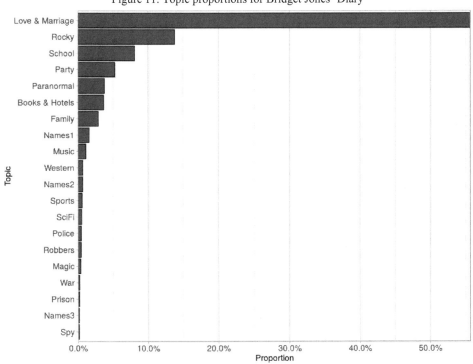

Covariates can be applied before or after modelling and can indicate patterns and temporal trends in topic distribution of use to the human analyst. In the examples shown in Figures 12 and 13, two author-named topics are visualised with corpus prevalence over time (K=20, random sample of 1000 movies). The graphs show the growth in the party topic over time and the relative shrinkage of the war topic in the sample with time. Certainly, for the movie corpus represented on Wikipedia at least, then, there is some indication that hedonistic themes may be overtaking warfare-related themes.

Figure 12: Changes in 'War' topic over time

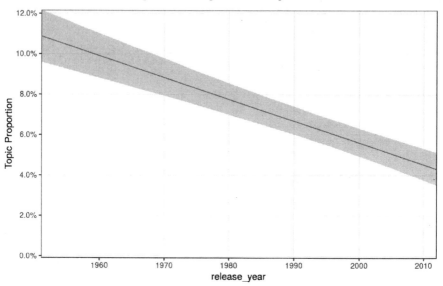

Figure 13: Changes in 'Party' topic over time

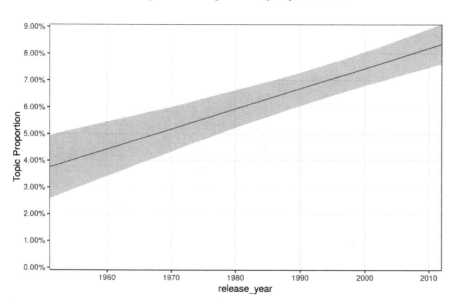

4. Discussion

In terms of the interpretability levels of Doshi-Velez and Kim (2017, Figure 2), topic modelling to date is often confined to the first two, certainly in machine-learning and computer science literature. The role of human evaluation is often to develop or validate automated evaluation metrics or is confined to discrete research studies. Information analysts, domain experts and general users tend to be progressively more shielded from the modelling process, though the review of recent work above does suggest some interesting ways forward. In terms of the analyst/researcher this means more control over model parameters and better understanding of the implications of model choice. For users more generally, this may mean the ability to take the model results as a starting point and "clean up" the resulting topics or provide new constraints for additional iterations. For both groups, better visualisation of model run results enables a greater understanding of how topics have been arrived at and can provide a range of views to allow meaningful labelling. Such tools start to approach a broader view of explainability that takes account of rich prior research and thinking in the philosophy and cognition of causal logic and social psychology (Miller 2017). This work has shown how people can struggle to link together high probability words into coherent themes and this effect worsens with a greater number of topics, even if this greater number leads to a better fit in a purely modelling definition.

Looking further at the sociotechnical design principles of Read et al (2015), there are clear strengths conferred by topic modelling, notably the efficiency and power to apply a structuration process to large text collections. Some iteration is also feasible, though this tends to be limited to repetition of model runs rather than direct, real-time intervention in the modelling process. In terms of validity, there is some doubt over the stability and reproducability of any particular modelling run (Agrawal, Fu, and Menzies 2018). To be useful, a model should be able to produce similar outputs on data from the same source (Greene, O'callaghan, and Cunningham 2014). While this study did not explicitly test this, it seems likely that better estimation processes provide better reproducability (M. E. Roberts, Stewart, and Tingley 2018). Choice is also an important meta-principle of sociotechnical design (Clegg 2000), but existing topic modelling approaches are not particularly good at communicating model options and their potential consequences (Boyd-graber, Mimno, and Hu 2017).

In terms of topic modelling as part of a holistic, integrated process, there are limited tools and systems available that are doing this:

...a holistic approach needs to be employed in the development of software that implements interactive Topic Modelling algorithms as qualitative content analysis aids. While the algorithm is the central element and interactivity plays an important role in helping the analyst to answer their research questions, the incorporation of tools to help the analyst interpret the derived topics are equally important and affect trust. (Bakharia et al. 2016)

For analysts with some statistical / coding knowledge, a promising open source toolset is the R Statistical STM package together with the STMInsights web application used in this study, and similar model-visualisation tools are available in Python.

A final design principle from Read's work, and the one judged most important by the experts polled, was creativity. It is here that there seems to be great potential for topic modelling to be part of an exploratively creative user-led process. What this study indicates is that the unsupervised nature of the approach can lead to interesting empirical findings that perhaps would not emerge so readily from the use of document-level metadata or a single set of keywords. It is in the sub-document patterns and distributions that we can start to look across documents in new and interesting ways.

5. Conclusions and further work

This work brought together some overall design principles for explainable machine learning with specific considerations for topic modelling and used the example of movie summary texts to investigate these. It seems that automated evaluation measures can get us some way toward one of the main modelling decisions, that of topic numbers. That said, the numbers suggested by automated processes are at the top end of what seems to be manageable and comprehensible for human users. In our example, while the modelling suggested something around 80 topics, our user testing and further analysis seemed better suited to a maximum of 50. Topic labelling—particularly with lack of context—was confirmed as an often challenging task and there was some indication that out of place words can easy detract from identifying connections, even where some can be discerned.

Using some examples of genre analysis against the topic distributions from the modelling stage, we see that the unsupervised nature of the technique can add potential value to existing, popular social categorisation. While a general topic signature corresponds well with several popular genres, we can also gain insight from examining particular instances and how they vary along different topic axes. A further step might be to develop tools that allow easier exploration of these and the comparison of outliers with prototypical examples.

There is also good potential to take this work further to look at how unsupervised might compare to semisupervised approaches when topic modelling is integrated into discovery and recommendation services. We might hypothesise that the use of labelled text might improve local coherence but limit creative exploration.

References

Agrawal, Amritanshu, Wei Fu, and Tim Menzies. 2018. "What is wrong with topic modeling? (and how to fix it using search-based software engineering)." *Information and Software Technology*, February. https://doi.org/10.1016/j.infsof.2018.02.005.

Arnold, Corey W., Andrea Oh, Shawn Chen, and William Speier. 2016. "Evaluating topic model interpretability from a primary care physician perspective." *Computer Methods and Programs in Biomedicine* 124: 67–75.

Bakharia, Aneesha, Peter Bruza, Jim Watters, Bhuva Narayan, and Laurianne Sitbon. 2016. "Interactive topic modeling for aiding qualitative content analysis." *Proceedings of the 2016 ACM on Conference on Human Information Interaction and Retrieval - CHIIR '16*, 213–22.

Bamman, David, Brendan O'Connor, and Noah Smith. 2014. *CMU movie summary corpus*. http://www.cs.cmu.edu/{~}ark/personas/.

Bamman, David, Brendan O'Connor, and Noah A Smith. 2013. "Learning latent personas of film characters." In *Proceedings of the 51st Annual Meeting of the Association for Computational Linguistics*, 352–61.

Blei, David M. 2012. "Probabilistic topic models." *Communications of the ACM* 55 (4): 77.

Blei, David, Andrew Ng, and Micchael Jordan. 2003. "Latent Dirichlet allocation." *Journal of Machine Learning Research* 3: 993–1022.

Boyd-graber, Jordan, David Mimno, and Yuening Hu. 2017. "Applications of topic models." *Foundations and Trends in Information Retrieval* 11 (2): 143–296.

Brezina, Vaclav. 2018. "Statistical choices in corpus-based discourse analysis." In *Corpus Approaches to Discourse*, 259–80. Milton Park, Abingdon, Oxon; New York: Routledge, 2018.: Routledge.

Chuang, Jason, Christopher D. Manning, and Jeffrey Heer. 2012. "Termite: visualization techniques for assessing textual topicmModels." *International Working Conference on Advanced Visual Interfaces*, 74.

Clegg, Chris. 2000. "Sociotechnical principles for system design." *Applied Ergonomics* 31 (5): 463–77.

Doshi-Velez, Finale, and Been Kim. 2017. "Towards a rigorous science of interpretable machine learning." *Arxiv.org*, no. Ml: 1–13.

El-assady, Mennatallah, Fabian Sperrle, Oliver Deussen, Daniel Keim, and Christopher Collins. 2019. "Visual analytics for topic model optimization based on user-steerable speculative execution." *IEEE Transactions on Visualization and Computer Graphics* 25 (1): 374–84.

Faisal, Ali, and Mirva Peltoniemi. 2018. "Establishing video game genres using data-driven modeling and product databases." *Games and Culture* 13 (1): 20–43.

Ganesan, Ashwinkumar, Kiante Brantley, Shimei Pan, and Jian Chen. 2015. "LDAExplore: visualizing topic models generated using Latent Dirichlet Allocation." *Arxiv.org*, no. March. https://doi.org/10.1007/BF00268510.

Giaquinto, Robert, and Arindam Banerjee. 2018. "DAPPER: scaling dynamic author persona topic model to billion-word corpora." *arXiv Preprint*, 971–76.

Grajzl, Peter, and Peter Murrell. 2018. "Toward understanding 17th century English culture: A structural topic model of Francis Bacon's ideas." *Journal of Comparative Economics*, no. October: 1–25.

Greene, Derek, Derek O'Callaghan, and Pádraig Cunningham. 2014. "How many topics? Stability analysis for topic models." In *ECML Pkdd 2014*. https://arxiv.org/pdf/1404.4606.pdf.

Hurault-Paupe, Anne. 2015. "The paradoxes of cinematic movement: is the road movie a static genre?" *Miranda*, no. 10: 0–15.

Jacobi, Carina, Wouter Van Atteveldt, and Kasper Welbers. 2016. "Quantitative analysis of large amounts of journalistic texts using topic modelling." *Digital Journalism* 4 (1): 89–106.

Lau, Jey Han, David Newman, and Timothy Baldwin. 2014. "Machine reading tea leaves: automatically evaluating topic coherence and topic model quality." In *Proceedings of the 14th Conference of the European Chapter of the Association for Computational Linguistics*, Pages 530–539, Gothenburg, Sweden, April 26-30 2014. Association for Computational Linguistics, 38:530–39. 1.

Lee, Hakyeon, and Pilsung Kang. 2018. "Identifying core topics in technology and innovation management studies: a topic model approach." *Journal of Technology Transfer* 43 (5): 1291–1317.

Lee, Tak Yeon, Alison Smith, Kevin Seppi, Niklas Elmqvist, Jordan Boyd-Graber, and Leah Findlater. 2017. "The human touch: How non-expert users perceive, interpret, and fix topic models." *International Journal of Human Computer Studies* 105 (July 2016): 28–42.

Miller, Tim. 2017. "Explanation in artificial intelligence: Insights from the social sciences." *Artificial Intelligence* 267: 1–38.

Morstatter, Fred, Marina Del Rey, and S Mill Ave. 2018. "In search of coherence and consensus: measuring the interpretability of statistical topics." *Journal of Machine Learning Research* 18 (169): 1–32.

Park, Sungrae, Doosup Choi, Minki Kim, Wonchul Cha, Chuhyun Kim, and Il Chul Moon. 2017. "Identifying prescription patterns with a topic model of diseases and medications." *Journal of Biomedical Informatics* 75: 35–47.

Pomeda, J. Rodríguez, F. Casani Fernández de Navarrete, L. A. Sandoval Hamón, F. Sánchez Fernández, and Ceci E. Bayas Aldaz. 2018. "A probabilistic topic model on energy and transportation sustainability perceptions within Spanish university students." *European Journal of Sustainable Development* 5 (4): 367–74.

Read, Gemma J. M., Paul M. Salmon, Michael G. Lenné, and Neville A. Stanton. 2015. "Designing sociotechnical systems with cognitive work analysis: putting theory back into practice." *Ergonomics* 58 (5): 822–51.

Ren, Fuji, Xin Kang, and Changqin Quan. 2016. "Examining accumulated emotional traits in suicide blogs with an emotion topic model." *IEEE Journal of Biomedical and Health Informatics* 20 (5): 1384–96.

Roberts, Margaret E, Brandon M Stewart, and Dustin Tingley. 2018. "Journal of Statistical Software stm: R Package for structural topic models" *VV* (Ii): 1–41.

Roberts, Margaret, Brandon M Stewart, Dustin Tingley, and Edoardo Airoldi. 2013. "The structural topic model and applied social science." In *NIPS 2013 Workshop on Topic Models: Computation, Application, and Evaluation.*

Roberts, M, M Stewart, and D Tingley. 2018. "stm: R Package for structural topic models." *Journal of Statistical Software* https://doi.org/10.18637/jss.v000.i00.

Röder, Michael, Andreas Both, and Alexander Hinneburg. 2015. "Exploring the space of topic coherence measures," In *WSDM 2015 - Proceedings of the 8th ACM International Conference on Web Search and Data Mining.* (pp 399–408).

Schwemmer, Carsten. 2018. *stminsights - A 'Shiny' application for inspecting structural topic models.* https://cschwem2er.github.io/stminsights/.

Sievert, Carson, and Kenneth Shirley. 2015. *LDAvis: A method for visualizing and interpreting topics.* https://doi.org/10.3115/v1/w14-3110.

Spohrer, Erika. 2009. "Not a gay cowboy movie? Brokeback mountain and the importance of genre." *Journal of Popular Film and Television* 37 (1): 26–33.

Wang, Lidong, Keyong Hu, and Xiaodong Xu. 2017. "Discovering symptom-herb relationship by exploiting SHT topic model." *IPSJ Transactions on Bioinformatics* 10 (0): 16–21.

Wickham, Hadley. 2009. *hadley/data-baby-names: Distribution of US baby names,* 1880-2008. https://github.com/hadley/data-baby-names.

Wikipedia. 2019. *Brokeback Mountain.* https://en.wikipedia.org/wiki/Brokeback{_}Mountain.

Fake News as an Emergent Subject Domain: conceptual and ethical perspectives for the development of a critical knowledge organisation

Rafael Cacciolari Dalessandro, São Paulo State University (UNESP), Brazil
José Augusto Chaves Guimarães, São Paulo State University (UNESP), Brazil
D. Grant Campbell, University of Western Ontario, Canada

Abstract

This paper performs a preliminary domain analysis of the emerging field of "fake news." Studying 136 articles published between 2014 and 2018, the authors determined that research on the phenomenon of fake news, misinformation, disinformation, information disorders and post-truth is largely concentrated in the social sciences, with information science claiming 18% of the total. The articles were grouped into five thematic categories: social networks, epistemology, ethical issues, political matters and critical view. Most of the articles fall into the categories of critical view, social networks and political matters. These three categories also contained the greatest number of articles that embrace multiple thematic categories. The greatest concentration of articles occurred in the years 2017 and 2018, coinciding with the Brexit referendum in Great Britain and the United States federal election. The rise of research related to fake news is matched by an increasingly urgent need within the professional and research communities in knowledge organization to confront the ethical challenges raised by fake news. These challenges can only be met by combining the ontological tradition of knowledge organization to confront what is "real" and what is "not real," together with the contextual tradition which acknowledges the cultural situatedness of these categories.

1. Introduction

Information Science (IS) has interacted with many scientific areas throughout its conception, and it has also been known for the speed and precision with which it provides information services within these other scientific fields (Borko 1968; Shera 1968; Saracevic 1970, 1995; Foskett 1996). Today IS faces a fresh challenge: to guarantee the reliability of information organized and disseminated in information units such as archives, libraries and museums which are now vulnerable to the harms caused by fake news widely spread by the press, by social networks, and even in scientific literature.

Reliability can be considered one of the most significant and determinant ethical values in the process of knowledge organization aiming at the retrieval and dissemination of information. However, the ethical issues do not stop at retrieval: information processes go far beyond the mere dissemination of information. They also work to achieve effective user satisfaction; they comprehend the appropriation of information and generation of knowledge in a process called by the authors an "informational helicoid". (Guimarães 2000, 2008).

It is precisely in this field of user satisfaction, and in the ways that users appropriate information, that we encounter fresh questions of an ethical nature regarding the origin and reliability of information organized, retrieved and disseminated, so as to avoid damages to the user. In this field, special attention is given to the deleterious effects caused by misinformation, usually spread through the so-called fake news that circulates in many kinds of means of communication (here understood as sources of information to the user). These sources are, for the most part, intended to deliberately produce or manipulate content and thus lead to the dissemination of false information.

The world wide web and its settings nowadays enables people to create the most diverse contents without demanding rigor and credibility in the process, which makes it easier for fake information to go viral. On the one hand information nowadays finds few barriers, thanks to the innumerable possibilities of instant messaging on the most varied platforms with internet connection, which brings knowledge and convenience with greater ease to people. On the other hand, all this ease favours the creation and dissemination of content which is not committed to the rigor and credibility that the process of creation demands. Psycho-demographic analysis and dark advertisements, coupled with the ability to design credible-looking information displays, can evade the skepticism of even the most cynical reader. Fake news, then, can spread rapidly, and those who read it can easily come to believe in rumors and other untruths which may later influence important spheres of society that directly affect citizens' lives, in areas such as politics, the economy, education and public health. The urgency of this problem gives rise to the need for close and specific analysis of the phenomenon: analysis which engages in an essentially ethical task of fighting the dissemination of false information to avoid the negative consequences that come from it (Volkoff 1999).

Fake news, then, has now consolidated into an effective domain of inquiry, having its own scientific literature, like the recent studies by Wardle (2017) and Lazer et al. (2018), and deserves to be studied from the point of view of knowledge organization, using domain analysis (Hjørland 2002) in order to understand its thematic nature, distinctive features and generic and specific themes, as well as the articulation between those themes. Given the size of the problem and the risk that false news offers to society as a whole, information professionals must actively participate in combating it. Archivists, librarians and museologists have the knowledge that enables them to identify dubious and tendentious information sources. They are therefore professionally equipped to contribute to the study of fake news, and their contribution forms one of the dimensions of ethical commitments of information professionals proposed by Guimarães (2000), more specifically with regard to the commitment to the content of the information itself.

In addition, information professionals, such as archivists and librarians among others (Mason 1990), have much to lose with the rise of fake news. Dealing as they do with the organization, retrieval and dissemination of information from diverse sources, thematics and users, their professional activities are especially vulnerable to the deleterious effects of the fake news. Information professionals must look critically and cautiously at the phenomenon of fake news and the research that has risen in response to it. Only by doing so will they retain their ability to identify the origin and veracity of the information treated, recovered and disseminated so that they can fulfill their social role (Richardson 1982), thereby minimizing and preventing user harm (Adler and Tennis 2013).

Even though we are aware of the harmful potential of fake news, little is known about the specific aspects related to this domain of knowledge and to what extent those aspects are being incorporated into the research universe of Information Science, especially if we consider that one of the main objectives of the research in Information Science is to produce and create knowledge (theoretical, methodological, applied) that can support the development of the activities of information professionals. Thus, this paper aims at conceptually delimiting fake news as a thematic domain, in the service of the ethical practice of information professionals in the field of knowledge organization.

2. Fake News: historical and conceptual considerations

The phenomenon we call "fake news" has always existed: despite its age, it has attracted fresh attention recently, especially after the North American presidential election in 2016. At that time, President Trump used his Twitter account to ridicule the press, using pejorative labels like "fake news "and" fake media", his intention being to attack the credibility of the media that was criticizing him, and to make people believe that he was the only reliable source of truth (Ross and Rivers 2018).

Also, in 2016, the Oxford Dictionary (Oxford Dictionaries 2016) chose "post-truth" as the word of the year. "Post-truth" is an adjective used to imply that objective facts are less influential in forming public opinion than appeals to emotion and personal belief. According to the dictionary, the concept of post-truth has existed since the last decade but came to light due to the referendum on the United Kingdom's permanence in the European Union and the presidential election in the United States.

According to the dictionary, the prefix "post-" refers not only to an event that follows another, as in "post-war." "Post-truth" carries the meaning of belonging to a time when the specific concept has become unimportant or irrelevant. In this way, the facts in the post-truth era are no longer consistent with objective reality that can be proven by evidence and become less important than people's personal beliefs and prejudices. According to McIntyre (2018), ideology precedes reality.

Lewandowsky et al. (2017) wrote that the post-truth world is the result of five important aspects which are considered mega-trends in society. They are: a decline in social capital, growing economic inequality, increased polarization, declining trust in science and an increasingly fractured media landscape. The authors suggest that dealing with these problems requires technological solutions which incorporate psychological principles, an interdisciplinary approach described by them as "technocognition."

According to Allcott and Gentzkow (2017), the emergence of fake news can be attributed to the relative ease with which content can be shared among users without rigorous processes, such as significant third party filtering, fact checking or editorial judgment.

Conceptually speaking, fake news is part of a broader thematic universe of so-called information disorders that focus on actions aimed at combating the dissemination of false information (Volkoff 1999). For Lazer et al. (2018), fake news is information that mimics news produced by specialized media (exhibiting the same format) but does not have the same rigor of standards and processes that guarantee the accuracy and credibility of what is being advertised. There is, then, a similarity in form to real news, but a huge difference in content. According to Lazer et al., fake news contains aspects similar to those of other problems that also affect the dissemination of information, such as misinformation and disinformation, both belonging to a group called information disorders.

Disinformation occurs when false information is deliberately created with the intention of harming a person, social group, organization or country, whereas misinformation occurs when the false information was not created with the intention to cause some damage or loss but results from errors (in photo captions, dates, statistics, translations) or when satiric treatments are taken seriously. Therefore, there is a difference in the degree of intentionality, although both may lead to damage.

Wardle (2017) adds a new species to the genre of information disorders - "malinformation", which although based on reality (with a degree of credibility as to its source) is directed at intentionally causing harm to individuals, organizations or countries.

3. Fake news as a subject domain in the international scientific literature
In order to better understand the fake news domain and its thematic configuration, the scientific literature in the format of articles indexed in the Scopus database was analyzed, from the years 2014 to 2018, that contained the term fake news as one of its keywords.

From a total of 136 retrieved scientific papers, content analysis (Bardin 1977) was applied to identify the conceptual relations between fake news, misinformation, disinformation, information disorders and post-truth, and also to differentiate between the distinctive features of fake news as a subject itself (considering elements such as nature, typology, origin, subjects, vehicles, consequences) and as a facet of approach applicable to different areas of knowledge, as it mainly happens in the field of politics.

The 136 scientific articles retrieved were distributed in the following areas of knowledge: Social Sciences; Computer Science; Arts and Humanities; Psychology; Engineering; Medicine; Business; Management and Accounting; Environmental Science; Decision Science and Neuroscience. It is worth mentioning that the Social Sciences area had the largest number of articles with a total of 98 articles (72% of the total publication), and that information science claimed 25 articles (18% of the total publication).

These articles were then classified into 5 groups that could be extracted from the papers after their analysis due to a connection with the topic fake news: social networks, epistemology, ethical issues, political matters, and critical view.

In the Social Networks group we classified articles that involve aspects related to the spread of fake news by social networks, such as Facebook and Twitter. Articles classified in the area of epistemology are those that deal with the formation process, motivations, effects and other aspects of the origin of fake news. Cultural, psychic, gender, educational, social, and economic aspects were taken into account - anything that can interfere with the way a person perceives the world and from then on proceeds to make judgments that are deeply affect by that change in perception.

The Ethical Issues category includes fake news articles that involve ethical, moral or other dilemmas, thereby invoking a deeper concern with right and wrong, given the harmful effect that fake news can have on the public. Political Matters encompasses articles linking fake news to political issues, its power to shape the electorate's view of candidates, and its influence over political parties, causing them to conceal facts in a misleading fashion.

The articles classified in the group of "Critical View" are those that present or seek to incite a critical eye on the theme of fake news, mainly through the problematization of the circumstances that generate or favour the appearance of such false news.

Figure 1. Article Classified according to Five Categories

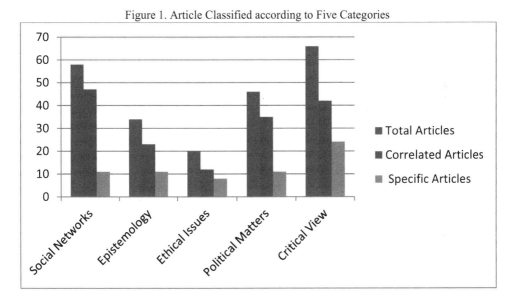

Figure 1 above shows the breakdown of our analysis. "Total Articles" refers to the total number of articles associated with a particular theme; "Correlated Articles" refers to those articles that dialogue with the other themes; "Specific Articles" refers to those that address only the one theme group to which they belong.

It was observed that the topics most covered in the scientific literature of fake news belong to the "Critical View" category, followed by "Social Networks" and "Political Matters". Further, we found that the articles in these three groups contain the greatest number of articles that dialogue with each other.

The journals that published Information Science content related to fake news were: Proceedings of the Association for Information Science and Technology (7 articles);

Profissional de la informacion (4 articles); Reference Librarian (3 articles); College and Undergraduate Libraries (1 article); Education for Informing (1 article); Education Policy Analysis Archives (1 article); Human-centric computing and Information Sciences (1 article); Informing Science (1 article); Journal of Documentation (1 article); Journal of Information Literacy (1 article); Journal of Museum Education (1 article); Library Management (1 article); Public Services Quarterly (1 article); Reference Services Review (1 article).

The distribution of the articles in relation to the analyzed years were: 2014 (2 articles), 2015 (3 articles), 2016 (2 articles), 2017 (31 articles) and 2018 (98 articles). There is a significant increase in the number of articles produced since 2017, which is justified by the fact that it is the year after the presidential elections in the United States and the referendum on the United Kingdom's membership in the European Union, events that took place in 2016 and popularized fake news.

4. Fake news and the ethical perspective for a critical knowledge organisation
The issue of fake news in its relationship to, and effect upon, information units such as libraries, in processes such as access, organization, retrieval and dissemination of information, raises an important ethical consideration that deserves a reflection on the part of the professionals involved. This consideration arises from a central paradox. Information professionals are ethically committed to critically analyzing information sources and combatting fake news, in the interests of serving their users and minimizing harm. And yet, we must, from the very start, accept that information is not neutral: it is always permeated by the values of those who created it.

This non-neutrality, in turn, extends to the field of organization and representation of knowledge. The processes, products and instruments developed for this field are the fruit of specific cultural contexts, and they may exhibit important differences from one another. Information production, mediation, processing and use can all vary between different cultural settings. And these cultural settings reflect moral values that often conflict.

Fernandez-Molina and Guimarães (2002) have addressed the ethical complexities involved in library processes such as the formation of collections, indexing and dissemination of information for almost two decades. These complexities persist today and are exacerbated by the deliberately misleading intent of fake news, which presents a fresh professional challenge, and a fresh ethical imperative, upon information professionals, demanding of them a still greater commitment to their profession and their users.

Fake news, deliberately false informational content created to inflict damage on others, embodies and represents a specific world view, a view most often marked by prejudice and discrimination typical of a hegemonic cultural pattern, thus hindering a transcultural ethics of mediation that considers information as an equally important input for a whole diversity of cultures, thereby promoting an effective cultural hospitality (Berman 1971; García Gutiérrez 2002; Beghtol 2002, 2005).

Resistance to this destructive hegemonic pattern extends not just to issues of access, but to issues of organization. As Hope Olson reminds us, an indexer possesses a power to name (2002). This power requires constant vigilance to avoid the consequences of ignorance and abuse. But it also implies another kind of power: the power to call out the false labels with which fake news claims a spurious legitimacy. In this way, information professionals possess a significant power to alleviate the damage caused by deliberately false information.

Challenging the false claims and false labels of fake news involves an important expansion of professional information work. While information professionals are trained to seek the origin of an information as a way to avoid the propagation of fake news, fake news often disguises its source. Information professionals must also learn to recognize the purpose of this information by interpreting it directly and recognizing and naming the values and idiosyncrasies exhibited by the information. As already noted, fake news behaves surreptitiously, presenting an outer form that is consistent with the usual features, both visual and rhetorical, of credible journalism and research. Information professionals must learn how to look past any false rhetoric of "impartiality" and the false layout of "an online newspaper," that lends fake news an air of credibility. They must learn to ask the question: "who is the master of this servant? "

To conclude, the phenomenon of fake news, as it concerns the ethics and practice of the information professional, presents a crisis that demands the contributions of all the approaches and faculties of knowledge organization. On the one hand, fake news raises ontological question of the type addressed by Ingetraut Dahlberg. What are the key disciplines in which fake news is being studied and addressed, and how does the information professional distinguish information that is "real" from information that is "false"? On the other hand, fake news demands from us a close attention to cultural context, as advocated by Birger Hjørland. How do we understand the various cultural contexts and contextual assumptions that are interacting within information sources that look the same and sound the same, but are proceeding from very different ethical, moral, social and political positions?

Fake news calls for an eminently critical and cultural dimension of the organization of knowledge, which characterizes the present moment, as demonstrated by Semidão (2019). Many different information domains, as we have seen, are addressing fake news in their various ways, and exploring the interactions of the various themes in this new domain. Knowledge organization must play its part as well.

References

Adler, Melissa & Joseph. T. Tennis. 2013. "Toward a Taxonomy of Harm in Knowledge Organization Systems." *Knowledge Organization* 40: 266-272.

Allcott, Hunt & Matthew Gentzkow. 2017. "Social Media and Fake News in the 2016 Election." *Journal of Economic Perspectives* 31: 211–236.

Bardin, Laurence. 1977. *L'analyse du contenu*. Paris: PUF.

Beghtol, Clare. 2002. "A proposed ethical warrant for global knowledge representation and organization systems." *Journal of Documentation* 58: 507-532.

Beghtol, Clare. 2005. "Ethical Decision-Making for Knowledge Representation and Organization Systems for Global Use." *Journal of the American Society for Information Science and Technology* 56: 903-912.

Berman, Sanford. 1971. *Prejudices and Antipathies: a tract of Library of Congress Subjects Headings concerning people*. Metuchen: Scarecrow Press.

Borko, Harold. 1968. "Information science: what is it?" *American Documentation*, 19 (1): 3-5.

Fernandez-Molina, Juan C. & José Augusto C. Guimaraes, 2002. "Ethical aspects of knowledge organization and representation in the digital environment: their articulation in professional codes of ethics." In Lopez-Huertas, M. J. (Org.) *Challenges in knowledge representations and organization for the 21st century: integration of knowledge across boundaries*. pp.487-492. Wurzburg: Ergon Verlag.

Foskett, A.C. 1996. *The subject approach to information*. 5th ed. London: Facet.

Froelich, T.J. 1994. "Ethical concerns of information professionals in an international context." In: Alvarez-Ossorio, J.R.; Goedgebuure, B. G. *New worlds in information and documentation*. pp. 459-470. Amsterdam: Elsevier; FID.

Froelich, T.J. 1997. *Survey Analysis of The Major Ethical and Legal Issues Facing Library and Information Services*. Munich: K.G. Saur.

García Gutiérrez, Antonio. 2002. "Knowledge organization from a "culture of the border": towards a transcultural ethics of mediation" In López-Huertas, M. J. (Ed.) *Challenges in knowledge representation and organization for the 21st century: integration of knowledge across boundaries*. pp.516-522. Würzburg: Ergon Verlag.

Guimarães, J.A.C. et al. 2008. "Ethics in the knowledge organization environment: an overview of values and problems in the LIS literature." In Arsénault, C.; Tennis, J.T. (ed.) *Culture and identity in knowledge organization*. pp.361-366) Würzburg: Ergon Verlag.

Guimarães, J.A.C. 2008. "Ciência da Informação, Arquivologia e Biblioteconomia: em busca do necessário diálogo entre o universo teórico e os fazeres profissionais." In: Fujita, M. S. L.;

Guimarães, J. A. C. (Org.). *Ensino e Pesquisa em Biblioteconomia no Brasil: a emergência de um novo olhar.* pp. 33-44. 1ed.São Paulo: Cultura Acadêmica.

Guimarães, J.A.C. 2000. "O profissional da informação sob o prisma de sua formação." In: Valentim, M. L. P. (org.). *Profissionais da informação: formação, perfil e atuação profissional.* pp. 53-70. São Paulo: Polis.

Hjørland, B. 2002. "Domain Analysis in Information Science: eleven approaches – traditional as well as innovative." *Journal of Documentation,* 58(4): 422-462.

Hjørland, B. 2002. "Epistemology and the socio-cognitive perspective in information science". *Journal of the American Society for Information Science and Technology,* 53(4): 257-270.

Hjørland, B. 2017. "Domain analysis." *Knowledge Organization,* 44(6): 436–464 (Reviews of Concepts in Knowledge Organization).

Hjørland, B. & H. Albrechtsen. 1995. "Toward a new horizon in information science: domain-analysis." *Journal of The American Society for information Science,* 46(6): 400–425.

Lazer, D. M. J. et al. (2018). "The science of fake news." *Science,* 359(6380), 9 Mar.

Lewandowsky, Stephan et al. 2017. "Beyond misinformation: understanding and coping with the Post-Truth era." *Journal of Applied Research in Memory and Cognition* 6(4): 353-369.

Mason, Richard O. 1990. "What is an information professional?" *Journal of Education for Library and Information Science,* 31(2): 122-138.

McIntyre, Lee. 2018. *Lies, Alternative Facts and Post-Truth.* Retrieved from https://thewire.in/world/lies-alternative-facts-and-post-truth

Olson, Hope. 2002. *The Power to Name: locating the limits or subject representation in libraries.* Dordrecht: Kluwer Academic Publisher.

Oxford Dictionaries. 2016. *Word of the year 2016.* Retrieved from https://en.oxforddictionaries.com/word-of-the-year/word-of-the-year-2016

Richardson, John V. 1982. *The Spirit of Inquiry: the Graduate Library School at Chicago, 1921-51.* Chicago: American Library Association.

Ross, A. S. and D. J. Rivers. 2018. "Discursive deflection: accusation of "Fake News" and the spread of mis- and disinformation in the tweets of President Trump". *Social Media + Society.* 4: 2.

Saracevic, T. 1970. *Introduction to Information Science.* New York: Bowker.

Saracevic, T. 1995. "Interdisciplinary Nature of Information Science." *Ciência da Informação,* 24(1):.36-41

Semidão. Rafael, A.M. 2019. *Abordagens Teóricas de Organização do Conhecimento: uma análise a partir do CSKOL da ISKO.* Marília: UNESP. Dissertation (PhD in Information Science).

Shera, J.-H. 1968. "An Epistemological Foundation for Library Science." In: Montgomery, E. B. (Ed.). *The foundations of access to knowledge: a symposium.* pp. 7–25. Syracuse, NY: Syracuse University Press

Sonnenwald, D.H. 2007. "Scientific Collaboration." *Annual Review of Information Science and Technology,* 41(1): 643-681.

Volkoff, Vladimir. 1999. *Petite Histoire de la Désinformation: du cheval de Troie à l'Internet.* Monaco: Éd. du Rocher.

Wardle, C. 2017. Toward an Interdisciplinary Framework for Research and Policy Making. Council of Europe report DGI(2017)09

Power, Truth and Creativity: the ethical dimensions of the knowledge organization of art

Deborah Lee, City, University of London, UK

Summary

Ethics is a highly topical issue in knowledge organization discourse. Work on topics such as power, gender and sexuality within knowledge organization systems are a significant part of current knowledge organization research (for example, Adler 2016, Adler 2017, Fox 2016). Furthermore, discussions about the information organization professional's ethical responsibilities show how the act of classifying and cataloguing each document has an ethical dimension (for example, Bair 2005, Shoemaker 2015, Snow 2015). The purpose of this paper is to look specifically at the intersection of ethics and creativity within knowledge organization, and to consider some particular aspects of the performance of ethical knowledge organization within the world of art. This novel focus on art and creativity enhances our general understanding of the ethics of knowledge organization.

The paper starts with an examination of the context of practitioner ethics in the field of knowledge organization, focussing on issues affecting the decision-making of those describing and classifying specific resources. Then, two examples within art knowledge organization are explored. The first concerns power: the organization of resources when there are questions about an artwork's attribution. Specific examples are used including a disputed artwork by Rembrandt. The issue of attribution highlights the power held by the classifier to enhance or diminish a false narrative. Furthermore, discussions about attribution illuminate problems when the accepted "truth" changes over time, and the consequential ethical implications.

The second example considers knowledge organization when creativity and truth are placed as adversaries. What happens when you are organizing a work, when that work's creativity is about blurring the lines between artistic world and reality? While some bibliographic works have a longstanding history of hiding or blurring their realities – for example, anonymous works, books written by fictitious characters – art examples are a fascinating window into this phenomenon when they imbue the subversion of truth as part of their artistic value. Some examples from documents of exhibitions involving North Korea, which may or may not document reality, are used to highlight how the knowledge organizers' remit of truthful description can be challenging when a document is deliberately, for artistic reasons, depicting a false reality. So, by examining the challenges wrought by the organization of art, we deepen our understanding of how practitioners perform the ethics of knowledge organization, which is a vital issue for current and future workplaces.

References

Adler, M. (2017). *Cruising the library: perversities in the organization of knowledge.* New York: Fordham University Press.

Adler, M. (2016). "The case for taxonomic reparations". *Knowledge Organization,* 43(8): 630-640.

Bair, S. (2005). "Toward a code of ethics for cataloging". *Technical Services Quarterly,* 23(1): 13-26.

Fox, M.J. (2016). "Legal discourse's epistemic interplay with sex and gender classification in the Dewey Decimal Classification". *Library Trends,* 64(4): 687-713.

Shoemaker, B. (2015). "No one can whistle a symphony: Seeking a catalogers' code of ethics". *Knowledge Organization,* 42(5): 353-357.

Snow, K. (2015). "An examination of the practical and ethical issues surrounding false memoirs in cataloging practice". *Cataloging & Classification Quarterly,* 53(8): 927-947.

Session 6B: AI AND TAXONOMIES

Paradigmatic Similarities in Knowledge Representation between AI and Ontological Systems

Jian Qin, Syracuse University, USA

Abstract

This paper reviews the development of knowledge organization and knowledge representation in AI in the last three decades during which schematic representation of data and information became the main focus and driving force for ontologizing knowledge organization and representation. The paper argues that the knowledge organization community has traditionally been guided by the integration and disintegration paradigms, while the rule-based, semantic networks and frames, and first-order logic paradigms have been prevalent in artificial intelligence research. The paper outlines the similarities among these paradigms and argues that ontologies as a type of knowledge organization system are bridging the gaps between the two parallel communities.

1. Introduction

Knowledge organization systems (KOS) are developed to represent knowledge in publications and in natural and societal environments. Depending on the purpose, a KOS may be general and broad, such as the Library of Congress Subject Headings (LCSH) which are used to index books and other publications in library collections, while others may be very specific, such as the National Center for Biotechnology Information Taxonomy that serves as a nomenclature and classification for organisms (NCBI 2018). Whether general or specific, traditional KOS are not designed for problem-solving purposes, but rather as standards to normalize vocabularies and as classification systems for organizing data and information in different systems. The capabilities of inference or reasoning are not part of the design of these systems, even though relations in hierarchical and associative systems may imply the possibility for this (e.g., the parent-child class relations in a hierarchical classification or the broader and narrower terms in a thesaurus). By contrast, knowledge representation (KR) in artificial intelligence (AI) applications produces a set of statements that express facts, relations, and conditions in formal languages or schemes upon which reasoning can be performed to determine actions or reach conclusions. The reasoning component is perhaps the most striking difference in KR between traditional KOS and artificial intelligence (AI).

Despite differences between traditional knowledge organization (KO) and AI-style knowledge representation, the similarities between the two are perhaps more interesting for the KO community for a number of reasons. First, KR in the digital data era is closely tied to language and technology, whether it is for KOS or for AI applications. Extracting or generalizing concepts and relations and expressing them in normalized, encoded formats have been extensively studied over the last 30 years. These studies have generated and established similar techniques and methods that have been applied in both KO and AI fields, such as graphical representations of knowledge or linked data (KO) and artificial neural networks (AI). Second, although the KO and AI communities have largely remained disconnected in the past, this disconnection is being narrowed, and the fields have converged through the advances in semantic web technologies and data science. The search for better and more effective ways to address the challenges that come with digital data and culture have prompted each community to look at the other for new ideas and methods. It is not uncommon, for example, to use machine-learning algorithms to extract semantic relations or concepts from social tags (Chen et al. 2008; Castano and Varese 2011) or classify concepts from research data (Kubat et al. 1993). Finally, there is an increase in KR convergence in the KO and AI communities, both from members' desires to understand the implications of AI on KO and the urge to utilize state-of-the-art techniques and methods within the KO community, as shown from a recent discussion about AI and information science on the community forum of the Association for Information Science and Technology (ASIST) (Toms 2019).

This paper will first review the historical development of KR in both KO and AI in the last three decades, during which schematic representations of data and information became the main driving force for ontologizing knowledge organization and representation. While the literature review allows us to see and compare KR paradigms between traditional KO and AI, it is important to understand where paradigmatic similarities exist and how the two parallel fields are converging. Following the review and analysis, paradigmatic similarities and convergence of KR in KO and AI will be discussed.

2. Knowledge organization (KO) or knowledge representation (KR)?
What is knowledge representation? The answer to this question can take several different directions depending on perspective. In the field of library and information science (LIS), the closest term to knowledge representation is knowledge organization, which in its narrow definition means "activities such as document description, indexing and classification performed in libraries, bibliographical databases, archives and other kinds of 'memory institutions' by librarians, archivists, information specialists, subject specialists, as well as by computer algorithms and laymen" (Hjørland 2008 p.86). The focus here is placed on organizing and representing documents that embody knowledge. Hjørland (2008) further articulates that knowledge organization in its broader sense is about how knowledge is socially organized and how such knowledge organization systems (KOS) reflect reality. The activities involved in knowledge organization can be divided into two areas: first, knowledge

is organized based on humans' understanding of the world in various systems or tools such as classification schemes and thesauri, and second, these knowledge organization systems are applied by humans or machines to represent the document content through a generalized set of terms as the surrogate for the document. The activities of representing document content by using KOS can be deemed as a form of human-mediated knowledge representation due to the fact that the terms or classes are assigned to documents mainly by librarians or information specialists, although fully automated document representation does exist, such as the indexing service at LexisNexis, and the purpose of such activities is to organize the documents based on topics, either on library shelves or in computer systems as catalogs and indexes for information discovery and use.

Figure 1. Paradigms in knowledge organization (Source: Qin, 2002)

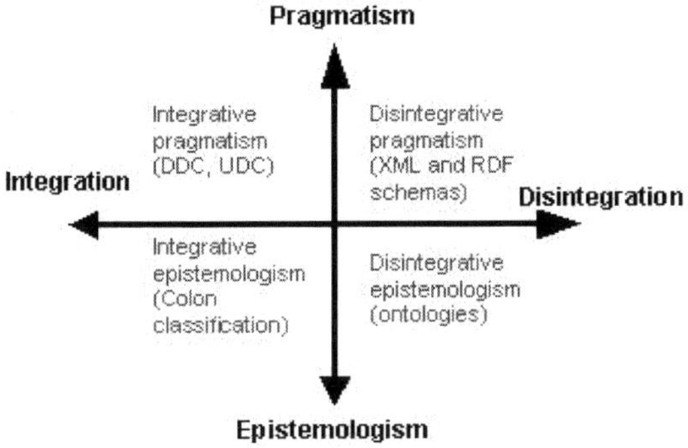

The deluge of digital data and information we have experienced in the last 20 years and our need to manage it puts traditional knowledge organization in the forefront. However, while "old tricks" in KO still work and are needed, they cannot keep up with the fast growth in the volume and complexity of digital data and information. Ontologies, as a special type of KOS, blend methods of classification and vocabulary control together with codified expressions and reasoning to handle the increasing complexity and volume of digital data and information, hence, they have quickly attracted the attention of the LIS community. Early ontology models that emerged from the LIS community started with re-engineering metadata models into ontologies, for example the ABC ontology that used Entity as the root class and Artifact, Event, Situation, Action, Agent, Work, Manifestation, Item, Time, and Place as direct subclasses (Lagoze and Hunter 2001), and the learning object ontology that remodelled the Gateway to Educational Materials (GEM) metadata schema into an ontological model (Qin and Paling 2001). Ontological models have also been developed and deployed to aggregate metadata from multiple sources and in multiple languages, as in the case of Europeana Data Model (Doerr et al. 2010), as well as in linking and opening datasets at cultural institutions to create broader access to art and archival collections, e.g., the well-known CIDOC Conceptual Reference Model (CRM) and the Linked Art Data Model (https://linked.art/model/index.html). After more than a decade's exploration and testing, the library, archive, and museum (LAM) communities have made significant progress in developing ontology theories and practices. The knowledge organization tradition in LIS has been summarized by Qin (2002) as falling into two paradigms: integration and disintegration. The integration paradigm has its root in the theory of "integrative levels" (Feibleman 1954), which views the physical world as cumulative with increased complexity, and classification systems such as the Dewey Decimal Classification (DDC) and the International Classification of Disease (IDC) are typical examples. The disintegration paradigm is the opposite: it does not use levels in organizing knowledge, but rather focuses on the concept and all aspects related to it, which is also called "polyrepresentation" (Ingwersen 1994). The spectrum from pragmatism to epistemologism represents the approaches utilizing the integration and disintegration paradigms. In the integration paradigm, both pragmatic and epistemological approaches share the same goal of organizing the universe of knowledge rather than solving problems (the left side of Figure 1), be it a hierarchical classification system, a faceted classification, or a system of controlled vocabulary with covert hierarchical relationships. In the disintegration paradigm, attention is given to data and problems in specific domains that require only relevant knowledge segments to solve the problems. As such, the scope of knowledge goes beyond publications to include data and other forms that embody knowledge. It is fair to say that, in the integration paradigm, the goal is to construct knowledge structures or systems to represent the knowledge universe by means of categorization, synthesis, and generalization, while the disintegration paradigm's goal is to solve problems by using knowledge organization as a means.

It is important to point out that KO activities and processes as well as KOS have some properties of KR, but they cannot be equated to KR in AI. Even though ontologies may be considered as the product of KR due to the fact that, in many ways, they resemble KR in artificial intelligence (AI), the objectives, methods through which KR is performed, and the outcomes differ fundamentally. Besides, not all ontologies are born equally in purpose, complexity, and function. In this sense, KO is not an interchangeable term for KR. What is knowledge representation then?

3. What Is Knowledge Representation?

There are many versions of the definition for knowledge representation in the AI field. KR has been defined as "a set of syntactic and semantic conventions that makes it possible to describe things", in which the syntax refers to "a set of rules for combining symbols so as to form valid expressions", while semantics are the specification of how such expressions are to be interpreted (Bench-Capon 1990, p.11). A more comprehensive definition is provided by Davies et al. (1993) who specify that a KR is a surrogate, a set of ontological commitments, a fragmentary theory of intelligent reasoning, a medium for efficient computation, and finally, a medium of human expression. Whether simple or comprehensive, these definitions share three core principles. First, knowledge about a domain can be represented systematically "in a sufficiently precise notation that it can be used in, or by, a computer program" and such a systematic representational method can be called a scheme (Hayes 1974, p.4). According to Hayes, such schemes include some programming languages, logical calculi, music notation, or "the systematic use of data structures to depict a world." The term *scheme* signifies a symbolic paradigm of AI (Bench-Capon 1990; Hoffmann 1998).

Another core principle for KR is the formality of representational schemes. The formality of KR refers to the fact that the schemes used for representing knowledge meet the criteria of adequacy and expressiveness. The adequacy criterion relates to things that the representation must have if it is to do what it is required to do. In other words, we need to produce an adequate number of representations of physical objects in the world, and such representations should enable us to both express the facts we wish to express and allow us to perform reasoning by using such representations in problem solving; additionally, these representations should be manipulable by computer systems. Semantically, the representations should be unambiguous, uniform, notationally convenient, relevant, and declarative (Hayes 1974; Bench-Capon 1990). The adequacy and expressiveness criteria for representation naturally lead to a third principle: reasoning or making decisions for solving problems must be based on the facts represented by the schemes. The expert systems that were developed during the late 1980s and 1990s are good examples; for example, the MedIndex system developed at the U.S. National Library of Medicine used the knowledge base frames to guide indexers in completing indexing frames for medical research publications (Humphrey 1989).

The principles above set the requirements for representing knowledge: they must be sufficiently precise and readable by computer programs to allow for reasoning in problem solving. Over the course of 30 years of KR research, the symbolic and connectionist paradigms have been prevalent in the AI field. While artificial intelligence has its intellectual predecessors from cognitive psychology, mathematics, philosophy of science, and cybernetics, the nature of intelligence and how to develop a formal theory of intelligence became the focus of early scholars in AI (Hoffmann 1998). This influence is also clear in the study of KR, which has produced some classical works by pioneers such as Patrick J. Hayes, John McCarthy, Brian C. Smith, Ronald J. Brachman, Marvin Minsky, and others (Brachman 1985). Three paradigms in KR emerged from research: (1) production rules (also called "symbolic paradigm" by Hoffmann (1998)) that are "the representation of knowledge as a set of condition action pairs," (2) semantic networks (or simply nets) and frames that are rooted in efforts to build systems to understand natural language by structuring objects in graphs (in mathematics) or networks and object-oriented frames, and (3) first-order predicate calculus (also first-order logic) (Bench-Capon 1990). Hoffmann (1998) named the semantic nets and frames as the "connectionist paradigm." Whether they are rule-based, object-oriented or logic-driven, these paradigms fulfill the expressive and adequacy criteria from different approaches and have strengths in different areas (as far as what these different approaches and strengths are, that would need another article to discuss).

4. Similarities between KO and KR paradigms

It is clear that paradigmatic differences exist the between KO and KR in terms of the goals, methods, and functions. In general, KO works at the conceptual level and uses language to describe concepts with phrases or terms, while KR focuses on formalizing the expressions in natural language as well as other types of data to enable reasoning as in human intelligence. This seemingly wide gap between the KO and KR paradigms is being bridged by ontologies that have become popular since Berners-Lee et al. (2001) proposed the concept of the semantic web. Ontology by its nature is "a specification of a conceptualization" (Gruber 1993). As a specification mechanism, an ontology defines classes of concepts or entities and relations between classes in a declarative formalism, which is then used to represent a set of objects. An example is the Gene Ontology (GO) that specifies about ten term elements and four main relations for gene terms from over 600,000 experimentally supported annotations. This central dataset offers "additional inference of over 6 million functional annotations for a diverse set of organisms spanning the tree of life" (Gene Ontology Consortium 2019). Another ontology example is Schema.org that contains a set of individual ontologies representing creative works, non-text objects, events, health and medical types, organizations, people, and other entities. From both ontologies, one can easily detect the inheritance of paradigms prevailed in the KO and KR communities. Table 1 provides a simplified summary of KO and KR paradigms based on goals, methods, and functions.

Table 1. Similarities in goals, methods, and functions between KO and KR paradigms

Paradigm		Goals	Methods	Functions
KO	Integration	Organize the knowledge universe	Categorize, classify generalize, synthesize	Represent knowledge in publications and organize knowledge about nature and/or society
	Disintegration	Organize the knowledge in a domain	Categorize, classify, generalize, synthesize, model	Represent knowledge in data and publications in a domain
KR	Production rules	Represent knowledge in condition-action pairs to solve problems	Use forward chaining algorithms to execute condition-action pairs	Represent fragmentary knowledge in entity-attribute-value (triple) format
	Semantic networks and frames	Represent semantic relations between concepts	Express semantic relations in triples	Connect knowledge nodes through attributes or slots to form a knowledge graph
	First-order logic	Formalize qualifier construction in natural language	Express declarative propositions using the first-order logic syntax and semantics	Produce a set of axioms for reasoning

The disintegration paradigm in KO as shown in Figure 1 is marked by the adoption of ontology as a methodology in developing knowledge organization systems (KOS). This turned out to be revolutionary for the traditional KO paradigm; it prompted the community to re-examine the KOS structures and explore ways for KOS to fully take advantage of technology advances. One of the most visible efforts in this area is transforming traditional vocabularies into linked open data. Remodeling controlled vocabularies into linked open data has made significant progress, as seen in linked data services offered by U.S. Library of Congress (http://id.loc.gov/) for its subject heading list and name authority file, among others, and the Getty Research Institute for its Art and Architecture Thesaurus (AAT), Thesaurus of Geographic Names (TGN), and the Union List of Artist Names (ULAN) (https://www.getty.edu/research/tools/vocabularies/lod/index.html).

Whether it is developing ontology from scratch (as in the cases of Gene Ontology and Schema.org) or remodeling existing vocabularies, it appears that the use of ontologies as a methodology for conceptualizing domain knowledge concentrates on two key features from both KO and KR paradigms:

- Formalism in representation schemes: the state-of-the-art encoding languages for ontologies offer a wide range of choices from Web Ontology Language to JSON.

These representational languages allow for inference through the creation of axioms.

- Structured objects as triples: The use of entity-attribute-value triples, for instance, (Jake age 18), is evidenced in rule-based paradigm as well as the semantic nets and frames. Although semantic nets and frames represent objects in a graph or network and are in a slightly different form from that used in a rule-based paradigm, the base representation is essentially the same triple structure.

Although the goals for KO and KR paradigms vary (Table 1), the similarities lie mainly in methods and functions. This new finding suggests that the KO community may look into the methodology and function similarities further to identify what new opportunities there may be for the KO community to make an impact in AI.

5. What Can KO Contribute to KR in AI?

The paradigmatic similarities in KO and KR provide some potential for KO to contribute its unique value to enrich knowledge representation. In KR, a well-known bottleneck problem is knowledge acquisition. Even though KR paradigms can produce well-designed and functioning formal representation schemes, these schemes need to have the facts and data decomposed, categorized, organized, and entered into the right places so the knowledgebase can be built and inferences performed. Natural language processing using machine learning has been one of the primary methods for acquiring knowledge from texts through clustering and classification (Fisher 1987). In a recent study, Qin et al. (2018) examined the results from manual and automatic detection of knowledge nodes (concepts) and relations from natural language texts in the domain of biomedical research. Their study found that, while manual and automatic tools (MetaMap and SemRep) generated comparable results in identifying knowledge nodes, the automatic tools either did not have the capability of detecting relations between concepts or did a poor job compared to human-generated relations. Acquiring and representing relations between concepts is the most challenging problem of knowledge acquisition in artificial intelligence. Even powerful machine-learning algorithms can fail to detect relations hidden in natural language that are critical for creating machine intelligence. The detection of relation patterns and development of new models and vocabularies for scaling up the relation detection task is an area that needs human intelligence.

Building the relation vocabulary does not need to start from scratch as many KOS can be utilized to aid the work. A good example is the Unified Medical Language System (UMLS), which has already identified a large number of relations as part of its vocabulary. For instance, Figure 2 shows part of the search result for the gene BRCA 1 (which causes breast cancer) in the UMLS. The UMLS provides a long list of relations for this concept and Figure 2 shows only five of them.

Figure 2. A UMLS example of a concept and relation representation

⊕ Concept: [C0376571] BRCA1 gene

⊖ Semantic Types

    Gene or Genome [T028]

⊖ Definitions

    MSH | A tumor suppressor gene (GENES, TUMOR SUPPRESSOR) located on human CHROMOSOME 17 at locus 17q21. Mutations of this gene are associated with the formation of HEREDITARY BREAST AND OVARIAN CANCER SYNDROME. It encodes a large nuclear protein that is a component of DNA repair pathways.

    NCI | This gene plays a role in cell cycle control, regulation of transcription and the maintenance of genomic stability. It is also involved in the inhibition of mammary cell growth.

⊖ Concept Relations (5)   REL | RELA | RSAB | String | CUI

    RO | | MTH | genetic analysis breast cancer gene 1 (lab test) | C2010863

    RO | | MTH | BRCA1 Protein | C0259275

    RO | | MTH | Hereditary Breast and Ovarian Cancer Syndrome | C0677776

    RN | | MTH | brca gene | C0596223

    RB | | MTH | BRCA1 wt Allele | C1704743

Utilizing the data from the UMLS, computer programs can be written to transform the data into the format suitable for KR. For example, the relations may be transformed into JSON format, one of the popular ontology encoding schemes:

```
{
        "@context": http://umls.gov/,
        "@concept": "BRCA1",
        "@semanticTypes": "Gene or Gennome",
        "@conceptRelations": {
                "@type": "genetic analysis breast cancer gene (lab test)"
                "@id": "C2010863"
                },
}
```

This simple example illustrates the potential for well-developed KOS to be restructured and/or remodeled to fit the needs of knowledge representation for artificial intelligence. But it is not trivial work to transform established KOS into KR-feasible structures. It is more than likely that new data and information will have to be added in order to make the transformation meaningful. As discussed above, relation representation and detection is still an area for much-needed investigation. Manual methods can do a finer job than current tools, but would not be able to scale. This gives rise to another area of research for the KO community: using AI techniques to mine data and documents to obtain sources for developing new vocabularies and knowledge organization systems.

6. Conclusion

The development of knowledge representation in AI provides ample opportunities and new perspectives for the KO community to re-examine the goals, methods, and products from KO activities. It is clear that some of the KO activities already stepped into the KR domain, such as the linked data services mentioned earlier in this paper. Although the prospects that KOS may contribute to KR can be exciting, there is a need for more research to locate exactly where the trajectory is for KO to converge with KR. The topic of KO and KR paradigms involves a great deal more than this paper has covered. The theory and methodology aspects in such a discussion will benefit both communities by broadening the research horizons in this field.

References

Bench-Capon, T.J.M. 1990. *Knowledge Representation: an approach to artificial intelligence.* London: Academic Press.

Berners-Lee, Tim, James Handler, and Ora Lassila. 2001. "The Semantic Web." *Scientific American*, Featured article, May 1.

Brachman, Ronald J. and Hector J. Levesque (Ed.). 1985. *Readings in Knowledge Representation*. Los Altos, CA: Morgan Kauffman Publishers.

Castano, Silvana and Gaia Varese. 2011. "Trust-based techniques for collective intelligence through folksonomy coordination." In *Next Generation Data Technologies for Collective Computational Intelligence*, ed. Nik Bessis and Fatos Xhafa, Chapter 4, pp.87-112. Berlin: Springer-Verlag.

Chen, Miao, Xiaozhong Liu, and Jian Qin. 2008. "Semantic relation extraction from socially-generated tag: A methodology for metadata extraction." In *Proceedings of the Dublin Core International Conference*, September 22-25, 2008, Berlin, Germany. http://dcpapers.dublincore.org/pubs/article/view/924/920

Davis, Randall, Howard Shrobe, and Peter Szolovits. 1993. "What is a knowledge representation?" *AI Magazine*, 14:17-33. http://groups.csail.mit.edu/medg/ftp/psz/k-rep.html

Doerr, Martin, Stefan Gradmann, Steffen Hennicke, Antoine Isaac, Carlo Meghini, and Herbert van de Sompel. 2010. "The Europeana Data Model (EDM)." In *World Library and Information Congress: 76th IFLA General Conference and Assembly* 10-15 August 2010, Gothenburg, Sweden. https://core.ac.uk/download/pdf/34626222.pdf

Feibleman, James K. 1954. "Theory of integrative levels." *British Journal for the Philosophy of Science*, 5: 59-66. (Reprinted in: L. M. Chan, Richmond, P. A., and Svenonius, E. (Eds.), Theory of Subject Analysis: A Sourcebook, pp.138-143. Littleton, Colo., Libraries Unlimited, 1989.)

Fisher, Douglas H. 1987. "Knowledge acquisition via incremental conceptual clustering." Machine Learning, 2: 139-172.

Gene Ontology Consortium. 2019. *The Gene Ontology and the Scientific Literature.* http://geneontology.org/docs/literature/

Gruber, Tom R. 1993. "A translation approach to portable ontologies." *Knowledge Acquisition*, 5(2):199-220.

Haug, Peter. 1993. "Uses of diagnostic expert systems in clinical care." In *Proceedings. Symposium on Computer Applications in Medical Care* pp.379-83. PubMed PMID: 8130499.

Hayes, Patrick J. 1974. "Some problems and non-problem in representational theory." In *Readings in Knowledge Representation*, ed. Ronald J. Brachman and Hector J. Levesque. Los Altos, CA: Morgan Kaufmann.

Hjørland, Birger. 2008. "What is knowledge organization (KO)?" Knowledge Organization, 35(2/3): 86-101.

Hoffmann, Achim. 1998. *Paradigms of Artificial Intelligence: a methodological & computational analysis.* New York: Springer.

Humphrey, Susanne. 1989. "MedIndex system: medical indexing expert system." *Information Processing & Management*, 25(1): 73-88.

Ingwersen, Peter. 1994. "Polyrepresentation of information needs and semantic entities: elements of a cognitive theory for information retrieval interaction." In *Proceedings of the 17th Annual International ACM/SIGIR Conference on Research and Development of Information Retrieval*, pp. 101-110. New York: Spring-Verlag.

Kubat, Miroslav, Gert Pfurtscheller, and Doris Flotzinger. 1993. "AI-based approach to automatic sleep classification." *Biological Cybernetics*, 70: 443-448.

Lagoze, Carl and Hunter, Jane. 2001. "The ABC ontology and model." In *Proceedings of the DCMI International Conference on Dublin Core and Metadata Applications 2001*, October 24-26, 2001, Tokyo, Japan, ed. Keizo Oyama and Hironobu Gotoda. Tokyo: National Institute of Informatics, 160-176. http://dcpapers.dublincore.org/pubs/article/view/655

NCBI. (2018). *Taxonomy.* https://www.ncbi.nlm.nih.gov/taxonomy

Qin, Jian and Paling, Stephen. 2001. "Converting a controlled vocabulary into an ontology: the case of GEM." *Information Research: An International Electronic Journal*, 6(2): http://InformationR.net/ir/6- 2/paper94.html

Qin, Jian. 2002. "Evolving paradigms of knowledge representation and organization: A comparative study of classification, XML/DTD, and Ontology." In *Proceedings of the Seventh International Society for Knowledge Organization Conference*, July 10-12, 2002, Granada, Spain, 465-471. Würzburg, Germany: Ergon.

Toms, Elaine. 2019. "Artificial intelligence and information science?" Discussion thread from *ASIST Open Forum.*

Should we Abandon all Taxonomies in the Light of New AI Tools?

Michael Upshall, UNISLO, Denmark

Abstract

Traditionally in academic publishing, libraries and publishers sought to facilitate the academic workflow, to solve problems such as information discovery, using some kind of classification, whether a thesaurus, taxonomy, or subject headings. The recent dramatic growth of corpus-based machine learning has created a very different methodology, with automatic identification of concepts "indexing" a document in a few seconds without human supervision. The technology of unsupervised cluster-based machine learning has made it possible for content owners to consider alternative approaches, not only for information retrieval, but also for a wide range of workflow tasks in academic publishing, which could include achieving business goals such as finding reviewers or identifying relevant journals. These new tools can provide a valid alternative to the creation and management of a formal taxonomy or ontology. This paper considers the main features, benefits and drawbacks of this new technology, and, via case studies, makes suggestions for the most appropriate tools for information management. Rather than identifying one methodology as a perfect solution for all use cases, the best tool for the job will depend on the circumstances of use: the existence of a formal public ontology, for example, or the balance of precision over recall (or the other way around).

1. Introduction

The rapid growth of academic content, particularly in STEM (science, technology, engineering and medicine) in the last hundred years has transformed the way that academics work. The processes of, for example, submitting an article for publication, of reviewing it for suitability, and of finding relevant literature, make it imperative to look for automated assistance. To take one example, that of content alerts (a tool for identifying relevant content), it is challenging, if not impossible, for researchers to keep up with the number of publications in their specialist area. Increasingly, researchers use some kind of automated assistance to identify new specialist articles. The days when an academic would browse through the latest issue of a specialist journal in the library are long gone. Several publishers provide an email alerting service by which academics can sign up to receive articles tagged for their specialist subject. However, such alerting systems vary widely in precision and utility, from the user simply requesting to receive details of any article published in a journal, to the setting up of a set of keywords that correspond with terms in a taxonomy used to classify each new journal article.

Content alerts are an example where the new technology of unsupervised concept extraction provides new choices for publishers, authors and information professionals. They comprise just one component of the scholarly workflow, which was linked by Kramer and Bosman into six main phases and over 101 separate innovative tools for managing them (2015).

Clearly there is a proliferation of new ideas and methodologies. For this use case, as for many others in academic publishing, should researchers now adopt the new tools and abandon existing taxonomies? Are the machine-learning tools reliable enough for widespread adoption? This article considers some case studies that have implemented different solutions, including publishers with private taxonomies used by organizations, the use of large-scale, public-controlled vocabularies such as MeSH, and some innovative business use cases that have been solved without the use of any classification system.

2. Using AI for information discovery and retrieval
The challenge of searching for content dates back hundreds, if not thousands, of years. The creation of the first library catalogue in the 18th century (Wikipedia 2019b) was an indication of the need for some kind of organised solution to the problem of information retrieval.

The rise of machine-learning tools to analyse natural language (the language used by humans, in this case in the form of academic articles) dates back to the invention of the term in 1959, but the widespread adoption of unsupervised machine learning dates from its separation from symbolist methodologies in the last few years of the 1990s, and moved to statistical and inference models, based on the use of large corpora (an example of big data, a large data set highly suitable for computer analysis), using natural language processing.

The symbolist approach to machine learning is based on the use of symbolic (human-readable) representations (Domingos 2015). These include expert systems, which comprise a set of rules and an inference engine which applies the rules to the knowledge base and then states some new knowledge. While expert systems were very popular during the 1980s and 1990s, they have become less widespread since then. The reason for the decline of symbolist approaches was because all the rules used by the algorithms had to be known in advance in order for the system to make use of them. As a result, symbolist approaches work best on very constrained problems, such as chess.

The alternative to symbolist AI is connectionist learning, loosely based on the way the human brain works: a collection of simple components working together as a neural network. Connectionist approaches can be divided by the kind of feedback given, broadly into supervised and unsupervised learning (Russell 2011, p. 694). Supervised learning requires some input, requiring an expert who can judge whether a link is relevant or not. Having once determined, for example, the field of quantum physics, it would be possible to use a supervised model to tag content to this field. But that requires a human stage: an expert is required to identify which documents require the relevant tags.

Unsupervised learning, in contrast, uses no human input at the point of classification. Once the algorithm is built, the process of tagging does not involve further human intervention, but more fundamentally, with the unsupervised methodology described here, there is no need to start from any rules. Given a large enough corpus, the system can identify what each document in that corpus is "about". The first stage is to analyse the corpus of documents, and to identify significant words and phrases from the text. These might be very similar to the terms that appear in a taxonomy, e.g. "heart disease", or a list of entities such as "Harvard University", but they might also be terms that, while significant for a document, are not terms that would be tagged in a taxonomy: for example "high temperature" might be very significant in a medical article. Once extracted, the concepts are then normalised for syntactic variations (for example, "disease of the kidney" and "kidney disease") and then used in groups, known as clusters. Similarity between documents is identified using overlap between clusters of concepts, rather than simply having one or two concepts in common. Mathematical modelling is used to identify members of a cluster which are "similar in some respect" (Pustejovsky and Stubbs 2012, p.22).

Unsupervised clustering concept extraction is a form of machine learning. According to Wikipedia (2019c), machine learning is defined as "the scientific study of algorithms and statistical models that computer systems use to effectively perform a specific task without using explicit instructions, relying on patterns and inference instead".

3. Unsupervised concept extraction

In contrast to a hierarchical organisation of concepts, the unsupervised concept extraction process creates clusters of related concepts for each document in the corpus. For some purposes, for example placing a book or article within a library hierarchical classification scheme, these clusters may not be very helpful because there is no one-to-one relationship between a single concept and a classification term, particularly a high-level term from a hierarchy such as "physics" or "chemistry". Yet the assignment of a document to a particular point in a classification hierarchy is almost never the end point of any academic use case. The typical academic article in any case is almost never about only one subject, but about a cluster of subjects. A typical academic article title reveals this clearly, for example, the title "Renal failure in septic shock: predictive value of Doppler-based renal arterial resistive index" contains at least four concepts, and no doubt the article full text contains many more (see the example in Figure 1).

Figure 1 Example of unsupervised concept extraction for an academic article (DOI: 10.1007/s00134-006-0360-x)

Intensive care medicine · 2006 · Journal Article

Renal failure in septic shock: predictive value of Doppler - based renal arterial resistive index

Lerolle, Nicolas · Guérot, Emmanuel · Faisy, Christophe · Bornstain, Caroline · Diehl, Jean-Luc · Fagon, Jean-Yves

Concepts mentioned in document

Top concepts   Matching only

| Renal Arterial Resistive Index | Scale For The Assessment Of Positive Symptoms | Resistive Index Measurements | Septic Shock |

| Arterial Lactate Concentration | Risk/Injury/Failure/Loss/End-stage Classification | ✓ Risk/Injury/Failure/Loss/End-stage |

| Renal Artery | ✓ Renal Failure | Lactate Concentration | Septic Shock Patients | Acute Renal Failure |

| ✓ Chronic Renal Failure | Vasopressor | Mean Arterial Pressure | ✓ Acute Kidney Injury | Arterial Lactate | Micromol |

| Positive Likelihood Ratio | University Hospital | « SHOW LESS |

Renal failure in septic shock: predictive value of Doppler-based renal arterial resistive index. 1553-9
Because acute renal failure (ARF) is frequent in septic shock, an early marker of ARF could impact on

A taxonomist using a hierarchical system adding codes to this document might add a maximum of five or six indexing terms, due to limitations of time, but it can be seen from the list of concepts in Figure 1 that there are many more that could be identified. Only the twenty more relevant concepts are shown in the figure, but the algorithm identifies many more. In other words, the clustering technique that identifies hundreds of concepts enables much more granular matching with related content to be achieved.

4. Benefits and drawbacks of unsupervised concept extraction
It should not be thought that unsupervised concept extraction is inherently right or wrong compared to the tagging of a document to a formal taxonomy. The best approach when evaluating the methodologies is to look at the specific circumstances.

Several criteria should be taken into account when choosing the best option for information-related tasks. Some of the main criteria are outlined below.

4.1 Cost and scalability and speed of execution

Human tagging is not easy to scale. While it is feasible to index 100 documents by hand, it becomes problematic to index 1,000 documents, and to tag one million documents would incur a prohibitive cost. In contrast, a machine-based algorithm is scalable in that once the algorithm has been created, the only cost remaining is the preparation of the data and the cost of running the servers required to run the process. The continuing fall in real costs of data storage and processing has enabled this kind of technology to become commercially viable in the last 20 years or so. Moreover, the quality of the concept extraction improves with a larger corpus.

As for the speed of execution, the time taken to tag one million documents by hand would be measured in human years of labour; the equivalent concept extraction can be completed in hours.

When considering costs, the full cost of a taxonomy-based system should include the cost of maintaining the taxonomy. These require continuous maintenance as new terms come into use.

4.2 Corpus and corpus size

In this area, machine-based tools become more and more preferable as the potential corpus widens. Until the development of open-access content, most academic content was hidden behind firewalls. The aim of any academic is to have access to the entirety of content in their domain, ideally with the full text available. As open-access content forms a higher and higher proportion of all academic content, it starts to become feasible to imagine the academic dream realised. Moreover, the advantages of tagging a vast corpus using a single consistent methodology are obvious. For many purposes, the entirety of academic content as the corpus would be ideal, for example when identifying peer reviewers.

Currently, the largest collection of full text content within a single domain is PubMed, which, although it contains over 26 million abstracts, has less than two million articles available with full text.

4.3 Replicability

One argument adduced in favour of Boolean search is that it is replicable, and hence more reliable. By replicable it is understood that the same search carried out on the same corpus would produce the same results. However, there are some caveats to this admirable principle. First, it is very difficult to demonstrate replicability. Studies have shown that search strategies for systematic reviews are frequently poorly documented; one study found only 22% of articles included one reproducible search strategy (Koffel and Rethlefsen 2016). Moreover, even when the search methodology is reproduced, it is often limited to title and abstract, which may leave out use of relevant terms in the full text. Secondly, it is difficult to demonstrate clearly that the Boolean search tools used do not miss any articles (false negatives). A typical Boolean search for a systematic review, for example, may be several lines long, and difficult to interpret clearly.

Unsupervised concept extraction can be similarly replicable, in that the concepts used to build a collection can be captured and re-run against the same time-limited corpus, for example all articles published between 2016 and 2018. In other words, replicability should not be a criterion for choice of tool if the concept extraction algorithm is implemented with transparency.

4.4 Need for subject-matter experts (SMEs)
Some expert involvement is required in any subject tagging, but once a subject cluster has been built, an efficient design of the algorithm should enable the process to run largely or wholly without human expert involvement. Although this sounds radical, many systematic reviews of medical topics using Boolean search are run by information professionals rather than by SMEs. One way to ensure more control over the result is to introduce a human-based stage in the creation of each collection, as described below.

4.5 Granularity
It would be reasonable to assume that the more granular the taxonomy, the more precise the classification of a document. But tagging by hand is expensive; roughly speaking, the granularity of the tagging varies in proportion with the cost. In consequence, human indexers tend to use a limited number of terms to tag content.

One of the most granular examples of tagging content by providing subject headings is MEDLINE, a bibliographic database of medical and life science academic content. Most of the approximately 29 million bibliographic citations in MEDLINE include subject codes, which were created by human indexers (National Library of Medicine n.d.). Each of the MeSH indexers is qualified at least to degree level in life sciences; in other words, they are all subject matter experts (SMEs). Nonetheless, the indexers only tag using a small number from the 27,000 descriptors available, typically using a maximum of ten to 12 terms per article (Chapman 2009). Depending on the use case, this may be sufficient for retrieval of content, but it is not difficult to imagine situations where a more granular list of concepts would enable a more precise set of results to be obtained. A relatively small number of descriptor tags would be insufficient to identify adverse reactions from the medical literature. The use of text mining of clinical reports and case studies for evidence of hitherto unnoticed interactions (see, for example Hammann and Drewe, 2014) is an example; taxonomies are insufficiently granular and locked into single disciplines for this kind of information extraction.

4.6 Ease of updating

One key requirement for commercial applications of this technology is the need to keep up with publications as they happen. Researchers are not satisfied with a delay of weeks between the first publication of an article and its indexing. This is a major challenge for any manual operation. In contrast, it is relatively simple to adapt a machine-based system to create a continuous ingestion model by which new articles are indexed within hours of their publication.

4.7 Flexibility

Classification systems, however much they may aim to be universal, are rooted in attitudes and ideas of their time. It is well known, for example, (see e.g. Qaisar 1974), that the Dewey Decimal Classification allocates far more space for cataloguing works on Christianity (divisions 220-290) than for works on Islam (division 297): there are several hundred more Dewey codes available for Christianity than for Islam. It is not feasible to change a classification system after it has started being used; the only solution is to use lengthy and inconvenient number strings to compensate. Moreover, the major classification systems such as IET Inspec (for engineering and physics) and Chemical Abstracts (CAS) (for chemistry) are typically based around a single domain, as well as being based on assumptions of how the material will be used, which may of course differ in practice.

4.8 Availability of public classification systems

In some domains, there is a large-scale public classification tool available, for example MeSH for life sciences and medicine. As a public list of subject headings, MeSH has the advantage that many different services and tools can point to it to ensure a compatible common terminology in the medical space; for example, MeSH lists under "heart disease" many related terms such as "cardiac arrhythmia", "myocardial ischemia", and "heart failure". The compilation of these related terms can be used to facilitate searching for related content. However, few subject domains have the unifying vocabulary available in medicine and life science via MeSH. In English history, for example, there is no resource that lists all the various ways of describing an English monarch, who could be referred to variously as "Henry the Seventh", "Henry VII", "Henry vii of England", "Henry 7th", "Henry Tudor", and so on.

It is possible to combine the two approaches, so that concepts from a public taxonomy such as MeSH can be introduced to the unsupervised concept extraction process, so that the algorithm searches for terms that correspond to the accepted terminology of MeSH. For most academic subject areas, and particularly across domains, with topics such as climate change or the history of medicine, a standard taxonomy will not be available, and an unsupervised approach is the most relevant.

4.9 Bias

Typically, machine-learning algorithms reflect the bias in the corpus that is used, even though the developers may not consciously incorporate any bias. This may lead to some surprising results, for example a search on Google for "most grand slam wins tennis" frequently displays Roger Federer's name first, although three women have won more grand slams than Federer, a statistic that is often only revealed when a gender qualifier such as "female" is added to the search. The bias may have occurred on the sites indexed by Google, but the result is bias, nonetheless.

It cannot be said that a machine-based approach is more or less likely to introduce bias; bias is omnipresent when dealing with content, and the only way to create an effective machine-learning algorithm is to be bias-aware.

There may be occasions where bias can be countered using this approach. For example, the recent Publons Global State of Peer Review Report reveals that Chinese academics review many fewer articles than their academic output would predict, or, to put it another way, editors disproportionately select reviewers from their own region (Publons 2018 p.14). There may be several reasons for this, but one possible solution would be an automatic tool that selects reviewers not from the reviews they have written (which would replicate the above bias) but to use academic papers they have written as a source. But to reiterate, it is only by being aware of bias that it becomes possible to counter the effects of bias, and this applies to any methodology for identifying content.

Figure 2 Bias in search engines: search on Google for "most grand slam wins tennis" (Google search 12 May 2019)

4.10 Measuring accuracy

When tagging a document by hand, for example in compiling an index or adding subject tags, humans do not agree completely. Studies suggest that two human indexers are unlikely to agree more than 70% of the time (see, for example, a review article by Leonard on inter-indexer consistency, Leonard 1977).

The standard measure of accuracy for AI tools is to use the F1 score, the harmonic mean of precision and recall (see, for example, Wikipedia 2019a). However, the F1 score typically uses a human-created set of gold documents against which the machine is evaluated. Given the limited agreement described above, the F1 score is not, therefore, a perfect tool for evaluation. There is a limitation in what is known as the "ground truth" – a comparison between what the algorithm predicts and what we know in reality (Manning et al., 2009, p.152). Strangely, the literature on measurement of machine learning tends not to mention this issue: the Wikipedia article for F1 score makes no mention of it. If the set of relevance judgements (the set of correct documents against which the test set will be evaluated) was created by hand, then the highest accuracy that can be achieved by a machine will be no greater than the accuracy of the humans who created the training set. To talk of "95%

accuracy" for an algorithm is therefore meaningless when even trained human indexers agree considerably less than this. More precisely, the score should be 95% of 70%, which is considerably less. As Manning states (Manning et al. 2009, p.206), "A human is not a device that reliably reports a gold standard judgement of relevance of a document to a query." Manning et al measured the "kappa value": "the kappa value will be 1 if two judges always agree, and 0 if they agree only at the rate given by chance". Using that scale, they found for medical collections of documents that "the level of agreement normally falls into the range of 'fair' (0.67-0.8)".

A further drawback of using the F1 score as a universal measure is that, depending on the use case, precision or recall might be preferable; the F1 score simply assumes they are of equal importance. Recall errors are when a collection is missing a document that should have been assigned to it, while precision errors are when a collection includes documents that do not belong with it. There are plenty of use cases where either precision or recall might be favoured, rather than keeping them with equal importance. For example, an academic who wants to be informed about recent articles related to their topic might promote recall over precision – better to have a few more documents that are relevant and to eliminate by hand a few false positives. When investigating medical diagnoses, a false positive will typically be less of a problem than a false negative.

4.11 Errors in the algorithm and the "black box" effect
Humans are wary, perhaps with reason, of any process that replaces humans by an entirely automatic operation which is not explained. A common criticism levelled at machine-learning tools such as unsupervised concept extraction is that the results have to be taken on trust; they are, effectively, a "black box" and cannot be modified. Once the machine has determined its results, there is no opportunity for feedback.

There are two kinds of potential error here. First, there may be an error in the corpus or in the algorithm, and there should be some means of communicating that error to the developers so that a fix can be identified. For example, a misspelling in the corpus, such as "Shakspeare" for "Shakespeare" may be identified by the algorithm as a discrete concept, and so there needs to be some kind of feedback to the developers to enable errors of this kind to be fixed.

Secondly, and more commonly, the human evaluator may not understand how the machine reached its conclusion or may disagree with the results presented. This problem can be dealt with by making the process carried out by the machine as transparent as possible, and by providing where possible a human feedback loop. For example, the initial results of creating a subject collection can be presented to the user for their evaluation and modification of the concepts included in that collection. In Figure 3, for example, the user can see clearly how many (and which) documents are included in a collection after identifying a number of relevant concepts. Using the selected cluster of concepts, the system "auto-approves" a number of matching documents, shown in the form of a histogram with three clearly delineated sections: documents auto-approved, documents highlighted for manual review, and documents auto-discarded because they do not contain enough of the concepts selected by the user. The user can then, if they wish, refine the cluster set and create a new histogram before approving the final collection.

Figure 3 Provision of a manual feedback loop for a machine-generated subject collection

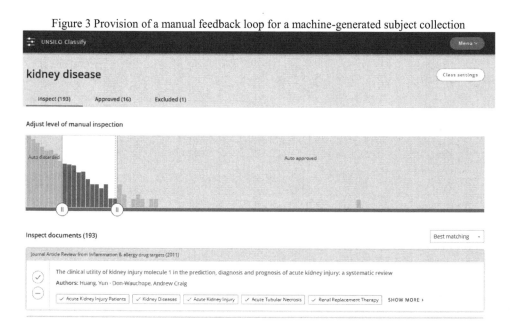

It is worth noting that both kinds of error can arise with documents grouped using human-generated taxonomies, but it is rare for any online system to provide a feedback mechanism of this kind for users.

5. Traditional use of classification systems

Fundamentally, classification is simply "grouping together things which are alike" (Batley 2014, p.1). The difficulty is how that grouping is done. Similarity on an e-commerce site is very different to similarity for scholarly articles about heart disease. An understanding of the use case is fundamental to a determination of the most appropriate tools. However, use cases are not often considered in textbooks on classification; the focus is typically on the "how", not on the "why".

Why do we use classification? Several reasons have been advanced to justify the classification process. Among the problems that knowledge organization sets out to solve, that of information retrieval is fundamental. David Tyckoson (2006 p.42) is typical in identifying the library catalogue and the Dewey Decimal system as two of the "top ten innovations in library history" but fails to mention anything about more recent techniques for finding content. The adoption of machine-learning tools has the potential to transform information retrieval (and other related activities), because well-designed tools are created to solve the user problem rather than to focus on a classification system that provides at best an intermediate solution.

Library classification systems, such as the Dewey Decimal Classification (DDC) and Library of Congress (LCC) systems, remain rooted in the paradigm of a physical library. Since a physical book can only exist in one location in a library, it is necessary for a cataloguer to determine what that location should be; in other words, the end point of the classification process is a single "best" code. To some extent, this limitation was remedied by the introduction of faceted classification systems, such as Bliss or the Universal Decimal Classification. These tools have the advantage of using more than one code to designate a work. Nonetheless, even faceted systems use only a small number of facets, and these can be insufficiently granular for many purposes, as described above.

6. Why use cases are important when making decisions about classification
As stated above, it is unlikely that a universal ontology for all subjects could be created; if it were, and general library classification systems are examples of this, it would be continually out of date and insufficiently granular for many purposes. It is very rare to find any academic author who agrees with the classification determined for an academic monography by the Library of Congress or Dewey cataloguers. But most importantly, decisions on classification should be based on use cases. Trying to address the issue of knowledge representation, one standard textbook on artificial intelligence (Russell 2011, p.462) presents various ways of encoding knowledge but then gives an example of e-commerce. Classification for e-commerce is very different to other kinds of searching: there is considerable use of faceted search, and the choice of a specific term for a facet is crucial. While for searching an academic article, it would generally be good to include synonyms in a search, but the opposite is often the case for e-commerce sites. Even though "king" and "monarch" are synonyms, searching for a "monarch-size" bed on an e-commerce site will

be much less successful than searching for a "king-sized" bed (Levi 2019). But for academics searching the web for references to "myocardial infarction", it might be very helpful to expand the search to include synonyms such as "cardiac arrest" and "heart attack", creating a semantic-based search rather than simply expanding the search to include syntactic variations such as plurals and inflected forms (for example, expanding "heart attack" to "heart attacks"). In other words, different uses entail very different solutions. Without an understanding of the use case, the choice of appropriate tools cannot be made.

7. Clustering compared with hierarchy

Traditional discussions of classification typically use hierarchical classification, such as the Linnaean classification of the animal and plant kingdoms, as a model. This classification model has in common with library systems that it is based on a single location: any individual species can only be placed in one location within the hierarchy of living things. However relevant that methodology may be for life sciences, it is not necessarily appropriate for all kinds of information.

Rather than a hierarchy with multiple levels and a single definitive code, the unsupervised concept extraction process has a much less rigid approach to identifying one or a small number of definitive concepts. Instead, an academic article is identified via a large number of clustered concepts. By aggregating clusters of concepts and then using that cluster to identify overlapping articles, it is possible to identify close relationships without the use of a taxonomy. An example of this clustering of concepts can be seen in Figure 4. A single concept identified in this way is not a definitive guide to the article, but the cluster of concepts may provide more precise links to related content than any single tag from a hierarchical taxonomy.

8. Case study: finding a peer reviewer

Finding peer reviewers is a good example of a use case that can be solved without the need for a taxonomy. In Figure 5, a submitted manuscript is shown on the right of the screen, and the system automatically identifies a number of relevant reviewers on the left. The process simply identifies overlapping concepts between the submitted article and other recent articles on the same concepts, sorted and displayed by person. A conflict-of-interest check ensures that the proposed reviewer is not based at the same institution as the author of the submission.

Figure 4 Example of related articles, identified using overlapping clusters of concepts, e.g. "patellar lateral shift"

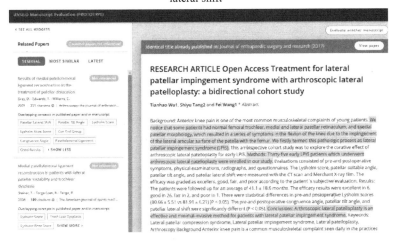

Figure 5 Example of unsupervised peer reviewer finder

What is interesting in this case is that no intermediary stage is required between the identification of the reviewers and the submission of the article. The unsupervised process uses concepts (such as "patellar lateral shift") that were identified as significant in the submitted article about the treatment of knee pain and finds papers that have the closest-matching cluster of concepts. A single click creates the transition from submitted article to suggested reviewer(s). In contrast, any other system using keywords and the tagging of an article uses two steps and is likely to be far less accurate.

9. Case study: The United Nations Sustainable Development Goals (SDGs)

Figure 6 The United Nations Sustainable Development Goals

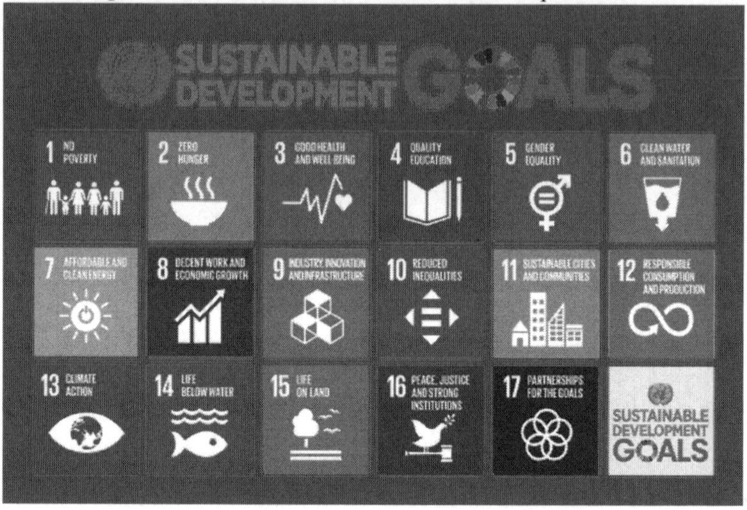

The United Nations Sustainable Development Goals (SDGs) (https://sustainabledevelopment.un.org/) is a set of 17 targets adopted in 2015. It is described by the UN as "a shared blueprint for peace and prosperity for people and the planet, now and into the future". These SDGs are being used by many intergovernmental organisations (IGOs) who wish to link their publications with the relevant SDGs, so that common goals can be identified. While the SDGs are a set of high-level priorities, they do not comprise or correspond with any existing formal taxonomy. Each goal is described in the 2015 Resolution, albeit in a very brief way; for example, "prosperity" is defined as "We are determined to ensure that all human beings can enjoy prosperous and fulfilling lives and that economic, social and technological progress occurs in harmony with nature". Such a document, however well intentioned, is challenging if an attempt is made to match it with a corpus to identify whether a document in that corpus is or is not concerned with prosperity.

In practice, there are a number of documents published by the UN that exemplify and describe the SDGs in more detail. This collection of documents can be used as a training set, giving examples in context of what constitutes relevance to each of the goals. Once a training set has been identified, the goal for the machine is to identify commonality across the corpus with each SDG. To achieve this goal by hand would be a major challenge; the OECD, for example, has over 250,000 publications available via its website. Instead, the training set of documents uses unsupervised concept extraction to identify common concepts. The cluster of concepts is then used as the basis of a trawl of the publications. The initial machine results are then partially curated by the use of an adjustable level of human supervision, as described above (0).

10. Adoption by the publishing industry

Whatever the potential of machine-based tools, they only become valuable when adopted as part of commercial publishing practice. A research article may find that a new methodology is fundamentally superior to earlier systems, and yet there are still good reasons for not adopting it.

The application of academic articles to operational practice is not a straightforward process, for the following reasons:

- Publishers, particularly society publishers, are cautious and perhaps not primarily motivated by cost considerations;
- Taxonomists are often unwilling to evaluate a methodology that changes their responsibilities;
- Publishers may be unwilling to engage with the challenge of rethinking their role with authors and institutions, when the current system appears to work reasonably well.

One of the paradoxes of scientific innovation is that new inventions are not always adopted by the industry they were designed for. XML, the mark-up language used by much of the world's academic publishing, was adopted widely only many years after it had been taken up in different sectors, such as the exchange of financial transaction information by banks; according to a Gartner report, around 50% of US banks were already using XML widely as early as 2003 (Knox 2003). Such a divergence between the ostensible use of a tool or technique and its actual adoption suggests the adoption of machine-learning tools may not be based around entirely rational criteria.

11. Conclusion

Given the limitations of the taxonomic and hierarchical approaches, does this mean that unsupervised concept extraction should replace them entirely? This article examined alternative ways of identifying relatedness, using traditional reasons for tagging and classifying content, and considered recent developments in machine learning, and suggests there is unlikely to be one universal solution to all information-related problems in the academic workflow. The two case studies considered here, tagging content to the relevant The United Nations Sustainable Development Goals, and finding peer reviewers for a new manuscript article, may be examples where machine-learning tools work well, but it is not suggested that all taxonomies be abandoned. Instead, there is an urgent need for information professionals in academic publishers and institutions to be able to evaluate alternatives, to be able to compare a range of options before making a definitive choice.

To quote from the recent STM report, discussing semantic enrichment (Johnson et al. 2018):

What has moved on is the assumption that a taxonomy is required [...] The more recent content analysis approaches (in semantic enrichment and AI) use more statistical and grammatical analysis, rather than analysis against a taxonomy or ontology. This makes them more flexible and potentially more fine-grained in their output. It also removes the need for the upkeep of such taxonomies and ontologies. There are cases where the use of a taxonomy or ontology are still appropriate, but this should no longer be the assumed starting point.

References

Batley, S. 2014. *Classification in Theory and Practice*. Chandos Publishing, Oxford.

Chapman, D, 2009. "Advanced Search Features of PubMed." *Journal of the Canadian Academy of Child Adolescent Psychiatry* 18: 58–59.

Domingos, P, 2015. *The Master Algorithm: how the quest for the ultimate learning machine will remake our world*. Basic Books, New York.

Hammann, F. & J. Drewe 2014. "Data mining for potential adverse drug–drug interactions". *Expert Opinion on Drug Metabolism & Toxicology* 10: 665–671.

Johnson, Rob, Anthony Watkinson, & Michael Mabe. 2018. *The STM Report 2018: an overview of scientific and scholarly journal publishing*. 5th ed. The Hague: International Association of Scientific, Technical and Medical Publishers.

Knox, M. 2003. *Measurement Improves FSP Data Quality*. Gartner Research Note. https://www.bus.umich.edu/kresgepublic/journals/gartner/research/118900/118970/118970.html

Koffel, J.B. & M.L Rethlefsen. 2016. "Reproducibility of Search Strategies Is Poor in Systematic Reviews." In *High-Impact Pediatrics, Cardiology and Surgery Journals: A Cross-Sectional Study*. PLOS ONE 11, e0163309. https://doi.org/10.1371/journal.pone.0163309

Kramer, B. & J. Bosman. 2015. *101 Innovations in Scholarly Communication - the Changing Research Workflow*. https://doi.org/10.6084/m9.figshare.1286826.v1

Leonard, L.E. 1977. *Inter-Indexer Consistency Studies, 1954-1975: a review of the literature and summary of study results*. University of Illinois School of Library Science, Occasional Papers, no 131 54.

Levi, O., 2019. *The Unique Challenges in Ecommerce Search: a case study at eBay*. Presented at the European Conference on Information Retrieval, Cologne.

Manning, C., P. Raghavan & H. Schuetze. 2009. *Introduction to Information Retrieval*. Cambridge University Press, Cambridge.

National Library of Medicine. N.D. *Frequently Asked Questions about Indexing for MEDLINE.* https://www.nlm.nih.gov/bsd/indexfaq.html

Publons. 2018. *Global State of Peer Review 2018.* http://publons.com/community/gspr/

PubMed - *NCBI.* n.d. https://www.ncbi.nlm.nih.gov/pubmed/ (accessed 5.5.19).

Pustejovsky, J., Stubbs, A. 2012. *Natural Language Annotation for Machine Learning: a guide to corpus-building for applications.* Sebastapol, CA: O'Reilly Media.

Qaisar, S.M.H. 1974. *Islamic Sciences: expansion of Dewey Decimal Classification ed. XVI, for Oriental Libraries.* Aligarh Muslim University, Institute of Islamic Studies.

Russell, S.J. 2011. *Artificial Intelligence: a modern approach*, 3rd ed.; International ed., Prentice Hall series in artificial intelligence. Addison Wesley, Harlow.

Tyckoson, D. 2006. "Top Ten Innovations in Library History." *Against the Grain* 18(6) Article 13. https://doi.org/10.7771/2380-176X.4690

Wikipedia. 2019a. *F1 Score.* https://en.wikipedia.org/wiki/F1_score

Wikipedia. 2019b. *Library catalog.* https://en.wikipedia.org/wiki/Library_catalog

Wikipedia. 2019c. *Machine learning.* https://en.wikipedia.org/wiki/Machine_learning

Algorithmic Relevance: a case of knowledge representation, organization and discovery systems

Lala Hajibayova, Kent State University, USA

Abstract

This paper calls for reconsideration of the current perception that knowledge representation, organization and discovery systems "know best" what resources are relevant to satisfy people's everyday information needs. This paper proposes that the impact of algorithmically-driven approaches in knowledge representation, organization and discovery systems is one of the hallmarks of the analysis of accountability, transparency and ethicality of these systems to ensure their human centered focus.

1. Introduction

In today's world, where knowing has become so closely associated with Internet access and, in particular, the ability to find information using search engines, information institutions seem to be in a race to embrace advancements of technologies to provide "Google like" services to satisfy individuals' everyday information needs. Huvila (2016 p.570) proposes three premises for understanding how knowing is framed in the contemporary search engine society: "easiness," i.e. the assumption of the primacy of convenience and emancipation; "solvability," i.e. the framing of information as a commodity that is embedded and available within technological infrastructures; and "appropriation of technologies and infrastructures for information needs," i.e. the significance of the diverse uses of information technologies rather than mere reliance on their asserted purposes of technologies.

The rapid advancement of technologies and the ever-increasing scale and breadth of digital collections have resulted in increasing reliance on machine or algorithmic approaches in knowledge representation, organization and discovery systems, from the most common manifestations of algorithms, such as the library catalogue's suggestions of relevant and/or similar titles, to more complex approaches in which web data are interlinked to enrich representation and discovery of information resources. Yet researchers have found cultural and gender biases in Internet data that are often utilized in algorithmically-driven projects, which affect the representation, organization and discovery of the resources.

This paper proposes that the impact of algorithmically-driven approaches in knowledge representation, organization and discovery systems is one of the hallmarks of the analysis of accountability, transparency and ethicality of these systems to ensure their human centered focus.

2. Algorithms and algorithmic culture

Algorithms are entangled in our lives through the recommendations, connections and suggestions across the various devices, applications and platforms on which we so heavily rely in our everyday lives (Ananny and Crawford 2016; Gillespi, 2010). Butcher (2018), indeed, claims that algorithms have become "performative intermediaries that participate in shaping the worlds they only purport to represent" (p.1) and emphasizes that algorithms ought to be scrutinized for the kinds of values and assumptions underlying their functions (p.36). Dourish (2016 p.2) proposes that understanding of how algorithms operate should be grounded on their relation(s) to other "computation forms, such as data structures", because they emerge in practice as well as in relation to these forms.

Foucault (1983) asserts that the most important aspect of power is not the control exercised by certain strong individuals over certain weak individuals, but the control that all individuals exercise over themselves and others through accepted forms of orderly behaviour. Foucault calls for full comprehension of the nature of power through investigation of "the relays through which it operates and the extent of its influence on the often insignificant aspects of the hierarchy" (p.213). In this regard, Foucault's reflections on power are aligned with the position of researchers investigating the social implications of technology, which Gerrie (2003) describes as the recognition that technology is not merely an "ethically neutral set of artifacts by which we exercise power over nature, but also always a set of structured forms of action by which we also inevitably exercise power over ourselves". In this vein, Mitcham (1994 p.209) asserts that technology can be "associated with diverse human behaviours, with distinctions among them often less clear than for either artifacts or cognitions".

In this regard, it is crucial for information specialists to acknowledge the necessity for a holistic approach to understanding of the complexity and multiplicity of algorithms, machine learning and big data.

3. Algorithms and knowledge representation and organization systems

The emergence of internet technologies has drastically changed the scale and accessibility of knowledge representation, organization and discovery systems. Among these changes, one of the most significant changes has been the shift from an institutionally-based paper catalogue to the online public access catalogue and one-stop discovery systems. Yet this shift has also introduced ambiguity into the individual's understanding of how knowledge is represented and why it is considered relevant and/or irrelevant to her/his search query due to the opaqueness of the algorithms behind these platforms, which screen the process by which particular information is discovered and retrieved. In this regard, the big data trends that utilize user-generated content, such as Goodreads book reviews, to enrich traditional representation of resources though linking and/or recommending user-generated content in such mainstream systems for representation and organization of resources as WorldCat, also raise questions associated with determining the relevance of suggested user-generated reviews as well as about data quality and ethical concerns related to satisfying one's information needs with user-generated content (Hajibayova 2019; Hajibayova and Salaba 2018). It is also unclear whether and/or how these algorithms further complicate the inherent limitations and biases of knowledge representation and organization by professionals and systems, such as tendencies to favor mainstream views.

Researchers have alluded to the biases inherent in algorithmically generated data (Pasquell 2016). For instance, Noble (2018 p.10) argues that while lack of social and human context in algorithmically driven decision-making is an issue for everyone engaging with information technologies on an everyday basis, it is of "particular concern for marginalized groups, those who are problematically represented in erroneous, stereotypical, or even pornographic ways in search engines and who have also struggled for non-stereotypical or nonracist and nonsexist depictions" for decades.

The question, therefore, is how knowledge representation, organization and discovery systems can reduce bias and amplify fairness in the provision of open access to the knowledge. This paper suggests the following premises for algorithmically-driven systems: transparency, accountability, ethicality and fairness.

3.1 Accountability

In the information world, where data are easily linked across various platforms and systems, accountability should be the regulating principle of knowledge representation, organization and discovery systems. That is, accountability must become one of the primary means by which agents address issues of appropriate use. When data have been either linked or recommended, it should be possible to verify, in accessible and understandable language, the policies and principles that regulate usage of the data and guide the provision of access to information resources across various systems and platforms, to ensure that accountability is activated when regulatory principles are accidentally and/or intentionally violated.

The assumption behind the call for accountability is assurance of *transparency,* referring to clarity of understanding the opportunities and obligations associated with provision of access to the knowledge.

3.2 Transparency

Transparency concerns are generally grounded on the logic that, in Ananny and Crawford's (2018 p.974) words, "observation produces insights which create the knowledge required to govern and hold systems accountable". Transparency in knowledge representation, organization and discovery systems implies provision of understanding how programs work within and across various platforms and systems. While system transparency entails boundaries that are set by corporate interests and security concerns, at a minimum, provisions for basic understanding of data provenance as well as relevance of information, as defined in relation to the system's requirements and individuals' information needs, should be in place.

Transparency also serves as "diagnostic for ethical action," because observers with more knowledge of how a given system works are more likely to properly assess whether a system works as intended or whether changes are needed (Ananny and Crawford 2018 p.974).

3.3 Ethicality

Ethical principles, interwoven with transparency and accountability, provide a solid ground for developing human-centered systems. The guiding ethical principles of knowledge organization systems should therefore be grounded in fundamental rights, values and principles of Beneficence (do good) and Non-Maleficence (do no harm), human autonomy, justice, and explicability (Draft ethics guidelines for trustworthy AI 2018).

Ethical principles, interweaved with transparency and accountability, provide a solid ground for developing human-centered systems.

4. Conclusions

This paper calls for reconsideration of the current perception that knowledge representation, organization and discovery systems "know best" what resources are relevant to satisfy people's everyday information needs. Even though a number of factors affect individuals' preferences for particular vocabularies to communicate and search for information, such as audience, background knowledge and culture, there should be a more comprehensive consideration of a systems' criteria for relevance in information retrieval and especially of how algorithms nudge, as they are extremely powerful and potent, due their networked, continuously-updated and pervasive nature (Gillespie 2018).

Developed on premises of accountability, transparency and ethicality, knowledge representation, organization and discovery systems should ensure that algorithmically-driven approaches are human-centered and put human rights and values first.

References

Ananny, M., & K. Crawford. 2018. "Seeing without knowing: Limitations of the transparency ideal and its application to algorithmic accountability." *New Media & Society,* 20(3): 973–989.

Bucher, T. 2018. *IF ... THEN: Algorithmic power and politics.* Oxford, UK: Oxford University Press.

Dourish, P. 2016. "Algorithms and their others: Algorithmic culture in context". *Big Data & Society,* 1-11. http://journals.sagepub.com/doi/pdf/10.1177/2053951716665128.

Ekbia, H., M. Mattioli, I. Kouper, G. Arave, A. Ghazinejad, T. Bowman, V. R Suri, A. Tsou, S. Weingart & C. R. Sugimoto. 2015. "Big data, bigger dilemmas: A critical review." *Journal of the Association for Information Science and Technology,* 66(8): 1523–1545.

European Commission's High-Level Expert Group on Artificial Intelligence (AI HLEG). 2018. *Draft Ethics Guidelines for Trustworthy AI.* https://ec.europa.eu/digital-single-market/en/news/draft-ethics-guidelines-trustworthy-ai

Foucault, M. 1983. "The subject and power." In H. Dreyfus and P. Rabinow (Eds). *Foucault: Beyond Structuralism and Hermeneutics.* Chicago, IL: University of Chicago Press.

Gerrie, J. 2003. "Was Foucault a philosopher of technology?" *Techne* 7(2): 14-26.

Gillespie, T. 2018. *Custodians of the Internet: Platforms, Content Moderation, and the Hidden Decisions that Shape Social Media.* New Haven, CT: Yale University Press.

Hajibayova, L. 2019. "Investigation of Goodreads reviews: Kakutanied, deceived or simply honest?" *Journal of Documentation,* 75(3), 612-626.

Hajibayova, L., & A. Salaba. 2018. "Critical questions for big data approach in knowledge representation and organization." In F. Ribeiro & M.E. Cerveira (Eds.), *Advances in Knowledge Organization: Challenges and Opportunities for Knowledge Organization in the Digital Age, Proceedings of the Fifteenth International ISKO Conference, Portugal.* pp. 144-151. Würzburg: Ergon-Verlag.

Huvila, I. 2016. "Affective capitalism of knowing and the society of search engine." *Aslib Journal of Information Management,* 68(5): 566-588.

Noble, A. U. 2018. *Algorithms of Oppression: how search engines reinforce racism.* New York, NY: New York University Press.

Pasquale, F. 2016. *The Black Box Society: the secret algorithms that control money and information* Cambridge, MA: Harvard University Press.

AI: Artificial Intelligence or Autistic Intelligence? Keeping knowledge organisation human

Patrick Lambe, Straits Knowledge, Singapore

Summary

The injection of artificial intelligence into organisational work can create radical work redesigns. But work must meet humans (employees and customers) at key points. Many forms of work that are imagined as simple linear processes actually have ecosystem effects and dependencies. Replacing human effort with work powered by AI can make processes leaner, more efficient, and less error prone. However, it can also create faithful propagation of errors without possibility of detection, and it can separate human curiosity, improvisation and sense of responsibility from the work outcomes. The redesign of complex work needs to take into account the special characteristics of human cognition and team cognition. Knowledge organisation professionals are positioned to do this, but the language of knowledge organisation (and AI) frequently ignores the human dimension of work, focusing on the logical, transactional and engineering aspects of devising solutions. In this presentation, I will discuss three cases where the digitalisation of work resulted in poorer organisational outcomes, and analyse where knowledge organisation work could contribute to better outcomes:

1. Singapore MRT breakdowns: separation of digital work from human work resulting in lowered sense of responsibility in maintenance staff
2. Copier machine call centre: mediating fluid customer enquiries with pre-set problem categories - disagreement that operator knowledge of the technology was required for accurate priming of a decision support system
3. Computerised physician order entry system: inhibition of error detection by nurses, and poor work affordances for laboratory staff

References

Allen, Davina. 2015. *The Invisible Work of Nurses: hospitals, organisation and healthcare*. London. Routledge.

Bowker, Geoffrey C. & Susan Leigh Star. 1999. *Sorting Things Out: classification and its consequences*. Cambridge, MA. MIT Press.

Brown, John Seely & Paul Duguid. 2000. *The Social Life of Information*. Boston, MA. Harvard Business School Press.

Butcher, Howard K., Gloria M. Bulechek, Joanne M. McCloskey Dochterman & Cheryl Wagner (eds). 2019. *Nursing Interventions Classification*. Seventh edition. St Louis, MO. Mosby Elsevier.

Forsyth, Rowena. 2006. *Tricky Technology, Troubled Tribes: a video ethnographic study of the impact of information technology on health care professionals' practices and relationships*. Thesis submitted for the degree of Doctor of Philosophy at the University of New South Wales, 2006.

Hutchins, Edwin. 1995. *Cognition in the Wild* (Cambridge, MA: MIT Press).

McDonald, Clement J. 2006. "Computerization Can Create Safety Hazards: a bar-coding near miss" *Annals of Internal Medicine* 144(7): 510-516.

Rochlin, Gene I. 1989. "Informal Organizational Networking as a Crisis-Avoidance Strategy: US naval flight operations as a case study" *Industrial Crisis Quarterly* 3 (2): 159-176.

Singapore Ministry of Transport. 2012. *Report of the Committee of Inquiry into the Disruption of MRT Train Services on 15 and 17 December 2011*. Singapore: Ministry of Transport.

Weick, Karl E. & Kathleen M. Sutcliffe. 2001. *Managing the Unexpected: assuring high performance in an age of complexity*. San Francisco, CA. Jossey-Bass.

Whalen, Jack & Erik Vinkhuyzen. 2000. "Expert Systems in (Inter)Action: diagnosing document machine problems over the telephone" in Luff et al. (eds.) *Workplace Studies: recovering work practice and informing system design* (pp 92-140). Cambridge: Cambridge University Press.

Session 7: DISCUSSION PANEL

In an AI-Supported World, Where Do the Opportunities Lie for Knowledge Organization?

Session 8: AI, KO AND RETRIEVAL

On Machine Learning and Knowledge Organization in Multimedia Information Retrieval

Andrew MacFarlane, City, University of London, UK
Sondess Missaoui, City, University of London, UK
Sylwia Frankowska-Takhari, City, University of London, UK

Abstract

Recent technological developments have increased the use of machine learning to solve many problems, including many in information retrieval (IR). Deployment of machine-learning techniques is widespread in text search, notability web search engines (Dai et al. 2011). Multimedia information retrieval as a problem however still represents a significant challenge to machine learning as a technological solution, but some problems in IR can still be addressed by using appropriate AI techniques. In this paper we review the technological developments and provide a perspective on the use of machine-learning techniques in conjunction with knowledge organisation techniques to address multimedia IR needs. We take the perspective from the MacFarlane (2016) position paper, that there are some problems in multimedia IR that AI and machine learning cannot currently solve. The semantic gap in multimedia IR (Enser 2008) remains a significant problem in the field, and solutions to them are many years off. However, there are occasions where the new technological developments allow the use of knowledge organisation and machine learning in multimedia search systems and services. Specifically we argue that the improvement of detection of some classes of low level features in images (Karpathy and Li 2015), music (Byrd and Crawford 2002) and video (Hu et al, 2011) can be used in conjunction with knowledge organisation to tag or label multimedia content for better retrieval performance. We advocate the use of supervised learning techniques. We provide an overview of the use of knowledge organisation schemes in machine learning and make recommendations to information professionals on the use of this technology with knowledge organisation techniques to solve multimedia IR problems.

1. Introduction

AI techniques, in particular machine learning, have become a significant technology in information retrieval software and services. Machine learning is defined as a method that learns from data with minimal input from humans. A key example is search engines (Dai et al. 2011) which use learning to rank algorithms to keep results presentation up to date given the inherent dynamism of the web. The web changes constantly both in terms of content and user requests, the data being documents, queries and click throughs etc. For text retrieval the machine-learning infrastructure is an essential part of the provision of a service that meets user needs, but the same could not be said of multimedia information retrieval where many challenges are still evident. By multimedia retrieval we mean search for non-text objects such as images, pieces of music or videos (moving images). Because of the semantic gap (Enser 2008), the features of these objects can be hard to identify and index, which leads to a separation of techniques in terms of concept-based retrieval and content-based retrieval (with text we have terms that represent both). In MacFarlane (2016) it was argued that human involvement is necessary in many circumstances to identify concepts recognisable to humans – the example being a picture of a politician in an election. Whilst the politician can be easily identified, the election is a more nebulous concept that is difficult to extract from an image, without context. Low-level features of objects are often difficult if not impossible to match with concepts, and this problem is likely to be one that persists for a significant length of time. Knowledge organization methods are essential to ensure that these conceptual features are captured and recorded in multimedia software and services.

However, recent advances in machine-learning methods such as machine vision algorithms (Karpathy and Li 2015) have provided the functionality to identify specific objects in images, giving multimedia IR designers and implementers the ability to address the semantic gap to some extent. It is argued that in conjunction with knowledge organisation, machine learning can be used to provide better and more relevant results to users for a given set of information needs that require the identification of specific objects. This paper puts forward an argument for a supervised learning approach in multimedia search, where a knowledge organization scheme is used as a rich source of information to augment the objects identified by any machine-learning algorithm. This is to provide an enhanced index of objects, allowing more effective search for those objects by the user. In this paper, we address the technological changes which have led to the potential for improvements in multimedia search and argue that knowledge organization can used with a supervised learning technique. We then review the landscape of multimedia search and show some possibilities for using knowledge organization and machine learning to improve results for users in some types of information needs. Features in various types of multimedia objects are reviewed, and we provide some advice on how to use these feature and machine learning in conjunction with knowledge organization in multimedia IR systems and services. We provide some ideas for the way forward, together with the practical implications for knowledge organization practitioners.

The contribution of the paper is a process that uses knowledge organization and machine learning to create a database of objects for the purposes of multimedia information retrieval. The proposed process uses both high level and low-level features identified for a multimedia object and the creation of an index within a database for the purpose of retrieval.

2. Technological developments in machine learning

What are the key developments which have led to improvements in technology, and which have significant implications for the use of knowledge organization in multimedia search?

In recent years, Deep Learning has become much more prominent in machine-learning circles (Pouyanfar et al. 2018), for a wide range of different applications such as speech processing and machine vision (Deng and Yu, 2014). As one might expect, there is a wide range of definitions of Deep Learning, depending on the context, but the most appropriate in this context is a "class of machine-learning techniques that exploit many layers of non-linear information processing for supervised or unsupervised feature extraction and transformation, and for pattern analysis and classification" (Deng and Yu 2014). Whilst the underlying technology for deep learning (Artificial Neural Networks) has been around for many years (McCulloch and Pitts 1943), it is only recently that the widespread use of the techniques has become widespread and available in open frameworks such as TensorFlow (Abadi et al., 2016). Over the years the AI community has developed a strong body of knowledge in the use of the techniques, but a key turning point has been the availability of Graphical Processing Units (GPUs), which are specialist chips that are able to significantly increase the processing of arithmetical operations (Singer, 2013). They are particularly useful for image processing but have become very useful generally for other types of applications such as neural networks that require significant processing of numbers. A benchmarking experiment conducted by Cullinan et al (2013) showed significant advantages for the GPU over CPU's (Central Processing Units) in terms of raw processing. The raw processing power from GPUs has proved to be the catalyst for a massive increase in Deep Learning algorithms in areas such as machine vision to detect features in images. This includes features such as the detection of neuronal membranes (Ciresan et at. 2012), breast cancer (Ciresan et al. 2013) and handwritten Chinese character recognition (Ciresan and Meier 2015). Whilst these unsupervised examples of feature detection are relevant, it is argued that knowledge organization can be used to augment feature extract to improve multimedia retrieval performance.

3. Machine learning and knowledge organization

As feature extraction from various media has improved in recent years, what are the implications of the use of knowledge organization techniques? Knowledge organization in its many forms (thesauri, taxonomies, ontologies) are human-generated schemes which provide a rich source of evidence to describe features of objects that are of interest – in this case multimedia objects such as images, music and video. The key to understanding the contribution knowledge organization can make in multimedia search is to consider the types of learning: unsupervised, semi-supervised and supervised (Russell and Norvig 2016). These are classed by their access to labelled or categorised data. Unsupervised learning (Russell and Norvig 2016, p.694) is where algorithms work without any labelled data, for example with clustering objects together based on the features extracted from them. This does not apply to our context, where we examine the use of knowledge organization techniques to the problem. Semi-supervised learning (Russell and Norvig 2016, p.695) does provide some access to labelled data, and it is possible to use this technique in some contexts where a limited number of multimedia objects have been manually classified by a practitioner. Supervised learning (Russell and Norvig 2016, 695) requires access to data that is completely labelled and is appropriate here – where we consider a large number of multimedia objects have been classified by a practitioner. Using supervised learning techniques, we can either match features detected by both the machine-learning algorithm and the practitioner (exact match case) or estimate the probability of features matching from both sources (best match case). We consider both examples later on the paper in section 6. In this paper, we focus on the user of knowledge organization and supervised learning in multimedia search, in the context of large amounts of data that have been labelled by practitioners.

4. Machine learning and multimedia information retrieval

There are limits to the use of machine learning/AI techniques to the application of multimedia information retrieval (MacFarlane, 2016). However, with the new advances in technology laid out in section 2 above and the ability of machine-learning algorithms to detect objects in media e.g. images (Karpathy and Li 2015), there is scope to improve multimedia search results using knowledge organization. In (MacFarlane, 2016) we argue that media of various kinds (e.g. images, music) require cultural knowledge which can often be only expressed tacitly, and thus require human input. The advantage of knowledge organization schemes is that they provide this knowledge which is hard for machine-learning algorithms to detect and can therefore be used with features extracted from multimedia objects to augment the indexing of that object.

The key to understanding the application of knowledge organization and machine learning to multimedia information retrieval problems is to consider different types of information needs in particular domains. One particular domain that provides useful examples is the creative domain, where various media are required on a daily basis e.g. video, music (Inskip et al. 2012) and images (Konkova et al. 2016) for advertising campaigns, or images for online news stories (Frankowska-Takhari et al. 2017). A specific example of information needs is the use of briefs in the advertising world which provide an overview of the media required and some specification of the criteria for the object to be suitable for that particular campaign. Analysis of these briefs has demonstrated that there are some aspects that can be easily detected by machine-learning algorithms, whilst others are too abstract for current techniques to work. For example, in music, Inskip et al. (2012), found that mood was a significant criterion for relevance in music briefs, which would be hard for an algorithm to detect. However, knowledge organization schemes with human input can help to resolve the need. Inskip et al. (2012) also found that music features such as structure are also important, which machine-learning algorithms can clearly be applied to. In terms of images, Konkova et al. (2016) found three categories of facets in image briefs including syntactic features such as 'colour' and 'texture' as well as high level general and conceptual image features such as 'glamorous' and 'natural'. These aesthetic features are an open problem in the field (Datta et al., 2008). As with music, there is a clear distinction as to which image facets can be detected using machine learning algorithms.

Machine-learning algorithms are very often used to detect features in a variety of different applications (Datta et al., 2008). The full range of algorithms can be found in Datta et al. (2008), Pouyanfar et al. (2018) and Murthy and Koolagudi (2018), but what problems are the algorithms applied to in the context of multimedia IR? Key problems which are addressed in many applications are classification, object detection and annotation. Examples include images where super-human performance has been recorded in the 2015 large scale visual recognition challenge (ILSVRC15) using deep learning methods (Poyyanfar et al. 2018), which has come about due to much improved object recognition (improving the ability to detect objects improves classification techniques). This has also led to techniques that can automatically annotate and tag images, including online services such as Imagga (https://imagga.com/). In music, techniques to apply classification and temporal annotation have been developed at low level (e.g. timbre), mid level (e.g. pitch and rhythm) and high level (e.g. artist and genre) in many music applications (Srinivasa et al., 2018). In video (which is moving images together with sound), problems addressed include event detection by locating scene changes and segmentation of the object into stories e.g. scenes and threads in a TV programme or film (Lew et al., 2006). A quick review of the literature shows that machine learning has been applied to many problems in multimedia successfully, but there are many issues to which the technique cannot be addressed (see above). The key therefore to augmenting any application that uses knowledge organization as its core with machine learning is to identify the features with which the technique can be used. The features that have been used successfully in the field are the ones that are known to bare fruit given the empirical evidence available. It is to these that we turn to next.

5. Features in multimedia information retrieval

Features are aspects of an object that can be used for multimedia search purposes. The key to the application of search on multimedia objects is to identify these features and provide an index for them, allowing for applications such as direct search and classification or categorisation. In this section we review the features for images, music and video and provide an overview of what machine learning can identify and what is appropriate for knowledge organization techniques, and when both can be combined. Our emphasis is on combining the features from both sources to improve multimedia search applications and services.

5.1 Image features

There is a wide variety of schemes that identify image attributes such as semantic (e.g. Panofsky/Shatford), syntactic and non-visual (Westman 2009, pp.65-66). Non-visual attributes (such as the metadata e.g. bibliographic data) can be useful (Konkova et al. 2016) but is not the concern here. Semantic information for an image will require human input to establish the 'aboutness' of a given object, through generic schemes such as the Thesauri for Graphic Materials (Library of Congress N.D.b) and specific schemes such as Iconclass (http://www.iconclass.nl/) which is focused on art images. Syntactic attributes can either be primitive visual elements such as colour, texture, hue and shape, or compositional e.g. the relationship between shapes, motion, orientation, perspective, focal point (Westman 2009, p.65). It is these syntactic attributes to which machine learning can be applied.

Specific application areas have particular needs. For example, the concept of 'Copyspace' is important in advertising, which is a clear space to insert text (Konkova et al. 2016). Further, studies from the user-centred tradition advocate that human image users in specific domains have specific image needs. Such studies aim to uncover the needs of users and identify which aspects of user needs can be used to facilitate automation of image-based tasks. For example, Frankowska-Takhari et al. (2017) investigated the needs of image users in online journalism. Initially their findings were similar to those from earlier studies e.g., Markkula and Sormunen (2000) and Westman and Oittinen (2006), and showed that users' descriptions of their image needs were often limited to their conceptual needs, and search queries tend to relate to concepts, while information about users' needs on the perceptual level was limited to descriptions of visual effects required in images. As suggested in Machin and Polzer (2015), it was necessary to reach beyond these descriptions, to identify the concrete visual features that engendered the required effects. Frankowska-Takhari et al. (2017) applied the visual social semiotics framework (Kress and van Leeuwen, 2006) to analyse images used in online journalism. They identified a set of 11 recurring visual features that engender the visual effect required in images used for illustrating news headline content. These included: a strong single focal point to draw readers' attention, the use of specific palette of colours depending on the tone of the news story, a photographic shot from waist-up including head and shoulders and close-up on the face, and a preference for a large object/person in the frame. Most of the identified features are detectable by currently available systems that make use of advanced computer vision. They could be implemented, for example, as multi-feature filters for image retrieval. Such a system. firmly rooted in the image users' needs, could be a step towards automating image retrieval with a purpose to support a specific group of image users carrying out specific illustration tasks.

5.2 Music features

Downie (2002) identifies seven facets of music information that can be considered as features to learn for a retrieval system, which can be further classified into low-level, mid-level and high-level features (Murthy and Koolagudi 2018). We merged these two schemes together as they provide a useful overall classification of features in which machine learning can be applied and where knowledge organization schemes are appropriate, as well as identifying the key features. The features are not mutually exclusive (Downie 2002), and low-level features are used to build mid level features, which in turn can be used to extract high level features (Murthy and Koolagudi 2018). Low level features are defined as the fundamental property of sound, mid level features the fundamental properties of music and high level features the human perceptual interpretation of the mid level features.

The low-level features are timbre and tempo. Timbre is defined as an attribute related to the tone that differs in the instrument being played (e.g. trumpet vs piano). It is the sound, tone quality and colour that make up the voice quality of a musical note (Murthy and Koolagudi 2018, p.7). Tempo is defined as the duration between two musical events (e.g. two notes). Timbre and tempo are strongly connected through frames, a short time segment of 10-100ms. These low-level features can fail to capture much information from a given song in their own right (Murthy and Koolagudi 2018) and mid-level features are required to build up a picture of music which can be used for an application. These mid-level musical features are pitch, rhythm, harmony and melody – note that in our scheme these features are still low level. Pitch is frequency of sound, the oscillations per second. Differences between two pitches are defined as being the interval between them. Harmony is detected when two or more pitches sound at the same time to create polyphonic sound, which is determined by the interval. Rhythm is defined by an occurring or recurring pattern in the music e.g. the beat. Rhythm and pitch determine a further important feature of music namely melody, which is a succession of musical notes. Murthy and Koolagudi (2018) do not classify this feature, but it is clearly a mid-level feature as it strongly related to other mid-level features but cannot be regard as a high-level feature. It is these mid-level features to which machine learning can be applied.

There is more ambiguity in terms of high-level features, and some can be detected through learning mid-level features, but others require human input. In some, both machine learning and knowledge organization can be used. High-level features include editing, text, bibliography (Downie 2002) and artist, genre, instrument and emotion (Murthy and Koolagudi 2018). Editing is defined as performance instructions of a piece of music such as fingering, articulation etc. Knowledge organization schemes such as the Library of Congress performance terms for music (Library of Congress, 2013c, 2014d), focused largely on western classical music, are appropriate. Text relates to any lyrics associated with a musical piece and can be handled via normal text retrieval techniques. It may be appropriate to use this feature to augment machine-learning algorithms (in conjunction with natural-language processing techniques). Bibliography refers to the metadata of the piece, which is determined by human entry of aspects such as composer, performer etc. Appropriate metadata standards in the field are appropriate here, and as with text can be used to augment machine-learning algorithms. Bibliography can determine the artist, genre, emotion and instrument features (depending on the metadata scheme used), but machine learning has been used to identify those high-level features from mid-level features extracted from a musical piece e.g. to classify it by the given feature ((Murthy and Koolagudi 2018). The Genre feature can also be augmented with knowledge organization schemes such as the Library of Congress music/genre headings (2013a, 2013b).

5.3 Video features

Video is multimedia in the complete sense, as it consists of moving images in sequence with audio. Image features identified in 5.1 above can be used here, and as we have extra evidence (e.g. a serious of images) we have more evidence to improve the detection of objects in the media being indexed. A practical example of the features that can be identified are outdoor and indoor shots, people and landscapes/cityscapes (Smeaton and Over, 2002). There are many features from audio that can be extracted via machine learning including speech to text (where text retrieval techniques can be used) and music (see 5.2 above). Whilst we can build on these features, there are unique features of video that can be used to classify or segment video objects. Video can be split up into scenes and threads (Lew et al., 2006), for example in a news programme where different news stories are presented to the viewer. The TRECVID track at the TREC (Text Retrieval Conference) investigated this in the shot boundary detection task (Smeaton and Over, 2002) by detecting different categories e.g. cut (short finishes, one starts right after), dissolve (one shot fades out while new one fades in), fadeout/in (one shot fades out, then the new one fades in) plus other categories which don't fit into these precise boundaries. Detecting shot boundary allows the detection of higher-level features such as events, embodied in LSCOM (LSCOM, 2011), the large-scale concept ontology for multimedia (Naphade et al. 2006). This is a knowledge organization scheme built via the empirical work carried out by the multimedia community, with TRECVID being particularly notable. Examples include people crying (007), maps (204) and people associated with commercial activities (711). These features can be augmented with other knowledge organization schemes such as the Library of Congress (N.D.a) scheme for assigning genre/form terms to films and video.

5.4 Summary of features
In this section we have identified two classes of features, one to which machine learning can be applied and one to which it cannot. The low-level features such as colour and hue in images, pitch and tempo in music and shot boundaries in video are ones that can be extracted using machine-learning techniques, whilst high-level features such as 'aboutness' require the use of human intervention via the application of knowledge organization schemes. Next, we consider the use of these different classes of features in conjunction with each other to improve multimedia information retrieval services.

6. Using machine learning and knowledge organization to enhance multimedia information retrieval
We propose a process by which the features for a multimedia object are identified (both high level and low level) to create a database of objects for the purposes of retrieval. We assume access to digital objects (analogue objects are not considered here). We identify five steps in this process (see figure 1). In step 1 we identify the corpus and knowledge organization scheme for the given corpus, which is split into two separate sub-steps: applying the knowledge organization scheme to the high-level corpus objects (1a) and using machine learning to identify the low-level object features (1b). In step 2, we combine both high and low-level object features to provide a comprehensive set of features for multimedia, which is richer for retrieval purposes (step 3). From step 3 we have the information to create the application of our choice, either a classification or categorisation system, or to support multimedia search functionality (step 4). A further step is considered (step 5), given two scenarios – either a new set of features is identified (by a change in the knowledge organization scheme or improved feature detection using machine learning) or a new set of objects is received and needs to be indexed. We discuss each of these steps below, highlighting the input and output data for each step.

Figure 1 – Process using knowledge organization and machine learning to index multimedia

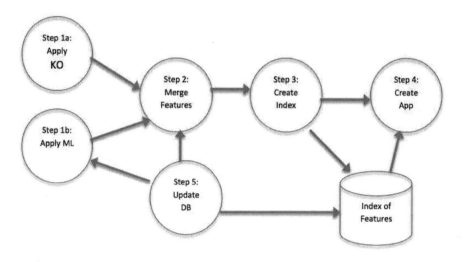

6.1 Step 1A: Apply knowledge organization scheme to corpus

Table 1 – Data required for Step 1a

Input Data	Output Data
1. Corpus 2. Knowledge organization scheme	Object features (high level)

The decision the information professional needs to make is to choose a relevant knowledge organization scheme for the corpus they are managing. This will either be a standard scheme (examples are cited in section 5 above), or a specialist in-house scheme derived by the organisation that requires access to the multimedia. Collection size is a concern here – unless there are significant human resources, manually cataloguing multimedia objects using the knowledge organization scheme might not be practical. In this case any metadata associated with the object can be used, with knowledge organization applied to the metadata to identify relevant features for the database. In other cases, the corpus will already have been indexed (perhaps over many years) and high-level features for each object will be readily available. If the media contains speech (if the corpus is either audio, or video which contains audio), machine learning can be used to detect text to which the knowledge organization can be applied. Whilst the word error rates might be high, the main bulk of concepts for the objects will be detected. This text might itself be indexed as part of the multimedia search service.

6.2 Step 1B: Apply machine-learning technique to corpus

Table 2 – Data required for Step 1b

Input Data	Output Data
Corpus	Object features (low level)

The next step for any information professional is to identify the low-level features using machine learning. This may require the assistance of technical staff with AI expertise, but the information professional should be aware of the process used to generate these features. A key decision is to identify training and test objects from the corpus, or a subset of the corpus. The training set is used to detect the features from the corpus, whilst the test set is used to validate the features detected. Getting this right is key, as poor decisions can lead to over-fitting of features, reducing their utility for retrieval purposes. In general, the standard way to split the corpus into training and test collections is two thirds for training and one third for testing at least. The training set should always be much larger than the test set. A further step is to split a corpus into a number of segments (say k) and spilt each of these k segments applying the machine-learning algorithms to each of these segments, by treating each k segment as a test set with other segments as the training set. This can be repeated with all of the segments and the results merged to create a set of features that is more robust. This is known as cross-validation.

The type and size of corpus is a consideration. The professional should consider appropriate features identified in section 5 for their corpus, and the training and test sets should not be to large (in some cases corpora with many millions of objects and large feature sets may be difficult to manage as machine learning is computationally intensive). It should be noted that in order to get an unbiased estimate of how well an algorithm is doing, it was common practice to take all the data and split it according to a 70/30% ratio (i.e., 70/30 train test splits explained above). These ratios were perfectly applied when dealing with small datasets. However, in the Big Data and Deep Learning era, where, the data could exceed millions of instances, the test sets have been becoming a much smaller percentage of the total. For example, if you have a million examples in the dataset, a ratio of 1% of 1 million (99% train, 1% test) will be enough in order to evaluate your machine- learning algorithm and give a good estimate of how well it is performing. This scheme is manageable for large datasets. However, any sample chosen must also be representative, otherwise the features will not be valid. At the end of this step, the low-level object features will be identified.

6.3 Step 2: Merge features for multimedia objects

Table 3 – Data required for Step 2

Input Data	Output Data
1. Object features (high level) 2. Object features (low level)	Object features (combined)

The data produced in step 1 from both sub-steps needs to be merged together to create a comprehensive set of features for each object in the multimedia corpus. It is this comprehensive set of features which provides the enhancement required for better multimedia retrieval. Getting the merge process correctly configured therefore is critical, and there are two cases to consider, one straightforward and one that requires a little more thought. The simpler case is the exact match case. In this case we have the same feature identified in both sources (e.g. text extracted from images) and can use that evidence to estimate the probability of the features utility. In most cases, the features will be distinct, and the information professional will need to think about which features to record from both sources. They may think it appropriate to record all features, but this may have drawbacks (features may not be useful for search). One way to get around this is to use machine learning to see which low and high-level features correlate with each other and choose the best set of features – this is the best match approach. This would work by applying a further step of machine learning (as outlined in step 1B above), in which an appropriate sample would be used to generate a set of features for indexing. The advice given in section 6.2 would apply in the best match case. At the end of this step a full set of features appropriate for search will be identified.

6.4 Step 3: Create index of features (database of objects)

Table 4 – Data required for Step 3

Input Data	Output Data
Object features (combined)	Database of Objects (Index)

Once a full set of features has been identified, an index of objects using those features can be generated. This can be either an inverted list or a relational or object relational database, depending on the context. The information professional could consult a technical person to assist with this. Examples of software available include Elasticsearch (https://www.elastic.co/), MongoDb (https://www.mongodb.com/), Neo4j (https://neo4j.com/), MySQL (https://www.mysql.com/) and PostgresQL (https://www.postgresql.org/)

6.5 Step 4: Create application or service with combined features

Table 5 – Data required for Step 4

Input Data	Output Data
Database of Objects (Index)	Object classification or categorisation

Once the database has been created, the application or service to meet user needs can be produced. For retrieval purposes. This may just mean writing an appropriate front end given users needs, together with a back end that matches user-defined features identified at the front end. However, if categorisation or classification were required, a further round of machine learning would be appropriate. This would be taking the machine-learning process overviewed in step 1b above but applying the algorithm to the combined feature set. An example can be found in Fan et al (2007), who combined WordNet and ontology data to support a surgery education application.

6.6 Step 5: Update database of objects with new information

Table 6 – Data required for Step 5

Input Data	Output Data
1. New Objects	1. Updated Database
2. New Features	2. Updated Features and Database

New information is generated all the time, and an information professional cannot assume that the corpus they manage will remain static. There are two scenarios to consider – one where new multimedia objects are received and need to be considered and one were new features are available. The first of these is easy to deal with as features can be assigned (high-level features in the knowledge organization scheme, low-level features extracted by an algorithm) and the object recorded in the database. The second is not so straight forward and requires a restart of the process – either because new elements have been added to the knowledge organization scheme or because machine-learning algorithms have been improved to provide a clearer picture of a feature already identified, or to identify new features. This will be an expensive and time-consuming process, so the information professional may wish to test the ideas on a sub-set of the corpus before restarting the whole process again.

7. Conclusion

In this paper we put forward some practical advice for information professionals who curate multimedia digital collections, and who are charged with supporting search services to those collections. We believe that information professionals should treat machine learning and/or AI techniques as an opportunity rather than a threat and should seriously think about using technology to improve the multimedia services they manage. Information professionals should be wary of the hype that surrounds machine learning/AI that has all too often been exaggerated in terms of impact, leading to AI winters. However, the process we describe in section 6, we believe, gives the information professional an opportunity to seize the initiative and build on their domain knowledge gained in working on images, music and video. We urge the community to consider this when considering access to multimedia digital objects for their users.

Acknowledgements
Many thanks to Sven Bale for his advice and clarification of features in music.

References

Abadi, Martin, Paul Barham, Jianmin Chen, Zhifeng Chen, Andy Davis, Jeffrey Dean, Matthieu Devin, Sanjay Ghemawat, Geoffrey Irving, Michael Isard, Manjunath Kudlur, Josh Levenberg, Rajat Monga, Sherry Moore, Derek G. Murray, Benoit Steiner, Paul Tucker, Vigay Vasudevan, Pete Warden, Martin Wicke, Yuan Yu, and Xiaoqiang Zheng, , 2016. Tensorflow: a system for large-scale machine learning. In *Proceedings of the 13th USENIX Symposium on Operating Systems Design and Implementation (OSDI;18)* eds. Andrea Arpaci-Dusseau and Geoff Voelker. 16: 265-283.

Byrd, Donald and Crawford, Tim. 2002. Problems of Music Information Retrieval in the Real World. *Information Processing & Management* 38: 249-272.

Ciresan, Dan C, Alessandro Giusti, Luca M Gambardella, and Jurgen Schmidhuber. 2012. Deep Neural Networks Segment Neuronal Membranes in Electron Microscopy Images. In *Advances in Neural Information Processing Systems*, eds. Leon Bottou and Chris Burges. 2843-2851.

Ciresan, Dan C, Alessandro Giusti, Luca M Gambardella, and Jurgen Schmidhuber. 2013. Mitosis Detection in Breast Cancer Histology Images with Deep Neural Networks. In *International Conference on Medical Image Computing and Computer-assisted Intervention*, eds. Terry Peters, Lawrence H. Staib, Sean Zhou, Caroline Essert, Pew-Thian Yap and Ali Khan. Springer, Berlin, Heidelberg, 411-418.

Ciresan, Dan C. and Ueli Meier. 2015. July. Multi-Column Deep Neural Networks for Offline Handwritten Chinese Character Classification. In *International Joint Conference on Neural Networks (IJCNN 2015)*, ed. Yoonsuck Choe. IEEE. 1-6.

Cullinan, Christopher, Christopher Wyant, and Timothy Frattesi. 2013. *Computing Performance Benchmarks among CPU, GPU, and FPGA*. URL: www. wpi. edu/Pubs/E-project/Available/E-project-030212-123508/unrestricted/Benchmarking_Final.pdf.

Dai, Na, Milda Shokouhi, and Brian D. Davison, 2011. Learning to Rank for Freshness and Relevance. In *Proceedings of the 34th International ACM SIGIR Conference on Research and Development in Information Retrieval*, eds. Richardo Baeza-Yates, Tat-Seng Chua and W. Bruce Croft. ACM. 95-104.

Datta, Ritendra, Dhiraj Joshi, Jia Li, and James Z Wang. 2008. Image Retrieval: ideas, influences, and trends of the new age. *ACM Computing Surveys*, 40: Article No. 5.

Deng, Li and Dong Yu. 2014. *Deep Learning: methods and applications. Foundations and trends in signal processing* (Book 20), Now Publishers Inc.

Downie, J. Stephen. 2003. *Music Information Retrieval. Annual review of information science and technology,* Wiley. 37, 295-340.

Enser, Peter G.B. 2008. The Evolution of Visual Information Retrieval. *Journal of Information Science,* 34: 531-546.

Fan, Jianping, Hangzai Luo, Yuli Gao, and Ramesh Jain. 2007. "Incorporating Concept Ontology for Hierarchical Video Classification, Annotation, and Visualization." *IEEE Transactions on Multimedia*, 9: 939-957.

Frankowska-Takhari, Sylwia, Andrew MacFarlane, Ayse Göker, and Simone Stumpf. 2017. Selecting and Tailoring of Images for Visual Impact in Online Journalism. *Information Research*, 22: 1.

Hu, Weiming, Nianhua Xie, Li Li, Xianglin Zeng, and Stephen Maybank. 2011. A Survey on Visual Content-Based Video Indexing and Retrieval. *IEEE Transactions on Systems, Man, and Cybernetics, Part C (Applications and Reviews)*, 41: 797-819.

Inskip, Charlie, Andrew MacFarlane, and Pauline Rafferty. 2012. Towards the Disintermediation of Creative Music Search: analysing queries to determine important facets. *International Journal on Digital Libraries*, 12: 137-147.

Karpathy, Andrej and Fei-Fei Li. 2015. Deep Visual-Semantic Alignments for Generating Image Descriptions. In: *Proceedings of CVPR 2015*, Boston, 7-12 June 2015, eds. Kristen Grauman, Eric Learned-Miller, Antonio Torralba, and Andrew Zisserman. https://www.cv-foundation.org/openaccess/CVPR2015.py

Konkova, Elena, Andrew MacFarlane, and Ayse Göker. 2016. Analysing Creative Image Search Information Needs. *Knowledge Organization* 43:1. 14-21.

Kress, A.G. and T. van Leeuwen. 2006. *Reading Images: the grammar of visual design*. London, UK: Routledge.

Lew, Micheal S., Nicu Sebe, Chabane Djeraba, and Ramesh Jain. 2006. Content-Based Multimedia Information Retrieval: state of the art and challenges. *ACM Transactions on Multimedia Computing, Communications, and Applications*, 2: 1-19.

Library of Congress. 2013a. *Genre/Form Terms for Musical Works and Medium of Performance Thesaurus.* https://www.loc.gov/catdir/cpso/genremusic.html.

Library of Congress. 2013b. *Genre/Form Terms Agreed on by the Library of Congress and the Music Library Association as in Scope for Library of Congress Genre/Form Terms for Library and Archival Materials (LCGFT).* http://www.loc.gov/catdir/cpso/lcmlalist.pdf.

Library of Congress. 2013c. *Introduction to Library of Congress Medium of Performance Thesaurus for Music.* http://www.loc.gov/aba/publications/FreeLCSH/mptintro.pdf.

Library of Congress. 2013d. *Performance Terms: Medium.* http://www.loc.gov/aba/publications/FreeLCSH/MEDIUM.pdf.

Library of Congress. N.D.a. *Library of Congress Genre/Forms for Films Video.* http://www.loc.gov/aba/publications/FreeLCSH/GENRE.pdf.

Library of Congress. N.D.b. *Thesaurus for Graphical Materials (TGM).* http://www.loc.gov/pictures/collection/tgm/.

LSCOM. 2011. *Large Scale Concept Ontology for Multimedia.* http://www.ee.columbia.edu/ln/dvmm/lscom/

MacFarlane, Andrew. 2016. Knowledge Organisation and its Role in Multimedia Information Retrieval. *Knowledge Organization.* 43: 3. 180-183.

Machin, D. and Polzer, L. 2015. *Visual Journalism. Journalism: reflections and practice.* London: Palgrave.

Markkula, M. and E. Sormunen, 2000. End-User Searching Challenges Indexing Practices in the Digital Newspaper Photo Archive. *Information Retrieval.* 1: 259-285.

McCulloch, Warren S and Walter Pitts. 1943. A Logical Calculus of the Ideas Immanent in Nervous Activity. *The Bulletin of Mathematical Biophysics*, 5: 115-133.

Murthy, Y.V. Srinivasa. and Shashidhar G. Koolagudi, 2018. Content-Based Music Information Retrieval (CB-MIR) and its Applications toward the Music Industry: *A Review. ACM Computing Surveys.* 51: Article No. 45.

Naphade, Milind., John R. Smith, Jelena Tesic, Shih-Fu Chang, Winston Hsu, Lyndon Kennedy, Alexander Hauptmann, and Jon Curtis. 2006. Large-Scale Concept Ontology for Multimedia. *IEEE Multimedia*, 13: 86-91.

Russell, Stuart J. and Peter Norvig. 2016. *Artificial Intelligence: a modern approach.* Malaysia; Pearson Education Limited.

Pouyanfar, Samira, Saad Sadiq, Yilin. Yan, Haiman Tian, Yudong Tao, Maria Presa Reyes, Mei-Ling Shyu, Shu-Ching Chen, and S.S. Iyengar. 2018. A Survey on Deep Learning: algorithms, techniques, and applications. *ACM Computing Surveys.* 51: Article No. 92.

Smeaton, Alan F. and Paul Over. 2002. *The TREC-2002 Video Track Report.* NIST Special Publication: SP 500-251. Proceedings of The Eleventh Text Retrieval Conference (TREC 2002). NIST: Gaithersburg, DC.

Singer, Graham. 2013. The History of the Modern Graphics Processor. *TechSpot.* 27 March.

Westman, Stina. 2009. Image Users' Needs and Searching Behaviour. In Information Retrieval in the 21st Century, eds. Ayse Goker, and John Davies. John Wiley & Sons, 63-83.

Westman, S. and P. Oittinen, 2006. Image Retrieval by End-Users and Intermediaries in a Journalistic Work Context. *IIiX'06 Information Interaction in Context*, 2006. Copenhagen Denmark. 102 – 110.

Rethinking 'Advanced Search': an AI-based approach to search strategy formulation

Tony Russell-Rose, UXLabs, UK

Abstract

Knowledge workers such as patent agents, recruiters and legal researchers undertake work tasks where search forms a core part of their duties. In these instances, the search task often involves the formulation of complex queries expressed as Boolean strings. However, creating effective Boolean queries remains an ongoing challenge, often compromised by errors and inefficiencies. In this paper, we present a new approach to query formulation in which concepts are expressed as objects on a two-dimensional canvas and relationships are articulated using direct manipulation. In addition, by combining machine learning approaches with manually curated ontologies, we are able to provide interactive support in the form of automated keyword suggestions. This approach eliminates syntax errors, makes the query semantics more transparent, and offers new ways to validate, share and reproduce search strategies and best practices.

1. Introduction

Many knowledge workers rely on the effective use of search applications in the course of their professional duties (Russell-Rose et al, 2018). Patent agents, for example, depend on accurate prior art search as the foundation of their due diligence process (Tait, 2014). Similarly, recruitment professionals rely on Boolean search as the basis of the candidate sourcing process (Russell-Rose and Chamberlain, 2016a), and media monitoring professionals routinely manage thousands of Boolean expressions on behalf their client briefs (Wing Pazer, 2013).

What these professions have in common is a need to develop search strategies that are accurate, repeatable and transparent (Russell-Rose et al, 2018). The traditional solution to this problem is to use line-by-line query builders such as that shown in Figure 1. The output of these tools is a series of Boolean expressions consisting of keywords, operators and ontology terms, which are combined to form a multi-line search strategy such as that shown in Figure 2.

However, the practice of using Boolean strings to articulate complex information needs suffers from a number of fundamental shortcomings (Russell-Rose and Chamberlain, 2016b). First, it is poor at communicating structure: without some sort of physical cue such as indentation, parentheses and other delimiters can become lost among other alphanumeric characters. Second, it scales poorly: as queries grow in size, readability becomes progressively degraded. Third, they are error-prone: even if syntax checking is provided, it is still possible to place parentheses incorrectly, changing the semantics of the whole expression. In addition, most proprietary query builders offer limited support for error checking or query optimization, and the strategies produced are often compromised by mistakes and inefficiencies in the form of spelling errors, truncation errors, logical operator errors, incorrect query line references, and redundancy (Sampson, 2006).

Figure 1: A typical form-based query builder

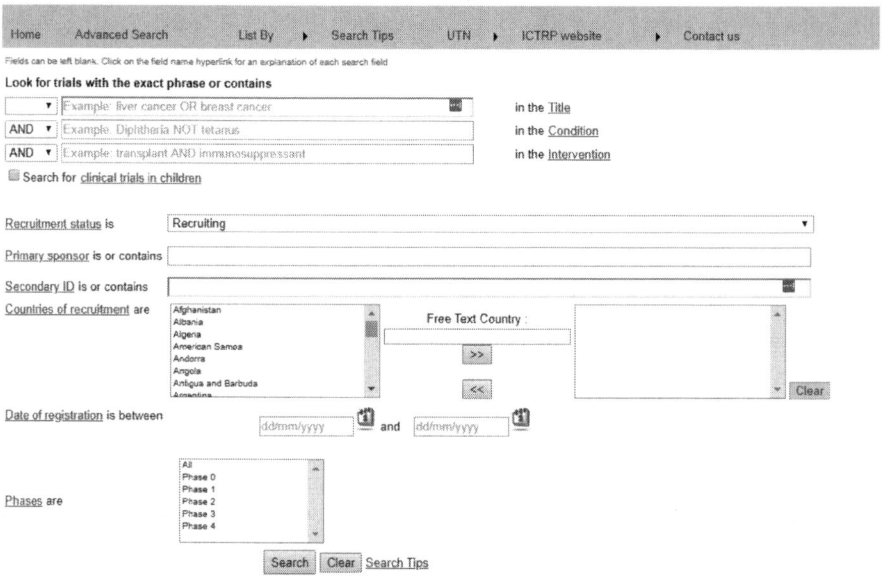

To mitigate these issues, many professionals rely on previous examples of best practice. Recruitment professionals, for example, draw on repositories such as the Boolean Search Strings Repository (https://booleanstrings.ning.com/forum/topics/boolean-search-strings-repository) and the Boolean String Bank (https://scoperac.com/booleanstringbank/newsignin.php). However, these repositories store content as unstructured text strings which are not directly executable in their native form.

In this paper, we propose an alternative solution. Instead of a one-dimensional search box, concepts are expressed on a two-dimensional canvas. Instead of formulating Boolean strings, queries are expressed by combining objects, and relationships are articulated using direct manipulation. Query suggestions are provided via an NLP (Natural Language Processing) services API which utilises machine learning approaches combined with linked open data ontology lookup. This eliminates many sources of syntactic error, makes the query semantics more transparent, and offers further opportunities for query refinement and optimisation.

Figure 2: An example patent search strategy

1	A01N0025-004/CPC
2	RODENT OR RAT OR RATS OR MOUSE OR MICE
3	BAIT OR POISON
4	2 AND 3
5	1 OR 4
6	AVERSIVE OR ADVERSIVE OR DETER? OR REPEL?
7	NONTARGET OR (NON WITH TARGET) OR HUMAN OR DOMESTIC OR PET OR DOG OR CAT
8	6 AND 7
9	8 AND 5
10	BITREX OR DENATONIUM OR BITREXENE OR BITTERANT OR BITTER
11	10 AND 5
12	9 OR 11

2. Related Work
2.1 Search query visualization

The application of data visualization to search query formulation can offer significant benefits, such as fewer zero-hit queries, improved query comprehension, and better support for browsing within an unfamiliar database (Goldberg and Gajendar, 2008). An early example of such an approach is that of Anick et al (1989), who developed a two-dimensional graphical representation of a user's natural language query that supported reformulation via direct manipulation. Similarly, Fishkin and Stone (1995) investigated the application of direct manipulation techniques to the problem of database query formulation, using a system of 'lenses' to refine and filter the data. Jones (1998) developed VQuery, a query interface to the New Zealand Digital Library which exploits querying by Venn diagrams and integrated query result previews.

Later work includes that of Yi et al (2005), who explored the concept of a 'dust and magnet' metaphor applied to multivariate data visualization. Nitsche and Nürnberger (2013) developed QUEST, a system based on a radial user interface that supports phrasing and interactive visual refinement of vague queries to search and explore large document sets. A further example is provided by Boolify (www.boolify.com), which provides a dynamic drag and drop interface on top of Google's search engine. Users build a query by dragging terms and operators onto a search surface. And more recently, de Vries et al (2010) developed Spinque, which uses a visual canvas to allow users to graphically model a search engine using elementary building blocks. They describe this as searching 'by strategy', although the term is used more in the sense of configuring the behavior of a search engine, whereas in our case a 'search strategy' refers to a sequence of connected Boolean search expressions.

Our approach combines elements of the above including the use of graphical representations, support for direct manipulation, and real time results retrieval. However, it differs from the prior art in that it focuses specifically on the needs of professional searchers, offers a generic framework for the representation of Boolean expressions and semantic relationships, and provides automated query suggestions with support for saving, sharing and re-using query templates and best practices.

2.2 Automated term suggestion

Query expansion is the process of reformulating or augmenting a user's query in order to increase query effectiveness, particularly with regard to recall (Manning et al, 2008). Selection of candidate expansion terms can be automated or interactive (i.e. guided by the user), and methods can be either local (based on documents retrieved by the query) or global (using resources independent of the query).

Global methods involve the use of domain specific resources such as thesauri, controlled vocabularies or ontologies to identify related terms in the form of synonyms, hypernyms, hyponyms, etc. Such resources may be either manually curated or automatically generated from domain-specific corpora using collocation and co-occurrence analysis techniques. Global methods can increase recall significantly but may also reduce precision by adding irrelevant or out-of-domain terms to the query (Manning et al, 2008). In the current implementation of our work, we will not always have access to the full text of the documents in the result set (other than result snippets), so local methods are less applicable.

Ontologies are considered most useful for query expansion when they are specific to the query domain. Universal resources such as WordNet are considered less useful as they are too general and may not distinguish class concepts from instances (Bhogal et al, 2007). However, ontologies may offer a productive source of related terms in the form of gloss words, i.e. words occurring in the term definitions (Navigli and Velardi, 2003). Moreover, in the biomedical domain, expanding queries with related MeSH terms has been shown to be useful (Rivas et al, 2014), while adding synonyms from the larger and more comprehensive UMLS has been found to improve recall (Giriffon et al, 2012), at the expense of precision (Zeng et al, 2012).

The development of efficient distributed word representations has revolutionized unsupervised natural language processing techniques for finding synonyms (Collobert et al, 2011, Mikolov et al, 2013). Given the value of distributed word representations in identifying related terms, a number of researchers have considered the utility of word embeddings for query expansion. Kuzi (2016), Roy (2016) and Diaz (2016) all used local embeddings trained on TREC corpora, with differing results. While Kuzi found that local word embeddings outperformed the standard RM3 relevance model, Roy found the opposite. Diaz (2016) compared local embeddings (TREC corpus) with global (generic Gigaword corpus) and found that local embeddings provided significantly better results for query expansion than global embeddings.

The fundamental problem with most query expansion techniques is that as many queries may be harmed (e.g. by introducing noise) as may be improved (Xiong and Callan, 2015). In addition, the user is unable to control how the expansion terms are used in the query. Cao et al (2008) argue that previous work, irrespective of approach used, only considers the effect of the complete set of expansion terms on retrieval and ignores the issue of how to distinguish useful expansion terms from useless or even harmful terms within that set. We address both these issues by treating query expansion as a recommendation task rather than an information retrieval task, i.e. given one or more query terms already entered by the user, can we provide a list of further recommended terms. Reframing the task in this way is particularly significant, since the visual approach offers an opportunity for the user to engage meaningfully with candidate expansion terms and thus exercise more informed judgment regarding their value and contribution to the current search strategy.

3. An Alternative Approach
3.1 Design Concept
2dSearch is aimed at knowledge workers who share a need to create search strategies that are accurate, transparent and reproducible (Russell-Rose and Chamberlain, 2019). The key design principles are to:

- Eliminate the syntactic errors associated with traditional query formulation tools, and provide a clearer mapping between the semantics of the query and its physical form
- Update search results in real-time as changes are made, and allow individual blocks to be enabled/disabled to see their effects
- Analyse and validate search expressions, and detect common errors (e.g. duplication, orphaned lines, redundant bracketing)

- Provide interactive query suggestions, avoiding the problems of phrase boundary detection and 'query drift' that undermine traditional query expansion techniques
- Offer multi-database support and a platform-agnostic representation to mitigate inefficient 'translation' of search strategies across databases
- Allow strategies to be shared as executable artefacts or imported/exported as traditional Boolean strings (so conventional and new ways of working can co-exist).

Taken together these principles reduce the likelihood of spelling errors, truncation errors, logical operator errors, incorrect query line references, and redundancy without rationale (Sampson and McGowan, 2006).

Figure 3: The 2dSearch application

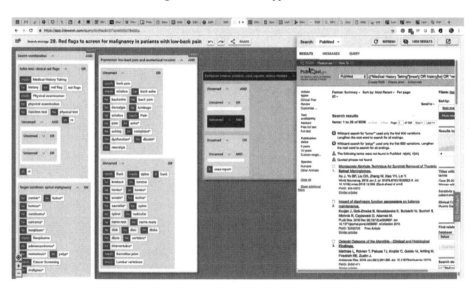

At the heart of 2dSearch is a graphical editor which allows the user to formulate queries as objects on a two-dimensional canvas (Figure 3). Concepts can be simple keywords or attribute:value pairs representing controlled vocabulary terms or database-specific search operators. Concepts can be combined using Boolean (and other) operators to form higher-level groups and then iteratively nested to create expressions of arbitrary complexity. Groups can be expanded or collapsed on demand to facilitate transparency and readability.

The application consists of two panes: a query canvas on the left and a search results pane on the right which can be resized or detached in a separate window. The canvas can be resized or zoomed and features an 'overview' widget to allow users to navigate to elements that may be outside the current viewport. Adopting design cues from Google's Material Design language, a sliding menu is offered on the left, providing file I/O and other options. This is complemented by a navigation bar which provides support for document-level functions such as naming and sharing queries.

Although 2dSearch supports creation of complex queries from a blank canvas, its value is most readily understood by reference to an example query such as the following from the Boolean Search Strings Repository, which was intended to retrieve social media profiles for data migration project managers located in Dublin:

(cv OR "cirriculum vitae" OR resume OR "resumÁI"') (filetype:doc OR filetype:pdf OR filetype:txt) (inurl:profile OR inurl:cv OR inurl:resume OR initile:profile OR intitle: cv OR initile:resume) ("project manager" OR "it project manager" OR "program* manager" OR "data migration manager" OR "data migration project manager") (leinster OR munster OR ulster OR connaught OR dublin) -template –sample -example -tutorial -builder -"writing tips" - apply -advert –consultancy

Although modest in length, this query is difficult to interpret, optimise or debug. However, when opened with 2dSearch (Figure 4), it becomes apparent that the overall expression consists of a conjunction of OR clauses (nested blocks) with a number of specialist search operators (dark blue) and negated terms (white on black). To edit the expression, the user can move terms using direct manipulation or create new groups by combining terms. They can also cut, copy, delete, and lasso multiple objects. If they want to understand the effect of one group in isolation, they can execute it individually. Conversely, if they want to remove one element from consideration, they can disable it. In each case, the effects of each operation are displayed in real time in the adjacent search results pane.

2dSearch functions as a meta-search engine, so is in principle agnostic of any particular search technology or platform. In practice however, to execute a given query, the semantics of the canvas content must be mapped to the API of the underlying database. This is achieved via an abstraction layer or set of 'adapters' for common search platforms such as Bing, Google, PubMed, Google Scholar, etc. These are user selectable via a drop-down control.

Support for query optimisation is provided via a 'Messages' tab on the results pane. For example, if the user tries to execute via Bing a query string containing operators specific to Google, an alert is shown listing the unknown operators. 2dSearch also identifies redundant structure (e.g. spurious brackets or duplicate elements) and supports comparison of canonical representations.

Figure 4: Using 2dSearch to visualize Boolean search strings

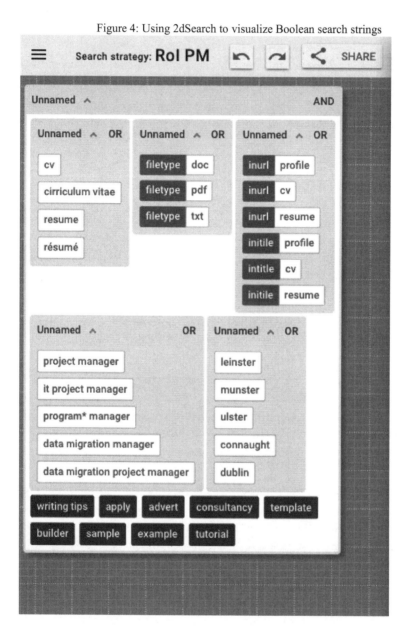

Figure 5: NLP system architecture.

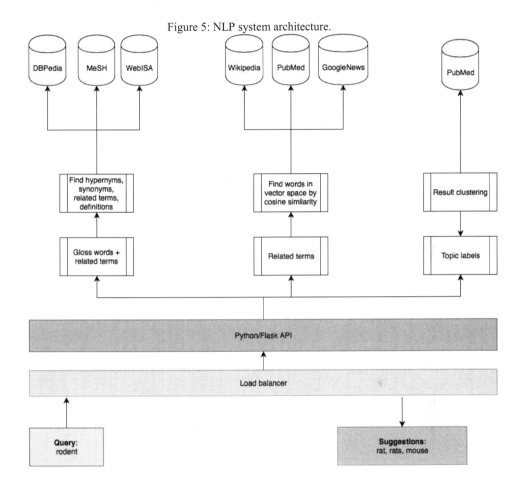

3.2 Query suggestions

The ability to generate useful query expansion terms for a given query against a third-party search engine without access to the source documents presents a challenge. Based on the review in Section 2.2, we implemented and evaluated three approaches to query expansion:

1. Global, using ontologies via a variety of SPARQL endpoints
2. Global, using word embeddings created from a variety of corpora
3. Local, using clustering and topic modelling of result snippets with Carrot2 '

(Osinski and Weiss, 2005)

Query expansion using ontologies

We developed a service that executes SPARQL queries to extract hypernyms, hyponyms, related terms, and term definitions from DBpedia, WebISA (Seitner et al, 2016), MeSH, and other public SPARQL endpoints. Keywords from term definitions are extracted using a variety of algorithms (TF-IDF weighted noun phrases, textrank (Mihalcea and Tarau, 2004), sgrank (Danesh et al, 2015), RAKE (Pennington et al, 2014), and neoclassical combining forms (NCF) (Diaz-Negrillo, 2014). Keywords plus ontology terms are then ranked and aggregated to form query expansion suggestions.

Query expansion with word embeddings

In addition to open-source, publicly available word embeddings for Wikipedia (Pennington et al, 2014), GoogleNews (Mikolov et al, 2013), and PubMed (Chiu et al, 2016, Pyysalo et al, 2013), we created new embeddings from the cleaned body text of around 900,000 full-text, open-access PubMed papers, optimized for multi-word expressions that typically occur in healthcare. Terms most similar in vector space to the input query terms are ranked and aggregated to form new query expansion suggestions.

Query expansion using clustering

As an initial experiment with healthcare data, we implemented Carrot2 as a service, and the cluster labels from PubMed search result snippets for the input query terms are ranked and returned as candidate query expansion suggestions.

The system architecture for the deployment of these NLP services is shown in Figure 5.

4. Evaluation

Recruiting suitable participants to take part in a qualitative evaluation of professional search tools can be challenging. Therefore, we have undertaken a quantitative evaluation of the query suggestion API, using an offline, Cranfield-style approach in combination with a publicly available test set and traditional precision/recall metrics. It is important to recognize that the query suggestion task in 2dSearch differs from traditional query expansion tasks in a number of important ways:

- The primary use case for 2dsearch is recall-oriented professional search tasks, so evaluation methods that focus on the effect of query expansion on search engine ranking are less appropriate.
- The suggested terms are being added to an existing term or set of terms within a larger search strategy, rather than to a single natural language query. This means that their effect must be considered within the context of that specific set of terms.

- Since the visual approach allows the user to select individual expansion terms and apply them in isolation, it is important that any evaluation method considers the individual contribution of each candidate term, and not just the overall effect of an entire candidate set

We have therefore based our evaluation on an approach that measures the extent to which the query suggestion API can generate terms found in existing (published) search strategies. For example, given the term *rodent* in the strategy of Figure 2, can it generate the related terms *rat, rats, mouse,* and *mice* (and only those terms). This particular search strategy consists of five such disjunctions (lines 2, 3 6, 7 and 10), each of which offers an opportunity to apply and evaluate the query suggestion API.

For our test collection, we used data from the CLEF 2017 eHealth Lab (https://sites.google.com/site/clefehealth2017/), which includes a set of 20 topics for Diagnostic Test Accuracy (DTA) reviews. Each of these includes a search strategy manually constructed by subject matter experts. Our overall evaluation approach is as follows: for every strategy in our test collection, iterate over each disjunction calling the query suggestions API on each term and calculating precision & recall based on the overlap between the original term set and the suggested term set. We then repeat this process for each of the methods offered by our API, and calculate macro precision, recall and F-measure. The results for the Ontology-based services are shown in Table 1.

Table 1: Precision, recall and F-measure for ontology-based related terms

Service	P	R	F
DBPEDIA	0.017	0.040	0.024
WEBISA	0.001	0.003	0.002
MeSH	0.045	0.012	0.019
BNF	0.002	0.001	0.001

At first glance these results appear quite low, since even the best performing ontology (DBPEDIA) returns an F measure of 0.024. However, this is in line with previous studies on recommendation system evaluation where precision in the range 0.5-7% can be expected using offline methods (Beel and Langer, 2015). Precision is relatively high for MeSH (0.045), reflecting the highly specialized nature of this resource (medical subject headings). Recall is relatively high for DBPEDIA (0.04), reflecting the broad coverage of this resource.

As mentioned in Section 3, DBPEDIA also provides term definitions that can serve as a further source of query expansion terms. These were extracted using a variety of algorithms

(Table 2). Here, the best performing algorithm was NCF regex, in line with previous results using this approach to extract entities from biomedical text (Gooch & Roudari, 2011). However, it is still inferior to the results obtained using the DBPEDIA ontology terms. This contrasts with the results of Navigli and Velardi (2003), who found gloss terms to be more useful than ontology terms for query expansion (although in their work WordNet was used).

Table 2: Precision, recall and F for gloss terms extracted from DBPEDIA definitions

Algorithm	P	R	F
NCF regex	0.011	0.025	0.015
nltk-np	0.007	0.015	0.010
textrank	0.011	0.018	0.014
sgrank	0.009	0.014	0.011
rake	0.003	0.005	0.003

We then evaluated a number of publicly available word embedding models and the bespoke models that we created (as described in Section 3). The results are shown in Table 3, with our two bespoke models in the final two rows. The performance of our first model (Pubmed unigram) is slightly better but comparable to that of Chiu et al (2016), which provides some evidence for the repeatability of the approach. The best performing model overall was our second bespoke model (PubMed trigram), which suggests that using higher order ngrams improves both precision and recall. A further contributory factor may have been our creation and use of a relatively clean corpus, which included only body text (no figures, headers, footers etc.) and removed numbers, punctuation, and other non-alphabetic elements.

Table 3: Precision, recall and F for terms suggested by word embedding models

Model	P	R	F
Word2vec (News)	0.016	0.025	0.019
GloVe (Wikipedia)	0.019	0.030	0.024
Word2vec (PubMed)	0.028	0.042	0.034
FastText (Wikipedia)	0.024	0.038	0.029
Word2vec (PubMed unigram)	0.031	0.047	0.037
Word2vec (PubMed trigram)	0.035	0.052	0.042

Finally, we evaluated the use of the topic labels generated by Carrot2 clustering search results from PubMed. The results for Carrot2's three clustering algorithms are shown in Table 4.

Table 4: Precision, recall and F for Carrot2 topic labels

Service	P	R	F
Lingo	0.002	0.005	0.003
STC	0.010	0.019	0.013
kMeans	0.008	0.016	0.011

Overall the STC (suffix tree clustering) algorithm performs best, although the F-measure is still some way short of that of the word embeddings and DBPEDIA. Moreover, Carrot2's results are much harder to replicate, as it relies on sending live queries to Pubmed which is subject to database updates, timeouts, latency issues, etc.

5. Summary and Conclusions
The results from our evaluation are encouraging in the sense that our PubMed Word2vec model returns results comparable with typical offline recommender evaluation tasks and outperforms the best publicly available embedding model. However, we should note a number of caveats. Firstly, we have assumed that all disjunctions in the data set are equivalent, whereas in reality some may contain synonyms while others may contain terms related in some other way. Clearly the nature of those relations will have a bearing on the most effective expansion approach. Secondly, we have assumed that the CLEF data is 'gold standard', in the sense that it includes all (and only) the 'correct' terms in each disjunction. However, there may be instances where a particular suggestion is absent from the data but would in fact be accepted by a human expert as a valid related term. This implies that our current results may be an underestimate of actual live performance, although only an interactive evaluation (or a comparison with human performance on the same task) could formally establish this. Thirdly, many of the query terms are polysemous, whereas our work so far has been agnostic of word sense. Evidently, there are many ways to utilize context to better disambiguate query terms, and this is suggested as an area for future work. Finally, our evaluation concerns only one data set and one domain. In future work we will extend this to other data sets and domains.

2dSearch is a framework for search strategy formulation in which information needs are expressed by manipulating objects on a two-dimensional canvas. Transforming logical structure into physical structure mitigates many of the shortcomings of Boolean strings. This eliminates syntax errors, makes the query semantics more transparent and offers new ways to optimise, save and share best practices. In due course, we hope to engage in a formal, user-centric evaluation, particularly in relation to traditional query builders. We are currently engaging in an outreach programme and invite subject matter experts to work with us in building repositories of best practice search strategies and templates.

References

Anick, P. G., J. D. Brennan, R. A. Flynn, D. R., Hanssen, B.Alvey & J. M. Robbins. 1989. A Direct Manipulation Interface for Boolean Information Retrieval via Natural Language Query. In *Proceedings of the 13th Annual International ACM SIGIR Conference on Research and Development in Information Retrieval* (pp. 135-150). ACM.

Beel, J., & S. Langer. 2015. A Comparison of Offline Evaluations, Online Evaluations, and User Studies in the Context of Research-Paper Recommender Systems. In *International Conference on Theory and Practice of Digital Libraries* (pp. 153-168). Springer, Cham.

Bhogal J, A Macfarlane, & P. A Smith. 2007. Review of Ontology Based Query Expansion. *Information Processing & Management.* 43(4):866–86.

Cao G, J-Y Nie, J Gao, and S. Robertson Selecting Good Expansion Terms for Pseudo-Relevance Feedback. *Proceedings of the 31st Annual International ACM SIGIR Conference on Research and Development in Information Retrieval - SIGIR '08.* New York, New York, USA: ACM Press; 2008. p. 243.

Chiu, B., G. Crichton, A. Korhonen, & S. Pyysalo. 2016. How to Train Good Word Embeddings for Biomedical NLP. In *Proceedings of the 15th Workshop on Biomedical Natural Language Processing* (pp. 166–174). Stroudsburg, PA, USA: Association for Computational Linguistics.

Collobert R, J Weston, L Bottou, M Karlen, K Kavukcuoglu, & P Kuksa. 2011. Natural Language Processing (almost) from Scratch. *The Journal of Machine Learning Research.*12: 2493–537.

Danesh, S., T. Sumner, & J.H. Martin. 2015. SGRank: Combining Statistical and Graphical Methods to Improve the State of the Art in Unsupervised Keyphrase Extraction. In *Proceedings of the Fourth Joint Conference on Lexical and Computational Semantics, *SEM @NAACL-HLT 2015* (pp117-126). The *SEM 2015 Organizing Committee

de Vries, A., W. Alink, and R. Cornacchia. (2010). Search by Strategy. In *Proceedings of the third Workshop on Exploiting Semantic Annotations in Information Retrieval (ESAIR '10).* ACM, New York, NY, USA, 27-28. DOI=http://dx.doi.org/10.1145/1871962.1871979

Diaz, F., B. Mitra & N Craswell. 2016. Query Expansion with Locally-Trained Word Embeddings. *Proceedings of the 54th Annual Meeting of the Association for Computational Linguistics.* Berlin: Association for Computational Linguistics. p. 367–77.

Díaz-Negrillo, A. 2014. Neoclassical Compounds and Final Combining Forms in English. *Linguistik Online,* 68(6).

Fishkin K. and M. Stone. 1995. Enhanced Dynamic Queries via Movable Filters. In *Proceedings of the SIGCHI Conference on Human Factors in Computing Systems (CHI '95),* 415-420, ACM Press/Addison-Wesley Publishing Co., New York, NY, USA.

Goldberg, Joseph H., and Uday N. Gajendar. 2008 *Graphical Condition Builder for Facilitating Database Queries.* U.S. Patent No. 7,383,513. 3.

Griffon N., W. Chebil, L. Rollin, G. Kerdelhue, B. Thirion, J-F. Gehanno, et al. 2012. Performance Evaluation of Unified Medical Language System®'s Synonyms Expansion to Query PubMed. *BMC Medical Informatics and Decision Making.*12: 12.

Jones, S. 1998. Graphical Query Specification and Dynamic Result Previews for a Digital Library. In *Proceedings of the 11th Annual ACM Symposium on User Interface Software and Technology (UIST '98)*. pp143-151, ACM, New York, NY, USA.

Kuzi S., A. Shtok, & O. Kurland. 2016. Query Expansion Using Word Embeddings. *Proceedings of the 25th ACM International on Conference on Information and Knowledge Management - CIKM '16*. New York, New York, USA: ACM Press; pp 1929–32.

Manning C.D., P. Raghavan & H. Schütze. 2008. *Introduction to Information Retrieval*. New York: Cambridge University Press

Mihalcea R. & P. Tarau. 2004. *TextRank: Bringing Order into Texts*. https://web.eecs.umich.edu/~mihalcea/papers/mihalcea.emnlp04.pdf

Mikolov, Tomas, Kai Chen, Greg Corrado, and Jeffrey Dean. 2013. Efficient Estimation of Word Representations in Vector Space. In *Proceedings of Workshop at ICLR*.

Navigli R. & P. Velardi. 2003. "An Analysis of Ontology-based Query Expansion Strategies". *Workshop on Adaptive Text Extraction and Mining*. http://wwwusers.di.uniroma1.it/~navigli/pubs/ECML_2003_Navigli_Velardi.pdf

Nitsche M. and A. Nürnberger. 2013. QUEST: querying complex information by direct manipulation. In *Proceedings of the 15th International Conference on Human Interface and the Management of Information: information and interaction design* - Volume Part I 240-249, Springer-Verlag, Berlin, Heidelberg.

Osiński S. & D. Weiss. 2005. Carrot2: Design of a Flexible and Efficient Web Information Retrieval Framework. In: Szczepaniak P.S., Kacprzyk J., Niewiadomski A. (eds) *Advances in Web Intelligence. AWIC 2005*. Lecture Notes in Computer Science, vol 3528. Springer, Berlin, Heidelberg

Pazer, J. (2013). *The Importance of the Boolean Search Query in Social Media Monitoring Tools*. DragonSearch white paper, https://www.dragon360.com/wp-content/uploads/2013/08/social-media-monitoring-tools-boolean-search-query.pdf

Pennington, Jeffrey, Richard Socher, and Christopher D. Manning. 2014. *GloVe: Global Vectors for Word Representation. Empirical methods in natural language processing (EMNLP)*, pp. 1532-1543.

Pyysalo, S. and F. Ginter, H. Moen, T. Salakoski, and S. Ananiadou. 2013. Distributional Semantics Resources for Biomedical Text Processing. *Proceedings of LBM 2013*, pp. 39-44.

Rivas, A.R., E.L. Iglesias & L. Borrajo. 2014. Study of Query Expansion Techniques and their Application in the Biomedical Information Retrieval. *Scientific World Journal*. 2014: 132-158.

Roy, D., D. Paul, M. Mitra, U. Garain & D. Roy. 2016. Using Word Embeddings for Automatic Query Expansion. *Neu-IR '16*. Pisa, Italy.

Russell-Rose, T., J. Chamberlain & F. Shohkraneh, "A Visual Approach To Query Formulation For Systematic Search". *Proceedings of the 2019 Conference on Human Information Interaction & Retrieval*. ACM, Glasgow, UK, March 10-14.

Russell-Rose, T., J. Chamberlain & L. Azzopard. 2018. Information Retrieval in the Workplace: a comparison of professional search practices. *Information Processing & Management* 54(6): 1042–1057.

Russell-Rose T. & J. Chamberlain. 2016a. Real-World Expertise Retrieval: the information seeking behaviour of recruitment professionals. In *European Conference on Information Retrieval*. Springer, 669–674.

Russell-Rose, T. & J. Chamberlain. 2016b. Searching for Talent: the information retrieval challenges of recruitment professionals. *Business Information Review* 33(1): 40–48.

Sampson, M. & J. McGowan. 2006. Errors in Search Strategies were Identified by Type and Frequency. *Journal of Clinical Epidemiology* 59(10): 1057–63

Seitner, Julian, Christian Bizer, Kai Eckert, Stefano Faralli, Robert Meusel, Heiko Paulheim & Simone Paolo Ponzetto. 2016. A Large Database of Hypernymy Relations Extracted from the Web. *Proceedings of the 10th edition of the Language Resources and Evaluation Conference*. Portorož, Slovenia

Shojania, K. G., M. Sampson, M. T. Ansari, J. Ji, S. Doucette, & D. Moher. 2007. How Quickly Do Systematic Reviews Go Out of Date? A survival analysis. *Annals of Internal Medicine*, 147(4): 224-233

Tait, J. 2014. An Introduction to Professional Search. In *Professional Search in the Modern World*. Springer, 1–5.

Wing Pazer, J. 2013. *The Importance of the Boolean Search Query in Social Media Monitoring Tools*. DragonSearch white paper (2013). https://www.dragon360.com/wp-content/uploads/2013/08/social-media-monitoring-tools-boolean-search-query. pdf

Xiong, C. & J. Callan. 2015. Query Expansion with Freebase. In *Proceedings of the 2015 International Conference on The Theory of Information Retrieval* (pp. 111-120). ACM.

Yi, J., R. Melton, J. Stasko, & J. Jacko. 2005. Dust & Magnet: multivariate information visualization using a magnet metaphor. *Information Visualization* 4(4) 239-256.

Zeng, Q.T., D. Redd, T. Rindflesch & J. Nebeker. 2012. Synonym, Topic Model and Predicate-Based Query Expansion for Retrieving Clinical Documents. *AMIA Annual Symposium Proceedings* 2012: 1050–9.

Intelligent Behavior-Based Techniques: do they have a role in enterprise search?

Marianne Lykke, Aalborg University, Denmark
Ann Bygholm, Aalborg University, Denmark
Tanja Svarre, Aalborg University, Denmark

Summary

Enterprise search is managed search environments that allows federated search and makes the content from multiple enterprise-type sources, such as databases, intranets, document management systems, e-mail, social media, searchable to a defined audience within an organization (White, 2015). Common to these systems are that they use advanced search technologies to facilitate information retrieval. Kruschwitz and Hull (2017, p. 6) state that it is a "wide-spread sentiment among users and search practitioners that enterprise search does not deliver on its promises". Schymik et al. (2015) conclude on the basis of their literature review that knowledge workers put a lot of time into finding information and that as much as 10 to 20 percent of that time is spent on unsuccessful searching for documents.

The purpose of the present study is twofold. First, the study investigates what problems the employees in a global biotechnology company face when they are using the enterprise search system to find information for their daily work tasks. Second, whether and how intelligent techniques such as behaviour based ranking can support the identified problems are analysed.

The empirical study of searching problems took place in an international biotechnology company that conducts research, development and production of industrial enzymes, microorganisms, and biopharmaceutical ingredients. We used a convergent mixed methods approach (Creswell and Clark, 2018) to study the employees' searching behavior. Our data came from three separate studies: log analysis of 288,363 search queries carried out by 5854 searchers' interaction with the enterprise search system in a six-month period; a questionnaire survey with 98 respondents (43% response rate); and individual interviews with eight of the most frequent searchers representing the five main users group.

The analysis of the usefulness of intelligent behavior-based techniques was based on a comparison of the identified problems with existing research about behavior-based information retrieval (Baeza-Yates & Ribeiro-Neto, 201; Ruthven & Kelly, 2011). The analysis showed that the behavior-based techniques on one hand is supported by the searchers' focused and very competent information retrieval behavior and on the other hand is challenged by the large variety in searching behaviour. The searchers switched competently between search moves and access points according to the specific search task and context. The results tell us that it is difficult to identify patterns in search behavior, e.g. use of search features, taxonomy filtering, document types, metadata, vocabulary, etc.

References

Baeza-Yates, R. & B. Ribeiro-Neto. 2011. *Modern Information Retrieval. The Concepts and technology behind search*. London: Addison-Wesley, 2011.

Creswell, J.W. & V.L. P Clark. 2018. *Designing and Conducting Mixed Methods Research*. Thousand Oaks,CA. Sage Publications.

Kruschwitz, U. & C. Hull. 2017. "Searching the Enterprise: Foundations and Trends". *Information Retrieval*, 11(1): 1-142.

Ruthven, I. & D. Kelly (ed.). 2011. *Interactive Information Seeking, Behaviour and Retrieval*. London: Facet, 2011.

Schymik, G., K. Cofrral, D. Schuff & R. St. Louis. 2015. "The benefits and Costs of Using Metadata to Improve Enterprise Document Search". *Decision Sciences*, Sept. 2015.

White, M. 2015. *Enterprise Search: enhancing business performance*. O'Reilly Media.

POSTERS

Retrieval and Visualization of Related Knowledge in Linked Open Data

Henrique Monteiro Cristovão, Federal University of Espírito Santo (UFES), Brazil
Luís Otávio Rigo Júnior, Federal University of Espírito Santo (UFES), Brazil

Linked Data in the Semantic Web make it possible to develop innovative and useful services for society. The Linked Data bases, composed of RDF triples and able to create links between different sources (Bizer, Heath, & Berners-Lee, 2009) are examples of information networks with ontologies that organize information and knowledge. The use of ontologies in this context supports interoperability. The present work proposes a Knowledge Retrieval on Linked Data bases, starting from an informational need of the user that has the desire to find relevant relationships for their search terms. The discovery of relationships between search terms uses Complex Network metrics for the ranking of relevant network nodes. The result of the search is presented by a concept map from a process of creation of meanings by a set of propositions (Novak & Gowin, 1984). In this concept map, the initial search terms and the other terms selected from the base that established the relationships are highlighted. However, the conceptualization of this resulting information is dependent on the interpretation of user, as a cognitive agent, and considering the context in which it is used (Capurro & Hjørland, 2003). The resulting information in a concept map format, which is presented to the user, has the power to modify their knowledge (Buckland, 1991) and thus enable the recovery of knowledge, considered a challenging task (Yao, Zeng, Zhong, & Huang, 2007). Links between search terms can be discovered directly where a predicate supports the relationship, or indirectly using multiple intermediate terms to establish the relationship. In both cases, the proposed algorithm chooses more relevant relationships. A prototype was developed to perform tests on the base of Linked Data DBpedia. The developed software receives a set of textual terms, does a search of these terms in the base and returns the first version of the information network. From this initial network, the algorithm ranks more relevant nodes using a combination of complex network metrics, such as betweenness, closeness and eingenvector. These ranked nodes are used to re-search the base that causes the network to grow over several cycles. In the next phase, the process of reducing the size of the network begins, i.e. the exclusion of less important nodes until the network reaches a viable size for presentation in a conceptual map format. Other complex network metrics are used at this stage, such as eccentricity and minimum path. The condition to unique connected component is required to get the conceptual map with all the terms connected. We are working to improve the present work by using interactive information retrieval to enable better knowledge discovery (Zhang, 2008) The interactive configuration in the process of growth and reduction of the network will be done by regulating the weight of the centrality metrics or by explicitly determining the nodes to be discarded according to the scope of interest of the user. The user's choices will feed a machine learning process based on Artificial Intelligence, where metric settings or node types for a given linked data base will be recorded and adjusted. Thus, in new search, the system will suggest new paths for the user based on the adjusted recommendation system through the set of the search already performed (Mahboob, Siddique, Akhtar, Asif, & Khanum, 2015). In addition, node types with a high statistical incidence of discard will not appear on the main track. It is believed that, in this way, the user's needs are better met.

References

Bizer, C., Heath, T., & Berners-Lee, T. (2009). Linked data - the story so far: *International Journal on Semantic Web and Information Systems, 5*(3), 1–22.

Buckland, M. K. (1991). Information as thing. *Journal of the American Society for Information Science, 42*(5), 351.

Capurro, R., & Hjørland, B. (2003). The concept of information. *Annual Review of Information Science and Technology, 37*, 343–411.

Mahboob, T., Siddique, N., Akhtar, F., Asif, M., & Khanum, M. (2015). A Survey and Analysis on Recommendation System Algorithms. *International Journal of Computer Science Issues, 12*(3), 7.

Novak, J. D., & Gowin, D. B. (1984). *Learning how to learn*. Cambridge, New York: Cambridge University Press.

Yao, Y., Zeng, Y., Zhong, N., & Huang, X. (2007). Knowledge retrieval (kr)., *IEEE/WIC/ACM International Conference on Web Intelligence*, 729–735.

Zhang, J. (2008). *Visualization for information retrieval*. Berlin: Springer.

Visualising Knowledge in Cultural Heritage

Mike Kelly, University College London, UK

This PhD project brings together academic and cultural heritage institutions for the collaborative development of visualisation resources which can assist with the representation and dissemination of cultural heritage research. The project aims to advance knowledge in the area of visual scholarship through a partnership with British Museum archaeologists, the University of Brighton and University College London.

The study of cultural heritage holds a particular fascination because of its position on the boundary between science and the humanities. This project looks to find a visual vocabulary which is appropriate for the representation of the interpretative humanistic aspects of cultural heritage research, as well as those aspects which are based on the physical sciences. Heritage science research data can often be complex, and visualisations can be an important part of making sense of diffuse datasets. Where data is used for interpretation, for example in the use of archaeological evidence to create narratives about historical human societies, standard visualisation techniques do not always give a full picture of the process of knowledge construction.

Drucker (2014) makes the case for greater intellectual transparency in the visual representation of data in humanities subjects, asserting that knowledge in humanist research is interpretative, often put together from data sources which may be fragmentary or from historical periods which we can never fully know. In her view, instead of presenting data as a direct manifestation of natural phenomena, we should make interpretative aspects explicit and allow space for subjective and contested interpretations.

In the case of data-intensive research, Leonelli (2014) suggests that the goal of fully automated reasoning remains elusive because of the necessary dialectic between propositional knowledge, which machines can process, and embodied knowledge, which is required for assessing the evidential value of data, but is derived from *in vivo* experience. When selecting data formats and visualisation tools, curators make choices that partly determine the significance that those data can have when 'automatically' mined.

For both writers there is a perceived danger of a loss of transparency in representations of knowledge as an outcome rather than a process.

This research looks to explore these areas at the limits of knowledge frameworks in cultural heritage, and to uncover the detail of where and how heritage researchers use evidence for interpretation. In the field of archaeological reconstructions, for example, the potentially misleading hyperrealism of computer models has prompted scholars to include measures of uncertainty in visualisations, and to document researchers' knowledge production processes, to allow for the verifiability and reinterpretation of visual representations. Similarly, Leonelli suggests that meta-data can become a tool to 'express the "knowing how" involved in the generation and use of data.' (ibid.)

The project will include practical outcomes, with visualisation examples which draw on the affordances of web technology and interactive computer-based media and test opportunities for distributed, pluralistic models of understanding.

References
Drucker, J., 2014. *Graphesis: visual forms of knowledge production*, Harvard, 2014.
Leonelli, S., 2014. Data Interpretation in the Digital Age. *Perspectives on Science* 22, 397–417.

Modeling Performing Arts Archives in South Korea Based on FRBRoo

Ziyoung Park, Hansung University, South Korea
Hosin Lee, Hansung University, South Korea
Seungchon Kim, Hansung University, South Korea
Sungjae Park, Hansung University, South Korea

Project Overview

The research project name is "Building Linked Data in Korean Performing Arts" and is being supported by the National Research Foundation of Korea (NRF) from 2017 to 2019. This project is initiated because archival information in the performing art field is not well organized and distributed compared to other art fields such as painting and music. Through the project, the research team is constructing semantic open data that can link the information about the performance itself and the performance record information as well as the original information that is the basis of the performance plan. In this proposal, we will mainly describe the ontology modeling and data mapping issues.

Ontology-Based Information Representation for Human Communication Supported by Artificial Intelligence

Floridi (2014) said that human-technology interactions will be replaced by technology-technology interactions in the fourth revolution infosphere. He also added that human will be beyond the technology-technology-technology loop not in the loop of technology's in-betweenness. Then, how do we communicate with each other in the future? Allemang & Hendler (2011) provides a clue of the answer by emphasizing the necessity of the semantic web and ontology. They offered three ways that semantic models support people to organize their knowledge as follows: 1) support people to communicate, 2) explain and make a prediction, and 3) mediate among multiple viewpoints. In other words, in the Semantic Web, information constructed by various people in different fields can be mutually understood and linked using a common model. A common model in the Semantic Web is represented by an ontology. Ontologies help artificial intelligence to understand knowledge in a particular field. The detailed descriptive information, such as the ontology specification, can support the way a person communicates through artificial intelligence. For example, Europeana created a TF to convert the Europeana Data Model (EDM) to FRBRoo (Doerr et al. 2013).

Arko Arts Archive: Performing Art Archive of Korea
Data collection
Arko Arts Archive (Arko) is an institution under the Arts Council Korea, established in 1979. Arko collects and preserves recordings and printed materials about performing arts such as plays and dance. In this project, the research team received materials on performing arts from Arko to build LOD. Arko performing arts archives consist of various information related to performing arts as follows:

- Information about other individual works such as original texts for plays (15,438) and dance (20,617)
- Information about performance plans for plays (27,351) and dance (31,392)
- Archival records about performance: DVDs (18,276), Programs (43,457+44,845), Posters (15,067), Drama Scripts (10,028), and Videotapes (12,079)

Data analysis
The type of data collected from Arko can be analyzed as follows:

1. Original work information that is the basis of performance planning
2. Information on planning and directing actual performances
3. Item information including performance recordings, drama scripts, etc.

For example,
1. An original work, Korean novel, "A Little Ball That a Dwarf Launches," was written by Cho Se-hui.
2. Lee On Ho adapted the original text for play.
3. Chae Yoon-il directed the drama, "A Little Ball That a Dwarf Launches," in May 1979 at the Sesil Theater.
4. The adapted script was collected by the Arko arts archive.

Modified FRBRoo for performing arts archives of Korea
FRBRoo as an ontology for LOD modeling
Object-oriented FRBR (FRBRoo) is a formal ontology for linking bibliographic and museum information developed by the International Federation of Library Associations and Institutions (IFLA) and ICOM-CIDOC (International Council for Museums – International Committee on Documentation). The first draft of FRBRoo was completed in 2006, and the model is formulated as an extension of the CIDOC CRM. In the harmonization process, the application of FRBR concepts to performing arts was also considered (CIDOC CRM [Web site]).

As a result, in FRBRoo, there are classes related to performing arts such as F20 Performance Work, F25 Performance Plan, and F31 Performance. For this reason, FRBRoo is selected for constructing the LOD of Korean performing arts materials. FRBRoo is characterized by applying time and event concept to static bibliographic information. This feature is useful for describing performing arts materials (Doerr, Bekiari, and Le Boeuf, 2008, 13).

Modification of the FRBRoo model for Arko performing arts data mapping
The data from Arko was analyzed according to FRBRoo classes and properties. We modified some of the existing FRBRoo models to reflect the characteristics of the Arko data. As a result, there are three types of cases in which the Arko data is applied to FRBRoo.

1. Restructuring Arko data according to the structure of FRBRoo: Arko regards the original text as work of FRBR and performing information as expression (realization of the idea of the original text). In this project, FRBRoo was applied, and original text was divided into F14 Individual Work and performance information was divided into F20 Performance Work, F25 Performance Plan, and F31 Performance.
2. FRBRoo is applied as it is: Arko adds information, such as the original novel which is the basis of the play. This part can be expressed as "F14 Individual Work (R2) is a derivative of - F14 Individual Work (Adaptation)."
3. FRBRoo is partially modified: F21 Recording Work is connected to F31 Performance and F29 Recording Event. However, Arko considers DVD and videotape recordings of the performance to belong to the performance itself rather than as implementations of the recording work.

References

Allemang, D. & Hendler, J. 2011. *Semantic Web for the Working Ontologist: Effective Modeling in RDFS and OWL*. Morgan Kaufmann.

Arko Arts Archive. [Web site]. [Cited 2019.04.23]. https://archive.arko.or.kr/

CIDOC CRM. [Web site]. [Cited 2019.04.23]. "FRBRoo." http://www.cidoc-crm.org/frbroo/home-0

Doerr, M., Bekiari, C., and Le Boeuf, P. 2008. "FRBRoo, A Conceptual Model for Performing Arts." 2008 *Annual Conference of CIDOC*. Athens, Sept. 15-18, 2008.

Doerr, M. et al. 2013. *Final Report on EDM – FRBRoo Application Profile Task Force Contributors*. Europeana Project.

Floridi, L. 2014. *The 4th Revolution: How the Infosphere is Reshaping Human Reality*. Oxford University Press.

Artificial Intelligence in Information Retrieval: forty years on

Linda C. Smith, University of Illinois at Urbana-Champaign, USA

The theme of ISKO UK 2019 is "The *Human* Position in an Artificial World: Creativity, Ethics & AI in Knowledge Organization." This theme echoes topics this author explored at greatest length in her 1979 dissertation, "Selected Artificial Intelligence Techniques in Information Retrieval Systems Research" (1), preceded in 1976 by a paper in *Information Processing & Management* (2) and followed in 1980 by a review article in the *Annual Review of Information Science and Technology* (3). The goal of this poster is two-fold: 1) to revisit the four artificial intelligence (AI) concepts proposed in my early work as having particular significance for information systems (pattern recognition, representation, problem solving, learning) and 2) to trace the evolution of interest in AI in library and information science over the past forty years, analyzing the literature indexed in *Library and Information Science Source*. This will yield a preliminary assessment of the ways in which my early work anticipated (or failed to anticipate) areas of AI application relevant to knowledge organization. The 1976 paper concluded with the statement: "Exploration and definition of the boundaries of artificial intelligence applications in performance of information retrieval tasks should give a better understanding of the roles of man and machine in retrieval systems made possible by the new technologies" (p. 220). Forty years on, we have a fuller understanding of "the human position in an artificial world."

The use of *Library and Information Science Source* as a data source is limited to a search for indexed items including "artificial intelligence" in the title. This yields 374 publications, with the author's 1976 paper as #1 and a paper published in May 2019 in *Information, Communication & Society* as #374. Titles and abstracts are analyzed and coded in order to identify themes and trends over time.

Nearly fifty years ago, authors of the UNISIST report from UNESCO (4) observed (p. 108):

Another open field of speculation, in a still more distant future, is more or less adequately described by neologisms such as *artificial intelligence,* "machine intelligence," and others. The methods covered under these names—problem solving, pattern recognition, logical inference, etc.—are sometimes presented somewhat naively, as the final answer to the more ambitious goals of information processing in science and technology. More than forty years on, we have reached that "more distant future" and have a better understanding of the relevance of AI to achieving "the more ambitious goals of information processing."

References

Smith, Linda C. 1979. *Selected Artificial Intelligence Techniques in Information Retrieval Systems Research*. Syracuse University, Ph.D. dissertation. 319p.

Smith, Linda C. 1976. Artificial Intelligence in Information Retrieval Systems. *Information Processing & Management* 12: 189-222.

Smith, Linda C. 1980. Artificial Intelligence Applications in Information Systems. *Annual Review of Information Science and Technology* 15: 67-105.

United Nations Educational, Scientific and Cultural Organization (Unesco); International Council of Scientific Unions (ICSU). 1971. *UNISIST: Study report on the feasibility of a world science information system*. Paris, France: UNESCO. 161p.

BuildVoc Simple Knowledge Organization System for Information retrieval

Phil Stacey, ICIOB, UK

Introduction

Information production and retrieval has become governed by many different systems and processes based on business requirements. One of the major challenges is that data is generated by individual businesses is captured in data islands. Simple Knowledge Organization System (SKOS) can join these islands of data together using the Resource Description Framework (RDF). This paper will identify how SKOS could be used to achieve consistency in file naming as a first step.

Simple Knowledge Organization System (SKOS)

The SKOS gives a platform for organizations to view and download concepts and terms in structured data. The goal of this classification system is to give the construction industry an introduction to linked data and its benefits. With the collaboration of existing classification systems such as Uniclass 2015, NBS create, RIBA plan of works being distributed in many different formats. The SKOS could aid in providing a unified platform for the distribution of these classification systems, in addition it would aid consumers of this data of the hierarchy, and phases of when this information is being generated using skos:related or rdfs:seeAlso type relationships.

Document data

The following example from the (The British Standards Institution, 2015) shows an example of the data which will be included are duty holders, uri, document type, work package, publication state. Also, the data has a subject by class is where the SKOS will be used to join the reference data libraries.

Figure 2 is an export in RDF format from a document repository, called Eprints which is an open source information system used to store university publications. This export shows how existing systems already have the capability of structuring data and files with the external subjects. This has given http://eprints.bimcoordinator.co.uk/id/eprint/11. Also a subject that has been imported from an external SKOS via a plugin gives dct:subject rdf:resource="c_2910" (Agricultural Information Management Standards (AIMS), 2018)

Figure 1 – Information model that represent relevant information about a document

PD ISO/TS 15926-11:2015
ISO/TS 15926-11:2015(E)

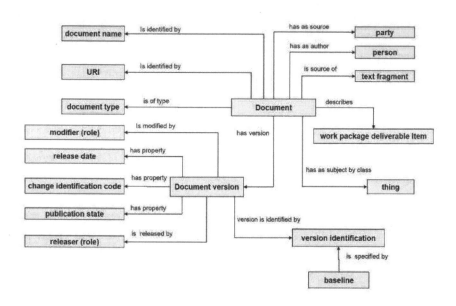

Figure 2 RDF export from an eprints repository

```
</rdf:Description>
<rdf:Description rdf:about="http://eprints.bimcoordinator.co.uk/id/eprint/11">
<bibo:abstract rdf:datatype="&xsd;string">(2006 edition incorporating 2010 and 2013 amendments) Approved Document B: Fire Safety covers building work
in England and Wales, such as the erection, extension or material alteration of a building, and how fire safety is designed into a building. The
Approved Document has been split into two volumes, Volume 1 deals with dwellinghouses and Volume 2 deals with buildings other than dwellinghouses.
Volume 2 includes amendments to the guidance on wall coverings and thermoplastic lighting diffusers and rooflights. Contracts and Management
Publications Update Service: To ensure that you have the most up-to-date Approved Document or Amendment to an Approved Document to hand, you can now
join our CAMPUS service. RIBA Bookshops will automatically send you copies of new releases as and when they are published. Visit our CAMPUS page for
further details.</bibo:abstract>
<bibo:authorList rdf:resource="http://eprints.bimcoordinator.co.uk/id/eprint/11#authors" />
<bibo:status rdf:resource="http://purl.org/ontology/bibo/status/nonPeerReviewed" />
<bibo:status rdf:resource="http://purl.org/ontology/bibo/status/published" />
<bibo:volume>2</bibo:volume>
<dcterms:creator rdf:resource="&epid;org/ext-ad11d8b47f69ab2f965c90c3a5de198c" />
<dcterms:creator rdf:resource="&epid;person/ext-dd6aad3eec54c6d42368164d19871d3a" />
<dcterms:date>2011-01</dcterms:date>
<dcterms:isPartOf rdf:resource="http://eprints.bimcoordinator.co.uk/id/repository" />
<dcterms:isPartOf rdf:resource="&epid;publication/ext-988c1a799fc843219ba2f1b4a6a5c188" />
<dcterms:subject rdf:resource="_:2910" />
<dcterms:title rdf:datatype="&xsd;string">Approved Document B: Fire Safetybuildings Other than Dwellinghouses Volume 2</dcterms:title>
<ep:hasDocument rdf:resource="http://eprints.bimcoordinator.co.uk/id/document/23" />
<ep:hasDocument rdf:resource="http://eprints.bimcoordinator.co.uk/id/document/24" />
<ep:hasDocument rdf:resource="http://eprints.bimcoordinator.co.uk/id/document/25" />
<ep:hasDocument rdf:resource="http://eprints.bimcoordinator.co.uk/id/document/26" />
<ep:hasDocument rdf:resource="http://eprints.bimcoordinator.co.uk/id/document/27" />
<ep:hasDocument rdf:resource="http://eprints.bimcoordinator.co.uk/id/document/568" />
<rdf:type rdf:resource="&bibo;AcademicArticle" />
<rdf:type rdf:resource="&bibo;Article" />
<rdf:type rdf:resource="&ep;ArticleEPrint" />
<rdf:type rdf:resource="&ep;EPrint" />
<rdfs:seeAlso rdf:resource="http://eprints.bimcoordinator.co.uk/11/" />
</rdf:Description>
```

Naming convention file retrieval

Files can be generated using a number of different software applications including Microsoft office, Autodesk and many other providers. The challenge is these files / records are being named and saved in an inconsistent manner. File naming convention can add real value when retrieving information in a folder-based system. When a consistent naming convention is implemented it acts as a metadata type definition in search. Also, the SKOS concepts could be used to assist in the development of a standard method of procedure (Stacey, 2018) a real simple starting point to using semantic vocabulary.

References

Agricultural Information Management Standards (AIMS). (2018, 06 16). *Fire Prevention*. Retrieved from http://aims.fao.org/aos/agrovoc/c_2910.html

Stacey, P. (2018, 06 16). *Standard Methods and Procedures (SMP)*. Retrieved from BUILDVOC - Thesaurus for the built environment: http://buildvoc.co.uk/resource/c_2e6cd3a6

The British Standards Institution. (2015). *PD ISO/TS 15926-11:2015 Industrial automation systems and integration — Integration of life-cycle data for process plants including oil and gas production facilities Part 11: Methodology for simplified industrial usage of reference data*. London: BSI Standards Limited.

Author Index

Ludi Price, City, University of London, UK 11
Jian Qin, Syracuse University, USA 221
Marcus Ralphs, Byzgen Limited, UK 144
Cecilie Rask, Danish National Police, Denmark 144
Jem Rayfield, Ontotext, UK 10
Luís Otávio Rigo Júnior, Federal University of Espírito Santo (UFES), Brazil 294
Tony Russell-Rose, UXLabs, UK 275
Phil Stacey, ICIOB, UK 303
Tanja Svarre, Aalborg University, Denmark 73, 291
Natalia Tognoli, Fluminense Federal University (UFF), Brazil 113
Michael Upshall, UNISLO, Denmark 232

Subject Index

Conference Organization

Programme committee

David Haynes, City, University of London
Stella Dextre Clarke, Independent Consultant
Judi Vernau, Metataxis

Review panel

Vanda Broughton, University College London
Helen Challinor, UK Department for Education
Stephen Dale, Collabor8now Ltd
Sylvie Davies, Robert Gordon University
Stella Dextre Clarke, ISKO UK
Francisco Javier García Marco, Universidad de Zaragoza, Spain
Claudio Gnoli, University of Pavia, Italy
Koraljka Golub, Linnaeus University, Sweden
José Guimarães, UNESP - São Paulo State University, Brazil
Barbara Kwasnik, Syracuse University, United States
Patrick Lambe, Straits Knowledge, Singapore
Andreas Ledl, Basel University, Switzerland
Deborah Lee, City, University of London
David Penfold, Edgerton Publishing Services
Vivien Petras, Humboldt University of Berlin, Germany
Pauline Rafferty, Aberystwyth University
Dagobert Soergel, University of Buffalo, United States
Renato Souza, Fundação Getulio Vargas, Brazil
Rick Szostak, University of Alberta, Canada
Douglas Tudhope, University of South Wales
Judi Vernau, Metataxis Ltd
Marcia Zeng, Kent State University, United States
Maja Žumer, University of Ljubljana, Slovenia

Conference organizing committee
David Haynes, Chair
Stella Dextre Clarke, Programme Committee
Helen Challinor, Posters
Niké Brown, Project Manager
Dave Clarke, Sponsorship
Vivs Long-Ferguson, Sponsorship
Tara McDarby, Publicity and Website
Duncan McKay, Treasurer
Judi Vernau, Co-editor of Conference Proceedings